RETURN TO SPIRIT

A WESTERN YOGI'S
FIRST - PERSON
ACCOUNT OF
SPONTANEOUS
KUNDALINI AWAKENING
AND CANDID LOOK AT
SPIRITUALITY INVOLVING
THE EVOLUTION AND
EXPANSION OF
CONSCIOUSNESS IN THE
21ST CENTURY

CHRISTOPHER B SOLTIS

outskirts
press

Outskirts Press, Inc.
http://www.outskirtspress.com

Paperback ISBN: 978-1-9772-1019-7
Hardback ISBN: 978-1-9772-1136-1

Outskirts Press and the "OP" logo are trademarks belonging to Outskirts Press, Inc.

PRINTED IN THE UNITED STATES OF AMERICA

To my parents for their unconditional love and raising my brother and I the way they believed sons should be raised.

Barbara Ann Soltis
January 18, 1949 – October 20, 2017

For the Love and Light in all of us.

ACKNOWLEDGMENTS

Cover art and interior images by Joiana Rose Iacono
Author photo by Michael Kravetsky of Watermrk Studios
Line editing by E.M. Levy of the Book Editing Network
Copyediting by Editage

TABLE OF CONTENTS

PREFACE

Disclaimer: If you are able to read this body of work keeping with the notion of having a completely open mind and truly believe ALL things are possible in the universe; then it may be a great benefit to you and possibly assist in alleviating any trivial stresses and anxieties in your life and potentially catapult you towards achieving your dreams. If you are close-minded, a cynic, identify more with your ego; judge others for their beliefs (and systems of) — feel free to return this or read it as fiction.

These words, thoughts, beliefs are not meant to offend, infuriate, belittle, frighten or sound blasphemous. We are all born free to believe, speak, write, and think what we want. Social conditioning, indoctrination, the way we were raised, other outside stimuli and negative influences can distort this fact. If anything you read comes across as egotistical, maniacal, ludicrous, vain: just absolutely negative—please trust me when I say it is for emphasis, humor and to make a point. When you truly believe in your heart of hearts that it is possible to exist without having any negative thoughts, words, actions, even towards people that do us harm then you are headed in the right direction.

Our perception of reality, how we live, exist is all we know. What if this is true after we die? What if our thoughts, words, actions, beliefs and deeds were directly correlated to the next existence on our eternal path? Wouldn't you want to live in a world of no pain, war, hostility, hatred, judgment, greed, poverty or misery?

This book is the direct result of having a spontaneous Kundalini awakening. I'm going to do my best to explain the whys and hows. My initial thought right after having this enormous volume of cosmic, universal, vital, spiritual energy surge up my spine, out my crown chakra and connecting to the Absolute/Source/Creator Universal Consciousness/Cosmic Consciousness/ Primordial Consciousness/Light of Pure Consciousness /A Higher Consciousness/A Higher Power/Holy Spirit/Great Spirit/God/ God Head/Universal Spirit/Higher Self/Supreme Soul/Universal Mind/ Jah/Jehovah/Yahweh/Om/The Divine/The Aten/The Eye of the Lord/ The Light (WHATEVER YOU WANT TO CALL IT—IT'S ALL THE SAME REGARDLESS OF CREED, CULTURE, RACE, GENDER OR SOCIAL STATUS) was to share the experience for the greater benefit of humanity and the universe. We are ALL capable of having this sacred experience. It is a marked sign of the evolutionary process of the human race and from what I've researched, the basis for many organized religions, shamanism and ancient royalty. I claim to neither be a wise man or a fool: just a regular guy who is trying his best to realize his own version of paradise on Earth. We don't have to wait until we die. We can all do our part by trying to be the best that we can be in everything we do. And if we fail? Know that your heart is in the right place and you will most likely have plenty of opportunities over the course of your journey to have it realized. Our planet is truly an amazing place. Let's work to keep it that way. If this book assists just one person in bettering their life then it has served its purpose.

Chapter 1

Introduction

WRITE WHAT YOU know. This is what I intend to do here. Please understand that everything in this book is coming directly from the heart. I've always lived by the belief that a man's word is his bond. If you can't speak the truth at all times or believe that pulling one over on someone is part of an ideal way to live your life, then hopefully this book will change your perspective on things.

The goals of this book are to try my best to explain spirituality and how it fits into our everyday lives and potentially assist in your own awakening. This evolutionary phenomenon is real and available to everyone. It is my understanding that any spiritual knowledge should always be shared for the greater good. Living a life full of creativity, joy, and love without letting nominal stresses and anxieties weigh us down is our God given right. It is easy to get thrown off track. One needs to understand and discern what exactly spirituality means for his or her self as it is different for everyone. To me, it means being present in every moment, consciously pursuing my passions and dreams without judgment. If it makes you happy and you aren't hurting anyone or yourself, you're on the right path. Having a solid understanding and balance of spirituality and materialism will be of great benefit in your life. If you are living a purely materialistic existence with a focus on money, social status, or "keeping up with the Joneses," then you are not, for lack of a better choice of words, "woke" or "conscious." When you wake up to the reality that you can't take any of it with you, and that Earth is a gigantic school and there are lessons in our everyday lives, it will have a profound effect on how you live your life. Of course, we all have materialistic needs such as shelter, food, clothing, and so on. Finding the right balance between the spiritual and the material will keep you moving in a positive direction.

You may come across a handful of topics that are repeated, since certain concepts apply to a broad spectrum of the topics under discussion. Bear with me and know it is for a reason. Keeping this in mind and making simple, complex, or abstract connections of said topics will definitely be of great benefit while reading this.

We are all connected. We are all God and have that element of the divine coded in our DNA. Some of us know this, but most do not. All the answers lie within us. It is up to us at the individual level to uncover and reveal our true selves, as we are all spiritual beings having a human experience. When we start living with the fact that our thoughts, words, actions, and deeds determine our circumstances and that our level of consciousness can be developed and is eternal, then it paints a picture that is easier for us to understand. There's really nothing to fear if you have unconditional love in your heart for all of creation, even for those that consciously and unconsciously wrong you or cause you harm. It is all part of a grand design.

A plethora of topics will be discussed in this book. Everything from organized religion, philosophy, astrology, astronomy, physics, metaphysics, chemistry, dreams, capitalism, history, ancient civilizations and cultures, the government, legal and justice systems, war, peace, music, art, love, loss, suffering, heaven, hell, psychology, drugs, healthcare, education, mathematics, geometry, technology, sports, biology, and evolution, pretty much anything you can think of that influences how we live our lives and what it means to be human. This includes the physical, emotional, mental, compassionate, expressive, and creative components that make us who we are.

I contemplated numerous titles for this book including *The Cosmic Orgasm, Embracing Your Eternity, The Eternal Self, This Way To Paradise, What The Fuck Are We Doing Here?!* (for comic relief), *Anatomy Of The Soul, Owning Your Divinity, Spiritual Amnesia, Universal Citizen, American Spirit, Memoir of a Spiritual Rock Star, You Are The Universe,* and *Deconstructing the Universe,* but settled on something more universal.

I have mirrored Gopi Krishna's autobiography in the sequence of writing this book. For those unfamiliar with him, Gopi Krishna had a Kundalini awakening while meditating in his bedroom. He began his book with the actual experience and then wrote about his life. This happened in India in the 1930s. He was brought up very differently than me in terms of culture, education, diet, and available technological resources (the Internet is a valuable tool!).

I am going to begin by describing, to the best of my ability, my Kundalini awakening by explaining what was going on physically, emotionally, mentally, and spiritually while it was happening. An autobiography will follow leading up to the awakening, since every major life event is tied in to why, where, and when it occurred. Please keep in mind that everything in life—thoughts, words, deeds, experiences, relationships, stimuli affecting our senses, and so forth has significance and purpose. You may find some of the details of my life to be completely mundane, but I ask that you remain patient and remember that it is a snapshot in time. In order to make this tangible, I came to the conclusion that my awakening was such a significant event that piecing together a memoir recollecting as much of my life as possible would paint a portrait for any reader to parallel my stories and life experiences to that of their own.

I have never kept a diary. Most of my writing is in a "stream of consciousness" style. My level of consciousness was heightened for a long period of time and the amount of energy and recall that came with it made it very easy for me to write in this manner. It is an accurate description of being born in the late 70s and growing up in a middle class family in the suburbs of New Jersey. After the autobiography—the main course, the crux consisting of universal and timeless knowledge, and symbolism that may be able to assist in your spiritual growth and development. Keep in mind that I didn't do much research as to why this happened to me. When Kundalini energy is initiated and raised from the root chakra, climbs up your spine clearing all the chakras, and opens up the crown chakra, your connection to The Divine is completely synchronous. It is as if a huge volume of energy is released into your mind and body, and a wealth of knowledge is downloaded into your system. You are pretty much plugged into the "Universal Mind" or Universal Consciousness. The modern accepted term is connecting with the Akashic Records. This theory states that everything ever known in the universe is available to anyone capable of raising his or her Kundalini energy to the crown chakra.

Please be advised in this book you will see a pattern of compulsive behavior involving chemical dependency and substance abuse. I am not glamorizing this lifestyle. It is a slippery slope and can be very destructive to family and friends. As a result, you will begin to see my life unravel in Chapter 6. This is a cautionary tale that leads to self-help, self-inquiry, wellness, and ultimately the physiological mechanism of Enlightenment.

Before continuing, I'd like to give a basic definition of consciousness, as you should really keep it in the back of your mind while reading this. This is directly tied into spirituality and Kundalini awakening. There will be many definitions in this book that I will use to clarify and expand upon.

Consciousness: the quality or state of awareness, or being aware of an external object or something within oneself. It has been defined as sentience, awareness, subjectivity, the ability to experience or to feel, wakefulness, having a sense of selfhood, and the executive control system of the mind.

You ready? Of course you are. You wouldn't have bought this book if you weren't so know you were meant to read this for a reason!

Some names and identifying details have been
changed to protect the privacy of individuals.

Chapter 2

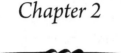

12.31.13

PHISH. NEW YEAR'S Eve. The Madison Square Garden run. The concert is halfway through the first set and I'm beginning to settle in. The venue is alive. Electrified. There is a current of energy surging all around, and on some level, everyone is able to feed off it and reciprocate. The versatile set closed out with Page's "Halfway to the Moon" (which by now seems like a profound prediction of the rest of my evening} and the very challenging "Fluffhead."

The band always does three sets on New Year's Eve while incorporating some unique theatrical component or prop. This year would prove to be no different. During the first set break, a flatbed truck drove onto the center floor of the Garden, which was clear of concertgoers. It housed a smaller stage reminiscent of the earlier days of the band. To top it all off, hockey sticks substituted for mic stands a la the band's first gig on the campus of the University of Vermont back in 1983.

As the howls of the crowd dissipated, the band opened the second set with the ever so playful "Glide." After the acapella ending and brief stage communication, Trey ripped into the opening chord of "Llama," a frenetic thrash groove that is technically part of the Gamehendge story. For those unfamiliar with the Gamehendge saga, it was Trey's senior thesis at Goddard College and tells a timeless story of, amongst other things, war, control, oppression, ignorance, love, and good versus evil.

The 27 months prior to this could easily be described as a living hell. During this time, the woman I fell in love with and had been with for the greater part of my adult life left me. This was in September of 2011. Five months later, she moved out of our house, which left her brother (who also contributed towards the mortgage and was an owner) and I in a bind. Since the two of us could not afford to live there, we contacted a realtor and rented out the house. We then had to move out all of our worldly possessions and seek housing elsewhere. Seven months later, Hurricane Sandy struck and destroyed the first floor of the house. Our tenants broke the lease, as the house was not fit for occupancy. With no leniency and misinformation from the bank or assistance from FEMA or local politicians, we were quickly behind on the loan by approximately $17,000. Not exactly chump change for someone carrying debt and living paycheck to paycheck. The options of a short sale and bankruptcy declaration were discussed. I borrowed money from my brother and parents, but this was just the financial headache. Where my mind, heart, spirit, and emotions were during this period was something altogether different. We finally got the house rebuilt and new tenants in September 2013. Things were getting back to normal.

Back to the second set. During the show, between periods of dancing without a care in the world, were moments when I was just taking it all in and marveling at the amazement of the event and life, reality, and existence in general. I started really going at it with my inner dialogue. You know, when you're thinking something but not saying it? It's your mind and it can play tricks on you if you let it get too far out of line. This wasn't going to happen that night. I really started to dig deep.

Just a week before on Christmas Eve, after an early dinner with my folks and before we traditionally head to church, I was having a cigarette with my mother in the kitchen. I forget exactly how the conversation started, but I told her without any fear or reservation that I wasn't a practicing Catholic. I explained that I were blessed to have been raised in a home by her and my dad in the way that they were raised and in the way that their parents before them were raised, and so forth. However, the dogma and beliefs were just not aligning with where my heart and soul were anymore. I understood Jesus' teachings, his message, and also honor those of other religions and cultures. She only inquired if I believed in God, which of course I do and that was good enough for her.

With that being said, during "Colonel Forbin's Ascent" (it is ironic that this song has the word ascent in it) I began to try to logically and creatively make sense of everything that had happened to me. I started to put the pieces of the puzzle together. It was as if a million thoughts started swirling around in my mind at an insurmountable speed, like stars and dust being consumed by a black hole. As I was gazing at the flatbed truck with Trey directly in front of me, I began to relax and started breathing deeply in a slow and steady rhythm. I said to myself, "I DON'T FUCKING GET IT." What did I ever do to suffer so much? No person should ever feel that type of pain. Why would God allow ANYONE to suffer? My heart has always been in the right place. All I ever did regarding the relationship with my ex was try to keep and make her happy in every way possible. Why did this hurricane seemingly land on my house? Why were there so many obstacles and hardships in my way to get back on my feet? This isn't fair. Life isn't fair. If karma is real, then the only possible explanation was that I caused the same amount of pain to my ex. Did she suffer silently? She never told me she was unhappy. Perhaps we were together in another life and I did the same thing to her then? That makes a lot of sense. I am not angry or upset anymore. Did I forgive her before I forgave myself? It doesn't matter. Either way, there is no sense in keeping a hardened heart. I'd rather the universe not exist than believe words spoken from my heart and soul, and the energy associated with them, didn't mean anything or would not reverberate throughout the cosmos forever. If it was meant to be and everything happens for a reason, then I learned my lesson. What the hell are we doing on this planet? I don't believe Jesus was the only Son of God. If the current stance of theoretical physics on the universe is the Big Bang and we all came from the same place and are made of the same substance and energy, then how can any ONE person be any better than anyone else? That doesn't seem balanced. That's not fair. We are all equal in every way possible. What about Buddha? What about Moses, Mohammed, Enoch, Noah, Jacob, and King Solomon? There are other cultures that existed before Jesus. The Mayans, Egyptians, the Druids, Incans, Mexico, the Romans, Greeks, Native Americans, those in Southeast Asia, and in Japan. None of them believed that Jesus was the only Son of God. They didn't even know who he was. Some worshipped the sun, others nature, and others had multiple gods that represented different facets of everyday life. We must ALL be sons and daughters of God. I'm not going to go to hell if I don't believe He was. I'm just trying to do the best I can with what I have. So, I've been lead to believe through social conditioning and indoctrination that you are born, go to school, get a job, get married, start a family, retire, and die. Is this the American Dream? That's it!? That's not MY dream. What if I never meet another woman interesting enough, attractive enough, understanding enough, passionately creative enough, emotionally stable enough, and intelligent enough to pass on my genes and accumulated knowledge and experiences and start a family? I don't have to settle. I am not settling. What is the basis for success? Money and fame? That's a bottomless hole. I earn enough money to be content. I don't need a Ferrari or a palatial estate. I know what my dream is and I am trying to work towards it every day. I am just following my heart. I have to believe that if I get hit by a bus tomorrow, I will still be able to work towards my vision of paradise. That's my only basis for eternal happiness. I learned my lessons. If reincarnation is true, then I don't want to be born again as a child and learn what I've learned all over again on a planet where war, famine and homelessness exists, the illusion of fear is rampant, and bad behavior and people with huge egos and destructive personalities are rewarded with money. There has to be something more to it!

I switched off my internal dialogue for a bit and just continued breathing and being present in the moment. The band did the classic "Forbin's" → "Fly Famous Mockingbird," which is one of my favorite Phish tunes. A deep wave of relaxation came over me. I'm with great friends and watching my favorite band kill it at one of my favorite live music venues. I'm enjoying a few beers and some quality cannabis to enhance the experience. The psilocybin mushroom cap and stem I ingested kicked in not too long ago. They are clean. I didn't take too much. I'm feeling fucking awesome! I've got a great job/career going. I get to play live music with my brother, my best friend, pretty much whenever we want. I'm in post-production on two albums worth of original material, which is a big part of working towards my dream. I cut down on the boozing and started a really great exercise and yoga program. I'm in the best shape of my life, physically, mentally, and emotionally. Even the house situation got worked out. THIS must be heaven.

By now I had a huge smile on my face. I continued my deep breathing and shut down my thinking mind for a bit and just stared at the stage. Wow. Am I in heaven? Because it really cannot get any better than this. What's left to do? I unwittingly and unthinkingly did a life review in contemplating every step that led up to this point in my life. I've developed enough self-love that I am satisfied in every part of my life, know what I want out of it, and who I'd be willing to share it with as far as developing a truly meaningful relationship goes. I am just going to keep doing what I have been doing because I believe working towards your dream with love in your heart is the only reason for doing anything. I guess the only thing left for me to do is to take what I can from how Jesus lived his life and I will have no fear when I die. Jesus died for his beliefs. I can only imagine that I'll end up in a better place than where we are now, and that living a life based on my own system of beliefs after all I've learned on this planet is a monumental reason for why I am even alive.

Around this time, a gooey, warm, fuzzy feeling started to become more evident in my body. I casually acknowledged it, continued to enjoy myself with an air of peace and contentment, breathed deeply and steadily, and truly believed in my heart that it REALLY can't get any better as far as where I'd rather be in my life or on the planet. This feeling intensified to the point where, in my mind's eye, a column of golden, silvery, fiery light began to make its presence known and ascended up my spine. There's really no other way to explain it. It started all the way at the bottom with a warm, tingling pressure. It was much like a pilot light before the gas valve is opened. My spine was the focal point, but as it gradually climbed, the rest of my body felt the effects. It was as if my spine was a power plant radiating its energy out to other sections of my body.

When it reached my navel, my thinking mind made an inquiry. I asked myself, "What's going on here?" I had a shit-eating grin on my face and never felt anything like it in my life. I've done hallucinogens before and am quite aware of the effects as well as the synergy involving multiple variables in my system, i.e. alcohol, tobacco, marijuana, and psilocybin. But THIS WAS NO HALLUCINATION. (Note: mind/consciousness altering substances have been used in religious and shamanistic rituals in many cultures going back millennia. There were no governmental laws classifying them as illegal. The current collective consciousness of society thinks of these substances as bad because the government deems them illegal even though they grow naturally on Mother Earth. For further study and reference, see Soma in the ancient Hindu Vedic texts or teonanacatl, Aztec for divine mushroom.) There were more components involved than just a compound of foreign substances in my body interacting with one another. The interactions as well as the heightened/altered state of my consciousness merely tricked my nervous system into allowing what was happening to me. Had I had any trepidations, there is a strong possibility that nothing would've happened. There were more universal elements involved here. The sound, reverberations, and vibrations of the band and the room, the magical light show, and the good vibes and energy of good people who were all there to let it rip and lose themselves. All these factors seemingly increased the positive electrical charge in the air. The overall state of my mind, body, breath, soul, and their alignment and assimilation with each other also contributed to this. Also, the physiological, biological, chemical, electrical, and magnetism of all the non-corporeal aspects of my being…I wondered, "Am I fucking dying?!" There's no possible way! I feel too good! It's indescribable! I truly have my shit together for the first time in my life. I can't check out now!

So I surrendered.

I just let go and let it flow. I didn't have a care in the world. If I was dying, there was no fear in my heart. I continued to breath and smile. My gaze was fixed on the stage and I was in a state of no-mind. This IS heaven! The fiery column pierced through my heart and a feeling of divine love washed over me. Within moments, I felt it in my throat and then in my head. At this point, my head felt like it was glowing on the inside and outside. There seemed to be a unique pressure, as if there was a magnet in the center of my brain, feeling the polarity of another magnetic agent.

Then it happened.

This effulgent column of light and energy shot out of the top of my head. This obviously wasn't visible or a hallucination. It was an internal vision, but the feeling of it exiting was absolutely profound. My entire body lit up on the inside. It was the most amazing feeling I have ever experienced, or for that matter, that I think is even possible to experience. It was pure bliss. It felt as if every cell in my body simultaneously turned to gold and had the most intense orgasm. Not that my physical body was experiencing an orgasm, but that every individual cell was having an orgasm at the exact same time! It felt like I shone like the light of a million suns. Another analogy that may offer a clearer description was the feeling of love between a child and a parent, but that feeling multiplied by the total of the number of people that have ever walked the Earth. My life seemed to flash before my eyes and in an instant, every important lesson I had ever learned seemed to be magnified. All the other crap, failures and wrongdoings by way of my negative thoughts, words, and deeds seemed to dissolve. They just burned up. A wealth of knowledge, which seemingly came from nowhere, was downloaded into my system.

This column didn't just shoot out into space: it connected with the Absolute/Source/Creator/Great Spirit/God/Universal Consciousness. Whatever you want to call it; the divine in me connected with the divine of ALL. It was as if the energy of my body matched a divine resonance and found equanimity with the universe. The experience was unequivocally supra mundane. Like I had been there before. There is no other possible explanation. My body felt as if it were impaled on this column of light, which originated from the core of the Earth and shot out infinitely through the cosmos. As my crown chakra remained open, I just basked in the Light of the Divine, the feeling, and knowing that we are all connected was coursing through my mind, body, and soul.

The next thing I know, I was AT the Light. It was in my mind's eye, this radiant disc about the size of a half-dollar was right in the center of my field of vision, which appeared to be 12 to 18 inches from my forehead. The physical world just dropped away. My consciousness merged with the Light. Here, there was no fear, pain, stress, anxiety, or suffering, only peace and pure bliss at the most profound level. I felt eternal—eternity coursing through every cell of my body. Divine love. The love and knowing that every friend and family member that had passed on was with me, and will always be with me. The feeling of being home and never wanting to leave came over me. God is unconditional love for all of Creation! I just really wanted to stay. Nothing else mattered.

The Light was all around me. It was the brightest white imaginable or that can be physically perceived. It seemed to pulsate or vibrate every color of the spectrum in it at, well, the speed of light. The closest description I can come up with is that it was like a shutter on a camera clicking 186,000 times a second. If you have ever stared at the sun during safe viewing times (an hour after sunrise and an hour before sunset), you'll start to see its outline, which appears to move around the circumference of the sun.

I continued to gaze at the center in pure bliss. Then something happened that I wasn't expecting to see. I had three visions that seemingly popped out of the center of the disc. The first appeared to be two atomic particles dancing side-by-side, interacting with one another. Both were a darkish green color that looked like marbles but they were not made of any physical matter and had a charge around them. Meaning, it looked like lightning or electricity encircled each of them. The colors of the charges were a composite of white, gold, and light green. As they came closer to one another, the charge intensified but they remained in this happy dance together. They never seemed to touch. Their respective charges kept that from happening. In an instant, they flew off to the right of my field of vision and the next one appeared in the center of this radiant disc of light. It was a spaceship approaching the Earth.

The Earth was at the bottom of my field of vision. The entire planet wasn't in view, only about a third of it was visible. The craft was in the middle of my field of vision, slowly advancing towards the Earth. It moved more towards the top of my field of vision, leaving space between the planet and the craft, and I really only caught a glimpse of the rear. I cannot possibly describe the size as there was no other object to reference other than the Earth and I don't how far away it was from the planet. It reminded me of a *Star Wars* star destroyer, but not as big. It definitely wasn't small. There were three burners in the back glowing in a mixture of white and gold light. There was nothing resembling exhaust emanating from the burners and the vessel appeared to be a dark metallic gray. As quickly as I took what I could from the vision, the Light outshined the Earth and the craft and it was gone.

The last was a holographic or transparent image of three other images overlapping each other. They were the Giza plateau with the Great Pyramid and the Sphinx, Stonehenge, and a pyramidal temple in the jungle of a culture in either Meso-America or South America. I'm pretty sure it was Mayan. The area around the temple was clear of brush and on the outskirts of the perimeter was lush vegetation. The image was absorbed by the Light, and I was left to discern my own hypothesis of why I saw what I saw.

I continued to bask in the Light. I stared at the stage but I wasn't hearing the band. There was sound but I just wasn't there. That may be difficult to comprehend, but my mind was still detached from the physical world. I looked to my left, right, and at the row behind me. They were all empty! It was almost as if the energy I was emitting forced people to move or their higher selves/souls knew on a subconscious level what was happening and it was understood that I had to be there alone, isolated. I spread out my arms so I resembled a 'T' and just let the Light continue to wash over me. I glimpsed at the stage again and felt like I was ascending or levitating. I say this because as I was looking at the stage, it was comparable to standing on my tiptoes to get a better view, except that the lift was one and a half to two feet higher. I looked down to see if my feet were still on the ground and the first thing I saw was what appeared to be a long and rectangular translucent pink jewel or gem. It was maybe three inches long by two inches wide and hovered over the center of my chest where my heart chakra would be located. I never got a glimpse to verify if my feet were still on the ground.

I turned my attention back to the truck. The Light was still in my mind's eye. In a flash, the Light seemingly returned to my body. It was as if this radiant disc, my inner sun separated into an infinite amount of stars stretched across the expanse of the universe with the realization of my, and every other being's equal connection to every atom within it. The vision reminded me of the Millennium Falcon entering or coming out of hyper drive in the *Star Wars* movies. Then it was gone. My friend Sean popped up out of nowhere. He asked how the seats were and if I was enjoying myself. We made some small talk. I couldn't even begin to explain to him what had just happened to me. But before he ran off, he said, "We gotta get you out of that corporate gig and just playing music." He mentioned that I was too talented to be doing what I've been doing for so long. Well, that is my dream and pretty much my greatest reason for living, so I thanked him and knew in my heart that I have been on the right path my entire life.

I'm guessing that the entire sequence of events from when the fiery column of light began to climb up the central channel of my spine to when the Light vanished lasted between fifteen to twenty minutes. I say this because I had no concept of time while this was all happening. It didn't mean anything to my thinking mind. In fact, the rest of the evening and show seemed like a blur, except that I had total contentment, joy, love, peace, and all other good things in my heart. I had a smile on my face and a glow about me for the rest of the evening. All I kept saying to myself was "only for good" and "people need to know about this." Those thoughts were reason enough to write this book. This was a life-changing event. I still have a smile on my face when I think about it. Now the real work begins.

Chapter 3

✹

GROWING UP

I WAS BORN on February 23rd in the year 1977 at 10:06 am at Overlook Hospital in Summit, New Jersey. It was a Wednesday. Two minutes later, my brother John sprang into this world, vacating my mother's womb. We are identical twins. My folks didn't know they were having twins until about three weeks prior to our birth, when the doctor informed them that there was another heartbeat in there. Technology was obviously not where it is today, so this is quite understandable. Our mom said we were conceived in New Orleans. That makes a lot of sense, as there is no other history of musical ability in the family, other than my mother's grandfather, who dabbled with the harmonica, and my father's mother who my father said: "thought she could play the organ." A couple years ago, over dinner, I joked that I remembered that day, a claim that my mother scoffed at. I then described the room color and what the nurse's uniform looked like, and she hesitantly agreed, with a puzzled look on her face. Maybe I was just guessing.

We were born a month premature, which puts us on the Aquarius/Pisces cusp. I weighed in at about four pounds, four ounces. My brother was a little healthier. Months of him stomping on me from above and crowding the area left me with banged up legs that required wearing corrective braces when I was younger. I also had an underdeveloped larynx, so that when I cried, I sounded like a little lamb, my mom said. John fared much better, since he didn't have any of the complications I had to work through.

Our dad, John, was born to Carl Soltis and Eva Capone in 1945. He has one brother, Carl, whose nickname his entire life has been Solty. They were raised in Garwood, N.J., a small borough between Westfield and Cranford. Carl's father, Karl, emigrated on the *Frederick Der Grosse* out of Bremen, Germany, in 1903 and was one of the first families to settle in Garwood. His first wife's name was Anna Szabol. She passed away in 1927, and he later remarried. My father's father had two brothers, John, for whom my father was named, and Frank. They all had blonde hair and light eyes. The name of the village on the naturalization records is Gollnitz, Hungary. Gollnitz is the Germanized name for Golniczbanya (which is the Hungarian name), which is synonymous with Gelnica, a town in the Kosice region of modern-day Eastern Slovakia. During the 19th Century, there was no Slovakia. This small mining town was part of the Austro-Hungarian Empire and further research shows that it was a Zipser German (also known as Carpathian German) settlement. Back in the 12th century, Hungarian kings invited German craftsmen, tradesmen and miners to settle on their land so they could have skilled laborers close. They were also to guard the empty mountain passes, as the area was part of an important trade route to the Baltic. Unfortunately, by the 19th century, Carpathian and Zipser Germans were forced to "Magyarize" or "Hungarianize" their names to fit in with Hungarian majority social class. They were often victims of genocide. Times were not fair to these people. Further genealogical research shows his baptized name to be Carolus (Medieval Latin for Charles) Scholtisz. He was the youngest child (he had four older sisters) born to Josephus Scholtisz and Anna Klein in Stara Voda, a village about 17 miles west of Gelnica. His sons would fall into the working class as contractors, carpenters and foremen–typical occupations for first-generation immigrants seeking opportunity in the land of milk and honey.

My father found an old picture of Karl dressed in what appears to be a military uniform. My father guesses he may have been a military deserter of the Austro-Hungarian Empire. For those growing up poor in villages where the only opportunity available was farming or mining, joining the ranks of the military was a way to survive. My father said he legally changed the last name to Soltisz to make it sound more American. Other surnames listed on my dad's father's and uncle's birth certificates as well as the 1920 and 1930 U.S. Censuses include Soltisz, Soltis, Soltes, and Schultes. They all roughly translate to "head of village", "village head man", "magistrate," or "mayor."

I did a majority of the genealogical research on my father's father's side of the family, as the mystery of his name and where he originally came from always fascinated me. (Additional genealogical research shows Josephus b. 1840, born to Andreas b. 1804, born to Mathias b. 1768 – all baptized Roman Catholic as discovered on church records scribed in Latin in neighboring villages in the Northern Kocise region of modern day Slovakia.) The other ancestors are less elusive, since more relatives from that side are still living, and names of villages in Italy are much easier to track back to.

Eve Capone was born to Dominic Capone and Estelle D'Amore. She had five siblings. Dominic started the first Italian-American club in Westfield, N.J. He was a successful businessman whose factory still stands on the border of Clark and Rahway. Carl and Eve owned a gas station on Route 22 West near the old Blue Star Mall in Berkeley Heights. One of my earliest memories was visiting my grandmother at the station on a cold day and her throwing some Pepperidge Farms cinnamon raisin bread in a toaster when we were hanging out in the office.

In 1971, when my father was still dating my mother, they were having dinner at my grandparent's house. Carl had a heart attack right there at the dinner table and didn't make it. Had they known to give him four Bayer aspirin, the end result could've been avoided. To lose a parent so young is devastating, especially a man that my father shared a bond with through golf. My dad said that the last round of golf his father played, he broke 80.

Our mom, Barbara was born to Leo Bertuzzi and Gloria Kalinowski in 1949. She has three siblings—two sisters and a brother. Our mom was the oldest and helped raise my uncle, who was 12 years her junior. They were raised on Verona Avenue in Newark, N.J., and then later moved to the Italian section that is located down the street from Branchbrook Park. Leo's father, Giuseppe (Joe), fought for the Italians during World War I then immigrated to the States. After he became a U.S. citizen, he fought for America. My mom was enthralled when she found his old draft card and still has his old army blanket. Joe married a lady by the last name of Losi (my mom called her 'Nawny'). My grandpa had a brother Al. The only other fact that stuck out about my great-grandfather was that he smoked cigarettes his entire life. I'm not talking about Marlboro Lights or Parliaments. These were heavy unfiltered smokes, like Pall Mall or Lucky Strikes. My mom said he used to wake up in the middle of the night just to have a cigarette. Well, one day when he was 76, he woke up, stated that his mouth felt like to bottom of a birdcage, and quit cold turkey right then and there.

Gloria was born to Ignacious Kalinowski (who later legally changed his name to John Collins) and Theresa Klunder, a descendent of German farmers. The Kalinowski's hailed from Golub-Dobrzyn, a town in what is today Central Poland. However, during the 19ᵗʰ century was part of the Prussian Empire. She had two sisters, Ruth (who passed away) and Dorothy. After Theresa died, Iggy (or John) remarried. I only knew her as Grandma Collins, but my mom said she was as real a grandmother as she could ever hope for.

As you can see, family history always fascinated me. Given the data, the melting pot make up of my brother's and my ethnicity is ½ Italian; 1/4 Carpathian/Zipser German, 1/8 German; and 1/8 Polish/Prussian. A pure European mutt and damn proud of every basis point!

Now that I've gotten my brief family tree out of the way, I'll resume the recollection and highlights of my childhood and growing up.

The most prominent themes of my childhood are family and the element of carefreeness. There were always extended family around and my parents' friends popping in to say hi. My mom would take my brother and me up to our grandparent's house in Newark on Tuesday nights while our dad bowled in his league. His high score was a 268. The parkway toll was a dime back then. Our father was an exceptional athlete and played football, basketball, and baseball.

From the date of our birth to about 1979, our folks lived with my dad's mother Eve and her second husband. Their house in Garwood had an upstairs, and this is where my parents started their version of the American dream. There's an early photo of my brother and me in typical cliché sailor outfits hanging out with Grandpa Leo who was over the house in Garwood one day. To this day, I still can't tell the difference between my brother and me in photos of that time. We were so identical that it was not until John's face started to fill in more than mine and the cowlick on the right side of my head became more prominent that I was able to start making heads and tails of us.

Our parents met "down the shore" as we call it. I say that because they were Central and North Jerseyans coming down for the season—a rite of passage for Jerseyans of any time period. Theirs just happened to be the late 60s. My mom told me of a dank, tiny room she remembered staying at in Belmar where there were millipedes and silverfish all over the place. They would listen to bands such as Salvation at the famed Osprey Night Club in Manasquan, slosh around in beer up to their ankles at the old Sea Girt Inn listening to Jimmy Byrne, or dance at Casablanca nightclub also in Manasquan. This was the time when the identifiable label BENNY (currently, it means a nonlocal or seasonal guest) actually stood for Bayonne, Elizabeth, Newark, New York. These days, people from all over visit the great stretch of beach in Monmouth and Ocean County.

Back to Garwood. Around this time, our folks were searching for a house to buy. They looked in Garwood, at a couple of places in Westfield, and, I think, even Colonia before settling on a dead-end street in Cranford with a lot of schools and parks within walking distance. They could never have afforded the down payment without the help of Grandma Eve.

Throughout her life, she would always help my parents out with some cash here and there. With her charity, she made our lives a little easier.

The Crane family, who built a mill there in 1720, founded Cranford (originally called Crane's Ford before the township was incorporated) in the mid to late 19th century. It is a beautiful suburb and welcoming community. I couldn't have been more blessed to be raised in such a lovely place. The town used to be called the Venice of New Jersey, an overstatement derived from the fact that the Rahway River runs through it. Folks from out of state would come to vacation in the early part of the 20th century, shop, and take a canoe trip down the river. These days, the school system, municipal amenities, diverse downtown shops, and proximity to Manhattan, Jersey City, and Weehawken via the train station make it an attractive place to settle and start a family.

The early days in Cranford are obviously fuzzy in my memory. I remember the yellow shag carpet in the living room, taking baths in the sink and tub with my brother and some float toys, being fed Gerber baby food and getting it all over the place, trips to the zoo, Branchbrook Park during peak cherry-blossom season, grocery shopping with my mom, and playing in the local parks.

At this early age in development, twins can begin to speak to each other in their own language. No one else can understand what they are saying; however, the siblings understand each other perfectly. That's what John and I did. No one had a clue what we were talking about, and we'd be laughing our asses off and having a ball. My mom said we sounded like aliens.

Three more stories around this time in my development and exploration as a toddler have been burned into my mom's memory, though I have only a vague recollection of them. One morning at Grandma Eve's, my mom left me alone for a hot second in the TV room adjacent to the dining area. I'm pretty sure it was mid-morning. Me, with my ever so curious nature, managed to make it up from the floor onto a chair, then an end table, and got my head stuck between two wooden Venetian blinds. I then lost my footing on the end table and ended up dangling by my neck in mid-air. I hung myself. Luckily, right before I started to turn blue, my mom came back into the room and saved my life. After that, my mom made it a priority to keep a closer eye on me. Who'd have thought you need childproof Venetian blinds?

When my brother and I were four, our folks decided that we were old enough to have a pet in the house. My mom always had dogs running around the yard growing up in Newark, and she can still name them all. Grandma Eve always had cats. One day, my mom and her sister Patty, I believe, took us out to a pet store on Long Island. She purchased a pure-bred Golden Retriever and named her Muffin. She would be the first of three Golden Retrievers my family would come to love over 30 plus years.

One morning Muff was lying in one of her favorite spots just chilling and being a dog. Between the kitchen and the family room is a step down. She liked to lie right where the step was in the family room next to the door that, at the time, led down to the covered patio. I decided to start taking running jumps over her and increased my distance each time I cleared her. This made her a bit nervous. The last running leap I took, I jumped on her. It wasn't a full-on landing where I could've caused serious injury, as that was never my intent. Either way, Muff decided she had had enough of my childhood game, and without warning reared up and around and bit me. At first, I didn't know what happened and felt no pain. There was an obvious disconnect between the injury and signals to my brain, most likely due to shock. The delay was similar to when a toddler injures him or herself, followed by a pause, and then the waterworks and wailing commence. I felt a sharp pain in my groin—Muff bit me on my scrotum. I saw blood seeping through my pants, started to panic, and ran screaming and crying to find my mom. "Mommmmm!!!! Muffin bit me!!!" She was horrified. Instantly and instinctually, she hurried me upstairs, started the shower, took off my clothes, threw me in the tub and called the pediatrician. The blood kept running down my leg and disappeared down the drain after dilution with the water. My mom did what the doctor told her to do regarding the wound, gingerly threw some new clothes on and off we rushed out the door to the doctor's office.

I loved Dr. Solomon Cohen. His practice was located in a nice residential area of Westfield. He was a brilliant, kind-hearted man and a natural when it came to medicine and dealing with children. When I was younger, I had partial deafness in one ear. Dr. Cohen prescribed steroids, and in time they remedied this condition. For a long time, I was always just a little bit shorter than my brother, as the medicine stunted my growth, but I am forever grateful for his diagnosis and treatment.

After dressing the wound and having a professional look me over, he confirmed that it was merely a flesh wound. Topical. The bite just broke the surface of the skin. That's a big area for blood flow and the reason I was bleeding out so profusely. My mom's biggest concern was that I would never be able to have children. Dr. Cohen told her I was lucky, because if Muff had gone another ½-inch deeper that might have been the case. Moral of the story: Let sleeping dogs lie.

The period between the ages of five and six, the nursery school and pre-kindergarten era, are a still a little fuzzy. Nursery school was at Osceola Church in Clark. My mom made friends very easily with the other kids' mothers. I don't remember any of it. Around this time, I did what every other kid that age was doing: play. I'd be outside on the jungle gym, on the swings; inside with toys, balls, and coloring books, watching cartoons or just using Muffin as a pillow. What else are you supposed to do, learn calculus? Around this age, John and I were obsessed with superheroes. Our neighbor, Mrs. Cirillo, made us Batman and Robin costumes. We were beside ourselves. It didn't even have to be Halloween. We'd wear them whenever around the house. I was Batman and he, Robin.

Another Saturday morning during cartoons I decided I wanted to cook breakfast for the family. My idea of this was putting a gallon of milk on the stove and turning it on. That's it. Not in a saucepan or pot—the unopened plastic jug. This caused a huge mess with melted plastic and burnt milk all over the stove as well as a little fire that smoked up the entire downstairs. My punishment included sitting in a chair facing a wall in the family room for like an hour and a half. Pure torture.

Our house was the last one on the block for years before the wooded area was developed to make way for six houses and a connection to another dead-end street that would allow motorists to drive through instead of taking a parallel street. The wooded area was a playpen for many of the neighborhood kids. We would go up there and wear ourselves out playing for hours. I'd come home with dirt all over my clothes, body, hair, and under my fingernails.

This was also the age when I was first exposed to parts of the female body that are supposed to be foreign to a six-year-old's eyes. Our neighbor was two years older than John and me, and one morning we found ourselves in her kitchen when her mother was out of the room. She offered a game of I'll show you mine if you show me yours. She went first, and then I obliged. It was completely innocent and is forever associated with my childhood.

With kindergarten, we entered the world of public education. Fortunately for me, Cranford had an amazing school system, with some amazing educators. When our mom walked us to school the first day, I was in tears. John and I also had speech therapy. I can only assume that stems from our unique twin talk impeding our language development. My mom's sister Terry would tease me all the time. "Chris, say can't smoke in school." My response was "can't foke in fool." Hardy fucking har!

I'm not sure exactly how old we were, but we started with recreational sports at an early age. Soccer and t-ball came first. Developing relationships, making friends, and learning about teamwork can never be taken for granted. This all seemed natural growing up in the suburbs. The orange slices to suck on between quarters were always a welcome treat.

~~~

My parents were raised in a religious household, as their parents were, and theirs before them. We attended church as a family every Sunday morning for as long as I can remember. The first church we frequented was St. Anne's in Garwood. My parents eventually joined St. Helen's of Westfield as some of their close friends, relatives on my father's side, and some of my friends' families were members there. It was also a bigger, more modern parish, with more amenities and was always kept clean. Our mother offered her services as a Eucharistic minister when needed.

John and I also became huge fans of the *Star Wars* franchise around this time. I think we saw *Return of the Jedi* seven times while it was playing locally. We had tons of action figures and some of the bigger toy models such as the At-At, Endor cruisers, walkers, X-wings and of course the Millennium Falcon. That year for Halloween I was Luke Skywalker and my brother was Han Solo.

Second grade was the first time I was ever struck in the face for butting into affairs that were none of my business. The students would line up outside the east entrance of Walnut School before the doors opened. One morning before entering school, two of my classmates were wrestling on the ground. From what I can gather, it was a primitive show of machoism to show off for one of the girls. It so happens I had a crush on the same girl at the time. While they were wrestling, I absent-mindedly began to prod them with my foot, and this may have been construed as kicking them while they were down. In an instant, they both got up off the ground and simultaneously, open-hand-smacked me in the face. The students went inside, and I remained outside for a little longer with tears in my eyes and red cheeks.

Around this age, I began my lifelong love of baseball. Cranford had, and still has, an amazing recreational league system for all ages. The south side (residents south of the railroad tracks) had the Memorial Field League and the north side had the Adams Avenue league. My brother and I would throw the ball around in the yard with our dad whenever we got the chance and developed our hand-eye coordination, basics, and mechanics during practice and games.

My first position was catcher, and my first baseball heroes were Gary Carter and Ted Williams. Gary was a role model to all young base ballers at the time. He truly embodied his moniker, "The Kid," and his youthful exuberance on the field and the way he lived his life off the field seemed to uphold core values of the American dream. I was drawn to Ted Williams for his record setting season average of .406 that I believe will never be matched and his lifelong batting average of .344. Even at my young age, I understood basic stats. Those are monster numbers!

For one of my first games behind the plate, I forgot to wear my jockstrap and cup. That was a tough lesson to learn. A fastball that fell short of the strike zone got under my glove and bounced right up where 'X' marks the spot. I played it off well but was screaming silently for about 20 minutes. I eventually moved to right field, then first base, and then third base early in my tenure in Little League.

One day, the Yankee Scooter Phil Rizzuto graced our fields with his presence and called one of the games in the next age-group league. I was walking with my grandpa, and he spotted Scooter before I did. He was walking toward the parking lot, and my grandfather told me to go shake his hand. I ran to catch up to him and the fellow he was walking with and said, "Excuse me, Mr. Rizzuto? I was just wondering if I could shake your hand?" He said "Why certainly young fella!" My right hand was soaked and sticky as the Coke I was running with spilled all over the place. I didn't want to get him sticky as well, so we shook hands lefty. I ran back to my grandpa who was smiling ear to ear. He had most likely seen him play fifty years earlier and was elated I was able to meet him.

Around this time, our mom's brother, Uncle Chris, was instrumental in getting us to follow the New York Mets. He'd always been a fan of the Amazins and still is. This was the era when Doc Gooden and Darryl Strawberry were making a name for themselves, and we started watching the 1986 season with fervor. I remember that fall watching the World Series game up in our folks' bedroom when Bill Buckner booted that grounder at first base. We were jumping up and down with excitement that the Mets had a chance at coming back. The momentum carried them to the championship. It was a brilliant series and further galvanized my love for America's Pastime.

John and I got our first bikes for Christmas around this age. They were the same model of Mongoose dirt bikes and really sleek. My friends and I loved the bike movie *Rad*, so no doubt that had a contributing effect on the type of bikes we got. I was so pumped that I had to take it out on that cold Christmas morning, with patches of ice on the ground. While riding around the block, I hit one of those patches and went flying. I still have a scar on my right knee as proof of my overzealousness.

Third grade was much the same as second at Walnut Avenue School, save for developing friendships and playing more often with the other kids from the neighborhood. We'd play wall ball outside the school on lunch break and develop enthralling games such as Push Down, in which the goal was to grab someone on our front lawn and push or throw him to the ground. This was pretty exciting stuff for a 9-year-old. I also purposely did poorly on an eye exam with the intent of getting prescribed glasses to make me appear more educated and refined, in hopes of impressing a girl I had a crush on. John and I also tried our hand at wrestling, but the leotards we had to wear and the fact that I had grappling all sweaty with one of my peers was a huge deterrent. Needless to say, that didn't last.

I was first exposed to alcohol around the age of nine. We were at my mom's parents' house in Newark visiting one evening and my Uncle Chris was drinking a Heineken. Naturally wanting to fit in and gain acceptance from my uncle, I asked if I could try one. I think my mom was in the other room at the time, but I started chugging what was offered to me. I didn't get sick. In fact, I enjoyed the sudsy taste; however, it immediately went to my head, and I got dizzy pretty quickly. By that time, my mom had found out what happened, and though she wasn't mad, she wasn't too pleased, either. I think she actually got a good laugh at what transpired. My uncle quickly passed the buck to me, maintaining that I was the one who expressed interest and that he had he clearly explained prior to handing me the bottle that it was an adult beverage and not for kids.

From kindergarten through third grade, I attended Walnut Avenue School, and then went to Livingston Avenue School for fourth through sixth. Both schools were pretty equidistant from our home. John and I were always able to walk home through the field or down our street for lunch. We had it pretty easy and were spoiled with healthy and delicious food prepared by our mom, who was the classic stay-at-home mom for much of our youth. Livingston was really where I started to consciously listen to music and was excited whenever music class was scheduled during the week.

Around fifth grade, I started wanting to pick up and learn how to play an instrument. The music teacher taught us the basics with *Every*, *Good*, *Boy*, *Deserves*, *Fudge* and *FACE* for the treble staff and showed us how to decipher key signatures. My first instrument was the alto saxophone. It was rented by my parents from a music store in Garwood that catered to students looking to expand their horizons and creative outlets.

At this age, I was exposed to the concept of what true love is and can and should be. That fall, one of my favorite movies was released—*The Princess Bride*. John and I went to see it with our mom and Aunt Pat at the Westfield Rialto. The repetitive phrase "As you wish," uttered by Peter Falk's character, and Westley, the Dread Pirate Roberts, took root in my subconscious. The ideals of selflessness and service in a romantic relationship always seemed to be chiseled in that phrase.

Our family got its first computer around this time. It was one of those boxy DOS operating system jobs with a floppy disk drive. I was curious, and ended up tinkering around on the thing long enough to try my hand at creative writing. I ended up writing a short story about a kid who was always running to and from school and eventually built up enough stamina and endurance to run a mile in under four minutes.

My first visit to an orthodontist and allergist was during this time period. I had scratch tests to uncover what else, in addition to cats, was causing my spastic sneezing, itchy throat, ears, watery eyes, and overall complete discomfort. For those unfamiliar, a scratch test is performed by puncturing the skin on the inside of the forearm with allergens to determine what agents are the culprits for one's misery. It was determined that cats, dust, dust mites, and pollen were the leading antagonists. I had 14 scratch marks on each arm. I felt like the subject of a mad scientist's experiment. For years, before the invention of effective oral allergy medication, I had to go to the allergist's office for shots. My only saving grace was the beautiful receptionist who was working there. Yes, I took notice at a pretty young age!

I got braces around this age as well. It was instilled upon me at an early age that good oral hygiene was important, and I took great pride in having strong, healthy teeth. My folks have horrible teeth. By horrible I don't mean crooked, jagged, chipped, or missing teeth—I mean weak. This was most likely due to lack of fluoride in the tap water at the time and other variables that are classic culprits of tooth decay. My mom's dentist was a drunk and often performed check-ups, cleanings, and minor surgery while inebriated.

Besides rec league baseball, soccer, and basketball, fifth grade was the year John and I entertained PAL football for the first time. Our dad, uncle, and two of our oldest cousins all played, and it was inevitable that we'd take a crack at the sport. The practices were a total turn off for me from the get-go. What 11-year-old likes to be screamed at and belittled by coaches who happened to be ex-jocks? I understand it's how you toughen up a team, but the practices were run like boot camp or basic training. I know the coaches had our best interest at heart, but that first (and last) year of playing football left a sour taste in my mouth.

We would often go with our friends to the field at Livingston School to take grounders or play a small pick-up game, just to stay active and improve our basic skills. The field had a backstop and makeshift pitcher's mound right. One day, I was running out to the field to take my position for grounders when I heard a metallic clanking sound. I turned around and one of my friends was banging my brand new aluminum Easton baseball bat against the metal post of the backstop. I was livid. I charged over to him as fast as I could, snatched the bat from his hands, and took a major league swing at his head. He ran home at top speed and most likely shit his pants. What he witnessed first-hand as a fit of maniacal rage wasn't that at all. Sure, my swing may have missed his head by inches, but I had no intention of putting a dent in it. I just wanted to scare him enough so he'd never fuck with my property ever again. He never did.

Growing up in a family that went to church every Sunday meant having to endure all aspects, initiations, and ceremonies of the faith. This meant christening and baptism, confirmation, and attending CCD, or religious education designed for children. Morals, ethics, and interpretation of parables were instilled upon me and many of my close friends over the course of the program. These classes were held and taught at different friend's houses by their parents, who were raised as my parents were.

I'm pretty sure I got my first musical instrument to own at this age. It was a Yamaha synthesizer, and I believe it was a Christmas gift. The keys were not standard size, but nonetheless, I had a lot of fun making sounds on that thing and really started to hear and see music from a different perspective. It started to seep into my subconscious.

That summer I landed my first kiss. It was at Unami Park, near the tennis courts. Actually, I went up her shirt that same day. What can I say? I was 12 and testing my limits. This was the girl I had had a crush on for so long. Classically and uniquely beautiful, with auburn hair, she was one of the only redheads in our grade. After graduating from checkers, I loved to play chess, and her father was a wizard at the game. I used to go over to their house and play him, and I'm pretty sure he let me win here and there. Either way, it had a bolstering effect on my problem-solving and analytical skills and use of logic.

~~~

My dad inherited a sizable chunk of change from his Uncle Frank after he passed and had a house built in Brielle, right on the Manasquan border west of the tracks in the late 70s or early 80s. When my parents weren't renting it out seasonally, we would spend weeks at a clip down there enjoying the majesty of the shore and all it had to offer. After the summer rentals moved out, they were tasked with cleaning the property, and my brother and I would help out with whatever was asked of us. John and I both got Walkmans the previous Christmas from Grandpa Leo and Grandma Gloria, and our musical library was slowly growing with each cassette tape we purchased. Our folks always had on an old-ies station in the car, so there was an early exposure to Motown and Top 40 from the 60s and 70s. I'm sure I bopped my head or sang along to whatever was popular at the time on the modern stations; however, our musical education was mostly influenced by what our friends' older siblings were listening to at the time. I remember working in the yard at the summerhouse and singing along to every track on Tom Petty's *Full Moon Fever*. Other notable tapes were R.E.M's *Eponymous* and *Green*, as well as *Simon and Garfunkel's Greatest Hits*, which I would listen to while doing my homework. Albums I remember being near the record player included Jimi Hendrix's *Are You Experienced*, *Led Zeppelin IV*, *The Eagles'*

Greatest Hits as well as Crosby, Stills, Nash, and Young's *Déjà vu*.

My sixth-grade teacher was a fox--tall, blonde, and thin with eloquent curves. She made it difficult to approach the chalkboard on more than a few occasions as the blood was flowing into different areas of my body at that time. I tested for the Gifted and Talented program, was admitted, and after a few classes decided it wasn't for me. The math equations they were putting in front of me looked like a foreign language and were obviously for a skill set a couple years beyond my age.

Kids in this time period were spoiled with classic movies that are forever embedded in our minds. Asides from rec sports, hitting a movie, attending a birthday party at the local bowling alley, or heading up to grab some pizza at Pizza Hut in town, we'd have sleepovers at each other's houses. These included playing video games, ordering Domino's Pizza, making prank phone calls, and watching movies such as *Vacation, European Vacation, Rambo First Blood*, Pt. 2, *Indiana Jones and the Temple of Doom, Ghostbusters, Commando, American Ninja, The Karate Kid, Goonies, Revenge of the Nerds, Back to the Future, Back to School, Real Genius, Weird Science, Predator, Better off Dead, Three Amigos, Back to the Beach, One Crazy Summer, Stripes, Spies Like Us, Roadhouse, Gung Ho, Wildcats*, and *Die Hard*, to name a few. My friends and I saw pretty much every classic movie that came out or made its way to HBO or was rentable at Blockbusters. A lot of us were so obsessed with martial arts, ninjas, and samurais that when visiting flea markets, we'd purchase Chinese stars to throw at trees or the sides of houses, just to watch them stick. Our friend's older brother even owned a samurai sword. John and I took judo lessons with the late Yone Yonesku, who coached one of the U.S. Olympic judo teams. He let me throw him to the ground to teach us that no matter how big or strong an opponent, proper technique will take care of the rest. We also started playing tennis at the local courts.

Our aunt Pat and uncle Chris decided to take us skiing one weekend. It was a day trip to Camelback Mountain in Pennsylvania. John and I had never gone before, but it looked like fun, and our uncle was an experienced skier. He'd done back bowls out West and even heli-skiied up in Canada. We rented our boots and skis and made our way to the bunny hill to get a feel for maneuvering, turning, and stopping. After a few runs on the hill, our uncle asked if we'd like to give an easy trail a try. I wasn't staying on the bunny hill all day, so I told him sure. Once we exited the chairlift, we followed our uncle to the top of a trail. Looking down, I couldn't believe it was an easy trail. It was steep and seemed to go straight down. I turned to him and asked if he was sure if it was a green trail, to which he replied, "Yeah, don't worry about it," and instructed me to make wide turns and, if I ended up going too fast, to put on the brakes. If I felt like I was getting out of control, he said, just fall down. So I followed him down and immediately was in complete fear due to the fact that I was gaining an incredible amount of speed. I didn't make any turns—I was careening straight down out of control. I heard my uncle yell "Fall down," but that wasn't a suggestion. That was going to happen eventually. My left leg angled to the left while my right stayed straight. Any skier will tell you that that, plus speed and no control, is a recipe for disaster. I totally ate it, smashed my face into the packed snow and garage-saled my skis and one pole. I watched helplessly as one ski sailed down the slope. My uncle pulled up with the other ski and a pole, and I said "There's no way that was a green trail--that was an intermediate slope," to which he replied "Yeah, if I told you it was a blue run, you wouldn't have wanted to go down it." It took me a long time to appreciate his logic. I later realized his rationale and what he was trying to teach me about overcoming the fear of skiing more difficult slopes, but sending an 11-year-old down a steep hill like that for his first time on skis is kind of fucked up! I ended up walking down the side of the slope, picking up my runaway ski, and sticking to green trails the rest of the day.

By this time, my passion for music was getting stronger. Out of nowhere, I told my mom that I wanted piano lessons. She hired a local teacher who would come once a week and go through lesson plans from a book. After I'd master a lesson or song, we'd go on to the next one. Eventually, I'd reach the end of the book, then start on the next-level lesson book. My Yamaha synthesizer was not an acceptable instrument to learn on, given the size of the keys, so my mom purchased a standard-key electric piano on a payment plan to get me up and running. Week by week, my proficiency on the piano advanced, and I became comfortable and confident in how I was progressing.

I was always interested in subjects that were on the fringe— paranormal and supernatural stuff that can't quite be explained or is just a head scratcher. Time Life released a series of books that catered to this area. These books would arrive every month, which was just the right pace to keep my thirst for the unexplained satiated. The name of the series is Library of Curious and Unusual Facts. The book titles are as follows: *Vanishings; Feats and Wisdom of the Ancients; The Mystifying Mind; Forces of Nature; Amazing Animals; Manias and Delusions; Mysteries of the Human Body; Odd and Eccentric People; Hoaxes and Deceptions; Lost Treasure; Shadows of Death; A World of Luck, Crimes and Punishments; and Inventive Genius.*

The week of graduating sixth grade the movie *Batman* came out. That was a graduation present in itself as the association with that particular superhero was still a part of me. We would also frequent a little play park on Route 22 called Boat Craft that had rides and an arcade. And we would also head up to Tuxedo, New York, to check out the Renaissance Fair and practice our archery and axe-throwing skills. That summer, the family, along with our mom's sister Patty, began taking an annual vacation to the Poconos. This resort had an outdoor and indoor pool, tennis courts, a lake on the property where guests could take paddleboats and rafts out, as well as spa services and an amazing dining facility that served great fare.

There wasn't much to gearing up for junior high school that summer. We weren't working any jobs or anything. Our friends and the local crew from the neighborhood would play simple games such as Tag or Ghost in the graveyard on our block. We'd ride our dirt bikes on trails throughout the wooded areas in town, hit the mall, play tennis, go into town, play Photon or Laser Tag, catch a movie, take a trip to the beach—all types of activities you could imagine doing growing up in the late 80s in middle-class suburbia. We did spend a lot of time at the community pool. Our parents met up with their friends, and so did John and I. I became a little more daring on the diving board, perfecting a flip from the low and high boards. Some of my friends were doing 1½s from the low board, but I never took the chance. I would do ¼ and ½ twists. The two times I tried a 1½ from the high board I landed first on my face and then flat on my back. Like hitting pavement.

Hillside Avenue was a K–8 school. It was a simple commute. John and I simply biked through the Walnut Avenue field, down a side street that led to a small bridge that went over a narrow section of the Rahway River, up the street, under a small tunnel that was beneath the train tracks and voilà—we were at school. When it was raining or snowing, we'd either be fortunate enough to get dropped off or grin and bear it on foot.

Adjusting to a new format wasn't too difficult. I liked not being stuck in the same classroom for an entire day and having a locker to keep all my stuff in. In the fall, I played on the school soccer team. I never ventured from defense, and the only position I can remember ever playing was sweeper.

The winter of my first year of junior high, I tried out for the basketball team. It seemed like a natural progression given the rec leagues I played in up until then, and anything to keep my brother and I occupied, out of our parent's hair, and out of trouble was always welcome. One early evening after a tryout I was in the locker room. I had just taken a piss and was about to change when two guys from CAP (Cranford Alternative Program) began roughing me up and throwing me against the lockers. They wanted to eliminate any competition to ensure their spots on the team. It was a pure after-school special episode. I think they said that if I told anyone what happened they would make the rest of my school year a living hell. One was twice my size and the other was affiliated with a local gang. They were thugs. CAP was for students with learning disabilities as well as troubled home lives. These two obviously didn't have the same upbringing as I did. Well, their threats worked. I didn't return the next day for the tryouts. I wasn't too keen on basketball anyway. I think the most points I ever scored playing rec league in a single game was 8 or 10.

My advantage was my height, which was good for hanging out under the basket to retrieve rebounds. I can only assume the thugs preyed on my passive disposition, which made me an easy target for a bunch of ruffians with a lack of ethics and moral turpitude. I'd never been in a situation like that before and really didn't know what to do or who to turn to for help. I was just minding my own business and trying my best. Anyway, I'm not sure what ever became of the bigger guy. I do remember hearing the gang affiliate was shot to death a couple years after I graduated high school.

Other than gym, where our favorite game was Hit the Pin, my favorite subject in junior high was music. I started on the sax, picked up a trombone for a day and settled on playing the xylophone, given my background with the piano. I don't remember much of what music class was like other than we had to march and play marching standards through town during parades.

Seventh grade was when the first guitar entered our home. Our Uncle Chris had a beautiful 1976 Hohner acoustic. He gave it to my brother after he expressed interest in it thus furthering our passion for music. I was still taking piano lessons and didn't have much interest in picking it up at first. I think there was a Mel Bay chord-chart book in the guitar case, so John started picking up shapes and names of chords. After hearing him pluck away for some time, I was curious and wanted a crack at it. It sounds funny, but I kind of knew how to play it before even picking it up. The piano lessons were paying off, and my music theory was expanding at a modest rate. All I needed to know was how the instrument was strung and I was able to construct chords from scratch. I may have scanned the chord book, but the shapes seemed familiar to me. I understood open chords and figured the shapes of bar chords were movable all over the neck, so I began to internalize them. I knew how major scales were constructed and their relative minors, so I was able to pick out melodies by ear. After my brother began to see my skill set surpass his, he decided he wanted to play bass guitar. He got a cheap starter bass and amp and began honing his chops.

My first experience with loss came in junior high. Our beloved family

Golden Retriever, Muffin, got cancer. It was in her snout, and the growth enlarged the right side of it. My folks did all they could for her, but it eventually metastasized. I was home sick the day Muff took a turn for the worse. She wasn't eating and had lost control of her bowels. She couldn't get up on her own. My mom carried her to the car to take her to the vet. I immediately ran upstairs to my bedroom, got on my knees, and began to pray for anything good that God or the vet could do for her. A little while later, my mom pulled into the driveway and came up the walkway carrying only her collar and leash. I'm sure my mom was rehearsing in the car how she was going to explain to me and my brother the decision to put her down, but at the time, I didn't really understand that there was nothing that could be done for her. I thought there was some surgery or medicine, or that they could keep her at the vet overnight for further analysis and observation. I wasn't expecting my mom to come back without her. Muffin was family, and we all treated her that way.

I was devastated when she told me. That was the first time I had ever felt a pain like that in my heart. I completely lost it. Wailing uncontrollably for the rest of the day, burying my head in a pillow on my bed—it was pure hell. When John got home from school, his reaction was similar to mine.

We wanted to get another puppy immediately and name her Muffin II. Our mom quickly shot that down, explaining there was only one Muffin and naming another dog after her wouldn't do any good in the long run. We relented, but the decision was still made to go out to the pet store on Route 22 the next day and pick out a puppy. John and I couldn't imagine being in a house without a puppy or dog. They just bring too much love and joy with them.

The next day after school we got lucky. There was a litter of 8–10-week-old Golden Retriever puppies. The employee removed them all from their cage, where they were just rolling around and playing with one another, and placed them in a gated pen so we could get a feel for which one was coming home with us. We were instantly drawn to the one female with the most energy, spunk, chutzpa, personality—you name it, she had it. Shanna came home with us that afternoon.

The spring rolled around, and John and I tried out for and made the baseball team. This time, no one was going to bully me off of the team no matter what. Baseball was my favorite sport. There was still a rec league going on, and we ended up pulling double duty, with practice and games for both teams, which many of the junior high team did as well.

During the summer months, a group of us got together in our free time, when we weren't taking day trips to the beach or hitting the community pools, to stretch our imaginations and enter a world of fantasy role-playing. This role-playing was known as Dungeons and Dragons. For those unfamiliar with it, a Dungeon Master set the course of play, and a roll of the dice determined each player's level of ability, including their strength, constitution, dexterity, intelligence, and wisdom. You could pick a race, be it human, elven, half-elf, etc., as well as a specialty or occupation.

Parties in junior high consisted of soft drinks (with the occasional hard-liquor spike for those who dared and were fortunate enough to raid their parents' liquor cabinet without getting caught), chips, pretzels, who had the latest pair of Cavaricci pants, girls dancing and singing their lungs out to New Kids on the Block and Vanilla Ice, as well as spin the bottle and closet time. It was all completely fun and innocent.

My brother and I expanded our group of friends as we met more people from Hillside Avenue. Cranford is such a tight-knit group that if you found a couple of things in common with someone, it wasn't too hard to strike up a conversation or start goofing around, as teenagers tend to do. John and I would jam with a friend who grew up in a more liberal home than ours. His parents were hippies, as was his older sister. We actually entered a talent contest held at a regional high school in Springfield and performed an original song we wrote together. John played bass, our friend played acoustic guitar, and I was on piano. I think we took second or third place, but to be involved in the creative process at such a precocious age was a total confidence booster.

Speaking of the creative process, I started to experiment with composition on the piano. I began to understand how songs were structured just from reading music and listening to them on the radio. In seventh grade,

I was sent to the Union County Teen Arts Festival at Union County College for a drawing I did in art class. In eighth grade, I was selected to attend again based on the piano piece I wrote. When I say wrote, I didn't write notes out on staff paper. All the parts were committed to memory. From my experience the previous year, I saw it as a free day out of school with the opportunity to meet some new and interesting peers from neighboring towns. We weren't required to be anywhere and mostly just roamed the halls of the buildings, popping in here and there to check out other students' work in sculpture, painting, drawing, etc. In one class, I was called up to the piano to perform my piece. I wasn't planning to play in front of anyone, as I was more interested in listening to students perform classical pieces by Mozart and Beethoven, given that their musical skill far exceeded mine. These are kids that started on the piano at early ages (like four) with a disciplined approach to learning the instrument. Nonetheless, the teacher in charge of the class insisted I come up and play what I had written. I was sweating bullets when I sat down to play. But I focused, got into it, and did my best. The composition was between and 3 ½ and 4 ½ minutes long. After I struck the last chord, I received a round of applause from everyone in the room. I heard some kid criticizing the song for its simplicity; however, the response moved me enough to decide to take time out of my day and work on writing something original, as opposed to playing someone else's piece.

Another confrontation also left me scratching my head. One day John and I were walking home from school and there was a group of kids behind us. They were all African American. One of them started shouting stuff at my brother for no reason. We just kept walking and ignoring the generic insults. This kid was obviously trying to pick a fight, knowing he had a crew to back him up if he got in trouble. He got closer and pushed my brother from behind. I was a little further ahead on the walk than John and actually kept walking. Nothing really came of it except for the perpetrator getting an ego stroke. My brother caught up to me, and I was a little embarrassed that I didn't turn around and stand by him. I just didn't believe in fighting. There was no reason for any of this. John never offended this kid, and we were always friendly and polite to him. Perhaps it was some sort of gang initiation deed that needed to be done. In any event, years later I heard the kid met the same fate as the bully during basketball tryouts—shot to death.

While on the topic of fighting, there's another incident that happened during junior high that involved my brother. Everyone knows how the stereotypical seventh and eighth-grade dances were. They pretty much consisted of all the guys on one side of the gym and girls on the other, with the DJ playing hits from the 80s or staples such as Meatloaf's "Paradise by the Dashboard Light." These dances were held on the north side of town at a school that was later converted to a community center. This meant students from Hillside Avenue commingled with students from Orange Avenue and Brookside Avenue. We rec-league guys knew a few of the north-siders by face or what team they played on, so it wasn't a completely foreign experience. Near the end of the evening one fall night, my brother was outside of the dance waiting for some friends and me. He was leaning over a railing when he felt a tap on his shoulder. He turned around, and the next thing he saw was stars. He got sucker-punched right on the side of his eye. He stayed on his feet but was in considerable pain, and the bruising started immediately. Apparently, what instigated this was somehow my fault. A girl that we grew up with and knew since kindergarten was hanging around with some kid from either CAP or a neighboring town and somehow sneaked into the dance. We later learned that I had somehow offended this girl by either saying something mean or pushing past her on my way to the bathroom. I know I didn't speak one word to this girl all night. She may have been near someone I was talking to and misheard what I was saying to my friend and heard something entirely different and thought it was directed at her. If I did push past her, I would've said excuse me and thought nothing of it. Perhaps I tripped over my feet in haste and put a hand on her to steady myself. I don't know. I did not see any of my actions as aggressive—certainly not enough to warrant someone taking a punch to the face. Diplomacy is a better course of action than violence. If she sought an apology I would've gladly offered one.

The boy's identity was eventually learned, and rather than pressing assault charges, my parents opted for his parents to just pay for John's medical bill. The kid was scolded by his parents and made him apologies for his actions. Afterward, whenever John and I saw him, he was always very polite and courteous, and we obliged.

~~~

Nearing the end of eighth grade, our class had an assembly on what we could expect when we got to high school. Being a freshman with three grades of students ahead of you seemed terrifying to me at the time, but the selected representatives and teachers that spoke did a good job of smoothing things over. The high-school band director came to the music class, as it was necessary to try out for band to get accepted. I played through a piece on the glockenspiel, and he seemed satisfied enough with my level of ability. As I was leaving, he told me to give him one more minute and asked that I turn away from the bells. He struck a note and asked me which one it was. I told him F#, which was correct, and he smiled and told me he'd be seeing me in the fall. I later realized that he was just testing my ears. Technically, this was a test of relative pitch or relative perfect pitch, where I was able to come up with the correct note from a referenced piece of music. In this case, the piece I was playing was in the key of D, and the F# is the third note in a D-major scale, so I heard that interval fairly easily.

High school started earlier than junior high and was on the north side of town, which meant John and I had to get up earlier to make it to class on time. We were fairly resourceful, either walking through town and grabbing a bagel with cream cheese and chocolate milk on the way and feasting when we got to our lockers while sitting in the hallway; biking; getting dropped off during the winter months; hitching a ride with our neighbors, who were a few years older than us and had their driver's licenses.

The high-school student body was composed of all junior high schools in town, so the north side and south side were combined. On average, each class had about 200 students. The high school had four floors, five if you counted the imaginary bowling alley and pool that the upper-classmen joked about. I enjoyed all my classes and began to develop an unquenchable thirst for knowledge. Band, gym, and science were leading the pack for my favorite subjects.

My day after school consisted of any chores that were required of me, such as raking leaves or sticky balls off the lawn, getting my homework done, dinner, shower, watching some TV and woodshedding on the guitar as much as possible. Woodshedding pretty much means playing for hours on end either working on chord shapes or scales on my own or learning songs by ear. My pianos lessons stopped before high school, given that I learned all I needed to know as far as the language of music and reading. My focus and passion were immersing myself in as much music as possible and playing until my fingers hurt. I still had the Hohner acoustic, and playing on heavier strings than an electric will toughen your fingers up pretty quickly. When I wasn't completely focused on a disciplined approach to learning something new, I was noodling while slouching on the floor in my brother's room watching TV. That was the key to my development at an early age. I always had the guitar working when I wasn't busy doing anything.

I got my first electric guitar for Christmas during freshman year in high school. It was colored midnight blue with a rosewood fret board and had triangular fret markings. It was sleek—an Ibanez X Series. Coupled with the guitar, my first amplifier was also part of my Christmas package. Aunt Pat picked me up a great starter amp. It was a Gorilla. A $100 jobber that had a great clean-and-crunch channel. Throw in a guitar tuner, a set of strings, picks-and an instrument cable and I was ready to rock!

I took a month of lessons at the local guitar shop. Once a week for a month I went down there seeking knowledge and technique to hone my craft. I was hungry and always a quick study when I had my heart set on something. My heart was set on learning everything I could about playing the guitar. The instructor, who was also the shop owner, set me up with a guitar tab booklet and showed me the basis of rock 'n' roll soloing—the minor pentatonic scale. From there, he added the b5 for the blues scale, and then we went on to the major pentatonic scale. He charted out some chord voicings, and he showed me how to transcribe songs that I wanted to learn just from listening to them. It wasn't rocket science. Put a tune on, figure out the key, and play along. If you didn't get it on the first pass, rewind, and keep going through the section until you do get it. Then, write it down.

After a month, I gathered enough information and technique to keep studying on my own. I bought a subscription to *Guitar World* magazine and couldn't wait for the issue to arrive in the mail. One of the very first issues to arrive had an awesome black and white photo of Pink Floyd (sans Syd Barrett) circa 1968 or 69. I was like "These guys are fucking cool!" The magazine had a transcription of "Comfortably Numb" off of *The Wall* album. That CD was one of the first that I owned, and that solo was one of the first that I learned note for note. Back in the day, there was no Internet. There were no YouTube instructionals. Everything was either written in staff/sheet music or tab. Tab was always easier for learning songs on the guitar.

Over the course of the school year, my brother and I met some other students who were interested in jamming. We knew them by face, name, and casual conversation as they all played rec league sports growing up. These kids were all from the north side of town, so it was exciting to branch out and connect with like-minded individuals who had also caught the music bug. We would set up in the basement of one of the kids, which was also his bedroom. This kid was devilishly handsome, a charmer, well mannered and raised properly. He was also a fucking maniac--like jumping off the walls, slam-dancing maniac. The perfect qualities for a front man! He didn't play an instrument. He just wanted to be Axl Rose. He completely idolized him and was a diehard Guns N' Roses fan. I believe he was famously quoted as saying he would suck his dick if he could. At the time, his ideal fantasy was a ménage à trois with Axl and Madonna. The other fellas who were always part of our jams were also full-fledged GNR fans as well as being into Metallica. They were all best friends growing up, and they welcomed my brother and me into their rock 'n' roll fraternity with open arms. There were a drummer and three other guitar players. At the time, we all had pretty much the same skill set.

Our jam sessions consisted of making sure everyone was in tune and doing our best to play along to songs we wanted to jam to. These included a handful of Guns N' Roses songs and whatever Metallica and AC/DC song we could piece together. I'm pretty sure the first tab book I ever bought was for "Appetite for Destruction." I'd bring it along as a guide and for the others to try to get the licks down. I don't believe we ever worked on writing original material. It was just a lot of fun playing with other kids and goofing around in the process. We continued jamming together whenever it made sense and also moved the location up the street to the drummer's house from time to time.

In school that winter, I decided to join the track team. My sole purpose was to stay active and get in shape for baseball season. Our practices were held indoors, and we would run through the school hallways as well as up and down the stairs. They were ass-kicking practices, but they did their job, as I shed some pounds and was able to keep my energy level up.

At the time, I wasn't much of a runner. I knew this prior to joining the team. I had no stamina and huffed and puffed my way through practices. I ran the 200-meter and made my attempts at what I believe were the 60-meter hurdles. The one incident that turned me off completely was a meet in Elizabeth. It was my first hurdle race, and by about the third or fourth hurdle my long feet caught the top of the hurdle and knocked it down. I fell, but got right back up and ran around the next hurdle, then cleared the remaining ones to finish dead last with the penalty and sloppy technique. I stuck to the 200-meter heats going forward but never did well. I had more fun gawking and flirting with girls from other teams and making fun of people from the bleachers with my newfound track buds than caring what my time was or if I was going to advance to the next heat. I never did!

Learning in school is easy if you have a disciplined approach and enough sleep the night before to pay attention. There's also an element of genetics involved. Our father graduated with a chemical engineering degree from Lafayette College and got his MBA from Rutgers University. Our mother didn't have the same opportunity as our dad did growing up in a lower economic status. She didn't get the chance to attend college or university. Student loans weren't readily available to everyone like they are now these days. However, she has always been sharp, bright, and wise beyond her years. I had a disciplined approach and paid attention in class. I always got As and Bs with the occasional C in a more difficult area of study. My GPA was always above 3.3, sometimes peaking to 3.7 or 3.8, and I prided myself on doing the best that I could and not slacking off. The only thing I had on my plate was school, guitar, sports, and hanging out with my friends.

That fall, through our church we had to attend a retreat with other kids our age as a prerequisite for confirmation. I was pumped because there were girls from other towns to flirt with. Not that it mattered much, as I was still a bit shy but was always game for rousing, goofy conversation if it happened to be in the cards. I always had fun at these functions. They had pit fires at night, and all the kids would be around just shooting the shit and getting to know one another. My brother met this one girl from Westfield and began a casual relationship with trips on the train to her town and long phone calls.

One of our neighborhood friends brought over an air rifle one day. His father was a police officer in town, and we were always into army stuff, G.I. Joe, and the infamous *A Christmas Story* when we were younger, so it was inevitable that one day we'd get our hands on a BB gun. We ended up trying to pick off squirrels and birds. I spied a blue jay perched on the highest branch of the willow tree in our backyard. We had no luck during the shooting session with our targets. This ended differently. I took aim, fired, and the bird just dropped from the branch and landed on the ground. I don't know what I was thinking. If you aim at something and keep missing, eventually you'll find your mark. I thought I would've been proud of my marksmanship, but when my friend picked up this poor bird and saw some blood and a partially splintered beak, my heart dropped. The bird was alive, but the pellet did some structural damage. The bird pecked my friend's hand and managed to fly away. This devastated me. Right then and there I decided I would never pick up any type of weapon ever again nor consciously intend to harm another living creature.

Back to school. Girls were pretty much out of the question. All the girls in my grade I would've hooked up with were into guys on the football or wrestling team or dated guys in older grades. There were a handful of girls I had crushes on, but nothing ever came to fruition. Aside from being shy and having a huge fear of rejection, I really had no idea what to do for dates other than grab some ice cream or pizza or catch a movie. Worst of all, I wasn't old enough to drive yet, so now we're talking having a parent drop off and pick up, etc., which to mean sounded lame. That kind of took the magic out of it all.

With dating out of the way the only other thing to focus on was the guitar, so I kept up my woodshedding and immersing myself in as much music as possible. I appreciated what popular music was on the radio or what MTV was setting into their rotation, but I always knew there was more out there. I sought out music that seemed to speak to me on a deeper level. In a way, certain songs at certain times shape your concepts and your whole perception of life. They are a part of being alive.

~~~

The spring came, and it was time for baseball season. I tried out for the freshman squad and made the team. This was also coupled with rec league, as my brother and I still played. I didn't start many games. My set position was second base; however, there was a player who was a little quicker and more proficient defensively at that spot, so I would go in late in games either at second or in right field. The coach was allowed to discriminate this way. In rec league, everyone gets a chance to play, but in high school, you're dealing with winning and trying to get to the state finals. I believe I had a total of 14 at bats while playing for the freshman team. I had three walks and four hits, which gave me a .364 batting average for the season.

John and I religiously watched MTV, as this was really the only channel on cable devoted to music at the time. Pearl Jam's album *Ten* came out the previous year, and their video for "Alive" received airplay and piqued my interest in the band. A few months later, their video for "Even Flow" started popping up in full rotation. I was hooked. Who are these skinny, longhaired maniacs playing and dancing around stage in fits of lunacy?! The music, vibe, and raw energy of that video were pretty much the catalyst that made me want to pursue music, guitar, and performance.

That summer was relatively pleasant. We had rec league baseball to keep us busy, day trips down to Seven Presidents Park in Long Branch, where John and I would boogie board with a local we made friends with, days spent at the community pools and biking all over the local area in our free time. We still met to play Dungeon's and Dragons and always found time to hit the tennis courts for some pick-up games. John and I started getting a little more serious about our golf game as well. By that, I mean heading to the driving range with our dad and going out for a few rounds here and there. Our dad's passion was golf. He learned from going out with his father and in turn planned to teach us everything he knew. His "bible" was Tommy Armour's *How to Play Your Best Golf All the Time*. He had subscriptions to the leading golf magazines of the day and played countless rounds throughout the year. We were fortunate enough to have him critique our swings and offer suggestions when necessary—which was quite often at that age.

Right before the start of the next school year, my parent's friends had a party to which we were invited. They lived in Westfield and were up the street from our house. Our father's cousin's kids, who were my age give or take a few years, were there, and I started talking to the oldest one about what music we were into. He brought up the Red Hot Chili Peppers, and I mentioned that the only stuff I knew from them were a couple tunes off of *Mother's Milk*. Their cover of Stevie Wonder's "Higher Ground" was always popping up on MTV. He wanted to play me a couple of tracks off their latest album *Blood, Sugar, Sex, Magik* and asked if I wanted to go for a ride in his car, to which I obliged. I was immediately awestruck by what he played for me. It was as if my musical universe expanded in an instant. The rhythm and intent of Anthony Kiedis's vocals, John Frusciante's unique style and choice of chords, Flea's bass bombs, and Chad Smith holding it all together was a feast that I ate wholeheartedly.

One of the bigger changes that fall was the introduction of a new style of music by way of the great Northwest: grunge. Besides becoming a huge Pearl Jam fan and collecting taped bootlegs, Alice in Chain's *Dirt* was released, and many of us were already listening to Nirvana's *Nevermind*. For some reason, that genre of music really spoke to me. Perhaps it was because I was at that age where you are searching for an identity that represents who you are at your core, but I found myself wearing flannel shirts, corduroys, and band shirts from groups like Mother Love Bone, and began to grow my hair long. The raw, organic nature of that music was refreshing in contrast to the pop music that was being played on radio stations such as 95.5FM (WLPJ) or 100.3FM (Z100) at the time. Other notable bands my brother and I were listening to at the time were Stone Temple Pilot's *Core*, Live's *Mental Jewelry*, and Rush's compilation album *Chronicles*.

Parties with alcohol came into my life sophomore year. One of my best friends from the south side of town was the host of such an event in the early fall. He had older sisters who had graduated a couple of years before, so he had an in to the upperclassmen conduit, and obtaining massive quantities of alcohol was never an issue.

I biked over, and when I arrived it was similar to something from an 80s coming-of-age movie: loud music, students from every grade with cans, bottles, or cups of whatever concoction they were sipping, boyfriends hooking up with their girlfriends in a far-off nook of the house, people dancing, people playing drinking games with cards . . . I was immediately hooked. There was a half-keg of beer out back, and a handful of classmates were playing Anchorman in the kitchen. This was a drinking game in which two teams compete to bounce a quarter into a tall mug full of beer. This wasn't any mug—it was a pitcher. A friend asked if I wanted in and I said sure. He then inquired if I could chug a beer. I'd never done so before, but I said yeah, no problem. I ended up losing the first game, as whoever I was pitted against sunk the quarter on the first bounce. I didn't even get a chance! The rule was that the losing team had to finish the pitcher in two drinking sessions, meaning once one teammate began drinking the beer, his lips were not to come off the pitcher until he gave what was left to his teammate. So, you're not capable of seeing how much is left to drink and are let to guess based on how much lighter the pitcher gets. Sure, you can look down the top of the pitcher while you're drinking from it, but the pitcher is so voluminous there's really no way to tell how much you've got left. I drank between 60 and 70 percent of the contents of the pitcher, meaning the "first" beer I had at my first high-school party was actually three to four beers. I may have played another game or two that evening, but I was so in awe of the overall atmosphere and vibe of the party that I was happy enough to shoot the shit with whomever I ended up talking to, and drank until it was time to head home.

We had a curfew, so I was typically always mindful of how much time we had before heading home. I definitely left before curfew time, as I was feeling the effects of the alcohol in my virgin system. Light-headedness, loss of balance, slurred speech—you name it, I was drunk. I'm not even sure if I said good-bye to the host, or anyone else for that matter. It could've been a classic Irish exit. I stumbled down the stairs and managed to find my bike on the side of the house in the dark. What lay ahead was pure disaster. Between the party and my home, short of going over my handlebars, I fell off my bike every possible way about a dozen times. I say it this way, because at the time, I specifically remembered counting. That and fucking laughing my ass off! There was nothing I could do about it. I would pedal, lose my balance and go over. Get back on, repeat, etc. I'm lucky that someone from the neighborhood wasn't watching or I wasn't hit by a car while crossing Walnut Avenue. It was obviously more fun falling in the field than the street. I had cuts, scrapes, and bruises everywhere and did my best to conceal them from my parents. I made it in the house and upstairs without incident or being spotted by my parents and immediately passed out with my clothes on in my bed. Later in the morning when I awoke I noticed my sheets and clothes were wet. Not surprisingly, I completely lost control of my bodily functions and pissed myself.

During that fall in band class, I met a set of fraternal twins who were freshman who became part of our crew. I say crew meaning that my brother and I both hung out with the same friends and started branching out to other areas, finding like-minded kids with similar interests. In our case, those interests were making fun of every conceivable aspect of life, as we knew it at the time. One of the twins was very collegiate, outgoing, and social; the other a true cynic, an introvert with very little respect for authority, although he wasn't one to act up in class. They seemed to be shadows of one another, meaning that if you combined them, you would have the entire spectrum of a complete 14-year-old growing up middle to upper class in the suburbs. The "preppy" one played trumpet, and the introvert was a drummer. I say introvert, but though he was shy around strangers once he was comfortable around people he trusted he opened up and was a riot.

Our mom took on some part-time work to help with the bills and have a little extra spending money. Of course, other than buying groceries, the majority of what she earned went toward my brother and me. She never spent anything on herself. She would work late on Tuesdays, and our dad didn't cook, so that was the night we'd hit Friendly's for dinner. I'd always get grilled cheese with tomato and bacon and a side of fries. We always had room for our peanut-butter-cup sundaes.

I frequented the local guitar shop from time to time, either picking up strings and picks or just thumbing through tab books. I always checked out the guitars on the walls. The owner had some vintage axes moving through his shop, and my eyes always lit up when I spotted a Fender Stratocaster from the 50s, 60s or 70s. By this time, I was getting more and more into bands such as Pink Floyd and guitarists like Eric Clapton. The guitar that he, David Gilmour, and Jimi Hendrix made famous mesmerized me. The shape was sexy and seductive; and when you gripped the neck and had one on your lap, flush against your body and underneath your right arm—it instantly empowered you. One strat caught my eye every time I went to the shop that fall. It had a rosewood neck, sunburst body, Floyd Rose floating bridge, two single coils set near the neck and middle positions, and a double humbucker pick-up at the bridge. It was a spotless 1992 American-made strat. I played it and immediately fell in love with its woody, earthen tone in the neck pick-up position, the twang of the split positions, and the heavy, chunky thuds of the bridge. I had not a dollar to my name, but Christmas time was approaching. It wasn't cheap either. I think it cost about $650 (before tax), which was a hefty chunk of change for my folks. They also didn't see any reason why I should own two guitars. My dad always had a good logical analysis of any situation. "But you already have a guitar." Yeah, but this is a Fender Stratocaster!" How could he not understand?! They eventually relented, and I believe my mom set up a payment plan at the shop, so it would've been paid off in time to sit pretty under the Christmas tree.

Our mom's father fell ill around this time. He was admitted to the hospital, and when elderly people with weakened immune systems take up residence for a few days, their risk of contracting pneumonia goes up. This is exactly what happened to him, and he passed away without my brother or I getting a chance to say good-bye. It was so sudden and unexpected. I'll never forget the pain and sorrow I witnessed from my mom at the wake. It hurt me to see her in such a state—I'd never seen her like that before. Our uncle was smiling, shaking hands, and thanking people for coming. He either held it together very well or was still in shock. People grieve in their own way, and I'm no different.

〜〜

That winter, some of the guys in band class as well as the soccer team (John played soccer freshman and sophomore years) got wind that we played guitar and bass. We were invited over to one of their houses while the parents were on vacation. Two of the guys were drummers, and the soccer guys were also in choir, so they could carry a tune. This led to writing a few original songs that we'd rehearse from time to time. I don't remember any of the original song titles other than one named "The Fetal Polka." It had vulgar lyrics set to a polka beat, and we fell over ourselves every time we played it, as the singers did their best Phil Anselmo (singer for Pantera) impressions.

In preparation for the spring concert, a trio from the madrigal class was selected to perform Eric Clapton's "Tears in Heaven." The madrigals were a separate class that members of the choir had to audition for. There were only six or seven spots for the guys and six or seven for the ladies. They would perform more intricate and complex chamber music, some pieces dating back to the 16th or 17th century and sometimes involving more than four harmonies and singing in rounds, as well as Toccata and fugue styles. The choir director asked the band director if there were any guitarists in class that could perform the song with the singers. The parts called for two guitarists, and I told him that I could do it and knew a friend in our grade that could also pull it off. The guitar tablature was in a recent *Guitar World* or *Guitar Player* magazine that I had, and I recently played through it. Now, it was just a matter of committing it to memory. This never seemed to be an issue, as the more you practice and learn songs; the more they are ingrained in your muscle and cellular memory.

I had maybe two rehearsals with my friend at his house and another couple with the madrigal singers. We played the song twice in front of an audience. The first time was for the students, as they always had a concert during school hours, and the next was for the general public, which included friends, family, and anyone who felt like attending. I took the lead part and my friend played rhythm. The performances went great, which bolstered my confidence and diminished any imaginary fears relating to stage fright. Up to this point, that performance was the most exposure I've had playing guitar in front of people.

Auditions to get into next year's jazz band were held. The song selected was "Cherokee," the standard written by Ray Noble and performed by various artists including Charlie Parker, Duke Ellington, the Count Basie Orchestra, and Sarah Vaughan to name a few. I was to play it in front of the band director. The spot wasn't a lock. Another student in my grade was auditioning as well. I took the sheet music home and ran through it maybe twice, then didn't look at it again until the audition a week or two later. I never even heard the song. I didn't think to purchase it or even ask for guidance after school to prepare for the audition. I figured I'd just be able to sight read on the spot and do a stellar job. Needless to say, my audition didn't go over so well, and I was not selected for jazz band. When I got that news, my heart sank. I felt ill and lightheaded and started to sweat. I walked out the front of the building and tears came rushing down my cheeks. By this point, I was seriously considering pursuing music in college and knew not playing in the jazz band would not get me to where I needed to be on a music theory level. Another minute or two passed and the band director came out and asked if I was OK. I explained to him that I wasn't and pleaded for a second chance at the audition, explaining that I just wasn't prepared and that I needed the class for my future in no specific terms. He said there was always next year, which made my condition worse. Before he left, he told me he'd have to think it over.

The next day in band, after the class was over, he pulled me into his office and said he had decided he would have two guitarists in jazz band next year and to not make him regret his decision. My eyes lit up. I told him he would not regret it and I left the class walking on clouds the rest of the day.

During baseball season, I played more often, since the starting 2nd baseman from the previous year's freshman team was called up to varsity. This suited me fine, as all I wanted to do was play as much as possible—which I did. I even took a crack at being a short reliever on the mound. I'd been honing my pitching skills in rec league and was fortunate enough to be given the chance on the junior varsity squad.

By then, the seniors from soccer and band that my brother and I had become friendly with were nice enough to invite us out on the weekends every so often. We were invited down to their rental in Seaside Park for prom weekend. It's tradition that immediately following the prom students headed down the shore for a weekend of mindless debauchery. I had an inkling of what we could expect, but it really evolved into something out of a movie. It was as if a party bomb had gone off in that town. Not only were there students from Cranford renting, but other towns from different states took up residence as well. New York, Delaware, Connecticut, Pennsylvania—they all had the same urge to really cut loose, shake it down, and be completely free for the weekend. People were boozing hard at all hours of the day. I've never been in a place where kids were knocking back shots and playing drinking games at 7 or 8 in the morning, or knocking back funnels of beer and doing keg stands before noon. It was fucking madness, but I loved every second of it.

There were plenty of landlord's in Seaside Park who were total slum-lords and shysters, so it was a crapshoot for some renters every year. I was pretty sure the house we crashed at was good until Sunday morning before the cops came and witnessed the types of activities taking place by underage kids. Not to mention that the certificate of occupancy was way over limit. John and I sneaked out before they were able to question us. The cops made whoever was left clean the place and get out with no fines or any type of tickets, so they were lucky in that regard.

Before the end of the school year, the Grateful Dead came to the Meadowlands, and set up camp for two days at Giant's Stadium. Sting was the opening act. That Saturday afternoon, one of the seniors from band who we were jamming with pulled up in his orange Volkswagen bus with about nine other guys in it and said we were going to see the Dead. At the time, I didn't know too much about them other than a few songs they played on the classic rock station or the *Touch of Grey* video that came out years prior. I was still in grunge mode and discovering guitar-ists that were prolific and really spoke to me. Our friend wasn't taking no for an answer, so my brother and I gathered what we could quickly, got permission from our mom and hopped on the bus. We were immediately handed canned beers. Up to this point, I've never had a beer in a moving vehicle before. The windows had curtains on them, so I figured, when in Rome. We pulled into the lot, and it was a psychedelic circus. Row after row of cars, trucks, buses; people walking around with drinks in their hands; grilling food; vending anything you could think of; smoke bil-lowing out of cars; tie-dyed banners and flags flying; music blasting, and people wearing clothing I'd never seen anyone wear other than in maga-zines and photos from the 60s peace movement. What the fuck is this?! It was like another planet. Within 10 minutes, I was lined up doing my first (and I think last) beer funnel. I didn't have tickets, not that it would've been hard to get them, but I was really enjoying the lot scene and didn't want to leave the party. We ran into a bunch of other people from town there and all partied together.

I picked up my first Fender amp around this time. After reading so many guitar magazines and seeing what combinations of guitars and amps my favorite players were using; as well as listening to their sounds, I settled into a lifetime of Fender amplification. The amp was a red-knobbed solid-state Fender Stage 185. That fucker got loud and was extremely heavy. But after enough tinkering and playing around with the knobs I was able to procure some listenable tones out of that thing. I felt way more big time upgrading from my little starter Gorilla amp.

Our next-door neighbor, who was in the same grade as our senior friends, asked if our little band of bards would be interested in playing at her high school graduation party. We increased our jamming schedule to the point where we were competent enough to string together a bunch of songs and come up with a set, so we all agreed it would be fun and said sure. It was to be the first time my brother and I played in a band line-up in public. We dragged our gear across the backyard onto her property and set up near the back of the yard facing west toward the house. There was no schedule of when we needed to play or for how long—no pressure whatsoever. Playing live music was new to all of us, and we were there to have fun and do our best. We played through a bunch of Pearl Jam tunes, Stone Temple Pilots, and God knows what else. Then we laid a couple of original tunes out there; most memorable was "The Fetal Polka." The crowd got a good laugh at our enthusiasm in playing such a ridiculous number. I'm pretty sure we played it more than once, as it was such a laughable creation.

The beginning of summer started a lifetime love of attending concerts and living for seeing live music. Lollapalooza '93 came through, and a whole mess load of us from our town went. We were fortunate enough to know cool people who drove, were able to procure alcohol, and had room to fit us in their cars. By this time, my musical tastes had expanded even more to include such bands as Tool, Rage Against the Machine, and Primus. I was exposed to elements of punk and hardcore as well, so my musical universe kept growing. Cassette tapes of The Descendants, All, Bad Religion, Quicksand, Fugazi, and The Gorilla Biscuits all found their way into the tape/CD Aiwa combo mini ghetto blaster John and I shared.

Much like the Grateful Dead show, Lollapalooza '93 was a shock and awe blitzkrieg for the senses. It was a beautiful sunny day, fun parking-lot scene with tons of familiar faces all rearing to let loose and party down. Rage Against the Machine, Alice in Chains and Primus headlined. Acts such as Fishbone, Arrested Development, and Dinosaur Jr. were also on the main stage. I wondered over to the side stage to check out Tool, who I started really digging on. They were loud and powerful and amassed a mosh pit that I had never witnessed first-hand before. It was hot and dry that day, so in front of the stage it looked like a whirlwind of dust, punches, and kicks. The people bouncing off of one another reminded me of sub-atomic particles in an excited state or what it would look like if there were more than one ball in a pinball machine.

After the Tool, set we all settled into the acts we were most interested in checking out. When the stage opened up for Alice in Chains' set, they were all dressed in white tuxedoes. The audience lost their shit.

～～～

That summer, my dad got me a job working in a factory at his company. The company had contracts with the government and big corporations such as Boeing. His company focused on electromagnetic shielding and other technical products of that nature. My hours were 7 AM to 3:30 PM, with a half hour for lunch. There was a 15-minute break at 10 AM and a 10-minute break around 1:45 PM or so. The job was monotonous, to say the least. The machine I was operating was a pneumatic press. I would take a 3-inch by 3-inch square of metallic mesh, place it over a hole, then plunge a lever down on it creating a rivet. It looked like a mini mesh donut. All day. That was it for a while, before the manager decided to try me on another machine of similar monotony. They kept me moving around to different machines ever so often. I can only imagine they did this at the request of my dad, as he knew I'd get bored easily. My co-workers were of Spanish, Mexican and Eastern European descent and for a majority of them English were their second language. I was friendly with many of them. They must've known my dad was inside wearing a collared shirt in an office. My pay was something like $9 an hour (before tax) paid every other week, which was considerable, given that the minimum wage at the time was a little more than half that. Signs such as BEWARE: PINCH POINT were all over the factory floor, reinforcing the number one rule on the job—safety. If one's mind was preoccupied and not focused, one could end up with a hole in his or her hand or actually losing one. It was a great lesson in responsibility, time management, and budgeting, as I'd never held a job before and I actually had money of my own to choose what I'd like to spend it on.

Near the end of the summer, I started smoking cigarettes. It starts with one and next thing you know you are smoking half a pack. Peer pressure had nothing to do with it. I caught a quick buzz initially then began to enjoy the feeling. It was relaxing. This, of course, led to other vices: marijuana. That summer, my brother and I smoked our first joint with our senior friends on a desolate neighborhood bike path at the end of a street. This would be a harbinger of things to come.

Sunday's that summer our crew would go to St. Michael's youth group just to hang out, play games in the gym like Hit the Pin, and smoke cigarettes outside. The man who ran it was a saint and good friends with our friends, who went to that parish. It was centrally located in town and just a good place to go and meet up with everyone.

We also started hanging out with a bunch of guys a year older than us to further expand our crew. The criteria were the same that attracted previous friends into the fold: a deep appreciation of good times, good music, laughs, and cynicism for the establishment or "man." We all liked to party and would go out together. If there wasn't one to be found, we'd somehow create our own. A couple of guys from the north side grew up surfing together and a fella from our side of town connected with them in high school.

Junior year started as the other years did. The high-school routine began to feel like an old shoe. Choir was an added class that year, as I had auditioned the last semester of sophomore year and grabbed a spot as a double bass. With choir and jazz band added to the mix, I had three music classes and gym. It was going to be an easy year.

I also made a new friend. He was in my physics class, originally from Cranford's north side, but had gone away to boarding schools in New England for a number of years and was back in the public education system.

This year, with the introduction of cigarettes, I had no desire to run winter track. Instead, I found myself in the outdoor common area between periods steaming a cigarette down, catching up on some gossip, and periodically engaging in a brief volley of hacky sack. This common area was better known as the smoking section. It had a couple of entrances from the ground level that led out to a courtyard of blacktop pavement. Cranford High School, I believe was one of the last high schools in the state to allow smoking on school property. One time, the track coach was traversing through the courtyard and spotted me taking a pull from a cigarette. Our eyes locked and he just walked away in disgust shaking his head. At that point, I knew I would not be back on the team.

That fall, with the inclusion of jazz band, I really started to listen to a wide variety of music. My approach was always this: If it moves you, if you connect with what the musician or artist is trying to say and you feel it behind your heart, it's got to mean something to you. At that point, there was no ego involved while discovering new music. If it sounds good, it didn't matter what the person laying down the track looked like or their background etc. I began to amass a sizable CD collection with a wide spectrum of styles. Most importantly, jazz and blues. Verve label's Wes Montgomery's *Jazz Masters 14* was the first jazz CD I purchased. I immediately fell in love with his style and the song "Impressions," with its simple head and ½-step sharp modulation, then, back down to the original key. I thought that was so hip. I picked up a live 1977 Albert King and John Lee Hooker CD because I knew Eric Clapton and Stevie Ray Vaughan were influenced by King. Little Feat's *Waiting for Columbus* found its way into our player as well as The Allman Brother's Band's *A Decade of Hits 1969-1979*, because I heard the haunting dual guitar lines of Duane Allman and Dickey Betts on "In Memory of Elizabeth Reed" and was instantly enchanted by the sound.

I was still listening to my favorite grunge artists as well as bands like

The Doors and Led Zeppelin. 88.3FM (WBGO) always had great jazz on throughout the day, and I used to listen to Marian McPartland's show whenever I found myself in the car during her program.

Hal, one of me and my brother's best friend's, and I volunteered through our church to assist in the kitchen during a retreat. It was a kill two birds with one stone deal, as our mutual friend (the one who accompanied me on "Tears in Heaven") moved to a town in New York a few miles north of the New Jersey border. He had just gotten his driver's license, and it was my first quasi-road trip without parental supervision. On the way up, he said he wanted me to hear this band, as he figured I'd really appreciate the guitar playing. The band was Phish and the album he threw on front to back was *Rift*. This was the first time I had ever heard of them or listened to any songs. I was instantly blown away by the title track. This bouncy, upbeat whirlwind of a song that sounded like nothing I had ever heard before instantly pulled me in. The composition of Trey Anastasio's solo and tone of his guitar opened up a whole new dimension of what a person and guitar are capable of. The outro build, tempo increase, and playful modulation at the frenetic end of the song hit me right behind the heart and ears. Needless to say, I was in heaven the entire ride up, listening to the album front to back.

Around this time, a friend had organized a bus trip to Killington, Vermont; to descend upon the mighty mountain for a weekend of skiing, snowboarding, and whatever else a bunch of high-school kids could sink their teeth into. The purchase price got you to and from the mountain by way of a decent-sized bus with tinted windows, comfortable seats, a bathroom, and TVs strung throughout the aisle; a spot in a room; and a weekend lift ticket. The rooms were at a local hotel a stone's throw from base lodge. The bus filled up, and the grade levels varied from sophomore to senior. We had packed all the necessary gear to have a fun weekend up north, including a ton of alcohol. We filled up one friend's hockey bag with a shitload of beer. There were bottles packed in, so we had to move some clothing around to hide the clanking. It was tucked underneath the bus in storage so the driver and chaperones didn't suspect anything. We boarded the bus on a Friday afternoon, and we all had carry-on bags with booze tucked in them. Once it got dark, consumption began. If an authority figure had to use the bathroom and walked back, we just tucked the can or bottle between our thighs or on the ground, secured by our feet and under cover of darkness.

There were a handful of younger girls from the sophomore grade on the trip and they started playing musical chairs, sitting next to people and talking. Eventually, one blonde sat next to me, and we pretty much hung out, talked, and drank the rest of the way up.

We got to the mountain, grabbed our gear, checked in, and then began to party. If security or a chaperone came knocking it was to tell us to keep it down. Once there was a knock, all signs of illegal activity were hidden from view. It started to get late, and the next thing I know I'm in bed with the blonde from the ride up. We hooked up, exploring each other's bodies; that was the first time I had slept in the same bed with a lady before. It was an unforgettable feeling.

Upon our return, I kept in touch with the blonde. I'd see her in school and we talked daily on the phone. For a period of three weeks, we were "dating." The thing is, I never followed through to hang out with her and do anything. Being carless was definitely a factor. She eventually got bored and broke things off. Nobody likes rejection, and I was no different. I felt a sharp pain in my heart, and I knew I felt it for a reason.

The fall and winter, John and I formed our first legitimate band. I was on guitar, John on bass, one of the fraternal twins from our crew on vocals, and Danny Donovan on drums. Danny was in band and had two older brothers who were also in band—and they all played drums. They lived right around the corner from us and I'd known them ever since our family moved to Cranford from Garwood.

We set up in our folks' basement and would jam together after school. Our dad usually didn't get home from work until a little before or after 6 PM, and our mom was very tolerant of the noise. For the most part, if she weren't preparing dinner she'd be upstairs where it wasn't too abrasive.

The material we worked up to build a repertoire came from what we were all listening to at the time. Songs by Pearl Jam, Stone Temple Pilots, Alice in Chains, Rage Against the Machine, and Tool were all rehearsed to the point where we would be comfortable enough to play in front of an audience.

After a few rehearsals, the creative side started to show, and we began writing original songs. It was more about having fun than being overly critical. We were 15 to 17 years old and just letting it rip. I think it was Danny who suggested a name for our band that we all agreed on. We called ourselves Doubting Thomas. We kept a fairly regular schedule of getting together to rehearse with the intention of eventually playing some shows.

~~

Christmas time, and lo and behold, the only item on my list was another guitar. I got skis one year, I just don't remember if it was part of a Christmas gift or for my birthday. By this time, I was really digging on Eric Clapton and wanted a guitar similar to, his named "Blackie," a black strat with maple neck. The local guitar shop had one that fit the description. It was a 1989 body but had two single coil pick-ups from 1974 that were still in good shape. The pick-ups pushed the purchase price of the guitar to over $800. I made a deal with my mom to use some of the cash I made over the summer working at the factory to split the cost of the guitar and she accepted the terms. Now I was on my way to really being a serious axe slinger—I was 16 years old with two Fender Stratocasters!

The winter cruised by with activities including, weekend day trips to the city. A bunch of us would take the train from Cranford to the PATH, get off at New York Penn Station, walk around until we found a bodega that would serve us beer, brown bag them, and hit up a couple of local record shops to obtain some rare finds and add to our music libraries. There were novelty shops where you could get a chintzy fake ID for $15. They were just a photo, name, address, and date of birth on a driver's license-size-piece of paper with a state of residence listed and laminate over it. I went into one of the shops one day and got a fake ID card. This actually worked at the liquor stores known to serve to underage kids in Elizabeth and Roselle. It was all a matter of confidence, acting and looking like you were older.

Three weeks before my 17th birthday, I went with two of my surfer friends to a tattoo parlor. I didn't have any design in mind or even know if I wanted to get inked up. After perusing the wall and books of designs I came across one that jumped out at me. It was a sun king. A drawing of a sun with a face that had blue eyes, rays emanating from his head, a long goatee, wearing a crown. I was instantly drawn to it, and all other designs faded from view. It was $65, took about 40 minutes to complete, and the guy didn't ask for any ID proving I was 18. I got it on my right leg just above the ankle. There was no searing pain; in fact, it was quite soothing. I was able to conceal it from my parents' view for a long time, either by just wearing pants or when I was wearing shorts to always stand slightly off center, in case their eyes drifted south.

Our 17th birthday came around and with it the driver's-license test. I aced the written part and got hosed on the driving section. It had snowed for a couple days before I went to the Westfield testing center and there were patches of black ice all over the roads the test was being administered on. My first fail was rolling through a stop sign. This was complete bullshit, as I stopped before the sign and the ice drifted me about a foot and a half forward. The employee administering the test did not give me a break on that. The second fail was my own fault. I was parallel parking and backed into a cone. I was livid and freaked out on the guy for calling me on the stop sign roll. The man sat stone-faced while giving me a report that read, "Fail" on it and told me I'd have to wait a month before coming back. My brother passed, and for the next month, if I needed to drive anywhere for short errands, he just gave me his license and I'd take one of my parents' cars. There are always some perks to being a twin.

It was baseball season, and this time I was in the rotation as a starting pitcher. When I wasn't pitching, I would be playing second base. The cigarettes didn't slow me down as they would have had I been smoking for five years. Funny, as an athlete in high school, there was not much said about the students who were seen lighting up in the smoking lounge between periods.

I passed my driver's license road exam with flying colors, and it was time to get a car for my brother and me to share. We were dead set on a Dodge Caravan. We wanted to be able to roll deep with our friends, and those vehicles had plenty of space in them. It was also convenient when lugging music gear from point A to point B. Our dad was dumbfounded that we didn't want the '70 Chevy Nova that had been sitting in the driveway forever. He eventually relented and we got this brown Caravan from a used-car dealer in Roselle. It had fake wood panels on the side. We named it Shit Brown. Looking back, we were young and naïve. Any 17-year-old with a brain would've jumped at the Nova, as it was a sure thing and free. Not to mention the car was a ballsy small-block V8 with a 350 cubic-engine engine. Our dad was great about offering suggestions but always remained passive enough for us to make our own decisions. It was a classic live-and-learn philosophy.

The parents of one of our surfer friend's had a family beach house on the lagoon in Normandy Beach. That spring, about 20 to 25 of us descended upon Normandy one Saturday night. We were armed to the teeth with beer, liquor, cannabis, and food to nosh on. It was all our crew plus a bunch of girls from our surf buddies' grade. About an hour in to getting the jam going, one of my surfer friends said he had picked up some magic mushrooms. They were called Oregon Gold. He asked if I was interested in trying some. I figured it was the perfect opportunity, so I popped a couple of stems and caps. They tasted like shit; not that I'd ever tasted shit before and not because, for the most part, they were grown on dung, but I managed to get them down without puking. An hour goes by and I start to feel tightness in my stomach. It wasn't completely uncomfortable—just a sign that my body was reacting to the food allergy. Gradually, throughout the course of a few hours, the psilocybin took effect and my entire body felt like it was humming. My visual and auditory senses were enhanced, and everything I saw seemed to have a sheen about it. The more I drank and smoked grass, the more everything seemed to get enhanced. I felt like a superhero with no powers. The beer and pot were fuel, but they be might just as well have been from a bottomless mug and bowl, because on mushrooms those things seemed to have little effect. I was just throwing back beers one after another and smoked a bowl whenever someone packed one.

At one point, all the lights were off in the house with maybe a candle or two lit. A bunch of us were lying on the floor listening to *The Doors' Greatest Hits*. "The End" came on, and I felt like I was in another time, another space . . . just floating in the ether. I took a walk, crossing a desolate Route 35 toward the ocean, and stood at the entrance onto the beach for a while feeling a cool wind cut through my body. It felt heavenly.

My energy eventually left me, and I ended up passing out slouched over on the step of the fireplace. When I woke, probably between 4 and 5 AM, there was some vomit on one side of me and a spilled beer on the other. I have no recollection of puking, and there was none on my clothing or face. There's a good possibility that someone puked there before I passed out and that I miraculously didn't slide into any of it. After I wiped the sleepy fuzziness from my eyes, the host of the party came into view right in front of me. He was pointing a double-barrel shotgun in my face, angry about the puke and spilled beer. Nothing happened, obviously, and I don't think it was loaded, but waking up to that sight can be quite harrowing for anyone. I was still too groggy to even be fearful, and I most likely pushed the barrel out of my face, called my friend fucking crazy, and passed out again.

The band and choir classes always had trips in the spring to compete against other municipalities. We had to raise money or pay out of pocket. The options for choir were fruit sales--mostly clementines, tangerines, and Florida oranges. I forget what the band used to sell, but we always targeted the usual suspects—family, neighbors, and friends. Most of the trips blend into one another. One year, the choir went to Virginia Beach, another year, to Quebec. Our groups always competed at a high level, and the trips were really great for bonding with fellow classmates.

The school year ended and I was once again back at my dad's factory for the summer. This time, management moved me to a different area of the factory floor. I would not be working with rivets or pneumatic presses, risking pinch-point injuries. Instead, I was assigned to a separate room with an electric saw that sliced material used for electromagnetic shielding and other technical products. It was a little assembly line that involved preparing heavy slabs and hoisting them onto the machine in preparation for the slicing. They were cut into different widths, either in millimeters, centimeters, inches, or fractions thereof. Two or three other employees manned the room with me, and these guys were a riot. They were all from different ethnic and socioeconomic backgrounds and we got along fine.

Throughout the course of the summer, we began taking more liberties in our separate room. This included taking mini-naps in while the rest of us covered the work of the person who was napping. There was a smaller room that you could access only through this one, which was perfect in the event a manager came in to check on us, which happened from time to time. Our added activities included gambling. We would roll dice and also pitch quarters against the wall. One day, the ante went up and I was into one of the guys for my radio cassette player, which I kept in the room and we listened to throughout the day. I don't remember if I won it back or the guy felt sorry and gave it back to me. But it was a valuable learning experience. Bet with your head, not over it!

Our band, Doubting Thomas, broke our proverbial cherry and played a couple of club gigs. Rooms such as Club Bene in South Amboy or Obsessions Night Club in Randolph always had shows for fledgling bands to perform in. There was one catch—the bands were in charge of selling tickets. Bands would get an allotment of tickets from the club and had to sell them prior to the date of the gig. If the money and tickets didn't add up, the band didn't play. We were in high school and could care less about making any money. We just wanted the thrill of putting our hard work and talent to good use and being able to get some stage time. Playing in front of friends and family and whoever else was there that would listen was payment enough. Our sound was raw but we played with conviction and from the heart.

Near the end of the school year, I came across a brochure for the Berklee College of Music's guitar sessions. This was a program for students interested in improving their guitar skills and theory with workshops scheduled throughout the day. It lasted a week and was held at their facility on Boylston Street in Boston. By this time, I was considering going to college to study music and I figured this would be fun and look good on my college application. I got the OK from my parents, and they helped me out on the tuition cost. I budgeted enough money from the factory job so that I didn't require too much assistance from them. My mom and I jumped in the car and rolled up to Boston on a Monday morning. I had my strat and a backpack. We reached Boylston Street, I got out, and my mom told me to have fun and she'd see me at the end of the week.

During orientation I saw a lot of kids who reminded me of myself, and I thought this was the greatest place on Earth. We were all there for the same thing—a passion for our instrument, music, and to improve our playing. We received room assignments, the schedule for the week, a t-shirt, and an ID tag.

I got to my room and met a tall Eastern European fellow with a bit of an accent, long black hair, and I'm pretty sure he was wearing either a Megadeth or Metallica t-shirt and black jeans. Soon afterward, a wily-eyed scrapper with big blue eyes and long wavy blonde hair, looking like a skateboarder from mid-70s California, walked in. The Eastern European said he was from Minnesota, and his parents moved there recently from either Russia or the Ukraine. The scrapper was from Rhode Island. While unpacking, we broke the ice and in no time were pretty comfortable with each other. The Minnesotan was into heavy metal, death metal, and progressive rock. The scrapper was a total hippie. He was into Phish, the Grateful Dead, Allman Brothers, etc. I appreciated it all and was in the middle.

Over the course of the week, we had classes scheduled every day. The downtime was ours to practice in isolation rooms that were on each floor of the dorms or to explore Boston. In one of my classes, I remember looking around the room and spotting a shy, quiet looking kid who reminded me of myself. He was thin with dark hair and got a smile and nod in, to which I obliged. To my surprise, years later I found out it was John Mayer.

Norman Zocher was one professor teaching a class on my schedule. He had a high, crackly voice, with hair that looked like he'd stuck his finger in an electrical outlet. Of course, none of this mattered to me after listening to the man shred jazz-fusion like he was taking a walk. Robin Stone rounded out the instructors whom I can remember. She was in charge of getting our class in shape to perform three songs on stage for our families, friends, and whoever else wanted to attend at the end of the sessions that Friday. Our assignments were Led Zeppelin's "Moby Dick," Jeff Beck's "Freeway Jam," and another I can't recall. We would go through the songs in class and pick out the place where each student would take a turn to add a fill or take a solo. Other classes learned other songs and were to do the same.

My roommates and I went out a couple of nights just to walk around the surrounding neighborhood and shoot the shit. We visited a couple of record stores and made our way to a head shop where I picked up my first bong. It was a foot-long Graffix, which was popular at the time. I was concerned about how to sneak it back home without getting caught by my mom, and discovered it fit perfectly in the neck of my guitar case.

Friday came, and our class was on stage prepared to play the three songs we learned. Staff and enrolled students were our backing band, which included drums, bass, and keyboards. All the session students played the song and when it came time to add a fill or take a solo the rest of us would drop out and the player selected for a certain section would let it rip. It was a blast. My mom, with brother in tow, made it up in time to catch my performance.

〜〜

Our family got a mini vacation in down in Wildwood. That part of the Jersey Shore is as touristy as it gets. People from all over the country, if not the world, travel there for an authentic taste of what a summer oasis can be in New Jersey. The boardwalk is enormous, much like Atlantic City's and Seaside Park's. Other than playing games of chance and skill on the boards, doffing quarters into arcade machines, and eating greasy food, the most vivid memory I have is buying a blue tie-dyed Pearl Jam shirt and a live Stevie Ray Vaughan CD from a show he played a few months before his untimely demise. The one track I kept repeating was "Scuttle Buttin.'" I'd never heard anything like that before. He was sober, so he and Double Trouble were spot on, and it was so fucking fast. I couldn't believe someone could play the guitar like that. Clean, mean, and ferocious fiery chops. There was a tab transcription of the main riff in a guitar magazine I had, so I was able to follow along. That is one upbeat blues shuffle that really turned me on to his style of playing.

By the end of the summer, I started delivering for a pizza joint in town. My brother had been working there through the spring and was making good money on tips for relatively easy work. That's a gig I could get used to. My first delivery I walked out the door with the pie bag under my arm—sideways. When I got to my destination and took the pie out of the warming bag, there was cheese oozing out the side of the box. I didn't think anything of it. As I was walking out the door, the purchaser told me to hold up. He opened up the box and the pie looked like it had been dropped. It was mangled. The guy said he wasn't paying for it, and I went back to the shop still clueless as to why it could've ended up that way. I brought a new pie back there 15 minutes later, and by then I figured out what the issue was and never stuck a pie under my arm again.

Senior year started up, and this time I had band, jazz band, choir, madrigal singers, gym, film, psychology, and English. It was going to be a fucking cakewalk. I met with my assigned guidance counselor as all seniors were obligated to do and she looked over my scholastic resume. By that time I was either 60th or 61st in my class out of about 208, had between a 3.65 and 3.85 cumulative GPA, an 1100 SAT score, played in school sports, was in every music class, and had a few clubs under my belt. She suggested I think about being a municipal employee or garbage man. (Not that there is anything wrong with that!) I looked her dead in the eye and asked if she was serious, to which she said yes. I started laughing and thanked her for her time and walked out of her office never to seek guidance from her again.

A few weeks later, my mom and I went to visit Moravian College in Bethlehem, Pennsylvania. I remember the ride on Route 78 that beautiful, crisp fall morning. The sun was brilliant, and the leaves were approaching full foliage. Everything seemed to shine with unlimited possibilities and potential. We arrived, took a tour of the campus, which included all buildings, dorms, and grounds on the property, then met with the head of the music department. He was impressed with my course load in high school and felt I'd be a fine addition to the music program there. I also informed him I played on the baseball team every year and was considering playing ball in college. He made a note of that and stated he would discuss anything they could do or offer me with the admissions department. My only concern after visiting was the size of the student body. There were about 1600 students enrolled there, and to me that meant attending high school all over again. At the time, I thought college was supposed to be a big place with lots of space, fraternities, and sororities (I'd been watching *Animal House, Revenge of the Nerds* and *PCU* at the time) and would give me a chance to meet people from all walks of life.

I had been doing my homework when it came to higher education regarding pursuing my passions for guitar and jazz. Berklee was an amazing school with a phenomenal reputation when it came to music and jazz studies. There was just one issue: at the time, obtaining a scholarship or any kind of subsidy to reduce tuition was pretty much nonexistent. The annual tuition wasn't cheap either. It was, at the time, something like $25,000 to $26,000 a year. For my folks putting two kids through college at the same time with a sole breadwinner and not much money allocated toward tuition—that school was pretty much out of the question. In my research, I had also come to discover that a state school in North Jersey, William Paterson College, had a reputation for one of the most accelerated jazz performance programs in the country, if not the world. It rivaled Berklee with a world-renowned faculty, advanced course offerings, and equipment. My mom and I went to an open house, took a tour of the campus, and watched a concert that the music department put on with current students performing in ensembles. The guitar work I witnessed blew me away. Like, "If I go to school here I can end up as good as that guy?!" Sign me up. For where I was and where I wanted to be as far as my playing and education went, there was no other alternative. The tuition was also manageable, it being a state school. I was pretty much set and submitted an application to enroll not long after. Rutgers University's Mason Gross School of the Arts was also in consideration; however, their jazz track was limited compared to William Paterson's.

I received word from the head of the music department at Moravian College that their dean of admissions and student aid department wanted to offer me a partial scholarship to enroll in the music program and play baseball for the school. Their annual tuition wasn't cheap, either, and was running close to $30,000. The small student body and the fact that I'd have to keep myself together and play baseball in college when I was more interested in partying and women was also a major deterrent. My dad wanted me to consider attending his alma mater, Lafayette College. There wasn't even a question of whether I'd get in, as he was an annual donor and knew faculty there. But to me, it didn't make sense, given their small and limited music program. I respectfully declined Moravian's offer and submitted only one college application, to William Paterson. This was a load off my parents' backs, as I pretty much did all the vetting and wasn't one of those kids who submitted applications to a dozen schools. That can get time consuming and expensive. I kept it short and sweet.

December 30th, 1994, I attended my first Phish concert. It was held at Madison Square Garden and was part of the bands' New Year's Eve run—the first for the band at that venue. I was with my brother and Hal. We had nosebleeds way up in the 400s section, but we didn't care and were just happy to be there. I was immediately blown away by the energy in the room. Everyone there felt like family. By then, I knew all the songs they played, as I had been listening to their studio albums for quite some time. The maniacal "Stash" made my jaw drop and showed what a four-piece band is sonically capable of pulling off. The jam kept building and building. It would get to a place of stability, and then fall apart, and the band would rebuild it, only for it to fall apart again. This was a strategy known as tension and release, and it can definitely be felt on a physical, emotional, and psychological level, even if the listener is unaware of what exactly is going on. Another standout was "You Enjoy Myself," but the entire show blew my fucking mind. We walked out of there feeling like a million bucks, almost as if we'd just left church on Sunday and were ready to change the world for the better. I had a newfound appreciation for the band. Their live performance seemed to be unmatched by any previous concerts or live musicians I'd seen. Of course, up to that time, my exposure to live music was limited, but that band set a pretty high bar and was the Gold Standard I used to judge future concerts.

Senior year chugged along quickly. I was excited to wake up every morning to a carefree schedule riddled with music classes. Our drummer was in school at Stockton State so Doubting Thomas was pretty much no more, which relegated me to more woodshedding and listening to a wider range of music. I picked up some names from listening to WBGO, so CDs by the Meters, Tower of Power, James Brown, Parliament, Sly and the Family Stone, Bob Marley and the Wailers, and guitarists like Kenny Burrell and Django Reinhardt started to find their way into my collection. My brother started collecting live Phish tapes, and he, Hal and myself would occasionally make a trip out to a hippie shop out on Long Island that sold bootlegs among their other wares. In addition to listening to live Phish, tapes by The Descendants, All, and Bad Religion still permeated Shit Brown's cassette player while delivering for the pizza shop. There were deliveries where I was rocking out, singing at the top of my lungs, and sure that anyone on the street could hear me from a block or two away.

That spring, I didn't play varsity baseball. It didn't matter, as I wasn't attending Moravian or taking any partial scholarship to play baseball at college. The coach had his favorites, and I knew how he constructed his line-ups, so I would've been riding the pine for most of the season. That didn't interest me, so I joined the golf team instead.

We would play the local county courses whenever we could with our dad, and if I was bored and had some extra money, I'd always find time to head to the driving range and whack a large bucket out there. At times, I was a driving-range hero, hitting the ball sure and straight with decent distance. Other times, I'd be a hack and hit toppers or skull the ball. When I was on, it was such a rush. My confidence got to a point where I'd line up on the canvas barefoot when addressing the ball. Unfortunately, my game didn't translate well from the driving range to the golf course. I was a horrible putter. If it weren't a horrible sway where my head would move, I'd either pop up on the ball when taking my backswing, not follow through on my right side when swinging through the ball, or roll my wrists. Pretty much, at least one defect that could ruin a decent round of golf would occur, if not many, when I played. I didn't care. I grew up loving the game and decided I would have fun that spring.

The choir trip was to Atlanta that spring. Other than crushing it in competition, the only memorable event that occurred was checking out an amazing band from our neck of the woods called God Street Wine. Hal was always two or three steps ahead of the curve when it came to discovering new bands and music. I trusted his ear and had been listening to their God Street's album *$1.99 Romances* for a couple of weeks. Hal convinced the choir director to allow a group of us to attend the Midtown Music Festival that was being held at a park while our class was down in Atlanta. Hal's father chaperoned us, while the rest of the class visited the Coca-Cola Factory. Snore. We made out like bandits.

The prom was coming up, and I needed to find a date. Luckily, there was this beautiful blonde girl in my grade who was in the same boat as I was, so we decided to kill two birds with one stone and go together. She was from the north side of town and had been in a few of my classes throughout the years. All of my friends in the grade were scattered so I didn't have a chance to pick whom I'd be heading over to the banquet hall in a limousine with—that was pretty much all the ladies' choosing. I ended up in a limo with her and her girlfriends and all of their dates. None of the men were part of my close-knit group of friends, but my brother and I got along with everyone, so it didn't matter. After a few photos, we all hopped in the limo, and within a matter of minutes I was drinking either a beer or vodka club.

The prom was put together well, a little bit like a wedding. The food was good, the DJ played songs that were popular at the time, and I may have gotten a dance or two in. Some of my friends brought flasks with them, so when we ducked outside for a smoke we'd take swigs to keep us in the partying spirit. I was outside when the DJ called last dance. I timed it wrong; as I thought there would be more time or another song before the last dance song. By the time I got inside, my date was dancing with one of her guy friends who she grew up with on the north side of town. I wasn't about to cut in.

Our crew had our own plan in place. In keeping with tradition, we had a rental for the weekend in Seaside Heights where everyone from our town was going. John and I were already packed, so all we needed to do was change and hop in Shit Brown. We had already bought beer, so there were a couple of cases in the van, and others that were heading down that night were bringing some as well. We got down around 2:20 AM and began partying with whoever else made the trip. The rest of our house wouldn't be showing up until mid-morning.

A few hours later, more and more of our crew began to show up, and each person brought enough booze to last the weekend. By about 1 PM, the cops showed up on a tip and told us to vacate the premises, as we were in violation of our rental agreement, given that none of us were of age to purchase or consume alcohol. It was a total scam. We weren't even in the house for 12 hours and we got the boot. We got word that it happened to another two houses, and we were clamoring to figure out an alternative plan when one of our friend's suggested heading back to Cranford, as his folks were away for the weekend. All any of us wanted to do was get wasted together, play drinking games and laugh our asses off, so the location didn't matter. We headed back up the parkway, and in a matter of a couple hours we were all holed up in our friend's house for the duration of the weekend.

High-school graduation took place at Memorial Field. Our class was seated on the football field and all friends and family were in the bleachers. The choir sang, speeches were given, and next thing you know, none of us were considered high schoolers anymore. We went home, changed, and got ready for our project graduation, which was held at Centennial Avenue Pool.

We had the pool grounds from like 7–11 PM or so and made the most out of a drug and alcohol-free gathering. Boredom eventually set in. The only thing I wanted to do that night was head over to our friend's house, where he and his older brother were having a blowout party. After doing some diving, eating, playing some games, including singing the Blue's Brother's version of "Soul Man" karaoke style, I gathered up my stuff and made my way to the exit. As I was walking out toward the bike rack a chaperone stopped me and asked if I was OK, due to the fact I was leaving about 50 minutes prior to the end of the event and I'd be the first one to leave. I reassured her I was fine, and it was just time for me to split. I made it over to the party and was greeted and congratulated by everyone I ran into. It was such a liberating feeling to be done with high school and onto the next chapter of my life. I also remember the drive home that night. It was hairy, and I had no business being behind the wheel. It was probably two or three in the morning, and I could barely keep my eyes open or the car in a straight line. I wasn't completely erratic all over the road but enough that, if I had I been followed for a couple hundred yards by a cop, it would've been curtains. Luckily, I didn't see one car on the road and made it home unscathed. That was a lesson unto itself and has stayed with me ever since. If you know you can't drive, then don't get behind the wheel. My mom always said if I couldn't drive for any reason, call her anytime and she'd pick me up no questions asked.

A day or two after graduation, Phish played at Waterloo Village in out in Stanhope, N.J. off of Route 80. It was a beautiful and hot day for that time of year. We had a caravan of people driving out together. Everyone ended up parking in the same area—the far lot, which required a hike or a hop on a shuttle bus to the venue. Once situated, our pregame rituals ensued, and I probably had a six of Sierra Nevada Pale Ales before heading into the show. Not a good start. Those are a bit heavier and all 160 pounds of me would surely feel the effect. The blazing sun didn't help much, and I wasn't too keen on proper hydrating techniques at the time, so I was already set up for a fail before the first note rung out.

Once inside, there was plenty of room to roam, and it was 1995, before the band started to get big, so the show was far from a sellout. The band brought some heavy hitters to the plate, including "Chalk Dust Torture," "Reba," a newly constructed "Free," and "Taste," "You Enjoy Myself," "The Lizards," "Harpua," "Llama," "Good Times, Bad Times" and "A Day in the Life" encore to name a few. Had I not been a neophyte to the pregame and tailgating rituals or been hanging around the Genesee beer trucks with my shitty fake ID the entire show I could've been in Phish heaven, as it was a rocking ass show.

I was by myself after the concert ended. I wasn't with our group for most of the show, as I had been digging the fact that my fake ID was getting me served all night. There were no cell phones or texting to rely, on so I had to go on sheer intuition to make my way back to the parking area. The problem was that it was pitch dark and I had no clue which road led to which lot. All I knew is that it took us a while to walk from where we parked to get in, so I figured I'd follow the masses down the road they were traveling on. The foot traffic stayed to the side of the road and the passing vehicles illuminated our way. After a while, I started seeing buses and people holding on to the back of them hitching rides. One slowed down enough for me to hop on, and I did the same. In my grossly inebriated state, this was a fucking bad idea. Some buses hit pretty high speeds, and drivers didn't know anyone was hanging on to the back. The day after the concert, word got out that two people died at the show. I know at least one was due to falling off the back of a bus. I held on for dear life, and the bus eventually hit its destination and dropped everyone off at the far lot. I wandered around for a bit. At the time, I didn't realize I had beaten all of our crew back to the parking lot. I couldn't find any familiar cars. I started to panic. Either I got dropped off at the wrong parking lot or everyone had left without me. I didn't know what to do. The best option would be to find a pay phone and call home for advice. I headed for the exit on foot and next thing I know I am on the on-ramp to Route 80 East. I was like fuck it; I'll just walk home. Walk home... wasted...on Route 80...In the dark of night...with all sorts of vehicles whizzing by, including 18-wheeler Mac trucks. Yeah . . . GOOD IDEA YOU FUCKING ASSHOLE!!!

Within two minutes, someone from a car shouted, "Hey Chris, need a ride?" I look over and it's a bunch of girls from Westfield we'd all been hanging out with. I said yes, hopped in, and explained my plan for getting home. My dad said he once hitched from Lafayette College to South Bend, Indiana, as one of his buddies was attending Notre Dame, and there was a big football game that weekend. I figured if he could get to Indiana from Pennsylvania, I certainly could make it from Stanhope to Cranford. Luckily, that reasoning and logic were squashed pretty early.

After getting dropped off at home, I walked inside and found my parents waiting for me in the living room. They looked furious and told me they received a call from my brother a short while ago telling them that he and our friends had been searching the grounds of Waterloo for over an hour, were the last car in the parking lot, and feared the worst for me. He called back and my folks told him I just walked in the door and was fine. I got yelled at for a while and was exhausted. Since I was 18, I wasn't going to get grounded, but it was explained to me I would be making it up to them and my brother by doing a lot of work around the house the next two weeks. I apologized, accepted my fate, and went upstairs to crash. When I woke up the next morning, one of my arms was in extreme pain and I could hardly move it. I thought it was broken. When my brother got up, he told me that as soon as he got home he marched up the stairs and started wailing on me. I was passed out, so I never felt a thing when he was hitting me. This was a small price to pay and a well-deserved punishment for my mindlessness. What a hell of a way to start the summer.

~~~

I'm not exactly sure when my brother and I started jamming again but a neighborhood kid a year older than us was interested in getting together with us and writing songs. He was very hippie dippy and played the bongos. John and I were used to playing with a kit drummer, so we asked another neighborhood kid whom we played rec league baseball with and were in high-school band with. We'd set up in our folks' basement, and I think there were times we rehearsed on the drummer's back deck. The percussionist tried his hand at singing, and we came up with a handful of originals songs. For the most part, they were instrumentals. I don't even remember any of the covers we played. We decided on the band name Shady Groove. I thought it sounded cool and didn't even realize the percussionist was a huge Jerry Garcia and Dead head. I'm pretty sure he recommended the name as a play on the 18th-century folk song that had been covered and recorded by countless artists, including Jerry Garcia and David Grisman. At the time, I'd never heard the song before or listened to any Garcia Grisman stuff, so I was in the dark. One of our first gigs, we set up in the backyard of a buddy's house while he was having a raging keg party during the day. The people at the party hardly paid us any mind. We were raw, and just working out the kinks, but had a blast doing it. We didn't even own a PA system. We had to borrow or rent one whenever there was a gig requiring vocals.

It was July 4th, and the family that owned a large farm on the north side of town near Union County College always had an amazing fireworks display. Our family would go every year with our grandparents and aunts. This year, I traipsed through some brush or rubbed up against something I shouldn't have a day or two before the fireworks, and my skin began to react. This coupled with the heat and humidity of the summer air forced me to head home early that night. It was either poison oak or sumac, because I've had poison ivy before and the patches that formed on the inside of my forearms looked nothing like an ivy reaction. They resembled a huge living scab—something out of a sci-fi movie. The patches began to ooze a yellow liquid when I needed relief and did an occasional scratch. I took an oatmeal bath for mild relief and applied bandages on the blotches on my arms and went to bed hoping the discomfort would subside by morning.

What I didn't realize that night was the poison was so contagious that wherever I touched a part of my body, it spread quickly. I had this stuff under my fingernails so that didn't make matters any better. I woke up around six the following morning to what felt like living hell. The poison had spread everywhere on my body. This stuff was on the palms of my hands, my junk, in my ears, on my eyelids, and worst of all—in my throat. My palms spread it to my junk when I took a leak, my eyelids when I rubbed them. To my throat since it was on whatever food I had before bed. My fingernails spread it to the inside of my ears because I must have had an itch and stuck my finger in there. I sat up in bed and didn't know what to do. I just wanted the pain and uncomfortable feeling to end immediately. I knew I needed immediate assistance, so I wandered into my parent's bedroom and woke up my mom. I was in tears and told her I needed to go to the doctor's office right away. I wasn't able to wait. It had to be now. She got up, made a call, got changed, and we were in the car within 10 minutes. The doctor shot me up with a large dose of cortisone. A topical cream would've been the equivalent of taking a piss on a 100-square-mile forest fire in high-wind conditions, and it would not have done any good given the location of some of my affected areas. On the ride home, I started feeling much better knowing the doctor took the most aggressive form of treatment available. To this day, there is still some minor discoloration on the inside of my forearms from the scratching.

August 9th, 1995. I got a phone call from my brother, who informed me that Jerry Garcia passed away. I was home in the AC at the time as it was a blazing hot day. I switched over to MTV and there was a news bit on it. I thought to myself, well, that sucks and didn't think much of it. As I was delivering pizzas later that day, the local classic rock station was playing all Grateful Dead tunes. The news channels showed people hugging and crying in the streets of San Francisco and other major cities throughout the country. At the time, I didn't listen to too much Dead. It began to dawn on me how much of an influence their songs, and music and general can impact people as well as culture and society at large.

Our boarding-school friend played hockey for the high school as well as club teams, and it turned out he was good friends with someone we'd grown up with. He was a south-sider and had a beautiful pool in the backyard with a lot of property. His parents were very cool and didn't mind us hanging out on their back deck grilling food and drinking beers as long as no one was driving home. This was fine, since for the most part we were all on bikes in the summertime.

Our crew spent a lot of nights, and even days, partying at this house that summer. When his folks went away, we'd have access to the inside and even crashed there when necessary. The deck was reserved for playing drinking games, listening to tunes (a lot of live Dead and Phish was played) and the pool area for just chilling and enjoying any additional extracurriculars.

I received a letter from college with orientation, room/dorm assignment and who my roommate was going to be. It had his phone number listed with the recommendation that we contact each other, so I called him. We spoke for a bit about what we were bringing to the dorm, and I invited him down to hang out one night. He lived in a town in northern New Jersey, relatively close to campus. He said sure, and I picked a night where I knew all of my friends would be hanging out together. He asked if he should bring anything. I said a case of beer wouldn't hurt, and he said done.

I really didn't know what to expect of my future roommate. That early evening, a cherry red, spotless Mitsubishi Eclipse pulled to my street. The car must've been not even a year old. Out pops a tall, chisel-chinned guy with product in his hair, sporting a white wife-beater, black pants, and dress shoes. The guy looked like a model for Calvin Klein. I'm sitting there with my Phish summer tour shirt, baseball hat, shorts and Birkenstocks. We were from opposite ends of the male spectrum. He came inside, introduced himself to my folks, was polite and well mannered, and seemed very comfortable in his own skin. We hopped in his car and headed toward our friend's house to pull a typical summer evening deck hang out. Once we arrive, he popped his trunk and grabbed a full cooler of Red Dog and Icehouse beer. We went around back, and I was waiting for that classic record-scratch moment where there's complete silence and judging eyes directed at my roommate, but it didn't come. Sure, he looked nothing like us, and a few of my friends may have made a couple of lighthearted discriminatory comments (all in good fun) to me in private (to which I objected), but for the most part he settled in to just telling stories, listening to ours, laughing, and drinking some beer.

At the close of the summer, one by one all my friends began leaving for college to begin new chapters in their lives. My brother turned down a music scholarship from the University of Rhode Island for tuba but opted to attend the University of Scranton in Pennsylvania. Hal went to Loyola College in Baltimore. My boarding-school friend headed for the University of Vermont in Burlington; another to Johnson & Wales, in Providence, Rhode Island; and a couple others stuck around town to attend Union County College to obtain associates degrees for future transfer to accredited places of higher learning.

I packed everything I was bringing to college, including a guitar, in my parents' Ford Taurus and hit the Garden State Parkway northbound for William Paterson College for the next chapter of my life…and destiny.

Chapter 4

COLLEGE

WE PULLED THE car up to the North and South Towers dorm entrance and it was a zoo. Lines of cars with their hazard lights on unloading suitcases, TV's, coffee machines and whatever else imaginable a freshman would be likely to bring when moving in for their first day of college. We secured a spot and I hopped out to run inside and check in. After receiving my room assignment, photo ID and key it didn't take too long to load everything in.

Once all my items were in the dorm room, I walked back outside, saw my mom off, and had a cigarette. Returning to the B floor of the North Tower, I noticed my room was diagonally across from the hall monitors. Great. Having loud parties in my room would prove to be difficult, so I'd have to make other arrangements. To fulfill that scenario, I'd also have to make friends first. I unpacked everything and set off for the student center. They had pool and Ping-Pong tables and arcade games, so I waited it out to get into a match of billiards and converse with some fellow students. There was student orientation in our dorm later in the day, so I took a stroll around campus and eventually made it over to see what that was all about. Then hunger called, and I headed over to the cafeteria to grab dinner with my newly minted college ID. The food was less than desirable. I once complained about a meal my mom made that I didn't like and my dad immediately chimed in, saying that one of these days you're going to be begging for a home-cooked meal that your mother makes. I didn't realize that was going to happen sooner rather than later.

I made it back to my room after dinner, took a shower, and didn't know what to do with myself. I wandered the halls of my dorm looking for friendly faces and popped outside a couple of times for a cigarette. I thought to myself, "It's college, where are all the party people?" I had no way of getting alcohol, no connections to get grass, and no car. I was pretty much landlocked, with no options.

With nothing left to do, I decided to christen the dorm room and my first day of college by jamming on my guitar and drinking by myself. I smuggled half a bottle of Dewar's White Label Scotch in my luggage and broke it out for my inaugural ritual. Within two hours, I was stinking drunk, stumbling all over the place, and laughing my ass off. I eventually made it to bed with the hope that things would be better tomorrow.

The next day, I studied my schedule and it appeared I was in the music track, but there were no jazz courses. I thought that was a little strange. I had beginner piano Monday, Wednesday, and Friday for forty minutes at 8 AM. I had a few years of piano lessons—why did I need basic piano? Didn't they know I could play? Class on Friday at 8 AM?! That seems fucked up. I'd never make it on a Friday morning after partying the night before. The confusion began to set in.

I don't know how my roommate did it, but he was able to keep his car on campus, so that was a little saving grace. We ran out and purchased some knick-knacks for our room and got better acquainted in the process. Word got around that there was a huge fraternity party that Thursday night. I was elated when my roommate asked if I'd be interested in going. Finally, some real-deal college party action!

That Thursday night, we hopped in my roommate's car and headed to downtown Paterson. Paterson was a thriving, bustling, industrial city back in the day. Over the years, it slowly lost some luster, with inner-city trappings and an elevated crime rate. I'd never been to a city like it before.

After parking in a lit area where other students were parking, we made our way to the address listed on a flyer posted in the dorm. We flashed our college IDs, paid a cover, got a wristband, and headed inside for our first taste of the college party scene.

Once inside, I realized the event was in a warehouse-type structure. Fraternity brothers and a giant-sized man you would think twice about ever starting anything with manned kegs. There was a huge stage and a band playing. I instantly recognized the sound of Kool and the Gang's "Jungle Boogie," as well as other funk classics by James Brown, Maceo Parker, Tower of Power, and other artists. The band and sound were amazing! I expected nothing less, given the amount of musical talent enrolled at the college. It reminded me of George Clinton and Parliament Funkadelic in the movie *PCU*. There was a drummer, bass, two guitars, two singers, keyboard, full horn section, and a whole mess load of sweat and energy. At its peak, there were easily 450 to 600 people at this party. It was starting to feel more like college. I relaxed, knowing I didn't have to worry about driving out of Paterson, and started swilling keg beer like it was my job.

The following day, I had plans to drive out to Scranton to stay with my brother for the weekend. My last class ended around 12:30 PM, and I had it timed so I was ready to go by the time my mom made her way to campus to pick me up. It was a two-step process, as I had no car on campus. My mom would come up to get me, and I'd drive her back to Cranford and get on the road from there. There was no MapQuest then, so my directions were written on a piece of paper and looked something like "Route 280W → 80W → 380N → 81N → Central Scranton Expressway, follow signs to University."

That first ride out solo to the University of Scranton was enchanting and brimming with possibilities. It's close to a two-hour drive from Cranford, and I had plenty of mix tapes and live Phish shows to keep me engaged and pass the time, while taking in the scenery of the Delaware Water Gap and eighteen-wheelers whizzing by in the fast lane.

I arrived on campus, found a place to park, and wandered around until I came upon my brother's dorm—McCourt Hall. He was expecting me, and we hung outside to have a cigarette. Once inside, he introduced me to his roommate, a shaggy, redheaded fellow with a short beard, wearing a baseball cap and glasses from a suburb of Hartford, Connecticut. He went by the nickname Harp, acquired from both his habit of always carrying a harmonica and his Irish roots. My brother took me to every room (three floors, about twelve rooms a hall, two students per room) in the dorm and introduced me to all his dorm mates. Within a week, my brother seemed to know every one of the guys at McCourt Hall. They all seemed to be like brothers. This was a far cry from my experience at the Towers. All his mates had either a nickname already or went by their last name. All of them welcomed me with open arms. Every one of them came from either a Catholic high or prep school and played sports, including rugby and lacrosse that were absent from our high school's curriculum. A majority were Deadheads, a handful were into Phish and a few played guitar. It was the quintessential on-campus hippie dorm.

After I got settled in and showered, we ordered some dinner. While we were waiting for the food to arrive, my brother informed me that a handful of people were dropping acid that night. A dorm mate knew a reliable source and was getting tabs for everyone in the dorm. He asked if I'd be interested, to which I said sure. When in Rome . . .

My basic view of college life was that you operate outside your comfort zone, expand your horizons, and take chances. I knew very little about acid, only that it produced hallucinations. One dorm mate offered some pointers, as he'd been a little more experienced in that department: "You control the trip, don't let the trip control you," and "Don't forget to breathe," along with "Fear is an illusion, and anything you see that looks like a hallucination is not real and can't harm you." Of course, these pearls of wisdom are easier to abide by when you are actually not tripping.

I was eighteen, visiting my brother for the first time at college. There was no way I was not going to experience that with everyone. My music and guitar idols of the sixties and seventies experimented with psychoactive substances, including LSD. I wanted to experience what they experienced. I thought of it as a rite of passage—something you were supposed to do in college.

The schedule of events for the evening started to take shape. Opening weekend at school, there would be a lot of options to hit up. The way the housing is designed for the school is unique to its location and the size of the student body. There are dorms available for freshman, but typically, after the first year, a majority of students rent houses off-campus. To give a picture of the size of the school: the enrolled student body at the time hovered between 5,200 and 5,500. Once you cross north of Mulberry Street, you are on off-campus grounds. The surrounding neighborhood is on the lower end of the socio-economic. You may have seen *Kingpin*. Some of the scenes in that movie portray this area realistically. You need to be very alert if you travel too far from campus alone at night.

On weekends, the college town swelled with people visiting their friends. Keg parties and other themed events were the norm, including kegs and eggs before college and pro football games. Some houses had parties even during the week. It seemed there was something to do every night.

Everyone ate his tabs and set out into the mystic. It was a mild night, with endless possibilities. Within that first hour, the acid took effect. It was much like the first time I ate mushrooms. A knot in my stomach formed, my pupils got enlarged, and the beer I was drinking felt like water going down. The measure of the effect depends on quantity and quality. Since I didn't know what to expect the first time, I heeded the advice I'd been given, went with the flow of things, and kept any fear and negativity to a minimum.

Psychedelics alter the user's consciousness and affect perception. As a result, I caught flashes of color out of the corners of my eyes, and depending on the lighting, whether it was indoor or outdoor objects seemed to be more vivid and enhanced. I had slight auditory hallucinations. Mid-conversation, I'd hear a whizzing or whirling sound. And my sense of touch was heightened, as if every molecule in my hand were connected to whatever I was holding or touching.

Smoking marijuana enhanced the effects. We had a couple of smoking sessions over the course of the evening, never ran out of houses to party at, and eventually made it back to the dorm as daylight was beginning to break. As the effects of the acid wore off, and before calling it a night, I stuck my finger down my throat to get anything out that I could. All I did was dry-heave.

I slept until close to 1 PM and dealt with "acid hangover" for most of the day. Over the course of an evening on acid, one can feel superhuman when it comes to ingesting alcohol and marijuana. But being on acid doesn't negate the effects of the toxins—your body and mind still have to process everything and clean your system out. That, and coupled with a foggy acid head kept me in a daze until my body was able to get some food in it to restart the party process for Saturday night. It was pretty much the same agenda and schedule of events as the night before, minus the hallucinogens.

When I got back home, my mom drove me up to school, and in the car, I told her about my weekend, obviously leaving out details regarding any illicit activities. I mentioned that I wanted to visit again next weekend if things didn't start to pick up for me socially that week. She agreed; in my mind I was already planning for her to come to get me that Friday.

I attended classes that week and went to the proper administrative department of the school to drop my beginner piano course and take up another required general education class. The class was way below my skill set. I felt like I was moving backward in development. I was already sick of the meal plan/cafeteria food and began ordering delivery. It was another uneventful week filled with watching TV, smoking cigarettes, and hanging out with my roommate when he was around or taking a trip to pick up stuff for our room. He explained to me that Willy P was a suitcase school, meaning no one hung around on campus on the weekends. That fact, coupled with being unable to have a few drinks and a slower than anticipated social scene geared me in the direction of repeating my weekend jaunt to see John and the McCourt boys out in Scranton.

That weekend was pretty much the same as the previous, save any hallucinogenic extracurriculars. John's friends and mates had started calling him Phish, given that his live tape collection surpassed anyone else's on campus at the time, and I took on the moniker Chips, which later morphed into Trips for comedic effect.

My priorities at William Paterson were a little backward. Paying attention to my studies and degree track took a backseat to developing a social circle and finding people to party with, as I had back in Cranford. At the time, I really had no true guidance to nudge me in the right direction for the jazz performance track. I thought I could just pick that as a major and then I'd be on my way. Sure, in retrospect, I could've scheduled time with someone from the department and explained what I was looking to do, and they could've carved out a solid program for me to follow. For example, I had no idea auditioning was a requirement or what I needed to perform or for whom.

The following week I started seeing signs for fraternity and sorority rush. This was the time the Greek organizations were soliciting for new recruits. For a couple of days, they had tables and chairs out on the quad in front of the student center. I stopped by a couple and chatted up some of the brothers. Some wanted to invite me up to the apartments where upperclassmen lived to party, and get a taste for what fraternity life had to offer. I was leaning toward one fraternity, since it seemed they were into the same things I was, when my roommate mentioned he was going to a rush meeting for Tau Kappa Epsilon (TKE) and wanted me to come along.

The meeting was held in a classroom in one of the academic buildings. There were probably a good forty-five brothers and about twenty-five rushes in the room. It was pretty much the melting pot of all the fraternities on campus. No two brothers looked alike. They explained the Greek social structure on campus such as the baseball fraternity, the football fraternity, and so on. There were guys from every walk of life. White, African-American, Hispanic, Muslim, Jewish, metal head, muscle head, hunter, preppy, Guido—they did not discriminate. They explained that they treated every single brother as if he was their own brother. They went to each other's weddings, children's christenings, and even wakes and funerals. One brother said that we might find ourselves in a job interview one day with a hiring manager who is a brother from a different chapter. Another brother, wearing a fraternity shirt with a skull on it, joked, "Look how badass we are?! We get to walk around wearing fucking skulls on our shirts!" That statement broke the ice, and the whole room was in stitches.

A couple of the brothers rented a huge loft in downtown Paterson. The rushes were invited over after the meeting, and there also were sorority girls in attendance. I started to feel more comfortable about attending school here, and my roommate and I had a blast. We were convinced after the party that we were going to pledge TKE.

At the second rush meeting, I noticed the number of rushes thinned a little. These were the serious students looking to dive in and get the pledging under way. The brothers explained that the program was seven weeks long, with a weekend away that was mandatory. Pledging consisted of knowing and understanding the history of the fraternity and why it came into existence, including its history of philanthropy and community service. Of course, as an eighteen-year-old with raging hormones and a sweet tooth for alcohol and marijuana, none of that seemed to register in my head.

After the meeting was over, I started rapping with a fellow rush I had spoken to at the previous meeting. His older brother was a senior, lived in the apartments, and was a huge Dead head. He asked if I wanted to hang out up there that evening and drop acid. Interestingly, that didn't faze me one bit, given my recent brush with LSD in Scranton. I said sure and he gave me his number and his brother's apartment information. After running back to my dorm room to clean myself up a little bit, I headed up to the apartments. A handful of people were there drinking beer and pulling tubes from a bong in one of the bedrooms. They had a good system down; toweling the doors and using fans to blow smoke out the window to ensure that none of it reached the hallway. These guys were listening to live Phish and one of them had an acoustic and was doing his best to play along. We began trading licks back and forth, and my friend from the meeting gave me my hit of acid. It was only half a tab, as it was pretty potent, not to mention that it was a weeknight. The blotter was a shade of blue and had a picture of a test tube on it with a cartoonish face and arms and legs that appeared to be dancing. That was the name of the particular batch—Dancing Test Tubes. I continued jamming, drinking beer, ripping tubes, and shooting the shit for about two hours after I ingested the hallucinogen. They had a 2 AM curfew at the apartments, and it was getting close. Guests had to sign in, and anyone that stayed past curfew ran the risk of having their host written up.

I walked back to the towers with my new friend, and once we got inside he said he was going to bed and took off. I was a little confused at that. There's nothing worse than tripping your face off by yourself. I thought we were going to hang out for a few hours and watch each other's backs. At that point, the acid was in full effect. It was strong. One can never know how long the effects are going to last when taking the drug. I didn't think it was going to be too long or too strong, as I had taken only half a hit. I was in no shape for going to bed, so I walked off-campus to the 7-Eleven across the street. I noticed a campus security guard parked in the lot keeping an eye on me. My paranoia set in, and I was convinced this guy knew I was on acid. I just acted casual and made it to the shop to pick up a few items and headed back to the dorms. Once there, I sat on a bench outside smoking a cigarette. Something happened as I stared into the shrubbery growing on the side of the building. It was as if within the snap of a finger I was in the middle of a jungle. It was unseasonably warm that night, and the crickets chirping sounded like a thunderstorm. I sat there in utter amazement enjoying the view. Everything seemed to move and was bursting with color and vibrancy.

After my cigarette and gazing into the jungle, I headed to my room. My roommate was sleeping, so there wasn't much I could do other than throw some water on my face in the bathroom or lay down on my bed. I tried to go to sleep. Anyone who's ever done acid knows that's not going to happen when you are peaking. I was peaking. I had a metallic taste in my mouth and a knot in my stomach. Within minutes, the shadows on the walls began to morph into clear visuals. I was in full hallucination mode. I saw a silhouette of what appeared to be Bart Simpson dancing in place, and then the wall turned into the Nintendo videogame Space

Invaders. My heart rate increased to the point where the beating sounded like tympani, and I thought it was going to burst clear through my chest. I got really nervous and thought I was going to have a heart attack.

My roommate heard me jostling around on my bed for a while. As I hopped out of bed to stretch my legs and pace a bit trying to figure out what I should be doing with myself for the next few hours, or until the acid wore off, my roommate threw on a light and asked if I was OK. I told him I took acid with one of the guys from the rush meeting, hung out in the apartments for a little bit, and here I am. I explained to him I was a bit frightened, didn't want to hurt myself or anyone else, and that the best thing for me right now was to just hang out in the room and wait the trip through. He was obviously concerned and decided to stay up with me for a few hours.

We talked the entire time. He asked what I was seeing and feeling and we had a pretty good time just shooting the shit. After a while and some good laughs, I was in a much better space and was able to actually lie down, relax, and close my eyes without bugging out.

I don't think I got any sleep that night. I remember walking to my 11 AM class in a dreamy state feeling the effects of the acid. I was still tripping a bit when I sat down to take a scheduled exam. I knew I had to take it. There was no backing out, so I decided to grin and bear it.

My weekend trip out to Scranton was becoming routine. By this point, I was seriously considering transferring there after my first semester. I felt I had way more in common with the guys my brother was hanging out with than anyone I had met so far at William Paterson. The only thing going for me there was to pledge TKE and see what happens. My roommate and I both decided that it was the right fit for us. The following week, the brothers decided whom they would accept as pledges. We were to wait at a certain time on a Thursday night for further instructions.

We were instructed to walk up to the top row of the commuter lot near the north end of campus or brothers came to the potential pledges rooms and grabbed us. We were all eventually led to the same location where every active brother as well as a large number of alumni waiting. This was the start of the pledge program. It was very ritualistic and made an impact on me. I knew right then and there that there was no turning back. I'm in it and prepared for whatever hell would be waiting for me over the next seven weeks.

My trips to Scranton continued even during the pledge season. If a brother knew you were in the dorms over the weekend, there'd be a good chance they'd come knocking for whatever they had up their sleeve. It was always best to get out of Dodge on Fridays. Out in Scranton, my brother started to meet musicians who were into the same music we were. We'd do some jamming and go to the off-campus parties, come back, and either party some more, jam, or pass the fuck out.

There was a trio out there that performed at some of the hipper and hippier off-campus parties from time to time. The tenants would clear out what little space they had and the band would set up in the living room. This particular band was called Goodfoot. They had unbelievable chemistry. John and I were fortunate enough to sit in at a few parties and perform some Dead tunes such as ""Scarlet>Fire" and "Eyes of the World," as well as what was becoming one of our favorite songs to jam to—The Allman Brothers' "In Memory of Elizabeth Reed." The haunting dual-guitar head recorded by Dickey Betts and Duane Allman took root deep in my heart and soul and has been a pillar in the foundation of my playing ever since. There was even a "Whipping Post" thrown in from time to time because we were just jamming and having fun.

One weekend, John and I decided to take a road trip to the University of Vermont at Burlington to visit our boarding-school buddy. This would be the first of many road trips to visit friends at their respective schools of higher education.

Once we arrived at our friend's dorm and found his room, there was a note on the door addressed to us. It read something to the effect of "Welcome to UVM. I am at a fraternity party," and listed the address of the house in downtown Burlington. We eventually found our way there and asked anyone who appeared to be helpful where our friend was. In no time, we found him on the back deck with a big smile on his face and about halfway to being three sheets to the wind. He later fell over the railing of the deck and inflicted a minor injury to his back and side which, he wouldn't feel until the next day, given the number of intoxicants that coursing through his body.

Back at school, pledging began to take over as a priority with studies and music coming in second and third. Unfortunately, I'm not one to discuss anything that occurred during pledging. I owe that much to my brothers and the organization that still holds true to its purpose of charity and philanthropy. I also held true to the notion of transferring to Scranton after the first semester, so all I needed to do was maintain a satisfactory GPA, and hopefully, the school would take pity on my parents' bank account and give my parents a discount, as they were already paying for one student there. I started the paperwork process to transfer. At this point, my sole purpose in attending WP seemed to be to make it into the fraternity.

What's the point of pledging a fraternity if you are only transferring out? Why not just quit? This, of course, is a personal choice. At that point in time, I wanted to join a fraternity so bad I could taste it. Those three letters hanging over my head were like a carrot you dangle in front of a donkey. As mentioned earlier, after viewing movies like *Animal House* and *PCU*, which had storylines based around fraternities, I thought that's what you were supposed to do in college. I thought it'd be fun, and I never had any intention of quitting. The best advice I can give is if you want something wrong enough you don't ever quit.

Aside from all the trivial knowledge a pledge is required to commit to memory during the program, such as the house's history and founding-father information, two major ideals hold truer now than they did when I was eighteen. The first is the fraternity's declaration of principles:

> Man is a social being. Our whole structure evidences the absolute interdependence of man. We believe the essential elements of true brotherhood are love, charity, and esteem; love that binds our hearts with the sturdy chords of fraternal affection; charity, that is impulsive to see virtues in a brother and slow to reprove his faults; esteem, that is respectful to the honest convictions of others and that

refrains from treading upon that which is sacred to spirit and conscience; these are the triple obligations of every brother in the bond. Finally, above all else, this fraternity stands for men!

At the time, these seemed to be just words to recite verbatim and commit to memory. I never really slowed down enough to contemplate what each section of the declaration really meant until later in my life. I will bring this up again in a later chapter, as it will help tie some things together.

The second ideal is the phrase, "Faith without works is dead."

Credos, mottos, and mantras have different meanings for different people. I like to think this one means that the end result will never come if you are sitting on your ass and doing nothing about it. Or, on a much broader universal scale, heaven isn't going to build itself.

The last week of pledging, the brothers had us in a common room at the end of the hall in my dorm. They were prepping us for the week ahead and also pumping us up. Last week. No turning back. I think at the beginning of the program we had seventeen pledges. Our class was now down to ten. During the pump-up session, one of my pledge brothers got super amped up. I liken it to a Viking berserker before a siege, where the logical thinking mind disappears and what's left is the primal, warrior mind of kill or be killed. He was in such an energetic state that he was literally jumping off the walls. In turn, he was pumping the rest of the class up. The brothers kept cheering him on, as that was the attitude they wanted us all to have. On one leap he missed the wall and broke the glass window. His leg went through, and on the way out one of his forearms caught the jagged glass that was still positioned in the sill. He turned to us with a gaping gash in his forearm. Blood was all over the floor. There was a look of shock and fear in his eyes. Someone quickly ran to the nearest phone and called 911. Another came back with towels to add pressure to the wound until the ambulance arrived. We were all speechless. I had never seen that much blood before in my life.

Our pledge brother was in the hospital, and word got out on campus that a brother threw a pledge through a window in the dorms. The information on the grapevine was obviously sour. Police took statements, and it was determined that there was no wrongdoing and the Greek Council would not be sanctioning the fraternity for what transpired. It was an accident.

Our class didn't get much sleep during the aptly named Hell Week. The required weekend getaway drew near—Hell Weekend. As mentioned earlier, I can't go into much detail, but we left the state, and there were about 12 to 13 inches of snow on the ground. There wasn't much opportunity for sleep, as pledge presence was constantly requested. Aside from the active brothers who were around, all alumni were welcome to join, so there were brothers who had graduated from years' past who we knew only from having seen an occasional photo, and heard their names, their family tree, and their scroll number (the scroll that every brother signed once he "crossed over").

There were rituals done that every brother in the chapter had to go through. Under cover of darkness, when the mind and body are at their most vulnerable, the final ritual was performed. Our spirits were shaken but not broken. It was the end. Our wounded pledge brother was still in the hospital, but I and the other eight members of my pledge class, Alpha Omega, crossed over and were full-fledged members of the Nu Omega chapter of Tau Kappa Epsilon!

It was a feeling of complete elation. The journey was over. I would never have to go through an experience like that again. It felt like stepping out of the tight grip of hell and into heaven in an instant. The brothers did an amazing job. As if someone threw a switch, all pledges were welcomed with open arms and were now equals with every other brother who went through the program. When available, the scroll numbers would coordinate with brothers in their family trees. Whereas brother to assist the pledge during the program) name was Chris and there was also another Chris in our line – my scroll number, #446, had some significance with each brother in my tree.

I don't remember much about the ride back to campus. I was still exhausted physically and mentally; however the emotional, psychological and spiritual aspects of my being were in a much better state than the previous day. When my roommate and I returned to our dorm room, we separated what clothes could be thrown out, what could be rinsed in the shared bathroom sink and shower, and what was salvageable enough to throw in our hampers. After my roommate got out of the shower, I had a nice, long, hot, soothing rinse. It seemed to melt layers of stress from my body. I hopped into bed and slept for about thirteen hours straight. To date, that was by far the most uninterrupted sleep I've ever had. I awoke the next morning with new vigor and a much sunnier disposition. I felt like a new man.

The rest of the semester flew by with get-togethers at the campus apartments, mixers with sororities at the older brothers' off-campus house, as well as loft parties where Greeks and whomever we wanted were invited. On a social level, it started to feel more like a college I could thrive and survive in.

My academics were another issue. I managed a 2.6 GPA for my first semester, barely breaking the required 2.5 for acceptance to transfer to Scranton. I received notification that I was accepted for transfer for the following semester; however, the university granted no financial aid whatsoever. This was the determining factor, and one possibility that my folks were very aware of when I submitted the paperwork. This weighed heavily on them but was not even going through my mind at the time. I had no concept of family expenditures and what my folks needed to do in order to send two sons to college. I was oblivious and thought there was enough funding there to take care of us. Little did I know my parents had taken out a second mortgage to free up some funds to pay tuition, in conjunction with whatever student loans we had. So that was that. I was stuck at William Paterson for my higher education.

I had general education classes to keep current with my degree audit; however, I was slipping away from my chosen major of jazz performance. Again, with no real desire to meet with anyone in the music department or my counselor— didn't think anything of it, and pursued the social aspects of the Greek life. The parties and mixers continued. A new pledge class came to the table, and I started to recognize the different groups within the fraternity. We were one organization, but there were separate factions that seemed to gravitate toward one another. All the jocks and muscle heads hung out together, the quiet and nerdy types the same. Fellas from North Jersey that were into club music and chasing women of that nature grouped together as well as the loners more interested in graduating in time, who didn't show their face much but would come to common hour at the student center or to a fraternity meeting or function. I found a handful of guys who were into the same music and extracurricular activities as I was. Ernie was a high school graduate from a town close to where I grew up and transplanted from Long Island to live with his father and stepmom. Nick was from a suburb of Northern New Jersey and was the high-school quarterback. These were the gentlemen, among a few others in our fraternity, with whom I spent a majority of my time when I wasn't attending class.

In fulfilling our charitable responsibilities through the church on campus, whose head priest was our chapter advisor, every week a handful of brothers were required to take the church van to the local nursing home and run a few bingo games over the course of an hour. It was volunteer-based, but a certain number of brothers were required to go and the youngest pledge classes were usually tasked with the duty.

We had to have fun and make the time go more smoothly, so Ernie, Nick, and a couple of other brothers typically pulled bong rips or smoked a joint before heading over there. The place stunk. It was completely institutional, with lime green walls, and very depressing. We always made the elderly feel comfortable in our presence, though, even if we were just joking around. They played for combs, notepads, and pens—little stuff of inconsequential value. The one thing that lit up their eyes when we walked in were the two or three dozen donuts we brought every week from Dunkin' Donuts. There was one lady we called the Cookie Monster (she resembled the Sesame Street character in her figure and mannerisms), who would beat us to the table before we even had a chance to put the donuts down, demanding "I want a donut, gimmee a donut!" until her needs were satiated. Sometimes she would go back for seconds, thirds, or fourths.

Our band Shady Groove landed a paying gig for a fraternity party at Rutgers University. Our singer/percussionist knew members of the fraternity, and they were in a pinch for any live music on short notice. We didn't rehearse much and didn't have much material, but we took the gig anyway. I think we got a check for $250. It was a raw, beer-soaked basement with horrible sound. The only people paying any attention were other musicians and drunks. We didn't know any pop or dance numbers and were relatively fortunate we didn't get booed out of there. I'm pretty sure our singer/percussionist knew people from his temple at the party, and possibly through that connection or a friend of a friend, my brother and I were introduced to Barry Karsh.

Barry lived in East Brunswick and before that was out in Oregon for a brief period. John and I hit it off with him almost immediately, given his carefree and humorous temperament as well as similar tastes in music. He mentioned he played percussion instruments, like bongos, congas, and timbales, as well as drum kit and said if we ever wanted to jam to hit him up. We exchanged numbers, told him that sounded great, and would be in touch.

～～～

The semester flew by, and before I realized it, it was summertime. I put in long days delivering pizza for a local shop. I'd do lunches, doubles, and night shifts but was pretty much always done by 10 PM on the weekdays and between 10 and 11 on weekends, which always left room for me to hang out with our crew. The money was great, too. Gas was cheap, and I'd have nights where I walked with over $120. For a nineteen-year-old, that was decent coin for easy work. There were always random parties going off and the occasional concert to prepare for and hit up. I remember catching Leftover Salmon at the Wetlands Preserve and talking to their guitar player/singer about hallucinogens while they were setting up the stage.

John and I took Barry up on getting together to jam, and we had an instant chemistry that felt just right for our skill set and level of music theory. Besides being a true hippie and loving The Dead, Phish, and The Allman Brothers, as well as bands like moe, String Cheese Incident, and other jam bands of the time, Barry was into jazz, jazz-fusion, and funk. He idolized and was directly influenced by drummers such as Billy Cobham, Dennis Chambers, Steve Gadd and any of the legends that played and recorded with such artists as Miles Davis, John Coltrane, and Art Blakey. He was also into groove-based music like Medeski, Martin and Wood, John Scofield, Charlie Hunter, and progressive-based fusion musicians of the likes of Pat Matheny. I can only credit Barry for giving me a direct connection to those genres of music and blowing the door wide open into the expanse of the musical universe. I'm sure I would've eventually found my way into those worlds, but at nineteen, my ears were light years ahead of where I would've been had I not met him.

I busted my ass working all summer and had enough extra spending money to purchase another guitar. I wanted something vintage, because all of my heroes played old guitars, and I considered myself a "lifer" when it came to being a guitarist, so I wanted to start collecting sooner rather than later. I was interested in a Fender Stratocaster with a specific year, 1977, the year I was born, so I was dead set on finding a guitar within my budget.

I traveled out on Route 22W to Outlaw Guitars. They were the closest shop that housed a decent inventory of vintage instruments. Any guitar enthusiast is a kid in a candy store when it comes to guitar shops. There were guitars of all brands, models, and years hanging on the walls with sticker prices hanging from their tuning pegs. Fender, Gibson, Danelectro, Rickenbacher, Gretsch, Martin – all there like ripe fruit on a vine ready for picking. I played a couple of Strats from the 50s and 60s, but their prices were way over my budget. I picked up a '77 strat with a maple neck, yellow-cream body, fat-70s-style headstock, and bullet-truss rod. I instantly thought of the guitar Mike McCready from Pearl Jam played in the "Evenflow" video as well as old footage of Jimi Hendrix. The guitar was all-original and came with the original case. It had some cosmetic dings and scratches, but overall it felt great given its fat neck and had a classic Strat tone with its three single-coil pickups and hard tail bridge. I played it for a while, screwing around with the pickup settings, tone, and volume knobs. It passed my inspection, and I bought it there on the spot for $900 cash.

The previous semester out at Scranton, my brother was caught with paraphernalia associated with marijuana in his dorm room. The classic spoof/toweled door/spray system so famous in college dorms failed when a hall monitor was sniffing around at the wrong time. They made John go to counseling, took his financial aide away, and as my brother put it, they pretty much asked him to leave. He needed to find another college to continue his education, and it was determined that the best bet would be for him to enroll at William Paterson. John was majoring in business, and Willy P had a decent program, so without much hassle, arrangements were made. He'd be coming up with me in the fall.

John and I kept in touch with Barry and we had some jam sessions together without the other fellas in Shady Groove. Both were in college, so getting together with them was tedious. I had a handful of original songs that John and I would jam to and Barry picked them up pretty quickly. We started to get them tight and picked a handful of covers to bolster our repertoire.

Barry is an amazing artist, and his area of study was graphic design. He was looking for a place to attend college and learn as much as he could in that field. John and I convinced him to come up to William Paterson. He could work on his degree, and we'd be able to jam as a three-piece and continue rehearsing and writing material with the hope of eventually getting some paying gigs down the road and whatever else may come our way with being in a band. A light bulb went off, and he was super into it. Within a matter of weeks, he was enrolled. Now we'd all be up there together.

Before the semester started, a handful of us went to Phish's first major camp-out show. The Clifford Ball was held in Plattsburgh, New York, August 16th and 17th. Five of us crammed into our buddy's Subaru Outback with rations for the weekend and hauled it upstate. The place was like a carnival. Whatever you needed was within walking distance, as tour rats set up vendor stands peddling grilled cheese sandwiches, veggie wraps, cold beer and water, clothes, and jewelry along with myriad other items one may need at a two-day Phish festival. The weather was superb, the band sounded unreal, and the entire experience was unforgettable.

$$\sim\!\!\sim\!\!\sim$$

My brother and I headed up to Willy P to start our sophomore year. We were both staying in the Towers—I was in the South Tower and he was in the North. Things seemed a little easier with my brother around. I got right back into the swing of things with all my fraternity brothers and John fell right in with all of them. We hit a couple of semester opening parties and had some fun. I told John that without a doubt, he was going to have to pledge the fraternity. There was no way around it. He didn't even balk or think twice. He was game and knew it was a necessity on that campus. This made things a little easier when I brought him around the brothers.

John and I continued our weekend trips to Scranton. He was still pretty close with his old roommate Harp, as well as a handful of guys from McCourt Hall or musicians he befriended, so it was never an issue finding a place to crash when visiting. Within a couple of weeks in the dorms I came across a few hippies, either by way of the patchouli smell in the hallways or the kind of tunes being blasted from open dorm rooms. This bait led me to a scholarly looking fellow with bushy hair, glasses, a hemp necklace, thin frame, and boisterous baritone voice. Josh Sternberg was from Marlboro, and we soon determined that his interests were similar to John's and mine. Aside from his sharp wit and sarcasm, Phish was one of the primary connections. However, he was more into artists such as Bob Dylan and other singer-songwriters. He loved the Dead as much as John and I had grown to love them and told us his first Dead show was in 1980 when he was on his dad's shoulders. After some bonding, Josh became a regular face, someone to hang out and chill with and his room a place to pop into.

Rush and pledging had begun, and my brother was thrown right into it all. It was determined, not by anyone but myself, that I would not be involved in any pledge education with his program. The other brothers had nothing to say about it, and respected my stance. The only advice I ever gave him was don't quit.

The weekends and spare time John and I had when we weren't heading out to Scranton were filled with jamming and increasing our repertoire with Barry. He had a great space in the basement of his parents' house with a kit set up as well as multiple percussion instruments. His parents were very easygoing and encouraging and didn't mind us doing what we did down there.

My brother took my only advice and came out on the other end with a scroll number of 456—ten after mine. The rest of the semester was filled with parties at the lofts, hanging out in the apartments, trips to Scranton, jamming with Barry, working on our repertoire, as well as hanging with our new friend Josh, who had bought a guitar and was teaching himself to play. I would sit with him and show him some stuff, as well as explain music theory, of which a lot seemed to sink in in a short period of time. He was brilliant, came close to acing the SATs and an eloquent speaker. He picked up theory much quicker than I had anticipated.

The year came to a close, and after the holiday fanfare and family and friends gatherings, it was back to campus for the start of the spring semester. I'm not exactly sure when it occurred, but due to a brief dinner conversation with my father, I moved further away from my field of study. My dad, mom, and brother were discussing college and our future, and I explained I wanted nothing more than to pursue music and jazz performance. My father, in a slightly annoyed and cynical tone asked, "What are you going to do with that?" I hadn't even thought of how I would earn a living after I got my degree. I knew I didn't want to teach, and I wasn't hip to the technological aspects of engineering and working in a studio, although I had a few classes related to prepping for that field. I just wanted to play guitar for the rest of my life. Perhaps my dad brought some bullshit from the office home with him and was subconsciously venting, and that's why his statement sounded so negative to my ears. It was crushing to my heart, as it felt as if I didn't have his full support in my area of study.

After that conversation took root in my heart, I thought it necessary to go to the office where my advisor was located and switch my major to business. I didn't even look through other fields or programs. Business seemed to be a logical choice, and that's what my brother was studying. I continued the general education courses and electives and picked up classes such as economic statistics and macroeconomics. The courses I took during my tenure at college felt as if they were all over the map, a potpourri or hodgepodge with no firm structure to cling to or clear path to travel on toward an end result. To name a few, I took philosophy, logic (classes I thoroughly enjoyed and did well in), Latin (thought it would help with my vocabulary), acting, public speaking, audio engineering and electronic music.

My close fraternity brothers Nick and Ernie were no longer enrolled in courses at the college. Ernie lived in the area, and Nick moved back home but would always pop over to campus to hang out and catch up with everyone. Ernie befriended a guy from my hometown who was enrolled at school. He lived in Paterson with his cat and sold marijuana. This man was very intimidating and hung out with the older boys from my neighborhood when I was a kid. He was African-American, between 6'3" and 6'4," with a slender but toned physique, had small dreads, was something like a fourth-degree black belt in karate, and walked around with a big walking stick. When I was a kid, he stole my Mongoose dirt bike from our backyard, but didn't have the proof or means of getting it back at the time. Anyway, bygones be bygones. We would drive into Paterson to hang out at his place, smoke, and buy marijuana.

One day, I was leaving the dorms to head to a class and Ernie's friend was coming up from the other direction. He stopped me, and we sat down on a bench along the walkway from the dorms to the student center. We started chatting, and he proceeded to light up a blunt. I was hesitant when he offered it to me, but I relented and puffed a bit and gave it back to him. I was all set to head to class, and he decided to about-face and walk with me. The only issue with this was he continued to smoke the blunt and pass it to me, and I continued to do the same. As we came up on the steps to the student center I advised him that it might be a good idea to put it out. To which he stated, "Nah man, it's legal! Just like cigarettes. We're just smoking. It's legal." He continued in this train of thought, adding in other pros regarding smoking grass. Against my better judgment, I kept smoking on the blunt and handing it back to him. I know either it was on a Tuesday or Thursday, as there was a period between 12:30 PM and 2 PM when a majority of students had no class and would congregate in the cafeteria to catch up with each other. Without a break in stride, we walked through the student center, up the stairs to the main level, and out the front door. We passed a campus security guard who either didn't smell the pungent odor in time (as cigarette smoking was still allowed indoors at the time) or didn't want to be bothered and just ignored us. We continued to walk across the quad toward the academic buildings. No one said anything or stopped us. We could've easily been arrested or thrown out of school, but we played it cool and acted like there was nothing wrong with what we were doing.

That semester, Shady Groove had a handful of power-trio gigs at off-campus bars. John and I had friends in other fraternities and sororities, so we were able to get a bunch of people out to support us. Our new friend Josh was always coming down and he'd bring a decent hippie contingent with him. There were always people that appreciated any type of live music or just something different from what the mainstream college kid was into at the time. We played a house party in Haledon at a friend's place. They cleared an area in the living room for us, and we set up and played to the partygoers who were ripping bong hits in the basement or Special K in the kitchen. We had a handful of original songs by now and early covers such as "In Memory of Elizabeth Reed", "White Room," by Cream; and Phish's "Run Like an Antelope" started to shape our sound.

The lofts in Paterson where our fraternity threw mixers and parties were given up as the alumni renting them moved out. The fraternity felt naked, as TKE loft parties were legendary at William Paterson. It brought us down to the level of the other fraternities who didn't have lofts and just threw parties at rented off-campus houses in towns such Haledon, North Haledon, and even Hawthorne. It was determined at a chapter meeting to find a place to rent for a one-off party. We eventually procured a gigantic floor at a warehouse in Paterson. The chips were in play, and everyone in the chapter did his part to put the pieces of the puzzle together, pull their own weight, and get the space party-ready.

We handed out flyers on campus, invited chapters from other schools in the area, such as Montclair State and Ramapo, and made sure our other Greek friends made an effort to show up. We were obviously allowed to invite any and everyone we wanted. My freshman-year roommate was the DJ, we had some lighting equipment, including strobes, and there were stations for hard-liquor drinks and shots. I think we had girls walking around with Jell-O shots as well. They wheeled in seventeen kegs of mixed beer up through an available service elevator.

The night of the party, people arrived in droves. All of the brothers had shifts throughout the night to make sure nothing got out of control and everyone was safe. Some were outside, some inside, and some had to man the door, take payment, and give out wristbands. No one was carding anybody, so for all I know there may have been high-school-aged kids there. John and I had a shift at the door, which was a landing at the top of the two flights of stairs. We had a cash box and welcomed everyone who came up the stairs. This included people from off the streets of Paterson, even a couple of homeless folks who didn't have money—we let them in. We were very fortunate no one tried to rob us or bring any weapons in and cause a disaster.

The party was going smoothly until the cops showed up about two hours into it. They made sure everyone left in an orderly fashion and wanted to speak to the person in charge, who technically was the president of the fraternity. Once word was carried to him that the cops were there, we made sure all the cash that was collected at the door left the premises immediately. He and a couple of other brothers split out a back stairwell to protect the take for the evening.

The mayor of Paterson showed up in her pajamas and berated the remaining brothers who were there about how reckless we were, and reminded us that if anything happened to anyone who was there or if any property in the neighborhood was damaged, we would be liable. It got comical near the end, and the cops seemed to be in a good mood. There were no arrests. The mayor made sure there weren't any news reporters there, as it could've caused a huge stir and threatened our chapter's standing with the school, city, and fraternal organization. Not to mention that it would have been a blemish on the mayor's reputation. All in all, over 1,100 people showed up, and our fraternity's coffers were healthy from the cash we took in at the door.

Our gigs around and on campus continued. I was still jamming with Josh in his dorm room. His progress and development with the guitar and workings of music theory came along at an exponential rate. It was eventually decided that he would join our band, as he had been writing songs on his own and working on them during our sessions. I started showing him the originals that we had already in place, as well as the cover songs, and we started rehearsing with him as a four-piece. The added guitar thickened our sound and freed me up to do more comping. He had a confident voice, had been working on his singing, and eventually came into his own with vocal duties.

In a filmmaking class I took with an esteemed professor who was known in the industry, I picked up the basics for filming with an 8 MM camera as well as editing film and audio. Our final project was a short film that every student who had the professor that semester would view during the last class. I took an avant-garde approach and didn't film much. I brought the camera to the bowling alley and filmed a bowling ball spinning on the floor. I scoured old reels of film housed in the department— footage ranging from parades, soldiers marching, war planes dropping bombs, and ducks swimming in a pond, and spliced them together with a numerical pattern of frames per second, such as 7fps – 12fps – 30fps – 12fps – 7fps, etc. For the audio, I recorded a layered loop with my guitar and multi-effects processor and transferred it with the help of Josh, who was a whiz and had taken the professor's class the previous semester. The audio track was soupy, archaic, and tense – which I felt was a great complement to the footage I had thrown together.

I was so eager to get out of Dodge when the semester ended that I dropped the film and audio off at the professor's office, left a note with a bullshit excuse saying I was unable to attend the final class for the viewings, and took off for Cranford.

When the grades came out, I received a C- for my project. I'm sure had I been there to explain my approach I may have had better luck with my grade, but at the time, I was just done for the semester and wanted to go home, see my friends, and get back into the summer swing of things.

Whenever we were all free, the band rehearsed at Barry's house. We booked a handful of gigs for the summer, including the anniversary party of a pizza-joint in a parking lot down the street from Barry's in East Brunswick. We also played at a dive bar off-campus at Rutgers, a place called Plum Street Pub that had a varied mix of college kids, hippies, and local blue-collar workers, as well as thugs, hookers, and drug addicts. It was a trip! I think at the time they served beer until 5 AM and shut down for an hour only to reopen at 6 AM for third-shift factory workers to come in for a drink after work. The place always had live music, and the curious music lover could always be found there on weekends checking out the goings-on.

It was Phish's summer-tour time, and there weren't too many shows to catch in our general vicinity. My brother ended up heading down south with a couple of buds and caught the Virginia Beach and Walnut Creek shows. The only other feasible options were Star Lake Amphitheater out in Burgettstown, PA, or Darien Lake Performing Arts Center in upstate New York. A handful of us opted for Darien Lake. The night before, a group of us ate mushrooms and watched the debut of South Park, so we were in prime form to keep the party going.

The first set was fun and bouncy, and I got my first "Tela." This is a love song sung by Page and part of the Gamehendge saga. During the second set, a bunch of characters began to make their way onto the stage. It was a colorful spectacle that was very reminiscent of a circus freak show. It was soon made known that Ken Kesey and other players from the legendary Merry Pranksters had joined the band on stage for some fun. Kesey and the Pranksters were instrumental with the Acid Tests of the sixties in San Francisco. They'd be held at house parties or in rented ballrooms, and the drug was typically administered via dosing of fruit punch, sugar cubes, or straight blotter. I had recently read a book published by Rolling Stone on Jerry Garcia and was familiar with the cultural scene in San Francisco, including Haight-Ashbury, at the time the Dead were up and coming. The Pranksters had their own view of reality and did not identify with how modern society was progressing and the conservative views of the time. They were added party favors to the Acid Tests and the antithesis of the cookie-cutter, white picket fenced, nuclear family model of the American Dream.

I was awestruck. Kesey, not only an icon of the 60s, wrote *One Flew Over the Cuckoos Nest* and voluntarily signed up for government testing of the effects of LSD. Along with other members of the psychedelic troupe, it made for an amusing and unforgettable concert. Kesey was up there with Prankster Ken Babbs doing a Bozo/Bolo bit. This stemmed from the Dead's touring buses, where the Bozos were on one bus and the Bolos on another. They would wear masks and fuck with each other while on the road. My jaw pretty much fell off my face when Kesey started into a "Two Bozos" bit and Trey dropped "Somewhere Over the Rainbow" and "If I Only Had a Brain" teases. It was complete lunacy.

After the concert ended, we headed toward our motel rooms in nearby Batavia. There was a diner in the vicinity, and we decided to pop in for some late-night grub. Once seated, we soon took notice of a section of the diner that was roped off and reserved. Further study revealed that it was Kesey and the Pranksters. Once we were done with our food we made it over to the section and thanked everyone for putting on an amazing spectacle earlier. I think they were a little stunned that a handful of twenty-year olds knew who they were or anything about the counterculture of the 60s. In the parking lot was the famed Further bus that the Pranksters rolled around the country in, filming their antics while in altered states of consciousness. This was the "magic bus" that the Who wrote and sung about, as well as the name of an incarnation of some post-Jerry Dead tour lineups. They were gracious enough to let us on the bus and take some pictures.

In a flash, the fall semester was upon us once again. This year, I was out of the dorms and able to live in the apartments that were designated for upperclassmen. They had a kitchen area with stove and refrigerator. Beyond those was a living room with a couple of couches. There were two bedrooms with two people per room and a full bathroom that all roommates shared. I lived with three fraternity brothers. One was my big bro.

With a handful of brothers graduating, that left a few holes to fill in the hierarchy of the structure of our chapter. I was elected Grammataeus, which was the position of secretary/scribe. My brother was Pylortes, or Sergeant at Arms, and one of my pledge brothers was elected Prytanis, or president. I pretty much just took notes during chapter meetings and other menial tasks when asked to.

John and Barry moved off-campus to an upstairs apartment a block from Celebrities, the local college pub in Haledon that all the fraternity and sorority members went to. Below them, in the first-floor apartment, was an Indian family. There was always an aroma of curry within a twenty-foot radius of their door.

Once we got our bearings and were situated, we would have writing sessions at John and Barry's place. They had a nice little area on the top floor where we'd all hang out, work on an idea that someone brought to the table, or come up with something right there on the spot. For the most part, the hooks and themes of songs to write around and develop came from Josh and myself.

~~~

Around the end of September, I sat down at my desk to read an assigned chapter about the French Revolution for a prerequisite history class I was enrolled in. I began reading and it was as if my brain ceased to function normally. I reread the first sentence of the chapter about half a dozen times and could not focus or digest any of the words that were in front of me. I was completely weirded out, shut the book, picked up my Strat, and began to noodle. My concentration was shot, and I didn't feel like my usual happy-go-lucky self. This feeling continued and seemingly got worse to the point that I called up my mom one afternoon and told her I thought I was depressed and needed to see someone.

Within a few days, I was in my family doctor's office explaining my symptoms and numbness to what seemed like the world. The doctor, assuming it was mild depression, gave me some Lexapro samples and a prescription. I felt a bit relieved that I was doing something about this and began taking the meds per the doctor's orders.

The following few weeks, my symptoms appeared to worsen. I felt weepy and anxious, and my sleep patterns were completely disrupted. I would lay awake in bed all night tossing and turning unable to get any rest. When I did get out of bed I was exhausted. There were days I would spend twelve or thirteen hours in bed, and it felt like complete agony. It got dark too. Negative thought patterns raced around. Feelings of worthlessness, doubt, fear, weakness—thoughts of suicide. My conscious mind, or voice in my head that sounded like me, was screaming "DO IT!!" I couldn't turn it off. It was too loud, and taking control of my life. The only saving grace was the thought of the pain I would cause my family and friends. I knew I was stronger than that and had to fight it tooth and nail.

My diet was nothing to write home about either. I would eat Burger King cheeseburgers and fries with a Coke for lunch two or three times a week because my meal plan allowed it. Dinner was usually take-out from a local Italian restaurant and typically consisted of pizza, chicken Parmesan, or meatball heroes or cheesesteaks. Fruits and vegetables were alien substances to me at the time.

Another factor that compounded my ailment was that I was drinking, on average, a six-pack a night, sometimes more. John had a part-time job at a liquor store in North Haledon and, being underage, I'd head over there and pull out whatever I wanted for the evening—at a discount. My brother knew the ins and outs of the way the shop ran its inventory and was able to finagle some shenanigans where I'd pay for a twelve-pack and walk out with two cases of beer, buy a pack of Camel Lights and walk out with a carton. It was totally shifty, but the entire time he worked there he never ran into any issues. I typically wasn't drinking light beer at the time, either. Premium brands such as Harp, Guinness, Anchor Steam, Sierra Nevada, Bass, Oregon, and Sammy Smith's all found their way onto the checkout counter.

We were spoiled in the marijuana department as well. A friend of the band had a connection in the City and would bring back ounces and glass jars of high-grade hydroponics. This was one-hit bud and if you took a full bong rip you were pretty much crippled for two hours. The grass looked like a work of art and had a bulbous, spongy feel to it. Its fragrance wasn't like anything my nose had ever smelled before. Eighths ran between $75 and $90 depending on supply and demand. Jars or glass vials held grams and ran between $20 and $25 a pop and contributed to a quick depletion of my savings account.

I had a follow-up appointment with the family doctor and explained that the meds he had prescribed made me feel worse. He suggested seeing a professional in the field and referred us to a psychiatrist. He said the guy was of Dutch origin and the Europeans treated depression a little more aggressively than American doctors. We scheduled an appointment, and my mom came with me and sat in the office while the doctor was asking me questions. I'm sure I left out the parts regarding marijuana and alcohol, but I gave him all my symptoms and told him I really had no interest in well, anything for that matter. This heavy, dark cloud descended upon me. I was in a fog and had no real way out on my own. I needed any and all the help I could get. The doctor prescribed me a very progressive drug called Effexor. He told me I should start to see an improvement in as little as two to three weeks. We scheduled follow-up appointments and were on our way.

One of the fraternity brothers in my brother's pledge class was pretty close to a brother in a different fraternity who, in turn, I'd become acquainted with. He lived in the apartments, and we got to talking one night. I dropped the fact that I'd been prescribed medication for depression and things weren't really going too well for me as of late. He mentioned that he was a practicing Buddhist, and I pointed out the fact that he was Italian and had to have been raised the same way as me. He just smiled said a few words of encouragement, handed me a book, and said it was a good read and might help me out and show things in a different light or perspective. The book was titled *Way of the Peaceful Warrior*, by Dan Millman. I read it with great intensity, inasmuch as it seemed to be more important than any of my assigned readings for classes.

During this time, I had also become friendly with one of the sorority girls. We'd chat here and there, at a mixer or in the student-center cafeteria. She loved the Dead and other classic rock bands I was into, told me her parents were total hippies and in my eyes—was the most gorgeous woman on campus. She was of German and Irish descent, had long dirty-blonde hair, green eyes, a slender figure, and was as much of a goofball as I was. She was dating a member of another fraternity, and I'm pretty sure he played football for the college. The man was a beast. She lived a floor above me and would swing by from time to time to say hi or partake in the occasional smoke session. One day she was hanging out in my bedroom and we were just shooting the shit. I had the Dead's *Without a Net* CD playing and was jamming to one of my favorite tunes, "Eyes of the World." Out of nowhere, she looked me in the eyes and told me she could listen to me play that song forever. My heart jumped, and I instantly fell in love with her. I had an extra for the December 2nd Phish show in Philly at the Corestate Spectrum, told her my brother and fraternity brother Ernie were going and asked her if she'd like to join us, to which she replied absolutely. I was super pumped and eventually mustered up the courage to ask if she'd also like to be my date to our fraternity's annual Red Carnation Ball, to which she also said yes. Wow! Two for two—I was on a roll and in better spirits.

Over the next couple of weeks, the Effexor really began to start working. The psychiatrist was right. I also didn't heed any of the warnings, as I kept drinking on top of the pills, as well as smoking very potent marijuana. My brother, a buddy from home, and Hal's brother and I took a road trip down to see Hal at Loyola College in Baltimore for a weekend. We got completely shitty both nights. The meds were working so well that my brain was firing quicker than it had ever been. In turn, my ego got the best of me. I was a complete fucking dick, and rather than being very fun I was probably the most sarcastic asshole I'd ever been. I hit on my friend's buddy's girlfriends and was an absolute condescending, negative terror to be around. What didn't help matters was that at one of the parties, they pumped a bottle of Everclear into a keg of beer. This was a dangerous combination to begin with but was exponential to someone battling depression on very progressive medication. I survived, but my brother and friends reminded me for a while afterward how scary I was.

That combination of boozing and meds continued, and I began testing the boundaries by performing social experiments for my own amusement. I convinced a number of people at a bar where all the fraternities and sororities where partying one night that I'd won the lottery. I was completely pathological and did it just to garner peoples' reactions.

Over the past year or so, our dad's mother, Eve, who'd been battling Alzheimer's disease, and whose condition had been gradually deteriorating, began acting more and more erratic. She would call the house constantly, drive by at all times of the day, and knock on the door when my mom was in no state to deal with her. There were times my mom would hide from view until she got back in her champagne Cadillac and drove off. She began forgetting names, people, personal history, and important events. It was very upsetting to our family, and it got to the point where, to fund her care in a specialized home, our dad and his brother had to sell the house they grew up in as well as the house our parents had in Brielle.

The Red Carnation Ball went well. My date looked like a model, an angel, and a goddess all wrapped up in one. The woman was absolutely stunning, with her golden hair done up, her grandmother's pearl necklace, and sleek black dress. We shared a couple of slow dances that drew me even closer to her.

Next semester, there was an opening at the Farm, one of the off-campus fraternity houses, so named because it was an old farmhouse back in the day. There was a lot of property, and it had a barn out back and vacant pens where livestock and fowl used to be kept. The upstairs had an unusual design. There were three stairwells and four bedrooms upstairs that were all connected. The only things separating the rooms were doors. One could walk in the back door and go up a staircase in the kitchen, walk through every bedroom upstairs and come down another staircase on the opposite side of the house. It kept things fun and reminded me of living in a maze. Beside myself, my good friend Ernie lived there, as well as my big bro and three or four other brothers.

No longer under the watchful eyes of any hall monitors or security guards, I felt liberated. Like anyone with a newfound freedom, I celebrated in grand fashion—with beer and marijuana. These variables, in combination with the Effexor, made for a chemical cocktail in my brain that boosted my communication skills, in turn boosting my level of self-esteem and confidence.

One weekend, John and I went out to Scranton in our usual fashion to hang out with his old college buddies. A handful of us ate some mushrooms and were going from house party to house party. We got to one house where some people were ripping tubes from a three-foot glass bong and I was concerned, as I felt that the mushrooms we'd taken were beat or on the weaker side. I pulled out the bag that had the dried remnants of the mushrooms in it and threw some in the bowl. I'd never done this before, but figured it'd have the same effect as eating them; only it'd get into my bloodstream quicker. I pulled a thick cloud of off-white, yellowish smoke into the column and took a huge rip. When it was time to leave and hit another house, my brother and I got up and proceeded to the door. It was dark in the doorway and dark outside. Right when I got to the doorway, my legs buckled and I went down. I got up and couldn't stand. My legs were like wet noodles. It felt like muscle paralysis. Something was definitely wrong. My nervous system went into overload. I thought I was going to have a panic attack or worse—a heart attack. John and I were on Mulberry Street, which is the main road separating the campus from all the off-campus houses. I got on the ground and crawled under the front of a car, as all I wanted to do was lay there and fight whatever nastiness was in my system. That or, like an animal on its last legs, die. I didn't know what was happening. My brother was probably more terrified than I was. There were groups of people walking by. Some were pointing and laughing. None offered any assistance. Within a minute or two, I pulled it together and began breathing deeply telling myself all is well. I'm good. It's all right. I popped up with a renewed feeling of vigor and began walking with my head held high and a smile on my face in just a t-shirt. It was probably fifteen degrees out that night but I felt impervious to the cold for a while afterward. Needless to say, I took it easy the rest of the night, as I knew deep down I had really pushed the limits of my mental and physiological constitution. In relaying this story to some of my fraternity brothers, a nickname they gave me my freshman year seemed to stick—Chris Shroomtis.

Back at the Farm in the early days of the spring semester, things were going super swell. I had check-ins with my doctor and had made considerable progress in maintaining a positive outlook on things. I continued my supplemental self-medication of beer and marijuana. I felt invincible—impervious to any outside negativity. My communication skills were superb, and I was very quick-witted and a total trip to be around. I had so much energy that there were days that I had all my schoolwork completed, did some guitar jamming, and would pretty much clean the entire house by myself because I didn't know what else to do.

Within a couple of weeks, things seemed to get out of control with the amount of energy I had. I was so charged up that I could sleep for only two-and-a-half to four hours a night. I was completely wired. Animated. I can only compare the feeling to what I've heard or seen about cocaine. The prescribed Effexor I was taking was like legal cocaine. I was firing on all cylinders, and my senses were heightened. My mind was racing a million miles a second. I had no control over the machine, as it seemed to be automatic and go into overdrive. At night, when I had nothing to do, I began writing in a notebook. It was a stream-of-thought flow. Whatever popped into my head, I wrote down. Within a couple of nights, the notebook was completely filled.

One of those nights, I just sat in silence on the floor. I actually focused enough to stop the automatic flow of my thoughts and just breathe. I lay on the floor and continued my meditation. After a short while, my body felt like it was humming. It was indescribable. There was a golden light that seemed to take over my field of vision. It was as if a veil had been draped over the rods and cones in my eyes. My room was awash in a faint golden glow. It soon seemed to emanate from my body. I felt really warm, and cracked the window even though it was freezing outside. After I cooled down, my body warmed up again in an instant, and I began to sweat. I stripped down to my boxer shorts and just lay on the ground.

There was nothing left to do but let whatever was happening happen.

The supercharged feeling continued for the next couple of days. My sleep pattern was affected dramatically, to the point where I wasn't sleeping more than two hours a night. I was a terror in class, acting like a complete asshole, making a scene and being disruptive. I was in a bad space. It felt as if a major change was coming over me that was going to last the rest of my life.

I stumbled into Ernie's room and confessed that I'd been battling depression and been on meds and that I felt like I was losing my mind and grip on reality. I broke down. I was on my knees crying, "Why me?" My big bro came into my room and was concerned enough to call my parents and explain to them what was going on. He hung up and said they'd be on their way up to get me and bring me home. I started to calm down and feel a little better, even joking with Ernie and my big bro over everything. I knew I needed help, and the course I was running wasn't doing me or anyone else any good.

Once we got home, my folks made arrangements for me to go to detox at Morristown Hospital. I wasn't home long. I packed some stuff, and we drove up there. Upon arrival, we made our way up to the appropriate wing of the facility. I believe it was called Franklin 5, denoting the floor and respective person the wing was named for. I immediately joked that a better name for it was Franklin's Tower, a reference my folks didn't get. An intake representative was waiting, and we sat in her office for about 20 minutes going through a checklist of questions to determine my current level of cognition. Questions such, as "Are these your parents?" The first thing that popped into my head was to say no just to garner their reactions and fuck with them, but I knew I had to play it straight. "What's today's date?" "What's your birthday?" Who is the president of the United States of America?" They all popped out, and I answered correctly, proving I wasn't completely delusional.

After I got checked in, I was assigned a room with a roommate who was close to my age. I never heard the numbers 5150, Psychiatric Ward, or saw anyone in straight jackets or padded rooms, so I can assume that what I was told was correct— I was there to detox.

They cut the Effexor immediately and started me on a different course of pills that each nurse made sure I took. They made me open up my mouth to make sure I wasn't hiding them under my tongue or against my cheeks. It was up at 7 AM, lights out at 10 PM and I had to be sleeping by 11 PM.

There really wasn't much to do between group sessions, meals, and shower time other than watch TV, read, play chess and other board games, and tinker on a rinky-dinky Casio keyboard that was lying around. I had so much free time, I recorded an instrumental song I had written out that Shady Groove had been playing titled "Wytunic".

I had a few visitors while I was there. My parents came, my brother, my fraternity big bro, and my sorority lady friend and her best friend. I was so thankful for the visits and wasn't even embarrassed that they saw me the way they did. My brother mentioned to me that once my sorority lady friend heard what happened, she burst into tears. Hearing that, at the time, weighed very heavy on my heart.

The rest of the time I was in there I did well. They leveled me off, finding the right combination of meds to dilute the Effexor in my system. I stayed for five nights before my folks came to get me. I left with a script for Depakote, which is a mood stabilizer and drug used to treat bipolar disorder. I had to find some humor in all of it, so I named the drug Deep Coyotes, as it sounded way cooler. I thought I was all set to go back to school and finish the semester out but my folks submitted an application for a leave of absence, withdrew me from my classes, and had other plans for me. They signed me up for mandatory AA meetings and told me it was state regulated. I was to go to a facility up on Morris Ave. in Springfield 2 or 3 times a week for a certain length of time and had to regularly pee in a cup for analysis. I was confused as to why I had to go to these meetings. I wasn't an alcoholic. I just drank a lot, as that's what I thought you did in college. Had it been explained to me the importance of not drinking while taking anti-depressants things would have been much different. So I dealt with the mandatory meetings and didn't drink.

This period was very difficult for my family. Not only were my parents dealing with my bullshit, Grandma Eve passed away during this time. It all seemed so heavy and dark that bitter winter.

My mom got me a job at the local Sunoco station a few blocks from our home. I was thankful, because had I been holed up at my folks' house doing nothing the cabin fever would've easily stirred me crazy. My shift was 6 AM to 11 AM and I worked some very blustery, bitter, bone-chilling mornings. It was usually just me and another person before the owner came in and relieved me of my shift. I kept my acoustic guitar in the office when it wasn't busy to keep my chops up. I joked around with the owner one morning after one of my shifts was done when I was counting out the cash in my pocket. I told her I thought I got to keep what I took in and she looked at me like I had two heads.

Given these recent events, I wasn't out of the woods just yet and still had some bouts of delusion. One morning I got it in my head that a friend was ill at Overlook Hospital and I closed up the gas station and just bolted. Once at the hospital I soon found out there was no ill friend, so I wandered into an administrator's office and told the woman I'd like to make a charitable donation to the hospital for one million dollars. She told me she'd be right back, as she needed to get her boss. Once she was out of view, I left her office.

Closing up the gas station mid-morning would have some consequences. I didn't want to go back and face the music. My mom ended up calling the owner, explaining my situation, and thanking her for the opportunity she gave me.

The time away from school and my studies afforded me time to clear my head as well as find constructive things to involve myself with. I was listening to the Dead quite extensively around this time and read in the Rolling Stone Jerry Garcia book that before he started playing guitar he was an accomplished banjo player. I had a burgeoning love for bluegrass music and decided I'd pick up the instrument and figure out the basics. I went down to the local guitar shop and spotted a brandless (no company name on the headstock) banjo hanging on the wall. I inquired as to how much, and the shop owner said he'd give it to me for $100; the case was another $35. Sold. He threw in a beginner's Mel Bay banjo instructional book, and I was on my way.

I didn't have any blocks when it came to diving into the instrument and learning different chords and scales. My music theory was at the point where all I needed was to know how any stringed instrument was strung and I was able to construct and internalize chords very quickly. I didn't put on any fingerpicks and just used my bare fingers and started to figure out how to finger-style roll on different strings to the point where it actually sounded like I could play the instrument.

My twenty-first birthday came, and I was unable to celebrate with my brother or friends. I stayed home, ended up setting up my first email account, and had one Guinness just for the sake of the special day. During this time, my brother had about twenty-six shots at the local college bar down the street from his and Barry's apartment, ended up punching a hole in the wall at the bar, and after getting kicked out, walked down the street backwards while pissing the entire time. I wasn't exactly upset I missed that night.

Near the end of the AA program meetings, instead of driving right home, which is what I normally did, I made a right out of the parking lot, hit Route 24W and drove around in unfamiliar neighborhoods. I just wanted to drive, listen to the radio, smoke a few cigarettes, and be alone with my thoughts. There were no GPS or MapQuest app to refer to. I ended up getting pretty lost in some of the rural neighborhoods such as Long Valley. Once I found my way on to Route 10W, I traveled on Route 206S past Trenton onto Route 130. I stopped at a grocery store and, for some reason; I felt it necessary to purchase a Bible. They didn't sell any there, so I asked a store employee who was mopping the floor where I could get one at that hour. I told him it was an emergency. He pulled a mini one out of his back pocket and handed it to me. I thanked him and promised that I would return it one day. After driving around Camden for a spell, I decided to head home.

Once off of the Parkway, I stopped at a Dunkin Donuts for a coffee and donut. I brought the borrowed Bible with me, sat at a table in the corner and started to read. A group of younger kids came in, took notice of me reading, and started pointing and laughing. One of them even threw something at me. I found it disheartening but just smiled and ignored them until they grew bored, stopped bothering me, and left.

After the mandatory AA program ended, it was recommended that I attend regular meetings close to home. I went to one in the basement of a church in a neighboring town. I didn't say anything and just listened to the stories. One man in his fifties went on about downing a fifth of vodka and chasing his wife around in a blind rage with a bat, screaming he was going to kill her. Everyone there laughed. That was the last AA meeting I ever attended. I wasn't the violent type. When I drank too much, I either passed out easily or pissed myself. I never had any intentions of deliberately causing anyone harm. I knew in my heart I wasn't like any of these people. I rarely drank hard alcohol save some celebratory shots, and I knew where I stood with beer. The synergy of the Effexor, alcohol, and marijuana in my system is what triggered my episode.

At the recommendation and referral of our family doctor, I started seeing a new psychiatrist. He was younger and a lot easier to relate to. My file was transferred from the Dutch doctor, so he was current on my situation. The plan was to wean me off of the Depakote and start taking Wellbutrin. This drug had the same active component as Zyban, a drug used to assist people who are trying to quit smoking. The weaning eventually went its course, and I was now taking only Wellbutrin as prescribed.

I stayed sober for about four months. I didn't drink any booze or smoke pot. I took my medication as prescribed. My only vices during this time were cigarettes and coffee—a classic combination for an AA meeting. My saving grace was writing songs and rehearsals with John, Barry, and Josh.

I also picked up a new job at this time. I was hired for the grand opening of the Guitar Center in Springfield on Route 22. I was like a kid in a candy store over there. I worked the accessories department, where they sold everything from tablature books, strings, and picks to effects pedals. I had fun working there and met some pretty amazing people and fellow musicians.

The four months of complete soberness eventually ended and I was back to drinking beer at a responsible level. I didn't smoke any pot, and told myself it was for the better, and perhaps one day when my mind is back to a respectable state I'd enjoy it once again.

~~~

The fall semester started up, and I was all clear to return and pursue my course of higher learning. I moved into a second-floor apartment with Ernie and Nick, located in a section of Haledon that was closer to Paterson than to campus; however, it was right down the road from the school. We also had a welcome mascot join us. Ernie's mom picked up a stray dog she came across on the side of a road out in Long Island. She was just a lost puppy and decided to take her in. The mutt had German Shepherd traits but was thin and long like a Greyhound. Either way, she was adorable. We decided on the name Tela, after my favorite Phish song. It took us a while to housebreak her and find the right combination of food for her diet. In the early days, we'd come home to steamy, soft piles of shit on the carpet.

Outside of class and fraternity functions, I was either jamming to blues CDs in my bedroom, writing with John, Barry, and Josh at John and Barry's apartment, or practicing darts in the apartment. A new pub opened up off of Belmont Avenue that was around the corner from campus called The Shepherd and the Knucklehead. We frequented the place often for their wide selection of craft beer on tap. The owner was a lover of all things artistic, and one could easily sit at a table or the bar and pick a book by Hemingway, Ginsberg, Whitman, or Joyce off the shelf and get lost while sipping on a Lambic. He had board games available to play, a great jukebox, and a huge poster of Jack Kerouac and Neal Cassady hanging on the wall. This place was right up my alley and our band developed a friendship with the owner, Chris, which eventually led to open jam nights tucked in a tiny section of what available space he had.

While in quarantine in Cranford a few months earlier, I came up with a chord progression and melody line that went over the changes but never found the right words for the song. During a rehearsal at John and Barry's, I lay down on a bed with the melody going through my head, cleared my mind, closed my eyes and just breathed. Twenty minutes later, I had the lyrics to the song memorized. It came from the ether, and I realized the power of concentration and meditative practices. The song, titled "Cabo San Lucas," painted a picture of disdain for the rat race and from a perspective of dropping everything and moving to paradise. I'd never been to Cabo, but the rhythm and cadence of the words fit perfectly.

Things seemed to be going OK. I was diligently taking my meds and watching the booze and marijuana intake. I'd see my doctor every four to six weeks for a few months. I was becoming a responsible student and actually attending classes, paying attention, reading assignments, and taking exams. The trips out to Scranton were becoming fewer and far between, but there were times we'd still make it out there and throw down. The band concentrated more on writing songs, developing our chemistry, and finding places and local bars to set up shop and let it rip.

That Halloween, a handful of us managed to get tickets for the Phish show out in Las Vegas. We were all college kids, dirt poor, and couldn't afford any room at a casino, so we ended up staying at a Super 8 on the outskirts of the Vegas strip. The room was something like $70 a night, and we had about six or seven of us crammed in there. The album being covered was still a surprise, and we all had high hopes it was something we all knew. They were on fire both nights. Halloween night's second-set cover album ended up being *Loaded* by The Velvet Underground. My brother and I were initially disappointed, given the logistics involved in getting out there, but any Phish Halloween show is legendary in its own right, so we quickly got over it. Sure enough, the next gig out in Utah, the band played the entire *Dark Side of the Moon* album. Fuckers.

The fall and winter flew by, and before I knew it, the holidays passed and I was right back into the swing of things for the spring semester. Ernie, Nick, and I moved out of our apartment in Haledon, since Ernie had taken a job at a swanky restaurant on the Embarcadero near Fisherman's Warf in San Francisco. Nick moved back home to focus on work and eventually getting back into school. Ernie's old room opened up at the Farm, and I jumped at the chance to grab it, as I felt it was the nicest room in the house. Once settled in my routine, I spent much of my free time watching

VH1 specials on rock documentaries on bands such as The Dead, guitarists like Stevie Ray Vaughn, and specials on the sixties scene out in California and other counter-culture programs, like *Summer of Love* and the *Monterey Pop Festival*. I became a voracious reader and ran through such books as Kerouac's *On the Road*, *Big Sur*, and *The Dharma Bums*. Other notable reads that captivated my imagination were William S. Burroughs' *Naked Lunch* (due only to the fact that Steely Dan named their band after a dildo in that book), *Junky*, and Hunter S. Thompson's *The Rum Diaries*.

The band also had a couple of gigs out of state at schools where Josh's friends were attending. We drove up to Union College in Schenectady, New York, and set up in the parlor of a gigantic mansion that was a fraternity house. To me, it was a dream come true. Play all night, take breaks whenever, party, get fucked up, maybe hook up with a sexy hippie chick and not worry about having to drive home. It was a success. Most of the students at the party were into what we were doing and we had a large crowd for most of the night. We also had a similar experience at a fraternity house at the University of Pennsylvania. We set up in a living room and on the other side of the house in a different large room was a DJ. The place was so big both acts were capable of playing at the same time and not sonically stepping on each other's toes. We played a searing "In Memory of Elizabeth Reed" and I was pretty much trying to jump out of my skin. There was so much energy one could feel it throughout the entire room. I felt it throughout my body, and my thinking mind shut off to the point where it was pure instinct. Right after we were done, I was sweating profusely while catching my breath and a guy came up to me and said "nice act" with a caustic tone. I just smiled, thanked him, and realized someone like that will probably never feel anything remotely like what I was experiencing ever in his entire life. That is just not something you can fake.

In April, we decided to record a three-song demo. We'd been rehearsing pretty regularly and had a handful that we considered were ready to be laid down. I forget how we hooked up with the engineer, but we traveled up Route 23 North to his studio in Butler and found it to be quite comfortable and affordable for the project. After about three sessions, we had the finished product for our songs "Top of the World," "The Perfect

One," and "Timeless." We played them all for our friends, who were very enthusiastic about what they heard.

The annual campus Spring Fest was right around the corner, and they were considering acts to play in front of the student center facing the quad. The entertainment committee was blown away with what they heard on the tape we gave them, and booked us immediately. We had fun cutting our teeth in front of the student body. It was a lovely warm spring day and here we were—a bunch of hippies playing jammy tunes, Allman Brothers, and Cream covers to a North Jersey crowd of students, most of whom were listening to pop, top 40, and dance music.

After the semester ended, a familiar pattern followed suit. This included delivering pizza, rehearsing, and playing gigs. Rooms were still sparse for an up-and-coming band with no management, so we took what we could get. This included parties in friends' basements, Plum Street Pub, and The Crossroads in Garwood, and by this time, we may have even snuck into the famed Wetlands Reserve in Tribeca. As we were total neophytes to playing in the City, we were relegated to the downstairs Lounge at the Wetlands.

We had to cut our teeth downstairs and prove our mettle in a very competitive scene. Friends would come support us, and soon we were making new fans that appreciated the original material, covers, and raw energy we were displaying. For one of our first gigs in the Lounge we did two sets. The first one clocked in at over three hours long and the second was close to two and a half. We stretched the material we had and took some jams into outer space.

The next semester kicked in and my routine was getting better. I didn't cut classes as much when I was living with Ernie and Nick or up in the apartments. There were days we'd get super stoned and head to the bowling alley for cheap games and pitchers of beer. Those slothful days were behind me. The band started a residency at Casey O'Tooles in Wayne. The place was a bar/restaurant and we knew a handful of people from school that either waitressed or bartended there. They had decent drink specials for students and we always brought some friends down to cheer us on.

That Halloween John and I decided to fly out to California to see Ernie. He was living in San Mateo, which is a good 25 miles south of San Francisco. He was still bartending and waiting tables at an upscale restaurant on the Embarcadero. Once we made it to his house, I noticed a cat litter box and some cat toys lying around. Ernie failed to mention his roommate had two cats. I am horribly allergic. By the time I was ready to call it a night and go to sleep, I was in such a state that I had to call a cab and stay at a Holiday Inn a few miles away. It was torture. My eyes watered up, I sneezed incessantly and my throat began to close up. I was able to hang out at Ernie's house for two hours tops at a clip when taking a handful of Allegras.

While Ernie was at work, John and I traveled to the Haight—the Haight-Ashbury district of the city. This was ground zero for the West Coast hippie movement in the sixties and synonymous with the Grateful Dead. We ventured to 710 Ashbury Street, where some members of the Dead and their friends, girlfriends, and members of management used to live back in the day. We hit up a local record shop near Golden Gate Park and had lunch and some beers at Magnolia, a gastro pub with amazing homegrown beers on tap.

John was flipping through some local entertainment magazine looking for a decent show to hit up while we were out there and noticed Strangefolk, a band from Vermont that Hal had turned us on to, were playing at the Great American Music Hall on the 30th and 31st. This was a no-brainer to check out. We'd been listening to two of their releases for a while, and the venue they were playing at was legendary. The Dead's *One From the Vault*, a show from 1975, was recorded there, and at the time, was one of my favorite CDs. I jammed to most of the double disc constantly. The show was packed with happy hippies in costume, and people were openly smoking grass in the venue. I got the feeling that most live music venues in San Francisco at the time looked the other way about weed.

After our return to the East Coast, my brother came up with some psychedelic lyrics to a jam that the band was working on. We eventually fleshed it out and named it "San Mateo."

A few shows that I put in for mail order over the summer were coming up, and that included a stop at Hampton Coliseum in Hampton, Virginia. After a couple of Philly shows, a whole slew of us from Cranford, and various other friends, descended on the town. The Coliseum resembles something out of a sci-fi film as it looks like a spaceship once it is lit up it all its glory. Hampton had a very liberal policy as far as policing the phans went. You could pretty much get away with anything so long you weren't destroying property, hurting anyone, or doing something you shouldn't be in plain sight of the police. The hotels and motels were mobbed with phans and the hissing of nitrous tanks sounded like an amplified snake pit. Local business always welcomed Phish fans with open arms, as we've always brought a boost to their economy.

Phish was playing a New Year's show to celebrate the end of the millennium down in the Everglades located in central south Florida. It was a two-night event situated on a Seminole Indian reservation. All my friends had tickets and had their plans in place. I was a last-minute addition. It took me a while to figure out that I'd be missing out on one of the most momentous Phish camp-outs in history. My close crew had no room in their cars for me, so I was relegated to finding a spot in a car with a girl from our crew, her sister, and her boyfriend. We got onto Alligator Alley, which runs east to West through the Everglades connecting the Florida coasts, and sat through crawling traffic for about five and a half hours before entering the reservation. We were fortunate as there were reports had we left earlier we could've been sitting in fourteen hours of traffic. Once inside, the campground was set up like a little village. There were signs for streets, potable water, and porta-potties, as well as vending areas. Campground employees handed out maps of the area when you entered the grounds.

I eventually hooked up with all my friends, and the millennial partying ensued. The 30th opened with a daytime set then a break and back to two long sets at night. The New Year's Eve was just magic. The second set started around 11:30 PM and ran nonstop until sunrise. There were occasional breaks where band members would hop off stage to use the bathroom, but that set was a feat unto itself. Fireworks went off at midnight to ring in the new millennium, and I found myself on a Ferris wheel with Hal while the band was playing "Bittersweet Motel." It stopped at the top for a while, and we just sat awestruck in befuddlement at the awesomeness and splendor of the event.

I kept my nose to the grindstone with the start of the new semester. I attended more classes than I usually did, paid attention in class, and focused on putting in a good effort to bolster my GPA. One of my favorite classes that semester, or for the entire time I was at school, was the anthropology elective titled Witches, Shamans and Magic. I listened with great intensity during class and read every assignment. That field always fascinated me and opened my mind up to different cultures and systems of belief (like vision quests by some Native American cultures), besides the Judeo-Christian upbringing I was familiar with.

During the course of the semester, we met an amazing keyboard player while hitting up some open jams at a bar that had a small stage in Ridgewood called the Underpass. His name was Shoheen Owhady, and he went by the moniker "Shady." He was half Iranian, half Irish, and his first name was ancient Persian for eagle. He had mad chops, was a huge Page McConnell fan, and dug everything from jazz to heavy metal. We got to talking, explained we were in the market for a keyboard player, and inquired if he would like to jam with us sometime. He obliged, and we eventually got together and had amazing chemistry. During the course of the semester, Josh and I would frequently head down to his off-campus house near Trenton (he eventually graduated valedictorian of his class at Trenton State College), and run through our original songs. He started to learn our repertoire, and soon we were rehearsing our originals and cover songs.

We had fun as a five-piece and were able to explore more sonic landscapes given the room a keyboardist afforded. While opening up a jam or when Shady was taking a solo, I was allowed to comp using different chord shapes inversions, melodic counterpoints, and polyrhythmic concepts. It was very freeing and added a much-needed dimension to our sound. One of the first gigs we had with Shady was at the Crossroads in Garwood. It was a last-minute booking, and we were hard-pressed to promote and get people out for it. We decided to play under the moniker The Costa Rican Surf Odyssey for shits and giggles. We all wore board shorts and island- and beach-themed shirts. We had no expectations other than going up there, experimenting, and having fun. We threw in a lot of jazz covers that we'd been jamming on, including songs such as "All Blues," "Back at the Chicken Shack," "Impressions," "So What," and even a Thelonious Monk tune.

My semester ended and we focused on picking up gigs and playing out as much as we could with our new lineup. We got ourselves an opening slot for a band called the Ominous Seapods at the legendary Stone Pony in Asbury Park. As this was Bruce Springsteen's stomping ground, we deemed it necessary to open the show with a Boss cover. We learned "Murder Incorporated," and I did my best Bruce growl before going right into one of our originals.

Given my growing love for the band Steely Dan and their original guitar players Denny Dias and Jeff "Skunk" Baxter prior to Walter Becker and Donald Fagen's use of session players on their albums, I felt it necessary to purchase a Fender Telecaster. Steely Dan were pioneers in blending rock and roll with jazz elements, and their albums are, from my perspective, sonic perfection. Both guitar players were associated with Telecasters, and that model is a classic American guitar. It was only a matter of time before I bought one. Like my '77 Strat, I budgeted my earnings from delivering pizza and eventually saved enough. I scoured a few stores to no avail and found myself on eBay doing a search. My eye caught a 1977 American Telecaster within my budget with a beautiful Nocaster finish. The finish was redone but I didn't care. Something about it called out to me. I put a bid on it, won, and in a few days it arrived.

One late summer night we were booked at the Wetlands Lounge and either Railroad Earth or Gordon Stone were on the main stage. I forget the complete details, but both musical acts featured banjo players. Gordon Stone was a wizard on the banjo and pedal steel. Halfway through our first set and after a very raw and experimental version of Steely Dan's "Your Gold Teeth," a friend of Josh's came up and told us to not look or freak out but Mike Gordon (Phish's bassist) was near the back hanging out and listening to us. We all looked at each other, smiled like little kids, and went on about our gig with newfound energy. Mike was also a banjo and bluegrass enthusiast, so it was inevitable once the main act was on break that he'd venture into the Lounge to check out the goings-on. He hung out for over twenty-five minutes, listening to what we were doing, probably getting the hint that his band had a major influence of every member in our band.

After a few short months, Shady quit the band. It may have had something to do with control and management. I think he may have wanted more of a role in band decisions or maybe things seemed too scattered for him. I was probably most shaken up over it than the other guys as I felt a strong chemistry with his style of playing.

My final semester at college was upon me, and I needed a place to stay, as there were no vacancies at the Farm. I got word that one of my pledge brothers had moved into a beautiful house in Wayne, north of the campus where older fraternity brothers were living. It was nestled on top of a hill in a secluded suburban neighborhood. The place had a full bar downstairs, a pool table, huge deck, and gigantic TVs. The alumni living there did well for themselves and liked to live large. The brother that lived downstairs had a vacant walk in closet and let me rent it out for $500 a month with all utilities included. It didn't have any windows, but that didn't faze me. I was desperate for a place and could suck it up for a semester.

Near the end of the summer I started talking to a little blonde girl from town. She was about four years younger than me and played soccer for the University of Georgia in Athens. We attended a Bob Dylan and Phil Lesh show at Waterloo Village together and stayed in touch over the course of the semester. I mentioned to her that I was thinking of flying down to visit for a weekend if it wasn't too much trouble and she was totally into it. Plans were made; I flew into Atlanta and took a fourteen-seater puddle jumper to the Athens airport. It was the smallest and loudest plane I'd ever flown in before.

That night, we pre-gamed at some of her team's off-campus apartments and went to a party that the baseball team was throwing and eventually a bar downtown. The night wound down and we headed back to her apartment. There was some confusion about the sleeping arrangements. I was half-naked, ready to hop into her bed, and she used some combination of words that expressed to me that she viewed me more as a friend than anything else. We hooked up a little bit, and I slept in her bed, but I was scratching my head as to why she thought I'd want to come down for a weekend to visit if there was no romantic element involved. We got our signals crossed; it was a case of complete miscommunication. The next day was a little weird, and by the time it rolled around to go out for Saturday night and repeat the drunken escapade, I didn't have it in me. She ended up going out with her friends, and I stayed at her apartment, cleaned the kitchen, and drank whatever beer they had in the fridge. The next day she drove me back to the airport, and it felt nothing short of uncomfortable. After returning to New Jersey, I wrote a scathing blues song aptly titled "Athens" about my awkward escapade.

My semester and with that, my college experience, came to a close. I finished out my degree audit and was informed by my counselor that I had been the last student at the university to graduate with a liberal arts degree. I was grandfathered, as they no longer offered liberal arts as a pure course of study. It came attached with a minor in communications, as the total of all my communication courses allowed for it. I put up my highest GPA for my final semester out of all the other semesters at school, sticking a 3.8. With my lackadaisical approach to my studies, it took me five years (five and a half, including my semester off). My brother had graduated in four and a half years and was currently working for New England Financial in Manhattan, learning the ropes to be a financial advisor. I pretty much took a hodgepodge of courses in college and didn't really learn anything other than time management and that took three and a half to four years on its own! Sure, my value was a little higher than that of someone with only a high-school education; however, I had no intention of securing employment in the "real world." My passion and dream were music and guitar. The sole purpose of attending William Paterson was to study music, and I no doubt, took myself out of that picture and got knocked off course. I now had to make my way on the lower end of the workforce and climb my way into a position where I could earn a living—with no real skills and nothing more than a piece of paper stating I'd graduated college.

Shady Groove was booked at the Wetlands on 12/30 as the opening band for Percy Hill. They were a New England band along the lines of the same genre and musical influences and styles that we were into, although more refined, with amazing vocals and a ridiculous keyboardist. The morning of our show, it began snowing. The precipitation came fast and dumped about one to two inches an hour. By mid-afternoon, there were between eleven and thirteen inches of snow on the ground, when the system tapered off and moved out of the area. This was right as we were all getting on the road. With so little plowing and slick spots, we feared the worst. Anything was possible, especially when riding in a non-four-wheel-drive vehicle on Route 22 headed east to 1 & 9 and the Holland Tunnel. Surprisingly, after getting out of the neighborhood and onto the main highways, the roads were clear and there were not many cars traveling. We flew in without incident.

We were concerned that the storm would deter fans from coming out but the true diehards made it in and there was a decent crowd by the time we took the stage. A highlight of our set was having Percy Hill's keyboardist Nate Wilson join us on stage for a searing 15 minute plus version of the Allman Brother's "In Memory of Elizabeth Reed." We played a solid set and warmed up the crowd enough for the main act to come out and slay it, which they easily did.

Chapter 5

<hr>

THE JERSEY SHORE

WITH COLLEGE IN the rearview mirror, the next logical step seemed to be finding gainful employment. It is very rare to jump into a career right after graduating from college unless there was a solid opportunity in place early in the planning process. That, or the old adage of "It's not what you know, it's who you know." I didn't know anyone and had no idea what I should've been looking for or in what field. All I knew was that I couldn't deliver pizza for the rest of my life.

I made my way down to the Cranford business park and set up an interview with Kelly Services, a leading temp agency. After discussing what line of work I was interested in (nothing), I sat down in front of a computer to run through an assessment of how well I knew Microsoft Office. I breezed through Word and Excel and my contact told me that if I knew Access and Publisher I'd be able to make more money. So I went through those assessments using the "Help" tab in the right-hand corner and scored fairly high.

A few days later I got a call about a work assignment. The corporate office of Blinds to Go, located near Metro Park in Iselin, needed someone to handle mailing out employee benefit packages to new employees once they hit their required 90-day waiting period for eligible enrollment into the available group health plans. The hours were 8AM to 1PM, five days a week and paid $15 an hour. Not too shabby considering minimum wage was about $5.25 an hour. I thought an abbreviated workweek was a great way to ease myself into the workforce. I didn't take any lunch breaks, only a few cigarette breaks, and wore khakis and polo shirts every day. The training was minimal and when I wasn't mailing out packages, I was putting them together from scratch. I ended up fielding benefit-related queries from employees who were looking for information, or who wanted to know if their doctor was accepted in this plan or that. These were all things that I really had no idea about but I slowly learned the process and got into a groove.

One of the more memorable purchases I made after college was Mark Levine's *The Jazz Theory Book*. I may have shit the bed on my dream of jazz performance and guitar studies at William Paterson but that didn't mean that I had to stop learning and educating myself. Music is infinite and I always considered myself a lifelong student of the craft. I dove in and read voraciously, memorizing and internalizing as much information as possible. Of course, there's no better process in learning and picking up new ideas than playing with other musicians, but at the time my focus was elsewhere. I loved to read and there were hours where I couldn't be peeled away from that book.

During the summer, our band picked up a manager. He lived in the financial district in Manhattan, loved music, and I believed he studied music management in college. He was a friend of a friend of Josh and started seeing us when we were playing at the Wetlands. He explained that we needed to play in other markets besides NYC and booked a bunch of shows at live music venues in college towns Upstate. We rented a white conversion van with a few rows of seats, piled our gear into the back, and took off for a club in Ithaca before we moved on to Syracuse and Buffalo. These venues were listed on Jambase and Jambands, websites exclusively for bands of our genre. A winter storm was predicted to dump upwards of two feet of snow in northern New York state over the period of our sojourn, but we had gigs booked and were sticking to our work ethic.

The snow didn't deter too many hardcore music lovers from making it out to the Ithaca show. We had fun, played well, and won over some local Ithaca and Cornell students. By the time we were done, there was over a foot of snow on the ground with more on the way. It didn't make sense for us to head to Buffalo or Syracuse, and one of the venues cancelled before we could even contact them to see what their status was. It was a little taste of what it was like to be in a working band and what life on the road entailed.

It was around this time that we had two shows booked up in Massachusetts. One was at a live music club called The Middle East in Cambridge. We were completely electrified that night to the point where I felt a different energy surging through my body during some peak points of our jams. My conscious mind switched off and it was as if something primordial took over. The music began to play me. I was merely a conduit. I was jumping up and down trying to shake my soul from my body and I got damn near close. I was sweating like I've never sweat before; it wasn't from external but from internal heat. I almost fell off the stage a couple of times due to my manic flailing. The crowd was mesmerized and our Boston friends who made it out told me that they had never seen anyone play guitar like that before.

For our other show we played a 50-minute opening set for legendary jazz drummer Bob Moses. He published a drum method book titled *Drum Wisdom* and has played with greats such as Roland Kirk, Jack DeJohnette, Larry Coryell, and John Medeski. John and I drove up midafternoon on a weekday, met up with Barry and Josh, loaded our gear, set up, played our 50-minute set, loaded out, and drove the four-plus hours back to New Jersey. We split a six-pack of heady beers for the trip back and I managed to make it to my desk at Blinds to Go by 8AM on only two to three hours of sleep.

A few months into my assignment at Blinds to Go, I received notice that the company had hired a full-time employee who would be taking over my position. After my two weeks' notice, I was back on the temp agency's list of eligible people to place for future employment.

It didn't take the agency that long to find me work. They secured a spot for me at an Orthodox Jewish synagogue located in Springfield. It was basic office work and learning proprietary software in accounts payable and accounts receivable. I worked closely with the temple's accountant who would come in a few times a week to check on me, make runs to the bank, and review the ledger as well as keep current on the goings on of the members. The sole purpose of hiring someone from the outside was due to the high holy days; a member of the faith wasn't allowed to work. They required a "gentile" in the office. The pay was the same as Blinds to Go, but it was a 40-hour a week position. It was my first real workweek since working in the factory in high school.

Shady Groove picked up another keyboard player and the process started over with the new guy learning our original songs and growing list of covers. He too didn't last that long. We continued playing gigs at the Wetlands, eventually working up to opening for larger and regional bands on the main stage. We became close with one particular act from the Boston area named Uncle Sammy. Another band on the scene that we shared the stage with was from the Philadelphia area, called Brother's Past. Other notable gigs we had around this time was opening for Amphibian (Phish lyricist Tom Marshall's band with a brilliant guitar player who attended William Paterson-Scott Metzger) at The Stone Pony, a downstairs slot at the Knitting Factory with Big Wu on the main stage, a show with RANA (Scott Metzger's band), and Colonel Bruce Hampton (of Aquarian Rescue Unit fame) and the Code Talkers at The Red Lion on Bleecker Street.

John and I were leaving the city after one of our gigs at the Wetlands. It must've been between 2:45AM and 3:15AM. We traveled through the Holland Tunnel and were on the Pulaski Skyway when up ahead I spotted headlights coming in our direction. That particular stretch of the 1&9 is a one-way road. A car was travelling in the wrong direction. My heart stopped. In a flash of slow motion, I thought of the battle of guts that was the game of chicken, and then steered the car into the slow lane. The other car whizzed right by us, going at least 15 to 20 miles over the speed limit. I was immediately concerned for anyone exiting the Tunnel after us. The trunk of our parents' Ford Taurus popped open due to a faulty latch and our guitars were right on top. They could've easily fallen out of the trunk. I found a spot on the highway to pull over and turned on the flashers. My heart was still racing and I was close to tears just thinking about how close to death we just were. It shook me to my core. How could anyone be so careless?

That summer, we played at another outdoor music festival called the Stonehenge Music Festival. It was out in Quaker country in Pennsylvania on a beautiful plot of land. It was two days and nights of live bands in a relatively free camp out setting. People were pretty much allowed to park wherever they wanted to in the designated areas, set up camp, meet other attendees, purchase goodies from vendors, and party. The weather was gorgeous that weekend and we ended up parking relatively close to the stage. There was a large pond on the grounds where some hippies went swimming and a lovely fog enshrouded the area in the morning. It was quite an experience. We had an early Saturday afternoon slot which gave us time to recuperate from partying the night before. Nitrous was rampant and all of us ended up doing way too much gas but … it was a gas.

⌇⌇⌇

The previous summer a handful of our friends rented a house (#554) on Brielle Road in Manasquan. The sleepy shore town had a history of turning into a summer-long party with young adults from all parts of New Jersey, New York, Delaware, Pennsylvania, and Connecticut renting bungalows from Memorial Day to Labor Day. I was in for a half share the previous summer and had a great time. This year, it was time to up the ante and go in for a full share. Our landlord was very laid back and allowed us to get in weeks before Memorial Day and stay until summer was over and the weather turned cold. Our surfer friends were stoked given our proximity to one of the best surf spots in New Jersey, the Manasquan Inlet. They made a handful of friends in the water, some from the city and some from Brooklyn, Queens, and Long Island. Our house was coded for eight or nine occupants, but most weekends there were way more people, with some crashing on couches, the floor, or even in the shower.

We rented the same house given its prime location between 2nd and 3rd Avenues and its proximity to the beach and local legendary watering holes Leggett's and the Osprey. On weeks when I was able to take Fridays off, John and I would head down to the house on Thursday after work. There was always an element of a three-day weekend with us either taking Friday or Monday off. We'd stop and get beer, load up the fridge, and pre-game until we all went out to the bars. Once last call came around, our late-night activities ensued and we'd pretty much drink until oblivion or until the sun came up. Sometimes oblivion came after the sun made its appearance. Manasquan was very reminiscent of a college town and we had heard tales of yore about how it was like the Wild West in the 1980s. That spirit never really left the town. You just had to be careful and not disturb the peace too much for fear of being written up by the cops and potentially being evicted. We made friends with our neighbors and met people who lived in the surrounding streets. But for the most part, our house was nothing like any other rental in town. My group of friends and our shared interests, crazy antics, warped sense of humor, and musical taste was a 180 from the other renters in the neighborhood. We were the house blasting Dead, Phish, Stevie Wonder, James Brown, and Iron Maiden while the girls next door were listening to club hits and whatever top 40 song was making its way up the charts.

On the morning of September 11, I was driving on my way up to the synagogue on Gallows Hill Road near the cemetery in Westfield listening to Howard Stern. He was reporting on an airplane crashing into one of the World Trade Center towers. My heart sank as my immediate reaction was for the passengers, crew, people in the building, and their loved ones. I listened with grave concern and shock as I made my way to work. Once in the office, my co-worker, an older woman, had the radio tuned in and we listened to history in the making. Eventually, they turned on a TV that was in a classroom down the hall and everyone at the temple periodically checked the coverage until the second tower collapsed. By then, we were all staring at the TV in utter disbelief. My supervisor made his way in and we continued to follow the news and talk about the horror for another hour or so without doing any work before I began to feel weak and heartsick. I told my boss I was leaving for the day, as the only thing I wanted to do was be with my family.

After having lunch with my mom and flipping between every available news outlet's coverage, I drove up to the Watchung reservation. There was a scenic outlook where the New York City skyline is completely visible near the top of the mountain. As I made my way up the hill, there were cars parked all along the road with people walking towards the top of the hill. I followed suit and by the time I made my way up to the zenith, I joined scores of others gazing out over New Jersey towards Manhattan. The section of the financial district where the two towers once stood was replaced with billows of dark smoke being carried off by the wind.

The attacks hit close to home for all of us. We soon found out that a man we'd grown up with, playing rec sports and spending childhood summers at the community pool, was on the top floor of the first tower. His parents were friends with our parents. My heart broke for his twin brother as I could only imagine that a loss like that would involve a long and painful grieving process.

Over the next few days I was hit by a bout of paranoia. Visions of terrorists making concerted assaults on synagogues throughout the country popped into my mind. Of course, these were completely unfounded fears. However, the United States was certainly dealt a haymaker on 9/11. The country and world were forever changed on 9/11 and repercussions and ramifications are still being felt to this day.

My world slowly went back to normal over the next few months. Our crew stepped up the Manasquan shore house rental process relatively quickly after the previous summer. Once May rolled around we were all licking our chops to get back down there and start the summer-long party all over again. This year, the house behind our old house was available. It had two stories, five bedrooms, and was coded for between nine and 12 occupants. The seasonal rent was relatively low compared to the other houses available in town. This made the per-head payments very attractive. We had full shares and half shares of which I was a full share and had my own bedroom, which was rare for a summer rental. I was supposed to let a half share stay in the room with me when he came down, but the one time he tried to enter the room I was with a lady and blew up on him. He stayed elsewhere in the house for the rest of the summer.

My desire for more musical equipment got the best of me again. I was dying to buy a Gibson ES-335. Clapton played one back in the day as well as Grant Green, a jazz guitar great I'd been digging. Freddie King was known to play one too and it was a main axe of Steely Dan session guitarist Larry Carlton. The list of players who had influenced me over the years and who had played this model is long and distinguished. I was searching for a smoother sound than what I was getting from my Telecaster. I did some research and came across a guitar superstore out of Nashville called Gruhn Guitars, named after the owner. They had an amazing online inventory of acoustics, electrics, basses, banjos, mandolins, and other stringed instruments from all the big names in the industry: Fender, Gibson, Martin, and Taylor. I was like a kid in an online candy store. After drooling over many of the vintage guitars and jaw-dropping price tags, I came across a beauty. An oxblood 1980 ES-335 with a coil tap switch on one of the horns to allow the humbuckers to split to single coil. It was listed for $2,200 and in fairly solid shape for a 22-year-old guitar. I kept my eye on it for a few days as I searched other sites, but this one kept calling me back. I spoke with the broker who was the point of contact at the store and he told me that it was in amazing shape, sounded phenomenal, and I could return it, no questions asked, in seven days if I was unhappy. Sold! In a few days it arrived packaged up in its original case. I tuned it, plugged it in, and fell in love instantly with everything about it. I added this charge to my mounting credit card debt.

One night at our local bar in Cranford, the Riverside Inn (aptly nicknamed the Dive), my brother and I got to talking with two older fellows from town, Lou Donovan and Todd Palumbo. We had grown up around the corner from Lou and his brother Danny was the drummer in our first band in high school. Lou graduated high school in 1992 from Cranford and Todd in 1991 from a private high school. Lou and Todd had been in a band together with a couple of other Cranford musicians back in the day and we started shooting the shit over several rounds of beer. This eventually led to the suggestion that we rent a rehearsal room at a studio and jam through a few tunes. Lou and Todd were huge Descendants and All fans, which was right up our alley. I think Todd suggested the name for the band, enjoy! titled after a short childish Descendants song about farts. We laughed our asses off at the name and all thought it represented our immature humor, so it stuck. We picked about six songs to learn, scheduled a two-hour block on a night the following week, and invited some friends to join us as we'd also be drinking and fucking around. We ripped through Descendants classics "Hope," "Clean Sheets," and "Silly Girl," then All's "Dot" off the album Percolator. We all felt an instant connection and the energy was undeniable. Our friends approved and we played a few more songs. We decided to do it again the following week with a bunch of different songs. Before we knew it, we had about an hour-long set of covers thrown together. There was an open mic night at a local bar in Kenilworth and we started showing up to play through some songs to get comfortable playing in front of people and to gauge their reactions.

Our first gig was the Friday of Memorial Day weekend at the Plum Street pub in New Brunswick. We opened for another act and blew them off the stage. After our set, some members of the headlining band told us they should've been opening for us! Immediately following our set, John and I set off for Manasquan and a long, wild weekend of boozed up debauchery with our friends.

After my brother left New England Financial, he found a position at Provident Mutual, which is an insurance agency that had an office located in the Cranford business park over on Commerce Drive. He started out doing administrative and middle management work before obtaining his Series 24 NASD license. This was the general securities principal registration and allowed him to, among various other responsibilities, supervise reps that were licensed by NASD.

One day in early June, he told me that a group of four reps (operating as a team) was looking for another administrative assistant and that I should come in and interview. It was a salaried position with full health benefits, 401(k), and a pension plan. It was a real job, so I set up an appointment. The reps all loved my brother and they figured the apple didn't fall far from the tree. I met with them all and they explained the position. My responsibilities would include processing service forms, scrubbing new business applications for insurance, annuity, and investment accounts, copying applications and policies, mailing policies and applications to clients, creating mailing labels and envelopes for bulk mailings, and so on. I told them I was game if they were and was hired on the spot. I was pumped. I gave my two weeks' notice at the temple and began learning about the position from the reps' two other administrative assistants who'd been working with them for quite some time. I was a quick study and picked up everything they threw at me.

We were let out an hour early on Fridays in the summer so John and I had our bags packed and bolted down the shore at 3:30PM. We would change out of our work clothes in the bathroom or a vacant office and into our standard t-shirt, shorts, and flip-flops. We'd hop in the car and crank up the tunes with the windows down to get pumped up for a fun, boozed up weekend. We'd typically pre-game at the house for a while before heading over to Leggett's. Once that got extremely packed, a handful of us would make it over to the Osprey. We never went in before 1AM, as there was a cover charge. Late night would be at our place or wherever anyone was throwing down where we could hang out.

~~~

I started noticing a young woman who was working as a badge checker on Brielle Road. She had fair skin, long curly hair with highlights, and a tattoo of a dreamy crescent moon design on her lower side. I couldn't make out her eye color as she always had sunglasses on. She wore hemp jewelry, which was a sure sign that she had hippie blood and tendencies. I was charmed and we always engaged in a little small talk while passing to and from our spot on the beach. The July 4th weekend was upon the shore and a bunch of us headed up to Brielle Road beach to watch the fireworks. As we crossed Brielle Road to get on the south side of the street, I noticed her walking with a friend. I turned around, made eye contact, and smiled. She wore a long floral dress made of light fabric, a plain white top that fit snug to her body, and sandals. I turned around one or two more times and noticed her smiling, talking, and laughing with her friend while occasionally glancing in my direction. That Sunday afternoon I was at Leggett's for a few beers while watching the Yankees and spotted her running food. It turned out she was a waitress. She flew by me a couple of times and we got our smiles and hellos in. I finally mustered up the courage to stop her in her tracks, introduce myself, and chat her up for a hot second. Before I left, I made sure to give her my name and number and asked if she'd like to come over to our house and hang out sometime. She was keen and I went on my way with an added spring in my step.

I got her email address and we started messaging during the following week. I told her I'd call her Friday or Saturday and make plans for her to come by and hang out, which I did on Saturday. The date was July 13. My new lady friend made her way up the driveway with the same girl she had walked with up to the beach the previous week. I got them some beers, gave them a tour of our pad, and introduced them to whoever was around. After chatting her up, I discovered that she was a recent high school graduate of a local shore town, and she was 18 and a-half years old. I had no idea she was that young. Her figure, eloquence, and maturity projected otherwise. I was 25. After they left for the evening, my friends gave me shit and good ribbings. I didn't care what they thought. I had a feeling and decided to pursue something more than a platonic relationship and wanted to see how it would play out.

This pattern continued all summer. We'd email during the week and hang out on the weekends, which eventually led to us becoming intimate. She was super cool, had knowledge of music history that was surprising for her age and was a thespian. Her singing voice was angelic and she had the same warped sense of humor as my friends and I. Over the course of the summer we got very close. There were weekdays where our shore house was vacant and I'd hop in the car after dinner up in Cranford to head down to the house. We'd hang out for a few hours before I got back on the road by 11:30PM or 12AM to make sure I was in the office on time the following morning.

By the end of the summer I realized that I was in the longest relation-ship of my life. In fact, it was my only real relationship. I haven't written too much about women until now. There were a handful here and there along the way but this one was different. The others were casual flings and one-night stands. Deep within, I knew exactly what kind of woman I would open myself up to emotionally and share my heart with. I was 25 and now was as good a time as any to take a chance. The only obstacle was that my lady friend was heading off to college in a couple weeks and would be staying on campus. One of my surfer friends saw the "writing on the wall" and told me to end it, to take it for what it was, a summer fling, and let her go. My heart didn't agree with him and I brushed off his advice.

One day before my lady friend was getting ready to head to school, we were hanging out with her friend in the driveway between the back and front house and they brought her Claddagh ring to my attention. I had no Irish blood, but she and her friend were brought up in Irish households and had a fair understanding of the traditions from the Emerald Isle. It was on her right hand with the point of the heart facing her fingertips. They explained to me that if that was the case, the wearer was single and we were to remain friends but were not in a romantic relationship. If the point of the heart was facing her wrist she was being courted and in a relationship. They asked me how she should wear her ring. I thought about what they said for a split second and had her turn the ring around, which made her excited. We were going to continue our relationship while she was at college.

The summer came to a close and my LF (lady friend) was up at college getting situated. Our gigs had slowed down but we were still booking. The manager we had been working with took a bigger role in managing John Mellencamp. It wasn't hard to see why he decided to jump ship. As we weren't gigging too much, my weekends were free to hang out with my LF. I had no other real plans at that time in my life. It was either get together with my friends, shoot the shit and drink, or spend time with a pretty cool chick.

The first few weeks she'd come home and we'd get together at the beach house. It was vacant and warm enough to still hang out there. Manasquan was a ghost town near the rentals after Labor Day, and the calm and quiet was much appreciated. She also introduced me to her family who consisted of her mother, step-dad, brother, sister and step-brother.

Shady Groove played an opening slot for an amazing funk band that I'd seen a few times called Deep Banana Blackout. They were booked at the Crossroads in Garwood and we were fortunate enough to get on the bill with them. We arrived early for the sound check and I found myself outside with their guitarist Fuzz. The man was a wizard on the axe and an amazing person to talk with. We hung out for a good half hour, shooting the shit and jamming on our guitars.

My girlfriend's schedule got settled and her roommate usually went home on weekends so we began coordinating weekends where I would come up and stay with her. We spent a lot of the time in bed. If we weren't being intimate and experimenting with ideas of a mature nature, we'd watch movies. I always snuck beer into the room in my backpack. We'd typically sleep in and then head out to a diner for brunch, come back to her room, have some more adult fun, nap, shower (if we didn't do that together earlier), and go out for dinner before having a few beers, getting naked, and passing out together. It was bliss and neither one of us had a care in the world other than each other.

During one weekend up at her school, we made love and simultaneously expressed that we loved each other. It was not pre-meditated, it just came out. Afterwards, while we were regaining our breath, I mentioned to her that she was glowing. She said the same thing about me. I then took a step back and noticed that the room had a slight pinkish golden glow to it, as if our bodies' energies had transferred to the surrounding objects. It was magical and a feeling and sight that I would never forget.

The New England band Uncle Sammy, who we had shared the stage with at the Wetlands for a couple of shows, were playing at the Crossroads in Garwood one night that fall. The last time they had played at that club I was fortunate enough to sit in on Steely Dan's "Bodhisattva." This time around, they had another band opening for them. We walked in and before we were able to grab a drink from the bar, someone told us that Kiefer Sutherland was hanging out at a table with a bunch of older guys. I'd been a fan his since watching the movies *Stand By Me*, *The Lost Boys*, *Young Guns*, and, at the time, his current hit *24*. I noticed he was sitting with one of the older brothers of a family that lived diagonally across the street from us. His younger brother babysat my brother and I when we were young and our families had a very friendly relationship. Kiefer got up to hit the head and I was standing in his way. As he was walking by me, he said hello and I replied, "What's up, Doc Scurlock?" (his character's name from *Young Guns*). He gave me an odd double look. A short time later my neighbor came by and we got to talking. He said that he and Kiefer shared the same close friend, had known each other for a while, and that he was in town for that friend's child's Christening. He asked if I'd like to be introduced and sit down with them. I agreed and we started discussing his guitar collection (as I knew he played) and also his hilarious role on Saturday Night Live when he dressed as Slash from Guns N' Roses and performed children's songs with Sebastian Bach doing his best Axl Rose impression. Before heading over to the Crossroads, I had invited Kiefer along and told him that he's more than welcome to sit in with the band for a cover if he wanted to. He never made it over.

After the Crossroads gig, the band came back to our house for a little late-night activity and to crash. Anything was better than four sweaty guys staying in a van overnight or hiking it back to Boston. Our folks were away and we didn't have to worry about being quiet.

The following morning, after prodding the guys in the band with a golf club to wake up and start making moves, I saw my GF off and my brother and I hopped in the car to head up to West Paterson to begin basic tracking of our debut Shady Groove album. It was a long time coming and money was always the 800-pound gorilla in the room as none of us ever had any. The hourly rates weren't cheap and there was always the element of finding the right engineer for the project.

We decided on Lester Holzapfel. He graduated from the audio engineering program at William Paterson and played guitar and keyboards. We shared mutual friends and he had become friends with us over the past couple of years. Les gave us a very competitive hourly rate and we all agreed that he was the right fit for us. He rented a second floor studio apartment in a residential area of West Paterson and converted one room into a control room that also had an isolation room attached to it. The main recording area was his living room and all the furniture was moved to the sides to make room for our gear and us.

We decided on eight songs that were very representative of our sound at the time. There were a few that I thought were stronger that should've been included, but I ultimately got outvoted. The first session was to get down all the drum takes and as much of the bass lines as possible (prior to any punch-ins and overdubs). The guitars, vocals, and other instrumentation would come later in other sessions, but our focus was on capturing the energy and feel of the songs. We had rehearsed a few times in the previous weeks at a local studio to get as tight as possible. This minimized false starts and bolstered our focus. We spent between seven and nine hours recording half a dozen takes of each song, some more, some less. After the end of the session and with exhaustion setting in, we packed our gear back into the cars and would await choice takes to be mailed to us (this was prior to being able to send huge files for free via cloud-based technology) so we could agree on the strongest takes for each song.

Around Thanksgiving, my GF decided to throw a wrench in the gears and broke up with me. I was stunned. We were having fun together and I treated her like gold. She gave no valid or sound reason for her decision, but I can only assume discussions with friends in her dorm may have swayed her heart as she discovered what the freedoms of being a college freshman housed on campus may bring. I only ever assumed the best in trusting her when I wasn't around and assumed she did of me. This was my first real relationship and the feelings I had for this girl were too strong to go down without a fight. We didn't fight. I pleaded with her and displayed enough of an emotional response for her to reconsider. After that, we were stronger than ever.

We decided to get out of dodge for a vacation in early February. I had come across a great deal on a travel site for both of us to go to St. Thomas. For the flights and a room at a beachcomber resort right near the airport on Lindbergh Bay, it was less than $1,200, which was a steal for a 26-year-old earning about $30K a year.

I'd never been out of the country and didn't have a whole lot of money to throw around, so that limited our recreational activities to pretty much working on our tans every day. Had I really planned it our right we could've been doing other stuff, but drinking Carib in the sun and doing nothing was just what the doctor ordered.

A few weeks later, a bunch of us went out to see Phish at Nassau Coliseum in Long Island. My GF had gone with me to see Trey's solo band (TAB) out in Lehigh a few months back, but this was the first Phish show we'd be catching together. She knew how much the band and Trey had influenced me as a guitarist and musician, so I was understandably excited for the entire show. The second song in they broke out "Destiny Unbound," a rare gem that hadn't been played live since 1991. For us old school heads this was like finding the Holy Grail. I screamed at the top of my lungs (to the point of almost losing my voice) at the first bent notes of the guitar, knowing exactly what it was. I immediately leaned over to my GF; kissed her, and told her it was a sign that this song was played at our first show together. Sure enough in the second set we got another surprise. The band busted out Bob Marley's "Soul Shakedown Party" for the first time in six years. A couple of weeks after that show, a handful of us got some rooms at the Tropicana in Atlantic City for what would be my first Bruce Springsteen and the E Street Band show. They played Boardwalk Hall and opened with "Atlantic City." The energy in the room was incendiary and it was definitely a top-ten concert for me.

I was in the market for another amp and I wanted something vintage, so I went hunting on eBay again. My Fender Hot Rod Deluxe sounded great but I always wanted an old classic Fender amp. I came across another gem: a late 70s Fender Twin. I ended up winning the bid and a few days later this beast was delivered to my parents' house. As always, I wanted a clean bill of health, so I started researching techs that specialized in vintage Fender amp repair and modifications. I found a guy out in West Jersey and told him to make it sound like fire. I picked it up a week later and the sound was exponentially better and cleaner than when

I plugged it in for the first time.

Guitar overdubs in the studio continued that winter and spring. It lessened the pressure in the studio going the multi-track route as opposed to recording all our tracks live. Josh and I would schedule time to head up to Les's; my brother had a few punch-ins he needed to do. The main focus was nailing the guitars so I could have a clean canvas to write guitar solos where needed.

With the help of Max, the bartender at our local bar in Cranford, we secured a gig at Leggett's in the spring. With regular enjoy! rehearsals, our repertoire had grown to over 40 songs. This was enough for a full three sets of music. We had learned that Leggett's was looking for a new Sunday night band in the summer. Max talked us up to some of the bartenders and got us a gig to audition for the slot.

Our repertoire was anything but top 40. We played what we loved to play and hoped the crowd understood that. Songs by Elvis Costello, Descendants, All, Al Green, Led Zeppelin, Sublime, Allman Brothers, Firehose, The Beatles, David Bowie, The Cars, Bruce Springsteen, Billy Idol, Prince, and Elvis Presley (to name a few) all came out of our speakers that night. We sounded a little rough and didn't have any monitors, just two Mackies on speaker poles and enough raw energy to make the crowd stop their conversations and actually take in a song or two. Todd was a natural front man. He had charisma coming out of his ears, amazing stage presence (he stood between 6'5" and 6'6"), and was a total class clown on the microphone, engaging the crowd and bartenders. The show was a success and we were eventually hired for the Sunday night slot.

Back at the office, the support staff and I had been working on a big life insurance case for two of our bosses. They were rolling a large cash value sum (1035 exchange) into a new universal life insurance policy (flexible premium, cash-value policy) for a business owner. I can't remember the particulars, like if it was personal, corporate, or trust-owned; however, the face amount was in the range of $11,000,000 to $14,000,000. They had been competing with other insurance brokers and won the case when the underwriting came back favorable. Not to mention my bosses were great guys and amazing salesmen. It couldn't have happened to more deserving gentlemen. My bosses had a 50/50 split on the commission and the day the commission check came in for around $198,000 the office was flooded with energy.

I thought about how agents got compensated in the financial services field. It blew my mind. To me, it appeared that they were just selling paper. Sure, it's a life insurance policy with guarantees from a claims paying insurer, but still. That commission check was a lot of fucking money! Within the following few days I entered one of the reps' offices that closed the big case and inquired as to whether he'd mind if I obtained my NJ life insurance license. He and the other guys in the office were all for it. I had too much mental faculty to work as an administrative assistant forever, so I figured that was a pretty decent step in the right direction.

I paid a fee and enrolled in a class to study for the license. Forty hours of classroom study was required prior to sitting for the exam. There was a school in Millburn that offered a flexible schedule, so for the next five or six weeks from something like 6:30PM to 9:30PM or 10PM on Tuesdays and Thursday evenings I was learning about life insurance. This was real life stuff. You couldn't cut or miss a class. I didn't approach this in the same way that I approached my college classes. I learned my lesson. I was in it to pay attention, learn, and pass the exam.

After the coursework was completed and I had passed the mandatory in-class practice test, I was able to schedule my exam. The exam was pass-fail. Either you knew enough or you didn't. Fortunately for me, I was an amazing test taker so I passed and was one step closer to potentially earning more than my salaried position allotted.

∼∼∼

We were back at 554 ½ Brielle Road in the summer of 2003. My GF was in on the share (I paid as she didn't have any money), which guaranteed us our own room. This year, the front house was occupied by a handful of fellas who graduated from Cranford High two years after my class. They were all rowdy jocks with good hearts and partied every weekend like the apocalypse was the next day. It was great. We had two full houses occupied by Cranford folk and everyone got along. I remember pulling into our driveway off of 3rd Avenue on Memorial Day weekend, walking up towards the house, and spotting a severed pig's head stuck on a fence post with one of the front house guys sitting in a lawn chair beneath it wearing a horned Viking helmet and drinking a beer. I thought to myself right there that it was going to be "that kind of summer." The Viking helmet eventually ended up on the pig's head that stayed on the post all weekend before it started to attract flies.

Our typical shenanigans ensued with pre-gaming, heading out to Leggett's or finding a house party, hitting up the Osprey at 1AM, grabbing a bunch of Gee Gee's $5 pies after last call, and sometimes post-gaming until sunrise. My GF was working with her step-dad assisting in dispatching for a local cab company and would get back pretty late on some weekend nights. It worked out pretty well as she was only 19 and couldn't make it out to the bars with everyone.

The weekly Sunday night gigs for enjoy! started the week after Memorial Day weekend. The nights typically didn't pick up until after the schools got out and teachers were able to make it out on Sundays. A decent local crowd and people who didn't have to work on Monday mornings usually came by in the early evenings. Industry folk would trickle in after their shifts ended and there was always the Parker House contingent that showed up between 11:30PM and midnight.

We started gaining momentum and getting comfortable playing in front of the shore crowd. The acoustics were less than desirable as the head bartender was always telling us to turn it down, but we did the best we could with what we had to work with. Week by week more and more people started coming to see us, and Sunday nights at Leggett's slowly started to become the place where shore party people liked to end their weekends.

Our shows were always three sets, which meant we took two set breaks. The sets would last anywhere between 45 and 50 minutes, sometimes shorter, sometimes longer. The size of our repertoire at the time meant that we needed to stretch out the night. A lot of our songs in the early days were pretty short. The ones we could expand and jam on helped us extend our sets a little bit. On our breaks we would stick around the bar for a brief spell, talking with friends and making new ones, before sprinting back to 554 ½ to partake in typical set break extracurriculars.

It was typically difficult getting out of there after the show. We'd play up to about 1:40AM and as late as 1:50AM on some nights, then take our sweet time breaking down and loading the gear into the car. Screwing around with the staff and conversing with the bartenders over nightcaps didn't help get us out the door any quicker either.

Work was another issue altogether. John and I worked together and had to make it to the office by 8:30AM. We usually got to bed anywhere between 3 and 3:30AM. We always had a celebratory beer and cigarette before hitting the hay after a Sunday night gig. My GF would be fast asleep and the energy surging through my body from the show kept me up much longer on some nights. This meant getting maybe two and a half or maybe three hours of sleep before groggily getting up and making the 50-minute trek north on the parkway to Cranford. Our saving grace was always a donut or munchkin cup from Dunkin Donuts and for me, a 20-ounce French vanilla light and sweet. Once those components and two cigarettes were coursing through my body, I had enough energy to maybe function at my desk for an hour before I started dozing off and laying down my head down when my bosses or the support staff ladies weren't looking. Mondays were rough and I was pretty much useless the entire day.

I continued my studio sessions up in West Paterson for our debut album. By now, Josh and I had all the rhythm guitar tracks laid down and I was focusing on the solos. When it came to solos, my work ethic as a guitar player was more along the lines of composing than letting the tape roll and taking seven or eight passes and deciding what the strongest take would be. I always felt that if I was going to lay down a solo, I wanted to be prolific since it would be there forever. I tried to come up with something meaningful that I could be happy with and wouldn't second-guess myself over. A cultured ear and mind can hear a well-constructed guitar solo and notice that a conscious effort and different process was utilized in comparison to a one-off take in real time. There were days I would come down the shore during the middle of the week to get out of town and be able to focus on writing at the beach house. I was way more productive without any other distractions. In fact, I ended up tabbing out a couple of guitar solos note for note on whatever medium was available (I didn't have tab paper and used the back of pizza boxes) and they ended up on the album.

A bartender at Leggett's that we all became friendly with came up with a shirt idea and was able to have a beer distributor pay for the production. He used a font similar to the Cocoa Cola logo (but not the same one for trademark infringement reasons) to letter enjoy! on the front and had some mock tour dates printed on the back with venues including Red Rocks, Alpine Valley, the Gorge, and the Arts Center. Beneath the fake dates it listed "Leggett's Every Sunday!" They were a rich red color and we immediately started disseminating them to our friends and the Sunday night regulars. Free advertising 101.

The Sundays got busier and busier and with that, more room for spilled beer, broken bottles, people falling down, and fights. Typically any fights that broke out were quickly squelched, as there were always a handful of floor guys who would descend on the offenders, and the bartenders would stop serving to hop over the bar and assist in expelling the antagonist. We would play through it unless on some rare occasion the rumble got too close to the stage or our gear and we had to fend for ourselves and make sure our equipment didn't get damaged.

The summer ended and our residency at Leggett's was a success. My GF was back up at college starting her sophomore year, and psychology would be her major area of study. Like the previous year, we were allowed to stay at 554 ½ until it became unbearable, as the place had no central heating. We decided to get a winter rental so my GF and I weren't locked away in her dorm room on weekends like the previous year. There was a house diagonally across the street at 541 Brielle Road that was available for $700 a month. It was a three-bedroom, one bathroom shack of a place. The one bedroom near the back door was the only room that was fully encapsulated, as the other two bedrooms' walls didn't go all the way to the ceiling. It was odd. You could throw something over the wall to the next bedroom and privacy was a bit of an issue. Hal moved out of the apartment he'd been renting in Lakewood and was looking for a place in Manasquan so he was up for the living arrangement. He took the back room. During the summer, I met a floor guy working at Leggett's and we quickly became friends. His name was Quinn. He grew up in the suburbs of a local shore town and attended a highly reputable Catholic high school. My GF, who was still waitressing at Leggett's, talked to him and he earned her seal of approval. He was also looking for a winter rental in the area so we offered him the open room and he took it. Rent was $233 each a month. I wasn't staying there during the week given my five minute commute in the morning from my parents' house, so it was just a place to go on the weekends so my GF and I could be together. Leggett's still had bands play on the weekends in the off-season and we started playing there every three weeks or so.

A handful of us caught the Steely Dan bug and decided to fly out to Las Vegas at the end of September to catch them at Mandalay Bay on the Strip. The acoustics were less than desirable at the venue; however, we were still boogieing and singing along to every song. Once again, we were also the youngest people in our section by about 20 years.

I decided to continue furthering my education in the financial services field. My brother started a couple years before me and had NASD licenses Series, 6, 7, 63, 65, and 24 under his belt. I figured if I was going to stay in the industry I should have a better understanding and knowledge base of how the industry works from a licensed perspective. Again, the thought of working as an administrative assistant for the rest of my career lit a fire under my ass to better myself. I screwed up enough in college and this was real life, not a dress rehearsal. It was time to put my brain to good use as I now had the time and no pressure on my back.

John gave me a brief overview of what each NASD license was about and which ones to pursue. He told me the way to go was to get the Series 7 first and then the 66, since the 66 was the Series 63 (sell across state lines) and 65 (charge a fee for investment advice) combined. I got the OK from my bosses as well as the managing director of the agency and used my brother's old study material. I made my own study schedule and had a very regimented approach, typically spending an hour a day reading through the chapters.

By the fall, we had all our guitar tracks laid down and were working on the finishing touches for the vocals. We all agreed that our sound needed keyboards to fill in the spaces and decided to hire a player to write his own parts for the eight songs on the album and to come into the studio to record. The keyboard player, Beau Sasser from the band Uncle Sammy, was our first choice and happened to be available and game for the assignment. We mailed him copies of the tracks along with chord changes and song structures printed out on paper, and he learned the songs and came up with his own parts on his own time. We didn't have much of a budget and the four of us were able to muster up $100 a song for his services. He was more than grateful for the work and consideration. We wish we could've paid him more, but for an early 20-something musician, that was good scratch at the time.

All the keyboard tracks had been recorded but we still felt that some extra flavor was needed. Barry recorded some percussion tracks, most notably on "Cabo San Lucas," to really spice up the overall feel, and we decided that we wanted a horn section on a few of the tracks. Les or Barry knew some cats from the jazz program at William Paterson and we met with one of the guys who would write and arrange the parts as well as hire two other guys for a full horn section. We got a very competitive rate and it felt like with paying Les for the sessions and contracting out other musicians we were really producing the album on our own.

Barry designed an ambient swirl of gold, bronze, chocolate, and other colors for the album cover in keeping with the theme to symbolize the shadiness of the music. He used his graphic design skills to come up with a simple design for the four-panel artwork that would be used by the CD manufacturer to print out the jackets. The design and masters were sent to the designated company, and within ten days or so our finished product of 1000 CD's arrived.

We were beyond ecstatic at how everything turned out and the fact that we produced the album with Les's help on a shoestring budget was all the more reason to celebrate. These songs signified our drive in pursuing our dreams and we wanted to share that with anyone who wasn't afraid to pursue their own dreams. The album was for anyone who could appreciate our sound that we had developed over the course of six or seven years. The CD's were quickly disseminated to friends and family and we always had a few on hand to anyone who was curious as to what we'd been up to for the past year.

~~~

At the beginning of the year, the team I worked for did a little reshuffling. It was decided that I would work solely for two of the reps, and the ladies who were my coworkers would be under the other two. My bosses moved upstairs to different offices and I was in the bullpen not too far from them. It became clear to me that the guys I was working under were most likely not going to hit their required minimum production for the agency. As a captive agent under an insurance company, reps had contracts and needed to hit a certain number selling proprietary products or they would be terminated. The reps I worked under placed a lot of outside business (which they were allowed to do). They also flipped a lot of old Provident Mutual (Nationwide Provident acquired Provident Mutual around this time) universal life policies into newer policies using the cash value (1035 exchanges) to bring down or eliminate premium payments while keeping a guaranteed death benefit. There was no question about the suitability of the transactions as they were doing right by the clients. Those old UL policies were in danger of "blowing up" (cost of insurance outpacing planned premiums), since the actuaries back in the day didn't anticipate that mortality rates would evolve the way that they have. I hoped for the best in that my bosses would step up their game and place more proprietary business.

The Series 7 exam is a two-part, six-hour, 250-question monster. It was scheduled for the first week of March and I could not have been more prepared for it. Nerves can play a big part in the test taking experience, so there was a bit of that to deal with, but in my mind it was now or never. This wasn't a pass/fail test. There was an actual score that needed to be obtained to consider passing. I breezed through both sections and didn't encounter any questions that looked completely different from the ones I'd seen on the practice exams. You find out your final score once you submit the computer-based test for processing. In an instant I saw the word "Pass" with a score of 78. I breathed a sigh of relief, obtained my print out from one of the proctors, and immediately went to the Dive for two beers. I got pretty sloshed that weekend in celebration.

Shady Groove had been practicing with another new keyboard player. We were working on our repertoire and got word there was a cancellation at Leggett's and that they were looking for a last-minute replacement. It was explained to the manager that we played more originals than covers and that our genre of music might not be too appealing to the typical bar clientele. They didn't care so we booked it and told many of our old college friends that we'd be playing down the shore for a random one-off show. We had a decent showing as far as the crowd goes. Old college friends travelled from North Jersey and the city to come down and cheer us on like they had back in the day. The acoustics were not very conducive to our style of music and associated energy, but we did our best not to pop anyone's eardrums. We had fun playing our originals to an unsuspecting and curious audience as well as covers such as "In Memory of Elizabeth Reed," The Beastie Boys' "POW," J. J. Cale's "Let Me Do It To You," and the Last Waltz version of "Further On Up the Road." Unknown to everyone except Barry, this would be our last Shady Groove gig.

〰〰

A couple of weeks later, Barry broke the news to us that he was moving back to the West Coast and setting up shop in California. He was making a new start and had other dreams and aspirations to chase. He loved making music and playing with us, but he felt that his creative energies and heart wasn't in it anymore. We decided that it didn't make sense to go on without him, as he was a driving member of the band and the best drummer I've ever played with. I took it hard. I was a wreck. The band and music we wrote and played gave my life more purpose than sitting in an office pushing paper all day. We had amassed a ton of fun covers and a great repertoire of original songs. Even though we had only recorded eight, we had a total approaching close to 30 originals. It ripped me apart to think that those songs would simply die and that all our efforts were for nothing. John was more headstrong than I was. I asked him what we were going to do, and without skipping a beat he told me that we could now focus our efforts on enjoy! At the time, that was the last thing I wanted to hear, but after some time I was able to see that option in a better light.

Leggett's wanted us back to play every Sunday in the summer and we all felt we could play more than just once a week. We got into Pat's Pub in Belmar, JP's in Wall Township as well as The Porch in Spring Lake Heights.

It kept looking more likely that my two bosses weren't going to make their contracts. My brother recommended that while I had the time and opportunity to do so I should obtain the Series 66 and then the Series 24 NASD licenses. I ordered the Series 66 study material and began a structured study schedule just as I had for the Series 7. I studied at my desk when my bosses weren't around.

When it was slow at work and I'd done enough studying, I started to write a movie screenplay. It was set in Manasquan at our summer rental and the main plot was a Jersey Shore-wide beer pong tournament. There would be different cup formations at each venue as well as rules for defense, blowing, scramble, physical contact, and so on. The venues were long-standing Jersey shore bars. My friends were the main characters, while "aggressive" cavemen types were the antagonists. The overall theme was comedy with adult humor. As I'd studied filmmaking in college and even took an acting class, I had a fair understanding of cinematic elements as well as stage direction. I added how the camera should pan, zoom, what type of cut would be used to get to the next scene, direction on how an actor should portray a certain emotion, and so on. I only wrote at work when I had the time so there were some days where I was too busy to get anything down, but I was determined to finish what I had started.

We were back at 554 ½ Brielle Road for the summer and my GF and I were able to procure the same room that we had the year before. We moved our stuff over from the winter rental a couple of weeks before Memorial Day.

I sat for the Series 66 exam at the end of June and failed by one question. I thought I was totally prepared, nailing all the computer-based practice exams that came with the study material. There are always a handful of questions that are based off of material that can't be found anywhere in the study guide. That's just the way the exams go. I had to wait 30 days to sit for the exam again, so I immediately had it scheduled for the earliest available date and started studying and prepping again.

By July, the Leggett's Sundays were in full swing. We made t-shirts again for our friends and fans and for the most part just gave them out to whoever wanted one. We paid out of pocket this year and figured it'd be a qualified business expense for the purposes of advertising and marketing ourselves. Between 11:30PM and midnight the bar would get so packed we'd have floor guys and bouncers keeping an eye on us while we were playing in the event that someone got too belligerent and felt like they could take over singing duties. Fights broke out from time to time and for the most part, we didn't skip a beat. Unless someone fell into our gear, we kept playing through whatever distraction there was, whether it was someone falling down, a spilled drink, broken bottle, or a stink bomb going off in the bathroom. The area in front of us got very crowded with people dancing, to the point that I had to duct tape my mic stand in place on the ground because people would knock into it and send it flying. There were times I had to duck from a falling stand in order to avoid having my teeth knocked out. It got pretty hairy.

The date for my rescheduled exam came around and I was just as prepared, as I had been the last time. I whizzed through the test and felt that the random sampling of questions were a little easier. I was fully confident when I hit submit to obtain my score, and sure enough I passed with a 78. I continued my tradition by hitting the Dive for two beers and immediately ordered the Series 24 study material, began a structured schedule, and immersed myself in the wonderful world of what a general securities principal does.

Mid-August brought the Phish debacle known as Coventry. A unilateral decision was made by Trey to discontinue the band that had been part of so many peoples' lives for so long. The four friends from Vermont changed the paradigm on what a live music act could encompass. The result was a farewell performance up at Newport State Airport in Coventry, Vermont. The Thursday before Coventry, my brother, GF, and I headed down to Camden to catch the last show before Coventry at the Tweeter Center. Our plan was to bolt out of the show at the last note, head to my folks' place, and pick up our already packed bags so we could make a midnight run up to Vermont and get a head start on the impending traffic up to the venue. We had mail order tickets for Coventry and had reserved a hotel in Rutland, a quiet town in South Vermont. We would make it to the hotel, crash, and have only about an hour's drive to the campground. We knew a handful of friends who were heading up after Camden and I called Josh to get a status on what the traffic situation was like while on the George Washington Bridge. He was already up in Vermont on one of the major highways and traffic was at a dead stop. I told him I'd call him back in a little bit to see if it got any better. I followed up close to 2:30AM near the southern border of Vermont and he told me they were about 35 miles outside the campground and had moved maybe one mile since the last time I called. He said to turn around, that it's not worth the hassle, and that there was an imminent rainstorm headed towards the area that wasn't going to make things any easier. I told him I'd call him in the morning from our hotel and if things didn't get any better we'd have to make a decision to either push forward or head home.

We checked in late to our hotel, had a nightcap, and crossed our fingers when we went to bed. In the morning, I called Josh for an update and he told me that they had moved maybe two and a half miles since the last time we spoke. Two and a half miles in about six and a half hours:

zoinks! Given the information and the heavy rain that began to fall, we made the decision to stay at the hotel for another night and head home the next morning.

Anyone who was at Coventry would agree that it was a pretty miserable experience. People left their vehicles on the highway and trekked some 15 or 20 miles to the venue, only to find a muddy campground and torrential rains pounding the area. Cars got stuck and people tried to take back country roads around the traffic and ended up leaving their cars and hiking from different directions into the show. The concerts were lackluster and low energy and everyone agreed that Coventry was not the way Phish should've ended their career.

Our singer Todd got married in August of 2004. That left the band with no singer for two Sundays at Leggett's as they went off on their honeymoon. We weren't about to have another band sub for us as we were building a following and had a work ethic to uphold. We managed to get local musician Mike Dalton to come out one Sunday. He had the weekly Thursday night gig at Leggett's and it got just as insane in there on that night. We emailed some songs back and forth during the week and came up with a set list consisting of most of our covers and a handful of songs that he performed. Everything went well. I remember looking over at Mike during one of the songs and he shot me this look as if to say "What the fuck?!" referring to the mayhem that was a Sunday night in August at Leggett's.

Lou lived out in Scottsdale, Arizona for a year or so, living with one of his best friends who moved out there around 1995. They had an original band and played part of the Southwest college circuit back in the day. His best friend Brendan Brophy was still out there living with his girlfriend and writing, recording, and performing original music. Lou talked him into flying back for the Sunday night gig that we didn't have a singer for. We had a few weeks to prepare and sent him our song list. His family was still up in Cranford so it gave him a good excuse to squeeze the gig in while visiting them. Notwithstanding a few minor musical snafus, he did a stellar job and even rocked a few Elvis moves during "Suspicious Minds."

Near the end of the summer I finished the screenplay that I had been writing for several months at work. It came to about 138 pages with lines, stage directions, scene descriptions, camera shots, and other cinematographic elements. I took what I had learned from my college classes, used my imagination, and created something from nothing. I had no idea what my next step was, so I did a little research regarding copyrighting and professionally editing the work as well as solicited and unsolicited submissions to a production company. I ended up just sitting on it and shelving it for another time.

Texas Hold'em poker started to become popular (again) with the nationally televised World Series of Poker tournament as well as the World Poker Tour events. A handful of guys who graduated high school two years ahead of me rented a house on the north side of town and began having weekly poker nights. The buy-in was always $40 with the rare instance of a $100 buy-in on special occasions. We played tournament-style Texas Hold'em where the buy-in got the player $1000 worth of chips and the blinds started relatively low at $5/$10. Third place usually won their money back, second place would see roughly 30% of the pot, and first place took anywhere between 50% and 60% depending on the number of players. We typically had between nine and 12 players a week. The nights where there were more than 11 or 12 we'd have two tables going, and on the rare instance when it got really packed, three tables. The regulars always showed up and everyone started to pick up on everyone else's modus operandi when it came to bluffing, slow playing, playing tight, and so on. I'd seen every conceivable bad beat and bluff one could think of. I've seen players go all-in on the first hand and double up or bust. We tried to start around 8PM, but in the early days of the games there were times we didn't get started until after 10PM. The latest I ever made it out was around 2:40AM after what felt like an hour-long heads-up contest. I was always a sneaky player and knew "when to fold 'em, and when to hold 'em." Over the years that the games ran, a majority of the regulars would have to agree that I cashed more times than many others who showed up to play. For someone on a miniscule salary and a fixed income, finishing in the cash could get you healthy.

Although I received no formal confirmation from my bosses, I determined that they were not going to be hitting their required minimum production numbers for the agency. The clues consisted of running envelopes for all my bosses' clients for a mass mailing that had an authorization for a signature transferring the clients' securities accounts to a new broker-dealer. This meant that I had four months until the end of the year before I would be out of a job, but more importantly, time to study for the Series 24. In the financial services industry, I understood the value of a general securities principal's license. All supervisory and managing associates were required to have one. It carried with it a lot of responsibility but also a lot of clout and would make me very marketable in the field. I may not have any supervisory experience but any hiring manager would understand the career path I was on. I ramped up my study schedule and made that my only priority for the time being.

Before I knew it, exam crunch time was upon me, and I was in full-on study/practice test mode. By then I was doing practice tests during Thanksgiving with the family and relatives. I was eating and breathing the material. The night before by scheduled exam, I got down on my knees and prayed for strength and fair questions in the exam, as I knew how tricky they could be. When it came time to submit for grading, I clasped my hands and said a little prayer before clicking the final button. In a flash I saw "Pass" and thanked God for the strength and guidance before looking at the actual score of 82. My tradition continued and I went to the Dive for two beers, but not before calling my GF, brother, and parents with the good news.

〜〜〜

My position with Bellmare Financial Group was terminated, as my bosses didn't make their contracts. They both went their separate ways and there was no room for me in either of their budgets. I was given two weeks' severance. After that was exhausted I cashed out what small retirement savings I had accumulated (with a hefty tax penalty) and applied for unemployment. I paid into the system so I was eligible for benefits.

I was required to go down to the unemployment office in Elizabeth and be processed through the system before I was able to begin collecting any benefits.

Todd informed us that he had applied to law school in Michigan and had been accepted. He would be ending his involvement with enjoy! and moving out there with his wife to become a full-time student. The rest of us were both excited for him and upset. We worked well together, had our own sound, and most of all had a lot of fun playing together. Lou, John, and I weren't ready to hang up our instruments. By this time, we had over 60 songs in our repertoire. The majority of them weren't being performed by any other band at the Jersey Shore. Lou mentioned that it might be a long shot but that he was going to ask Brendan if he was interested in moving back from Arizona to become a full-time band member. Lou needed time to come up with the right approach for selling points and knew it wasn't going to be a quick decision. Brendan's girlfriend was from Arizona and had family there. John and I waited with fingers crossed and bated breath while Lou worked his magic and had multiple lengthy conversations with Brendan.

Lou's approach eventually worked and Brendan was able to convince his girlfriend to make the move back East. She had gone to school for chemistry and was interested in the pharmaceutical industry and New Jersey was a hot spot for companies in that sector. They began making arrangements for the move. Brendan needed assurance that there would be enough work in New Jersey for him to support himself as well as opportunities for writing, recording, and performing original material. We were all for it. In the meantime, my job, in addition to finding work in the financial services field, was to mine some bars between Manasquan and Belmar to drum up more work.

We were late to the party in finding a summer rental. All of our regular Brielle Road crew had scattered. Some weren't coming back while others had bought houses so we didn't have the numbers to come up with the required lease. Those of us who were left had to find another option. I asked one of the head bartenders at Leggett's, who was also a property manager for the bar owner who owned rental real estate, if he knew of anything available for the summer. He mentioned there was an apartment open in Seabreeze, the complex diagonally across from the Osprey Night Club on First Avenue and Main Street. He showed me the place and I liked what I saw. It had two bedrooms, two full bathrooms, central air, a clean kitchen area, as well as a decent living room. A balcony overlooking First and Main was attached to the living area and the complex was located behind Gee Gee's Pizza, right on the Manasquan boardwalk (blacktop). I was sold. The location was great, it had central air, and the place wasn't a dump. That was all I needed. The property manager informed me that the apartment wasn't available just for the summer but that it was a year-round rental. I had to come up with some selling points for the others I'd be renting with if we were going to pull this place off. I told the property manager there would most likely be a few other people staying there over the summer, much like full and half shares over at Brielle Road. He didn't have a problem with it as long as the rent was in the mailbox on the first of the month, so I told him that I'd get back to him in a few days with an update.

After doing some calculations, I came up with a share price that was affordable for six people. It was comparable to a full summer share over on Brielle Road. It would be my GF and I in the smaller bedroom, our friends who were a couple in the bigger bedroom, and my brother and a fellow from Cranford who graduated two years ahead of me jockeying for the sofas. Everyone was on board. The manager couldn't hold the place until May so we had to sign the lease for March 1st and drum up cash from everyone. As my name was on the lease and I was responsible for the rent ($1,800 a month), I had to come up with a plan for after Labor Day when the other couple and sofa riders would be moving out. The plan was this: the other couple would pay their share through the end of the year at which time we'd find another renter for their room. My brother would pay to crash there and the lone Cranford sofa rider would be out. It seemed like a solid plan where no one was going to get fucked so we rolled with it.

I got the keys, set up the utilities, and my GF and I started furnishing the place with basic necessities. We bought some cheap dressers from

IKEA, had fun putting them together, and slept on an air mattress the first night we stayed there. Slowly but surely we moved more stuff in and it began to look like a real apartment.

My only source of income at the time was unemployment so I was going to have to come up with something legitimate soon if I was going to avoid running into issues with the rent. I was searching online job postings, going to financial service company websites, and scrolling through their career pages every day. One late afternoon I got an email from someone who searched posted resumes on Monster and came across mine. It was for a position similar to what I had been doing at the Cranford agency based out of Livingston, which wasn't too far of a commute from Cranford. I scheduled an interview and went up there to see what the gig was all about.

An agent of the Guardian Life Insurance Company owned the firm. He'd been with them for close to 30 years and was a large producer, but didn't focus on life insurance. He earned a majority of his income selling and servicing group health insurance plans. My job was to assist in the renewal process as well as service related issues and … answering the phone. I never wanted to work in a position as a glorified receptionist (not that there is anything wrong with that), but I knew in my heart that I had more to offer with the proper training. The position came with a salary that was higher than my previous job and health benefits after a 90-day waiting period. I had one stipulation. Between Memorial Day and Labor Day I wanted Mondays and Fridays off. I explained my new venture as a performing musician and the late hours that came along with it. It was a gamble on my part but the boss seemed to take a liking to me and the fact that I was licensed for life insurance and had three NASD registrations, so he agreed to my request. I also requested that my NASD registrations be affiliated with his broker-dealer. In the securities industry, if a recognized securities firm does not pick up your registrations within two years you lose them and are required to re-test. There was no way I was going to let that happen given the time and effort I put in over the previous year and a half. He said he'd look into it and get it squared away with his broker-dealer. We had an agreement and I was to start the following week.

Brendan and his girlfriend drove back from Arizona and found a small place to rent a couple of doors down from Leggett's, which was within sight of our balcony. After they settled in, the four of us started rehearsing our repertoire, new songs we had selected, as well as working on original material that Brendan had recently written. His music theory wasn't where John and mine were, but he had an exceptional ear and could pick up anything I showed him relatively quickly. Our new band was rapidly getting it together to where we'd be firing on all cylinders come Memorial Day weekend.

The rooms we played in that summer in addition to Leggett's on Sunday nights were the Boathouse, 507 Main St., Connolly Station, and the Porch. Brendan and I also picked up Friday happy hours at O'Neill's located on Main Street in Manasquan. It was an acoustic gig and I played the Hohner acoustic our uncle had given us back in the day for a couple gigs with a removable pick-up before buying a mid-range priced Martin acoustic-electric.

The weather was amazing that summer. Being within a stone's throw from the ocean, we'd make it up to the beach to lie out whenever possible. Having Mondays and Fridays off added to the ease of beach living.

After Labor Day, my work schedule returned to five days a week and I stayed at my folks' place in Cranford. My GF began her senior year at college and was already discussing and planning her next step to further her education in working towards her master's degree closer to home. She didn't need me to tell her that the extra time and money would pay off handsomely in the future. Psychology was a tough field that required many hours of study as well as in the field. My GF was smarter than I ever was and had a more focused approach to her schoolwork. I was her biggest supporter in her scholastic pursuit of bettering herself.

Enjoy! continued learning new cover material in the fall as well as playing gigs on the weekends down the shore. We also kept working on more original material that Brendan had written. By this time, the couple that was renting the big room had moved out and my friend Quinn had moved in. My Cranford pal who was couch-surfing stopped coming down, but my brother still chipped in monthly so he had a place to crash since my GF and I also stayed there on weekends. My brother also started seeing the wait staff manager at Leggett's who was also a teacher in a local community's school system.

In March of 2006 I was let go of the administrative position I had at the insurance agency up in Livingston. My boss explained that they really needed someone working five days a week during the summer. I told him I would suck it up and do the full 40-hour work week, but he also added that my salary was an issue. He never got around to having my NASD registrations associated with his broker-dealer even though I kept reminding him so that may have been another factor. I had no hard feelings and kept my head up on my last day of work. I immediately went home and applied for unemployment benefits and would continue my health insurance coverage through COBRA at a whopping $350 a month. I reactivated my resume on Monster and Career Builder and started searching the career postings for financial services firms and insurance companies.

I was enjoying my free time while being unemployed. I stayed down at the beachfront apartment during the week and often went out for beers since Leggett's was a skip across the street. John left his job up in north Jersey because his boss was dragging his feet about letting him mine his book of business and service his lower net worth clients. He was hired by AXA Advisors and worked out of their Manasquan office.

In my free time I also took trips out to Trenton and spent hours in the office of vital records researching my father's side of the family's genealogy. I wanted to know more, and if I had to dig into hundreds of years of our ancestry, I would. Trenton was the first logical step. I came across my grandfather's birth certificate as well as that of his two brothers. There was different information listed on each microfiche regarding my great-grandfather's name and country of origin. My father loved the fact that I took the initiative. I don't think he knew his Uncle Frank's legal name was Franz Ferdinand!

My friend Quinn didn't last long in the beachfront apartment. Turns out his routine didn't sit too well with my GF. Of course, this wasn't the sole reason. Her brother was looking for a place to live and she felt more comfortable with him than a former co-worker. She made me break the news to him and it was really difficult for me. I explained the situation with my GF's brother and that she wasn't taking no for an answer. I was stuck between the proverbial rock and hard place. By the end of my talk with him, tears welled up in my eyes. He knew it was a tough position to be in and took the eviction as gracefully as he possibly could.

Right before the summer season got under way, one of my old bosses from Bellmare Financial Group contacted me and told me that a couple who were in the fee-based advisory business and renting in the same office building as him asked if he knew of any registered principals who may be looking for a consulting job. He immediately thought of me. I called, set up a meet and greet, and brought my resume to their office on Route 22 in Springfield. After pleasantries were exchanged they told me that they primarily operated a fee-based investment advisory business and recently transferred their book of business to a small broker-dealer based out of Georgia. There was one major stipulation that was ordered by the NJ state securities administration: they were required to have a NASD registered principal (Series 24) on site. The husband had some reportable events (fines, judgments, complaints, etc.) on his U-4 (every registered associated in the securities industry has a profile that lists specific information related to their work history as well as complaints, financial liens, bankruptcies, settlements, legal judgments, etc.) and the State Securities Administration (SSA) would not let him operate as a registered representative in his current capacity without an on-site principal. I explained my work schedule in the summertime and that I would need Mondays and Fridays off to which they had no objection. We discussed a number that was reasonable for both parties and the total was a little more than what I paid for my monthly health insurance and beachfront rental. I would be paid twice a month and would be "on call" if a member of a regulatory authority (SSA, NASD) or compliance associate from the home office visited. It was set and I started going into the office the following week.

I filled out my U-4 for the broker-dealer to process and my NASD registrations were safe and associated with the firm. A compliance manager from the home office visited for a couple of days to get the ball rolling on what I would be expected to do and to give me some pointers. He advised me to, if I had the time and drive, obtain more NASD registrations as they could only help me further on down the road. I took that under advisement.

My bosses were wonderful and had a young son who they were raising together. They were in their mid to late 40s, but better late than never. They were very knowledgeable about the business, professional and responsive to their clients, and a hoot to talk to. The wife went to the University of Michigan and told that she saw The Police in some dive bar where there were like 15 people in the audience!

My GF graduated from college and took a summer job locally. She would start her master's program in the fall. My brother took a trip to the Bahamas and ended up proposing to his girlfriend on the plane. The cabin all cheered after she said yes. It was quite a story!

At the start of the summer, I found myself with three sources of income for what seemed like not much work or stress. I had the bi-weekly check from the investment advisors, an adjusted bi-weekly unemployment benefit check, and cash from gigging. I was styling.

Enjoy! kicked off the summer playing our first wedding. It was for a local Manasquan couple that dug good music. It was held at the Columns and introduced us to a lot of the locals our age that also enjoyed good music, beach culture, and partying until they fell down. Our type of people indeed.

My GF's step-dad had a good friend who was a tattoo artist and her family decided to have a tattoo party in her parents' kitchen. I had some time to figure out what I wanted so I did some searching online. As I'd recently uncovered the fact that my great-grandfather was of German descent, I stumbled across the coat of arms for Germany, the Reichsadler or "Imperial Eagle." It had a rich history dating back to the Holy Roman Empire and just screamed "ink me on your body!" I was smitten with it and couldn't imagine having anything else tattooed at the time. I settled on my left shoulder blade. It's mostly black with some red for the eagle's talons and beak. I haven't gotten a tattoo since I was 16, but the feeling of the needle buzzing in the skin is unforgettable.

One Sunday at Leggett's we noticed a couple checking us out in the first set and really paying attention to what we were doing. They were digging it and I could tell they were into the same genres of music that we were into. At set break, they came over and we got to talking. They were Sean and Jill and had recently moved back from Burlington, Vermont. We hit it off instantly. They both worked at Higher Ground, which is a popular live music venue near Burlington. They were looking for a local band to play their wedding next year and they loved what they heard. They asked if we could play any Phish and we broke out "First Tube" in the following set. We exchanged information and knew we'd be seeing them again soon.

Going with the home office compliance manager's advice, I purchased study material for the NASD Series 53. This was the Municipal Securities Principal license and dealt with, amongst other things, 529 Plan products and municipal bond underwriting. My duties, when I came into the office, were scarce. Other than setting up correspondence files and reviewing what they were sending to clients, for the most part, I shot the shit with the couple I was consulting for. There were days where I'd come in for an hour and a half and days where I'd be there for four or five hours. It was a very easy-going gig. I couldn't just sit at a desk for a long period of time and surf the Internet. I knew I had to do more with my free time so I invested in my future and buckled down with the new study material.

The summer was in full swing and once again Sundays started to blow up. We had our nights down to a science, escaping through the kitchen and hightailing it to my apartment on breaks. By now we must've been pushing between 90 and 100 songs in our repertoire. I started keeping track of what songs we played at what venues so we didn't bore the staff with the same show. A lot of bands played Jersey Shore bar standards such as Springsteen's "Rosalita," The Violent Femme's "Blister in the Sun," Tom Petty's "American Girl," and Rick Springfield's "Jessie's Girl." We didn't view ourselves as a typical Jersey Shore bar band and didn't believe we needed to the play songs that every other band were playing. We all listened to a wide variety of music and wanted to share that with our audiences. More and more people started approaching us during our set breaks and informing us that they'd never heard this or that song played in a bar before. The musical universe is vast and diverse. There is so much amazing music out there that the general music listener is not familiar with. I saw us tasked with the responsibility of opening up the doors for them to expand their musical horizons.

Following the theme of musical horizon expansion, around this time I came across a cache of music that found its way onto my iPod. Complete works by musicians such as Django Reinhardt, Joe Pass, Barney Kessell, Kenny Burrell, Grant Green, George Benson, Tal Farlow, Albert Collins, Albert King, Art Blakey and the Jazz Messengers, Art Tatum, Bill Evans, B. B. King, Charlie Byrd, Charlie Parker, Curtis Mayfield, Frank Zappa, Freddie King, Herbie Hancock, John Coltrane, John Scofield, Miles Davis, Pat Martino, Stevie Wonder, Thelonius Monk, and Wes Montgomery all swirled on my shuffle option. I had heard many of the artists on the local jazz station WBGO 88.3 but had no way of getting my hands on their music other than listening and hoping something sweet would come on. This, of course, was before the time of Internet radio and subscription based music streaming services Pandora and Spotify. I soaked up the sounds like a sponge and began to hear music a little differently. The colorful chord options jazz musicians use and the flurry of notes over their changes can have a profound effect on the way your brain perceives music and trains your ear after some time.

~~~

One weekend we played a gig at 507 Main Street and there was a beautiful young girl hanging around making eyes at me all night. She hung around after we were done and asked if she could have a t-shirt.

We didn't have any left inside so I had her follow me to the parking lot through the kitchen. Once we got to my truck I pulled out a size small and she asked what I wanted for it. I told her a kiss would do and we started hooking up. When I got into bed, my GF woke up and said she had a dream that I cheated on her. My heart sank and I lied through my teeth. I was completely mystified by her statement. No one saw us in the parking lot earlier that evening. There were obviously some cosmic forces at play.

Another successful summer came to a close. By then, Brendan and his girlfriend moved to an apartment complex up in Tinton Falls. We were back into our schedule of rehearsing new cover material as well as working on original songs that Brendan was constantly writing. I was also going up to his apartment during the week and working on songs for our acoustic duo gigs. We continued our tradition that started with Todd of dressing up on Halloween gigs. One year, John and I dressed up as crazed-looking clowns, Todd was in drag, and Lou was a caveman. The first Halloween with Brendan we all dressed up as the Cobra Kai skeleton crew from "The Karate Kid," complete with full-face paint, white hoods, and skeleton costumes. This gig was held at Leggett's and was a blast for all in attendance. We even learned the song from the soundtrack "You're the Best Around" to add to the authenticity of our show.

New neighbors moved in across the hall from us at Seabreeze. One was a local fellow who had grown up in the area and lived down the shore his entire life, and the other was a sound engineer. Brendan was excited about the latter and we soon found ourselves hanging out really late into the evening after gigs, having nightcaps and puffing on some cannabis. We'd listen to tunes and even started recording some demo tracks when the engineer's roommate wasn't around.

My Series 53 window was open and I had been studying full on for months, mostly during the week at the office. I sat for the exam in early December and the questions seemed trickier than they had in previous exams. When I got to the end to press submit for my final score, I wasn't too sure if I was going to pass. I took a deep breath, clicked the button, and in a flash the word PASS shot across the screen with a score of 78. I was elated. I didn't hit the Dive this time. I headed right back down the shore after calling my parents, brother, and girlfriend with the good news and decided to celebrate in Manasquan with a few beers.

A similar pattern began to take hold in 2007. This included rehearsals for new material to cover as well as original songs and booking gigs throughout the year. Dates were more sporadic in the offseason that allowed me to spend some weekend nights with my GF. There were also plenty of times she was in bed early and I'd spend my late nights across the hall with our new sound engineer friend. Some nights my priority was getting hammered because I could simply stumble across the hall to my place and make it to bed in a few short steps.

Sean and Jill eventually hired us to play at their wedding scheduled for Memorial Day weekend. He'd been checking us out throughout the summer and into the fall. We eventually started hanging out as he was good people and we shared similar interests. He wanted to meet with the band and offer a proposition. The proposition was to take on management and soundman duties for enjoy! After hearing his pitch and talking things through with everyone, we gave him the opportunity. Within two or three weeks he had purchased $20,000 (borrowed from his stepdad) worth of PA equipment, including a 16-channel Mackie board with firewire capabilities (interface to record and mix live music down to a compatible laptop), JBL towers, subs, monitors, rack-mounted effects and power amps, a slew of cables, a gear chest, and a road case for the mixing board. We were shocked. Sean started to dig in and learn how to use the equipment. It became a baptism by fire and within a couple of weeks he was pretty comfortable running sound at our gigs.

My brother, who had been studying for the Certified Financial Planner designation, passed the exam. It is held three times a year and there are requirements that need to be met in order to sit for the exam. At the time, it was a college degree from a four-year school, three years of industry experience, proof that you were involved in one of the six steps of the financial planning process, an education requirement from an accredited institution such as The American College or Kaplan, and so forth. The education requirement was self-study in the six areas of the financial planning process and an exam was taken online. All exams had to be passed prior to sitting for the final exam. My brother took a 40-hour crash course (ten-hour days over four straight days) to prepare for the exam by a CFP who specialized in getting people through the exam with a passing grade. It was a load off his shoulders and he was able to focus more of his energy on his pending nuptials.

In late winter I began planning for my brother's bachelor party. He was one of the first of our entire Cranford crew to get married, so most of our friends' schedules were pretty flexible. I managed to get about 17 of us rounded up and committed to a Saturday night in April. I rented a luxury party bus to take us down to Atlantic City. We barreled down the parkway to our first destination, a strip club that a Cranford native's family owned, and we skipped the line and cover while wheeling in coolers of beer. I never had enough money for lap dances so I was just drinking and taking it all in. My beer muscles got flexed given the crew I was rolling with and I pushed a guy from behind who kept stepping backwards onto my bare toes as I was wearing flip-flops. It was a warm evening. A bouncer spotted this and I was out the door in a heartbeat. A bunch of us wound up drinking on the bus while others stayed in the strip club or ventured into the casinos to try their luck.

My brother's wedding was the following month and I was obviously the best man. Since I had time to prepare and using what I had learnt from my public speaking class in college, I wrote a speech using flash cards and began going through it two weeks before the wedding. The ceremony and reception were held at Bonnet Island Estate in Manahawkin. When it came time for the speeches, I tucked my flashcards into my suit pocket because I had them memorized by then. My speech was about four and a half minutes long and garnered a lot of laughs from the guests. My brother and his wife sat nervously (his wife more than him) awaiting the end, since they thought I was going to add some remarks that would've been in poor taste. They had an 11-piece band and enjoy! sat in for a few songs. Everyone had a blast and after the reception was over. We ended up closing the night out upstairs, drinking with our folks, the brides' folks, groomsmen, some of the bridesmaids, and a handful of our closest friends.

My GF and I had settled into a comfortable routine that summer. It wasn't like the first two years when we spent every weekend together. The honeymoon period was over and we both enjoyed what free time we could find to hang out and do couple things together. We went out for lunch and dinner whenever we could, but our free time was marred given the bands' ramped up gig schedule and the pursuit of her master's degree and work schedule. Our love life wasn't as incendiary as it had been or should have remained for two people who were madly in love with each other and told each other so whenever possible. A part of that was due to developing a condition that complicated physical intimacy. We made do with other options and I only ever remained patient, positive, and supportive.

Career-wise, I decided to start studying for another NASD license. The NASD became FINRA in 2007. The next principal's license that made sense to purse was the Series 4, Registered Options Principal. An option is a contract that gives the buyer the right, but not the obligation, to buy or sell an underlying asset at a specific price on or before a specific date. This exam was more math-based than the Series 53 but it was not an exam to be taken lightly. I purchased the study material from the same company I used for the Series 53 and started with my studies at the office as I had for the previous exam. I used the "if it ain't broke don't fix it" approach. My old boss who introduced me to the husband and wife investment advisors rented an office in the same building, and he'd pop in from time to time to shoot the shit. He started duffing off lower-end clients on me who were looking to purchase life insurance, as he didn't have the time to assist them. I didn't mind one bit. I wasn't exactly working too hard as a consultant and knew the life insurance business like the back of my hand. I placed a few policies (including two for my brother and his wife) and enjoyed some commissions from it. The commissions were like found money.

The summer flew by and the band started to hit its groove. Our growing repertoire made it easy for us to stay engaged and invested as we were constantly mixing up our shows. We never got bored and each song that had room for jamming became a platform to jump off of and create music out of the ether. Sundays at Leggett's were just as packed as always. I always managed to hit a late night after a Friday or Saturday gig as my GF was fast asleep by the time I got home and she trusted me. Hal, who moved over to Ocean Avenue, always had people over late at night or he'd just have a good ol' summer time party with Corn Hole, darts, and barbecue where everyone was welcome. The late nights would mostly consist of MJ (Michael Jackson) dance parties with the lights down low, hat parties (guests wearing different hats that he had collected and had in his closet, including a mullet wig, Viking helmet, or lampshade), or just a few guys drinking beer and either listening to live music or watching a DVD of a live show (mostly Phish) from his vast collection.

~~~

The summer came to a close and with that, all the Benny's cleared out of the surrounding shore towns' rental properties. My brother's wife and her sister owned a house on 3rd Avenue in Manasquan, which is two blocks from the beachfront. It too was vacated and my GF suggested moving out of our rental and into their house. We checked it out and the place was in pretty good shape. As you entered the front door, there was a decent size living area and stairs to the left leading up to a second floor loft with a full bathroom. Downstairs, beyond the living area, was a small bedroom to the left, kitchen to the right, and beyond the kitchen, a bigger bedroom on the left. Across the hall from the bigger bedroom was a full bathroom. Further down the hall was the back door that led out to the driveway, back yard, and garage. The rent was another $50 a month and we were all pretty taken by the house so I contacted the property manager and asked about getting out of our lease with 30 days' notice. As we'd become close given his employment at Leggett's, there was no issue and we began to make preparations for our move.

I rewarded myself for another successful and busy summer by buying another guitar. I found a 1974 Gibson ES-335 with a walnut finish on eBay that was in really good shape and I had to have it.

I had some free time on my hands and decided to take a guitar lesson. I'd felt I had hit a bit of a wall and knew someone else's perspective may be all I needed to get over the hump I was lingering on. I searched a bit online and found the contact information for the touring guitar player of Steely Dan, Jon Herrington. I scheduled a lesson at his mini studio apartment about two blocks from Madison Square Garden. He asked what I wanted to work on. I explained my current dilemma and was looking for anything new to work on. He immediately started going through inversions of certain jazz chords (major 7th, minor 7th, half diminished, 9th's) up the neck of the guitar. I thought that was awesome, as I'd never worked through those before.

Not too long afterwards I emailed the head of William Paterson's jazz department inquiring if there were any guitar professors that gave private lessons. The man gave me contact information of a fellow by the name of Paul Meyer. I sent him a message and we arranged a time for me to come up to his apartment in Jersey City. He asked what I wanted to work on and I explained to increase my knowledge of jazz guitar, comping, and soloing. He broke out sheet music for Wes Montgomery's "Sun Down" which I was familiar with, as well as handwritten changes and the modes that went along for the standard "Stella By Starlight." I'd seen music broken down this way in *The Jazz Theory Book* that I bought a few years ago. Things started to make sense and fall into place for me as far as modal jazz goes. Overall, I got what I needed from both guitar lessons, increased my theoretical knowledge of the fret board, and was grateful for my instructors' time.

The exam for my Series 4 was scheduled for the end of November. Exam day came and a lot of the questions were easy, since options calculations are fairly simple once you understand the logic behind them. I did the same thing I had done for the previous exams when it was time to submit for grading. I took a few deep breaths, said a little prayer, crossed my fingers, and clicked the button. PASS with a score of a 77. My structured study schedule paid off once again and with that license, I knew I was done studying for another FINRA exam for a while, if not forever.

That December my GF decided to get a rescue dog. I think she found one on a pet adoption site and the next thing I knew we were at her parents' house with this little black wolf looking thing prancing and sniffing around. The breed was a Schipperke and they originated in Belgium back in the 16th century. The breed name translates to little boatman and they were bred to hunt vermin on barges and fishing vessels. My GF named him Pedro. He was anywhere between six and eight years old and we soon learned that, through his body language and temperament, that he must've been abused. He was very skittish and it took a while for him to warm up to guests. He barked and ran towards the door at any approaching sound, but once he was relaxed and hanging out on the couch, all he wanted was have his belly rubbed and to be petted and pampered. A dog's life.

One day in early February I was home from work when my boss called me up and told me that I might want to sit down. I obliged and he informed me that my old boss from Bellmare Financial Group passed away suddenly. I was completely shocked. My heart sunk and I immediately got lightheaded and tears welled up in my eyes. After our brief conversation I burst into tears and fell to the ground. Apparently, my old boss was driving out on Route 78, pulled his car over, and walked into traffic. He had a wife and two young boys at home and was a very intelligent and personable man. I didn't want to believe that he took his own life. I said to myself that it must've been a terrible accident where he may have lost his bearings for an instant while talking on the phone, but that line of logic didn't hold up for too long after having some time to process and talk with my bosses at work. A week or two later his wife visited the office and inquired if he was acting or saying anything unusual, to which we replied no. He seemed normal and happy-go-lucky.

My GF wanted to go on vacation before the summer season picked up and decided on Cabo San Lucas. I wrote a song about the place and she figured if there were any destination that we should travel to together it would be there. I had recently consolidated all of my credit card debt through a credit counseling company. Over the years, I amassed close to $12,000 in credit card debt and my minimum payments became astronomical. On top of my car and student loan payments it became too much of a burden to continue this way. The counseling company paid off my cards and sent me a coupon book with a lower monthly interest rate. The timing of my GF's planned vacation to Cabo could not have come at a worse time. I explained my situation and told her a trip like that just was not on the cards for me. I really had to work on budgeting my income and as much as I wanted to go, it was not going to happen. She understood and managed to convince her sister and brother to go and they had a blast.

Summer came back around and with that more gigs at the usual spots. We picked up a new room at the Parker House and had a handful of high-energy, super packed gigs there. Our Sundays were in full swing and with that came a change of scenery for the band. The bar hired a local carpenter to build a moveable stage that covered the handicap ramp near the 1st Avenue entrance of the building. It was designed like a jigsaw puzzle. There were nine pieces that the floor guys dragged from outside and they all locked together perfectly over the ramp. We were pumped. This cut down on the potential risk to our gear from spilled drinks. It also reduced the possibility of someone falling on us, an amp, or knocking over a speaker. We could hear ourselves so much better and our levels were easier to manage. The bar also hung specialized curtains that were designed for soundproofing. They had been getting noise complaints from a crotchety tenant across the street on the beachfront and decided to be proactive about the situation.

My GF and I bought new bikes from a local shop in town. I picked up a sweet royal blue 21-speed hybrid that really trucked. Given my proximity to outdoor drinking establishments such as the Union Landing and Riverhouse, I started heading up there during the week for some drinks and Yankees baseball games after my GF went to bed. I'd roll solo and meet up with some of the locals or my friend Quinn would bike over and we'd head up together.

My GF's brother and I cleared out and cleaned the garage. It was the perfect pre- and post-game summer spot and we'd throw the occasional party. It had a beer pong table, fridge, colored lights, and personal effects such as posters and beer mirrors. We'd crank up the tunes and all of our friends would converge to throw down. On nights after gigs where there was no one hanging out in the garage, I'd bike to Hal's house on Ocean Avenue for other late-night activities. There were times when I'd leave his house, bike up to the boardwalk which was two blocks away, crank some Bob Marley from my phone, and take a long lap up Brielle Road before making the right turn onto 3rd Avenue and heading home. By then, the sky would be brightening with the coming sunrise. We also began to book more private parties and weddings, which happened mostly because of word of mouth, from people visiting our website, or music lovers who had seen us at the bars.

One of my favorite bands, The Police, reunited for a world tour and I had to catch a couple of shows. Tickets sold out pretty quickly but that didn't stop me from paying a premium on Stub Hub. I had all of their albums and credit Andy Summer's style and sound as a major influence on my guitar playing and musicianship. They sounded amazing and it was so refreshing to hear their songs live, full of renewed energy, and being performed by the artists who wrote them.

∼∾∼

That fall, Brendan's girlfriend of over seven years left him. I'm not too firm on the particulars but I believe she was looking for the next step in their relationship and wanted to get married and start a family. Brendan was still getting situated in New Jersey, learning how to help in managing affairs with the band, and budgeting his time and money. His girlfriend had a solid job with a pharmaceutical company and was making decent money; however, Brendan just was not ready for the future to come his way so soon. She packed up, moved back to Arizona, and he got a rental with one of his good childhood friends who rented with us on Brielle Road and bartended locally.

I still had a lot of free time on my hands given my consulting schedule so I decided to bite the bullet and pursue one last exam, the Certified

Financial Planner designation. I figured that I had the time to study for it just as I had for the FINRA registration exams. I might as well invest in my future, since only good could come from the hard work. John gave me all his study material and I started slowly with a few pages a day. I had no schedule for when I was planning to sit for the exam, so I kept the same study schedule that I had for the past two years and started filling my brain with new information about the financial services industry. There wasn't even an element of sibling rivalry. I always believed that one should never stop learning. I didn't have the resources or the drive to pursue an advanced degree in graduate school. This made the most sense given my future career path.

I had been making good on getting my debt down and hadn't been on vacation in a while. My GF and I decided to get our passports and we booked a trip to Punta Cana in the Dominican Republic in January of 2009. There were always decent travel deals listed online and we found one for an all-inclusive resort right on the beach. Just as with our trip to St. Thomas a few years earlier, we didn't have much money for any specific extracurricular activities and were advised not to leave the resort for safety reasons. This was verified during our van ride from the airport to the resort. There were scores of shoeless people in ragged clothes on the sides of the road waiting for work and armed military men making sure no one got out of line or rushed passing vans full of tourists and money.

Once we checked in and got settled, we didn't care too much about doing anything too special other than having some good meals, laying out in the sun near the water, and drinking cocktails. It was a vacation away from reality and we checked out of our minds once we boarded the plane.

One night we were having dinner at an Asian fusion restaurant in the resort and my GF mentioned that she wanted a ring. It caught me off guard but I wasn't too surprised. A few months ago she had asked me out of the blue where I saw us in five years. I didn't have a solid answer. I'd been busy investing in my education in the financial services industry as well as building up my own business with the band. I never thought too much or too far into the future. I told her that I saw us pretty much doing the same thing that we were doing now, only in a better position career-wise where we could support ourselves. We'd go out to dinner and on the way home she'd say how about this name for a boy or that name for a girl. I'd humor her but deep down I was in no position to be thinking about starting a family. I had a consulting gig that covered my basic expenses and worked my ass off playing gigs with the band. Not to mention I was still in party-mode given the frequency with which I consumed large amounts of alcohol and marijuana. My primary focus was to settle my credit card debt, study for and pass the CFP exam, stay healthy, and keep her happy. I took her ring request under advisement and certainly didn't flinch or try to change the subject. She had a valid point. We had been together for over six and a half years. She was pretty much saying shit or get off the pot.

Not long after getting back from our vacation, my GF stumbled upon another dog she had to have. It was a rescue puppy about eight or ten weeks old and it was the size of my shoe when she brought him home. The rescue shelter was not sure what breed it was but it looked like a mix between a Lhasa Apso, Maltese, and a Terrier. He looked like a baby Ewok and we instantly fell in love with the little scrapper. The folks at the shelter said a woman came in with a couple of pups from the same litter and said she didn't care what they did with them, including putting them down. We were trying to come up with a name when I recommended Bowie (in honor of the iconic musician and the Phish song). It stuck immediately and we were now the proud owners of two dogs. While my GF was at work and I wasn't at the office I took him up to the Manasquan beach and let him dig deep holes in the sand to wear him out. He was high energy as most puppies are and always brought a smile to our faces when it was time to play.

The next couple of months the ring conversation bounced around in my head and my heart. It was always in the back of my mind but I was still nowhere near a position to save for a ring, much less a wedding. Something needed to change in order for me to dive headlong into the next step of our lives together.

I reevaluated my current situation and decided to start looking for a real job (40 hours a week) with full benefits (health insurance, 401(k), pension, etc.). I had been in the financial services industry for over seven years, had five FINRA registrations, and was moonlighting as a compliance consultant. There were surely a handful of positions out there I might be suitable for. I spruced up my resume and posted it to Monster.com and CareerBuilder.com. One day I came across a listing for a position with MetLife. The job title was Senior Agency Compliance Consultant and the job dealt with every aspect of agency compliance including signing off on new accounts, reviewing incoming and outgoing correspondence, trade reviews, and keeping tabs on sale representatives. The job also required continuing education requirements. The job involved significantly more responsibilities but I was up for the challenge. The office was located in Wall out on Route 34 and was about a 15-minute drive from our house. I went in for an initial interview and met with the managing director and director of operations. I got a second interview the following week and they offered me the position, beating out about 20 other candidates. My starting salary was $55,000 and they told me the biggest selling point for them was the number of FINRA licenses I held. I knew my hard work would eventually pay off and I was right.

Phish got back together and their debut shows were held at the famous Hampton Coliseum in Virginia. Most of our friends got shut out for the public ticket sale months before, but that wasn't going to stop me from hitting those shows. I immediately went on Stub Hub and started scouring for tickets and ending up paying a hefty premium for every single one. I bought three for each night, covering my brother, GF, and myself. Hal had reserved multiple rooms when the shows were announced, so we were set on lodging. A handful of us went down the night before the first show, stayed in Baltimore, and went out for some drinks before making our way to Hampton. It took us over 50 minutes of waiting in line to get in for the first night and everyone tightly gripped their tickets. Some people were offering up to $1,000 for a single ticket and there were no takers. The venue only held close to 14,000 people and everyone knew how momentous the three-night run would be. Once inside, we procured spots in the stage left area (Mike side) up a bit, but not all the way to the back, for all our friends who made it down there. That's where we set up shop each night. When the band took the stage to a thunderous applause and Trey struck the first chord of "Fluffhead" it was game on and we were back to catching many future shows of the best band ever.

With my starting date of April 6th looming, I had about three weeks to figure out how to break the news to my bosses. I'd been with them for close to four years with no major incidents or fires to put out. Sure, when the home office sent an auditor to the office and when an associate from the state securities administration came by I hadn't been there, but I was ready at a moment's notice to head up to the office to deal with anything that needed my attention. I sucked it up and waited for them to both be in a good mood and at the office together. I then shut the door and told them I had something important to tell them. The wife knew immediately and they were both very excited for the new chapter in my life. Tears welled up in my eyes. They had been unbelievable and I knew I would miss their company and ridiculous office banter. I gave them two weeks' notice but I don't even think they cared if I came back the following day.

The job called for business attire meaning a suit, tie, and dress shoes. I was 32 years old and didn't own a suit. I had always borrowed one from my brother when I needed it. I went down to Joseph A. Bank, got measured, and bought three suits during their buy-one-get-two-free deal.

I started my new job and began to soak up every aspect of what the position entailed as well as meeting the reps and office associates. They even gave me an office with a nametag on the door. I learned what was required of me relatively quickly and brought any questions or concerns I had to my direct supervisor, the operations manager whose office was adjacent to mine.

With my new job, I had to reward myself with some new music equipment. This time it was another amp. I did some research on classic Fender amps and the '65 Deluxe Reverb was right up my alley. I searched on eBay and came across an authentic one and had to have it. I bought it and when it was delivered I plugged my 335 in. It sounded exactly as I had hoped. I took it to my amp guy and told him to clean it up and get it firing on all cylinders.

The band's summer schedule was booked up relatively early that year and was busier than ever. There is typically a balance, meaning if we lose a room, we'll pick up a new one. We were back for our seventh straight summer playing Sunday nights at Leggett's. The new stage was back in full force, which was such a relief.

Brendan slowly began drinking again. He saw how the rest of us operated on stage and figured he may be able to make it work. He had been clean while he was with his girlfriend, but when she left his sobriety gradually began to deteriorate. He started hanging out with a new group of people, including enablers. They would get fucked up and frequently stay up past sunrise and on some occasions past noon. There was a hot tub at the back of their house and people from all walks of life were invited over for little soirees at all hours of the day and night. Brendan met the definition of an addict and would do just about anything (except heroin) that was put in front of him. The rest of us didn't see it and he hid it well for a while.

Early on in the summer, the ring conversation came to the forefront of my mind. It was like a bolt of lightning. I had just landed a real deal job, was busy with the band, and had been with the woman I love for close to seven years. Her parents, siblings, and friends loved me and I couldn't imagine being with anyone else. Everyone knew how we felt about each other. We had such amazing chemistry and were both complete goofballs. What was I waiting for?! I decided that I was going to propose on our seventh anniversary, July 13, 2009. That gave me a good five or six weeks to come up with the money for a ring and to plan how I was going to propose.

I only had a small amount of free cash saved and knew it wasn't going to be enough for a decent wedding ring. Sure, I could've made it work, but you want the woman you plan to spend the rest of your life with to be happy with what she wears on her finger. I brought my plan to the dinner table one night up at my folks' place with my brother in attendance. I told them I needed to borrow some money for a wedding ring and they were happy to write a couple of checks. They knew I'd be good for it and would eventually pay them back now that I had a steady full-time job and still raked in gig money. Now I just needed to find a reliable jeweler because I didn't know the first thing about wedding rings. Brendan's sister was a jeweler but I reached out to my friend who threw the first party I got drunk at. His wife told me that I didn't need to go anywhere else. Her family had a friend in the diamond district that did her parents' wedding rings as well as hers, and she guaranteed that he was an honest person. There would also be an appropriate inventory for me to decide on and she assured me that I'd ultimately be happy with what I chose. I couldn't say no after hearing that, so we made plans to meet at the jeweler's shop the following week. She insisted on coming with me so that I'd feel more comfortable and also wanted to see what kind of taste I had in rings.

I took a day off of work and met my friend's wife at the shop, which was located in Manhattan right in the heart of the diamond district. We went upstairs and got buzzed into this small front display room by an elderly man in his early 80s wearing a jeweler's eye loupe around his neck on a chain. He was very pleasant and we started looking at stones. My GF wanted something classy, old fashioned, and traditional. The jeweler showed me a few stones of different cuts, grades, and clarity but I kept going back to the same one and eventually decided that it was the perfect diamond for her. Princess cut, 1.13 carats, with a G rating by the GIA. The actual ring had five little diamonds on each side of the center stone for a total of eleven. I was mesmerized. It was classy and traditional. My friend's wife was impressed and told me that my GF would love it. I was sold on the ring and the jeweler drew up the paperwork. I left a deposit with the remainder to be paid in full by a cashier's check upon pick-up, which would be in approximately two to three weeks. I thanked the jeweler and my friend's wife and went on my way with added energy in my stride.

On the way home I started to realize synchronicities associated with the ring, my proposal date, and our anniversary date. The ring was rated G by the GIA, which is the seventh letter of the alphabet. There were a total of 11 stones and the weight was 1.13 carats. I was going to propose on our seventh anniversary, July 13th, and there was a 13 associated with the weight of the ring. If you added up the month and day of July 13th, it added up to 11 (7+1+3). In my heart, all of these synchronicities added extra magic to the ring, the proposal date, and our bond. I felt that there were higher forces at work and it served as reassurance that I was on the right path.

Less than a week before I was to propose, my brother and his wife's first child was born. John Peter entered the world on July 7th, 2009. He was named for his father. John was also our father's name. His middle name was that of his maternal grandfather. He would be called Jack. My GF and I hopped in the car that night and headed up to Monmouth Medical Center to meet up with my brother and his wife, our parents, his wife's two sisters, her father, and stepmother, as well as his wife's mother and stepfather. After greeting everyone I peered into the nursery. All the newborns were resting quietly and my brother pointed out which one was theirs. Tears instantly welled up in my eyes and I felt an electric sensation in my heart. I knew the newest addition to the family was in great hands.

Monday, July 13th came upon us. My GF and I decided to head over to Klein's Seafood in Belmar for an anniversary dinner. This was all part of the plan. I had the ring in my shorts the entire time. I forgot what she ordered but I was into Alaskan king crab legs at the time and figured I'd eat like a king on such an important day.

After dinner, we headed back to 3rd Avenue. I suggested we take a walk up to Brielle Road beach and she agreed. The sky was split with sun in one half and threatening clouds in the other. It looked like a sun shower was inevitable. Once we turned onto Brielle Road and walked past our old house at 554½ we reminisced about our time there. I brought up the first time I really took notice of her walking with her friend up to the beach in 2002 for the fireworks display. I demonstrated my little lookback in the same spot on the sidewalk when I spotted her and described what she was wearing and the look she gave me. There was an element of electricity around us, energy unlike anything I'd ever felt before. I was completely present and my heart felt warm and was buzzing. The butterflies in my stomach were fluttering wildly. We passed the entrance to the beach from the blacktop and I pointed out to her where her badge checking beach chair was and described what she was wearing the first time I came up to her while she was working. We continued further towards the ocean and the sun shower began. There were dark clouds over us, but clear blue sky in our field of vision. I suggested we take off our sandals and get our feet wet and we headed down to the water's edge. After a brief moment and a kiss we headed back to where we left our sandals. The sun shower started coming down heavier and we just laughed it off. She turned to look towards the road and that's when I grabbed her hand, whirled her around, and got down on one knee. As she peered down, I had the box open, displaying the ring. She gasped and appeared paralyzed. Her eyes were wide and bigger than I'd ever seen. I told her I was so in love with her, that I couldn't imagine being with anyone else, and that the past seven years had been truly amazing and the best years of my life. "Will you marry me?" popped out and she said yes!!! I put the ring on her finger and the exact moment our lips locked the sun shower ceased. Light began to shine on us and I spotted a double rainbow in the sky. I pointed to it in complete amazement and declared that it was surely a sign. We headed back to our house as she marveled at the ring on her finger and headed to her parents' house to share the good news. I texted friends and family and she did the same. We decided that there was no rush in planning a wedding. We still didn't have a pot to piss in and given enough time, we'd be able to save for something memorable. She was still glowing and staring at the ring as she lay in bed before packing it in for the evening. She gave me kudos for my taste, reaffirmed that she loved the ring, and thanked me for an amazing proposal.

Newly engaged, we both had a renewed sense of energy and interest in our relationship, but things didn't change too drastically. We still had our routine and I hardly had any weekends off with our ramped up schedule. She was still taking classes for her graduate degree and working full-time. We were both trying our best to get ahead given our circumstances.

One Sunday night at Leggett's we were about four or five songs into our first set when the manager came over between songs and told us not to freak out or say anything, but Bruce Springsteen was having cocktails with two or three buddies outside on the patio. We played it cool and the next song we did was "Prove It All Night." After our set was over, one of the bouncers who was between the bar area and the doors to the patio told us that Bruce had listened to our entire rendition of his song and afterwards commented to the bouncer "those boys did that song justice" and "that guitar player's real good." We all appreciated the compliments, added it to the bank of band lore, and played with a higher sense of purpose for the rest of the night.

Mid-August, The Allman Brother's came to town and played at PNC Bank Arts Center. My friend Sean, who'd been working for Live Nation, called me and asked if my fiancée and I would like to come up to the show for a little congratulatory concert given our recent engagement. I agreed and we headed up to Holmdel and met him outside the venue to pick up our passes, which were good for a section in the seated area. Once we got to our section, the area was jam packed with other concertgoers, which made for an uncomfortable experience. We headed to the side aisle and stood for a good 40 minutes before Sean came back down and told us to follow him. The next thing we know we are on stage right, standing with about 15 other people, all of whom were friends and family of the band. We only knew Sean but no one seemed to mind us hanging out there and watching the concert from a different vantage point. I looked out to the sea of people and it was just an awesome sight. The place was packed. My gaze was pretty much fixed on Warren Haynes and Derek Trucks the entire time. At one point, my eyes locked with Derek's for a few seconds. I'm sure it was due to the fact he knew everyone on the side of the stage except my fiancée and I. I kept a grin on my face and didn't waver. Later in the set, Greg came out from around his B-3 organ and was a good three feet from me, soaked to the bone in sweat. He took his t-shirt off and was taking a breather during a drum break. I remember thinking to myself, "That's Greg Allman RIGHT THERE. Dude damn near sweated on me. That's Duane's brother." It was a truly unforgettable evening.

Over the next couple of months my fiancée and I had conversations about setting a date and also brought up the whole having children thing. I recommended July 13th, 2012, as it would be our tenth anniversary. That date stuck and gave us time to hustle and save for the expenses. At the time, kids and starting a family was still not a priority given our financial situation and hectic schedules but I needed to keep my fiancée engaged with that possibility.

With Phish back in full swing and touring again, a bunch of us hit up shows like we had over a decade ago. This time we had more resources, money, connections, know-how, and wisdom to make every show an everlasting experience. Phish shows felt like a homecoming to many of us. They had become ritualistic and encouraged an atmosphere of freedom that was unparalleled. Other revelers and I traveled down to Merriweather Post Pavilion in Maryland, Philadelphia, Albany (where they debuted TV on the Radio's "Golden Age"), and three shows at MSG. The MSG tickets weren't an issue since Sean was employed through Live Nation and was able to procure tickets that they had holds on. We even had a luxury box one night. The band played Frank Zappa's "Peaches en Regalia" for the first time in over a decade, which coincided nicely as I had recently read his autobiography, which was a gift from my fiancée. The band was on top of their game and they sounded like fire, playing with renewed energy now that Trey had banished his inner demons and darkness.

New Year's came around and Phish had booked four nights at American Airlines Arena in Miami. I had to go and would not take no from my fiancée. It turned out that Sean and his wife, a good friend of mine who attended UVM and his wife, as well as a local Manasquan cat and his girlfriend were all going. I got two tickets for the 30th and the 31st, booked our flights and hotel room (which was within walking distance of the venue), and prepared for an epic time.

It was epic. We all got to hang out together, grab dinner, catch some sun on the beach, and my fiancée and I made a day trip to South Beach and walked around visiting some local art galleries and other boutique shops. The 30th and 31st shows were two of the best I had ever seen. The band opened the 30th with Bob Marley's "Soul Shakedown Party" and continued to bust out songs they typically hadn't played in a while. I was more than happy that I had made the trip down, glad my fiancée was with me, and felt satiated in having attended a number of Phish shows for their triumphant return. I could rest soundly until their next tour was announced.

My studies for the CFP exam continued at a structured pace. When I could sneak it, I would have my study material under my desk at work. If I knew my boss was going to be busy and I hit a slow period where I was on top of my work, I would break it out and try to get as much in as I could. After work, I'd come home and take the dogs down 3rd Avenue so they could find their spots in the reeds to do their business, and then have dinner with my fiancée. Afterwards, I dedicated between 45 to 90 minutes to studying in isolation upstairs on a couch in our bedroom. I was prepping to take the required education program exams. These were self-study and the exams were submitted online. My only focus during this time was to study my ass off and pass the exam. I was planning on sitting for it that June since it is only offered three times a year.

~~~

Over the next couple of months my fiancée talked me into making this year our last year renting in Manasquan. She wanted us to buy a house together and get situated prior to getting married. There was an added incentive given somewhat lower interest rates, the FHA program, and first-time homebuyer credit of $8,000 that the federal government was still offering. We did the math and it appeared to be only a couple of hundred dollars more than what we had been doling out in rent every month. She viewed paying rent as throwing money out the window when we could be building equity and working towards home ownership. She had a point and that was the next big life event for us.

I managed to pass all of my required pre-education exams and was ready to submit my application to sit for the CFP exam. They required a certified copy of my college transcript, proof of three years industry experience, and demonstration in one of the six areas of the financial planning process as well as ethics requirements. This meant no felony convictions or anything related to fraud. My application was approved to sit for the June exam so I had another three months of intense studying ahead of me. I also planned to pay for the 40-hour crash course seminar with the same guy that my brother had used. I ramped up my study schedule to between one and a half to two hours a night and would continue this pace until the crash course seminar.

Sometime around April my fiancée wanted to go to Paris. Travel was the last thing on my mind given the staunch focus I had on my studies. There was also the matter of paying my folks and my brother back for the engagement ring. She had a general idea of how much it cost but didn't realize I added to my debt in the process. She decided to go with her sister and upon her return, ramped up the search for a house, and obtained information about the FHA program, and first-time homebuyer credit.

My four-day, 40-hour crash course seminar came and was approximately two weeks before the scheduled CFP exam. I had to take two vacation days from work since it was held on Thursday, Friday, Saturday, and Sunday in a huge conference room with about 70 other people in a hotel in Newark, about a mile and a half from the airport. It was grueling. Ten-hour days discussing everything from life insurance trusts, defined benefit pension plans, Medicare and Medicaid rules, the time value of money calculations, bond laddering, and tax and estate planning. Anything and everything you could imagine in the field of financial planning was covered. The planner running the seminar was funny, animated, easy to relate to, and had an amazing success rate. Something like 85% of people who took his crash course passed the exam. This made me breathe a little easier, even as I was dozing off at my table while he was going over generation-skipping tax planning.

Somewhere within the two-week window after the seminar and prior to the exam I broke down. I had been busting my ass for over a year and a half studying and preparing for this exam and the notion of failing crossed my mind and got to me. I had a borderline anxiety attack and tears started to flow as I was talking to my fiancée after dinner one night before heading upstairs to study. She calmed my nerves, reassured me that everything was going to be all right, and said that it's not worth working myself into such a state. I eventually calmed down and agreed with her.

Exam day came and it was now or never. I had studied enough, used flashcards, and ended up looking at them in my car prior to entering the location to check in. The exam was held at a community college out near Princeton and was a two-day event. There was one section on Friday and two the following day. An appointed proctor monitored the classrooms. I got through the first day feeling pretty good. I went home, laid down for a bit, had dinner, and then started my flashcard routine and went through problem topics for a couple hours as my head was on fire. I then crashed and got a decent night's sleep.

The following morning I was up a little after 6AM and ran to Dunkin Donuts for a coffee and munchkin bites before heading out on Route 195 West for the 8AM exam time. I think the allotted duration for each of the two sections was four hours with a 45 to 60 minute break in between. Section one felt a little easier than the previous day's section. The afternoon section was the most challenging of the three. I finished up with about 50 minutes to spare and went back through my answers, reviewing some of the questions that were head scratchers with the hopes of seeing them from a different perspective, but in the end I didn't change any of my answers.

I handed in my exam, checked out, got to my car, and sighed a heavy sigh of relief knowing I did my best and hoped I beat the curve. The CFP Board of Standards uses a bell curve to determine who passes the exam. The previous exam had something like a 52.4% pass rate and the one I just sat for would not deviate too much from this percentage. In my heart, I had to figure that I had put in enough blood, sweat, tears, and heart to beat out the lower 48% who thought they could wing it and breeze through without working as hard as I had. Now all I had to do was wait. Exam results would not be distributed for six to eight weeks. The exam process is similar to the bar exam in that respect.

Within the next few weeks, things progressed quickly on the home purchase front. My fiancée's brother, who had been living with us for a few years, was now part of the plan. She had convinced him that it would be easier to qualify for more money to borrow from the bank if we had his income included on the loan. In other words, he would be a third person on the mortgage. He understood the logic of it all since we would be building equity instead of throwing money away paying rent every month.

My fiancée was searching listings online like it was her job. Monmouth County, close to the shore, was out of our price range. The properties that had been affordable to us were too small, too run down, and just not places I would want to call home. She searched in Ocean County spotted a couple houses, found one she really liked, did a drive by, and scheduled a viewing with our realtor. It had been a ranch and a second floor was built onto it in the last few years with five bedrooms (one being an office that could be converted to a bedroom and three bathrooms. It had no basement but a lot of property and a fence around the perimeter. The place was beautiful and my fiancée loved it. The price was a little steep, just south of $400,000, but doing the calculations it was possible to fit it in our budget. My fiancée wanted it and I only cared that she would be happy there so I agreed. We didn't even try to bargain or negotiate to lower the price. I was naïve in that respect. My father taught me better than that, but the realtors felt that the asking price was fair and it could be a simple transaction. The owners moved out of state and were already getting situated there with new home furnishings. I asked if they could throw in most of the furniture and appliances and they happily agreed. That was a huge selling point. The house was practically already furnished.

The next step was coming up with enough cash for the FHA required down payment of 3.5%. Again, I didn't have a pot to piss in so I liquidated my IRA, borrowed the maximum from my 401(k), and asked for a small loan from my brother. My folks also gifted me money towards the down payment. My fiancée had no money and her brother was able to borrow a little bit from his retirement plan.

The day came to meet with the lawyer to review all the paperwork and to sign and initial where needed. The section where our mortgage payment was discussed came up and the escrow additions for insurance and property taxes brought our monthly outlay to close to $3,000. This was a huge bump from what we were paying in rent at $1,850. I think my fiancée thought our monthly mortgage payment was going to be closer to $2,200. Once she heard the figure her eyes bugged a little bit. She wasn't making too much money with her current job and her portion of the mortgage was a huge dent in her monthly income. I knew we would get some money back on our taxes and I was busting my ass with the band so I reassured her everything was going to be fine. We negotiated our move-in date for September 1st so we could finish out our last summer in Manasquan. I was now a homeowner.

The summer was as busy as always. Our growing repertoire kept us engaged and we picked up a few new outdoor venues including the Union Landing in Brielle and Wharfside Patio Bar in Point Pleasant. Both were early starts (6 to 10PM) because we played outdoors. We loved the UL. The local crowd was really into the music we played and the owners and staff were phenomenal people. Patio Bar's clientele were from all walks of life so we catered to the crowd with our song selection. We always played something for everyone at that venue.

I received an envelope at work from the Certified Financial Planner Board of Standards. It was my test results. I carefully opened it and the only words that jumped out at me were Congratulations and PASS. I was elated! I immediately called my fiancée, brother and my parents to share the wonderful news. I decided I was done with pursuing additional certifications and designations in the financial services field. I had done a lot in a short period of time and was ready to kick my feet up.

We received an email asking if we'd be interested in playing a wedding in San Luis Obispo. The man was a year or two older than Lou and Brendan and his father was a judge in Cranford. He was also related to a girl from Westfield who my brother invited half of Cranford High School to her house for a party back in the day. We were all for it but the matter of logistics and budgetary constraints were the obvious first and second hurdles to get over. Our terms were realistic and minimal:

we would require round trip airline tickets, a van to get from the airport, the venue, and back, lodging near the reception area, a PA, backline (full drum set, bass amp, and two guitar amps), and $200 each for the service. We would gate check our guitars and pack what effects pedals we needed in our carry-ons. The future groom and bride did the math and decided to go forward with the plan. This was the farthest we'd be traveling for a gig and I had never gate checked my guitar before. We all knew a ton of the wedding guests so we felt very comfortable.

We flew out of Newark and touched down in Los Angeles. After picking up our reserved SUV from the car rental agency, we set out of LA eventually making it to the Pacific Coast Highway. We then travelled north through Santa Barbara, making it to San Luis Obispo in about three and a half hours. After checking into the hotel and getting cleaning up, we headed over to a house party where a handful of wedding guests were catching up and throwing down. We then hit a bar in town that was a few blocks from our hotel and stayed up pretty late after ripping some tequila shots and downing a few nightcaps. The following morning we headed to the reception and ceremony location. It was on the grounds of a ranch nestled in a valley. We were to set up outside on the lawn facing the house with a makeshift dance floor in front of us. We looked over our gear, everything seemed to check out, and then proceeded to set up our "stage" area. The area where we were to set up was located in a shady section of the lawn that still had morning dew on the grass. The sun had not yet dried out the area. There were some soggy sections of the lawn so we found the driest, most level area to set up on. Once the gear was in place and we got everything up and running, we headed back to the hotel for some down time and to get ready for the gig.

Once back on the ranch grounds and all the guests had taken their seats, the ceremony took place followed by a cocktail service. The best man's speech ran a good 35 minutes before the groom cut him off and explained to all the guests that he hired a band to play and wanted to get to the festivities and live music. That was our cue. We played four or five sets over the course of the evening and everyone had a blast. We played until the bride and groom were the last people on the makeshift dance floor. It must've been close to 3:30AM. A patrol car showed up and explained that they had gotten a noise complaint from the other side of the valley. This made complete sense as sound travels in odd ways when you are outside. We headed back to our hotel room and eventually called it a night.

The next day we grabbed a bite to eat, said our goodbyes at the ranch, and headed back to LA. Once in town, we had a couple of hours to kill so we grabbed a few beers at a local bar on the Sunset Strip before heading to the airport. It was quite an experience and our lives were enriched for having played so far away from the Jersey Shore and being part of an amazing wedding for an amazing couple.

Brendan continued to go at it hard that summer. It didn't help that he was surrounded by a handful of enablers. He didn't understand that he was an alcoholic and fell off the wagon hard. There were a few gigs where he'd shamble in after waking up at 7 or 8PM and we wondered if he would even show. There were days he'd sleep until 2 or 4PM, wake up, start partying with his friends, and show up half in the bag. He never missed a show. His performance and energy may have suffered here and there but it's not like he was a train wreck at every gig. The rest of us kept a watchful eye on him. We weren't of the mindset to tell anyone how to live their life unless it was completely affecting our reputation, or worse, becoming an abominable detriment to his health.

The summer flew by with gigs, late-night beer pong games in our garage; weeknight bike rides to the UL, and late-night dance parties at Hal's place on Ocean Avenue. Like the previous summer, my favorite times were hitting up the boardwalk shortly before sunrise, shirtless on my bike, listening to Bob Marley after a late-night sesh and cruising up Brielle Road on my way home, acting as the night watchman.

Our move to our new home began on Labor Day weekend. My fiancée's brother borrowed their father's pickup truck and we began getting the bulkier stuff out of the 3rd Avenue house and dropping it off at the new house. We were prepared, having had enough time to box up our personal effects. After several trips we had all of our worldly possessions in our new home. Moving is never an easy process but this couldn't have gone any smoother. Our house was already mostly furnished and ready for us to move in. It only took about a day to organize the rooms, hang what needed to be hung, and put the rest in the garage or attic. Next thing I know we were sleeping on a California king bed in a spacious master bedroom with a beautiful bathroom attached. We settled in fairly quickly and I slowly made my way out to the local shops to get a feel for our new neighborhood.

We eventually settled into our home. We had a nice long front deck with furniture so we could hang outside when the weather was nice. My fiancée and I would walk the dogs in the local neighborhood and toss around ideas about our wedding reception. In addition to work, she had to put in the required hours for the advanced psychology certification that she was pursuing. She jumped right into it after obtaining her master's degree. There were days she'd be up at 6AM and not get home until 9 or 9:30PM. She was always in bed between 10 and 10:30PM and was sound asleep shortly after her head hit the pillows. I couldn't get to bed that early and was usually up until 12:30AM and 1AM on work nights, at which time I'd catch up on some TV shows, have a couple of heady beers, and practice on the guitar.

Back at work, we got word that all New Jersey MetLife agencies would be consolidating under one branch. The managing director at the Cranford agency would take on a co-managing director and they would be at the helm of the pending new super agency. Meaning salaried employees (including myself) did not know what the future had in store. Some of the reps I talked to asked if I was concerned about losing my job. One veteran was pretty sure of that outcome and suggested I start sprucing up my resume as he'd heard of stories like this before. I remained optimistic. Since I started working there, I had mastered the role and responsibilities of the position and focused on performing them better and more quickly every day. I would hope that any new manager would view me as a valuable asset and think twice before slipping me a pink slip.

Within the coming weeks, I learned that my position would be absorbed and central compliance duties would be performed at the Cranford agency. My direct supervisor was safe as they needed someone at the Wall office and she also had over 20 years with the company. When she broke the news to me. I can't say I was too surprised. I just thought it could've gone either way and hoped for the best. I saw the tears well up in my boss's eyes as she was telling me because she knew I had recently bought a house and proposed to my fiancée. Anyone and their mother would've shown sympathy since it's a shitty hand to be dealt.

I packed up my personal effects, said my goodbyes, and was walked out of the office. I also received a severance package commensurate with how long I was employed with the company. To top everything off, we got dumped on with about 27 inches of snow at the end of December. John and I were supposed to see Phish up in Worcester but the timing of the storm made travel impossible. Instead, my fiancée and I spent a greater part of the day shoveling our driveway. We hit the New Year's MSG shows, which were a treat. That was the end of 2010. I could only look forward and make 2011 as great as possible.

～～

Once at home and unemployed, I had a lot of free time on my hands. One of the first things I did was file for unemployment benefits as I had done in the past. I kept a regular schedule and knew going out for drinks every night wasn't going to help anything so I started going to the gym regularly. I received a discount through work on my membership to the Atlantic Club in Manasquan, so I began a routine with the elliptical machine, stepper, and weight training.

On January 8th, our drummer Lou got married to his longtime girlfriend. They had a beautiful ceremony and reception up in central Jersey. Later in the evening, while outside with a handful of people smoking cigarettes, Brendan was crying his eyes out and hugging his close friends who were consoling him on the loss of his uncle who had recently passed away. I'd never seen him like that before and it broke my heart. I knew he was in good hands with friends he'd grown up with.

Back home, while searching employment sites and financial service firms' career sections on their websites, I logged into the MetLife portal as I still had access to it, and, on a whim, went to their internal link for listed job opportunities. I searched compliance and a couple of positions popped up. The one that stood out was "Senior Controls Analyst." The job location was work from home. I had to look twice because, at the time, I couldn't possibly imagine working from home. I viewed the job description and, among other tasks and related duties, it was for email and trade reviews. I had done this in the agency but the compliance department was centralizing the duties and all of those employees would now work from home. I applied immediately and received a call from one of the managers of the unit the following day. He gave me the details of the role and went over my resume. He felt comfortable that I'd be a good fit for the role given my work experience and told me that his manager would be following up with a call. There was no in-person interview; it was all done over the phone. The next day his manager called to feel me out and next thing I know he offered me the position. I was beyond ecstatic. My heart jumped for joy and I couldn't wait to tell my fiancée, brother, and parents. It was for the same salary I had with my previous agency job but working from home meant that I could create my own schedule and didn't have to worry about commuting. I never wanted to work where all the bigger financial service firms' offices were located, such as Jersey City, Weehawken, or Manhattan, but was prepared to bite the bullet in the event that things started to get desperate. This solved that issue in an instant.

My start date was February 15th so I had a few weeks to chill before diving into a new position. As I was rehired within the same company, my severance package was off the table. I kept up a decent schedule with hitting the gym and laying low with my evening routine. For as long as I can remember, I had always ended the evening with milk and cookies. That was always the icing on the cake.

My start date came and I received a work laptop, printer, and port and began getting everything set up and configured through the

IT department. I then started training with my new boss who lived in California. After I proved my competency, they let me run free on my assigned agency queues that were located in California and Texas. We turned one of our spare bedrooms into my office and I got pretty comfortable in there with a desk, futon, and guitar for when the mood struck. I worked my queues diligently under minimal supervision and found myself working some odd hours, so I was able to free up my days for errands and hitting the gym. I quickly realized that this was the best job I had ever had and told myself I could never go back to working in an office again.

At the end of February I went down to Leggett's to confirm our Sunday nights in the summer with the manager, and he told me that they were planning on going in a different direction that year. I thought he was joking. We'd done a bang up job every summer since we started and I couldn't process his decision. He told me it wasn't personal it was business. Not only were we completely insulted and infuriated, we all relied on the steady summer work as a source of income. This left us with three months to find a new room, set up shop, and start building a night again.

I hunkered down in my new job and got comfortable in my duties. Our house started to feel more like a home. My fiancée's brother had been dating a nice girl since the summer and she started staying over more frequently. The band stayed relatively busy in the off-season and we eventually got our summer dates booked, including a last minute Hail Mary by the Manasquan Beach House. The ex-manager of Leggett's left and acquired O'Neill's and eventually changed the name to the Manasquan Beach House. He got word of what happened to us at Leggett's and offered us every Sunday night. We only wanted to play in Manasquan on Sunday nights in keeping with tradition and happily took the gig.

Memorial Day weekend was upon us and we geared up for another busy summer. A handful of friends from the Shore and Cranford headed up to Bethel Woods, New York for three nights of Phish. We were booked in Toms River that Saturday night, and near the end of the first set, Lou got a text message from a friend who had heard through the grapevine that a guy named Max from the Jersey Shore had died up in Bethel earlier that day. We only knew one Max from the Jersey Shore who could've fit the description and prayed it wasn't our friend. He had been instrumental in getting us in at Leggett's and served us at the Dive in Cranford for so many years with a smile on his face and amazing live music pumping through the bar. By the end of our set we got confirmation that it was our friend. John and I went outside and just fucking lost it. It felt like all the blood left my body and in an instant I was completely numb. We all knew the lifestyle he chose to live and unfortunately it caught up with him just as he was starting to make healthier changes in his life. He died doing what he loved: going to see his favorite band with his friends. We mustered up the strength to play through the rest of the night and by the time we got to my house I was in shambles again with my fiancée consoling me. We had a drink on our porch and shared a couple of Max stories before turning in.

A couple of days later at PNC Bank Arts Center, we played in the VIP tent before Phish took the stage. This was coordinated through our old manager Sean and we had our old Shady Groove keyboard player Shoheen with us. We had reconnected a few years back and whenever we had a party or bigger show that required keys, he was our go-to guy. We powered through our set then quickly broke down and loaded our gear back into our cars so we could make it down to our seats to enjoy the rest of the show with our friends. We hustled and made it down by the end of "The Moma Dance" before the band started the PNC favorite cover of the Velvet Underground's "Rock and Roll." After that, Trey stepped up to the mic and dedicated the next song to Max and mentioned that he had recently lost his life. The band ripped into one of the most scintillating renditions of "Sand" I had ever heard. This was one of Max's favorite Phish songs. Some of the vibrato and bent notes Trey used mimicked the wails of a banshee or the absolute pain of total loss. Right when Trey spoke Max's name, our entire section (Sean had been able to procure a large number of tickets in the lower orchestra so the Jersey Shore and Cranford crowds had a large presence at that show) erupted with screams, howls, and whistles. I felt heaviness in my heart, looked over to my fiancée, and tears started to well up in my eyes. I had to sit down for a brief moment, as my knees felt weak. I looked down the line at all my friends and we all had the same look of utter amazement and bewilderment. There was an energy in our section that felt as if Max was right there with us, rocking out as if he had never left. The rest of the shows were fire (pun intended as they encored with Hendrix's tune of the same name).

Sometime in the middle of the summer I decided to treat myself and buy another guitar. Of course there had to be a significant reason to shell out over $3,000, but I found one to celebrate 20 years (it was actually 21, but I was the only one counting) of playing the guitar. We had been busting our asses and I actually had enough free cash where I didn't have to lay it all on a credit card. I've always been a sucker for Gibson semi-hollow bodies and liked the idea of a smaller sized body since the 335s were fairly large. Gibson made Les Paul-sized semi-hollow bodies and I had been doing my research. I settled on a CS-356. I found a beautiful rare sunburst on eBay that didn't have a lick of wear on it and had been manufactured that year. The only "new" guitar I had ever owned was the first Strat I got, a 1992 American Standard. It seemed fitting to purchase this one. It felt like coming full circle. It was on my doorstep within a week.

Chapter 6

∼✦∼

THE DARK NIGHT OF THE SOUL

I AM NOT going to detail the specific series of events and conversations that led to the dissolution of my relationship with my fiancée. I will cite various examples that, in looking back and having done much soul-searching and introspection, are pretty clear. One thing was certain: it was a complicated situation. Unfortunately, it should not have been. I had been dealing with mental health and chemical dependency issues for half of my life, and had been unconscious of how that pattern of behavior affected the people I loved. I hid it well for a long time. From the outside looking in, you are the last person to see it. That is the disease. You believe your behavior is normal. That being said, it is still a disease, like any other such as cancer or Alzheimer's. They all need to be treated with care, compassion, patience, hope, and understanding.

My behavior was less than exemplary for a great duration of our relationship regarding the overuse of alcohol and marijuana. Alcohol was always prevalent, but over time the marijuana crept back in with more frequency. Anyone in the field of psychology could easily view the relationship from a clinical perspective as codependent. Our signals got crossed and it became a perfect storm of textbook cohabiting codependency that led to a complete communication breakdown.

At the time, I was not an ideal candidate to be a responsible husband or father. This was what my fiancée wanted: a healthy and normal life plan for our future. The timing could not have been more perfect. We owned a house and were within ten months of our planned wedding date, but I failed to properly engage in the important conversation of the family planning process and put any fears and doubts she may have had about marrying me to bed. My focus was work and earning enough money to ensure financial stability, not defaulting on our mortgage, reduce my debt, and saving for a wedding. That is the great irony of this scenario. Responsibilities of every day life required for survival in the 21st century can inhibit any relationship. There were years where I was working what seemed like every weekend with no end in sight. In effect, giving way to no sound work-life balance. As a result, an accumulated level of exhaustion became commonplace and I believed I was young enough and strong enough physically and mentally to not let it wear me down. It is extremely difficult to climb out of that haze once you've been in so deep for so long. Without knowing it—I spread myself pretty thin. I'd work until last call and get home around 2:30AM, and would get to bed between 3AM and 3:30AM if I were lucky. We were like two ships passing in the night. Our circadian rhythms were clearly out of sync.

When presented with a dilemma of the heart, I was in such a fragile state, overworked and self-medicated, that I was not thinking or seeing things clearly. My judgment was grossly impaired and my fiancée had no idea where my headspace was at or the shape I was in. She attempted to logically and clearly communicate that a change was necessary, but my comprehension was distorted. There was a disconnect between my logical and rational thinking mind and heart. A delay in processing what my head heard and heart acted upon. I needed a different form of communication, such as a punch to the face. The absence of self-awareness, my level of emotional intelligence, and common sense regarding her wants and needs were lacking. At one point she might as well have been talking to a wall. From an energetic perspective, my heart (4th) and throat (5th) chakras (the energy centers of the subtle body associated with compassion, empathy/seeing things from someone else's perspective and honest communication from the heart, respectively) were blocked. I was operating from a space of lower evolution of the 2nd chakra where fight or flight and reacting to emotional responses are associated. (More on this in Chapter 9.)

The habitual use of alcohol and marijuana cut me off from my feelings and made me indifferent to certain stimuli, which is not conducive to growth, healthy relationships, and the development of an ongoing emotional, intimate, and loving bond. Over time, it brought me to a lower vibratory state or frequency that did not match my fiancée's. That definitely has no business being a part of starting a family and raising children. From a place of utter confusion, I did say and do some things that I am not proud of, were immature, misconstrued, didn't mean, and weren't true. For example, I was scared to death of children. With that, I only pushed her further away and gave her no reason to stay in the relationship. I panicked. This exasperated an already delicate situation and my responses only confused her more. My fight or flight response took hold. The darkness comes out in times of great stress and anxiety and the shadow self manifests. I was trying to develop professional relationships and build a small business while holding down a career and do what I truly believed in my heart I was supposed to be doing. I was trying to keep my passion for music alive while earning additional income.

I studied insurance, securities, investing, and financial planning for over a decade and understood how to plan for life events, including a family. At the time, I wasn't capable of viewing the situation from her perspective and didn't take into consideration that her biological clock was ticking away. I had been nearly flat broke in my early 20s. When the opportunity was there to earn money, I wasn't one to hesitate. In my mind, I thought what I was doing was right for us, but had no foresight to actually sit down, take stock of everything, see the bigger picture, have a discussion with honest and clear communication, strategize, and put a plan in place to eradicate the toxic substances and people that easily come from the environments that working musicians are exposed to. It's an unfortunate occupational hazard. Living where we did for so long didn't help either. Being within walking and biking distance to bars is a trap for anyone with addiction and chemical dependency issues. Without question, I certainly was not the best version of myself and needed to do a lot of work.

From the heart, I would have done anything for my fiancée and thought that this along with my level of patience was understood. I am a fixer by nature and was not able to make this right. As I never considered for our relationship and bond to be challenged, and in conjunction with my mental health history, the shock of the event triggered a nervous breakdown. If there were any shots at redemption or conflict resolution they were not apparent or I potentially self-sabotaged them given the fog I was in.

Hindsight is 20/20. I can say without a shadow of a doubt that the physical pain, emotional strain, heartache, psychological, and spiritual turmoil I experienced from the loss of a great love and someone I planned to be with for the rest of my life was the biggest life lesson I have learned to date and one of the primary catalysts for growth, change and ultimately my Kundalini awakening. This experience was not for nothing. It was a blessing in disguise. Socrates said, "The unexamined life is not worth living," and it is a statement that certainly deserves further reflection.

~~~

Before the summer got under way, I decided that I wanted to go back into the studio and record an album of a handful of Shady Groove songs that we had written and used to play quite frequently. I was proud of those songs and the collaboration with my brother, Josh, and Barry, and found it difficult to just let them disappear from the sonic record. Creating music and the art of recording them was, to me, right up there with playing music in front of people and sex; there was no greater pleasure. The recording process was extremely fun and being at the helm with complete artistic control for the first time was something I was looking forward to. Another reason for this endeavor was that I had hit a creative roadblock with songwriting. Ever since I went into financial services and enjoy! began to occupy a lot of my free time, I didn't have time to spare to focus on letting my ideas germinate and flow. When I was younger with less responsibility, the ideas flowed out of me more easily. I was an open channel. Either sitting in my brother's room in Cranford noodling around, or drinking beer and pulling tubes in the apartment he shared with Barry and Josh in college. It was so easy back then! In my heart I knew I had to do this before the next creative project manifested itself. It was my destiny.

With Barry in California and Josh married in Brooklyn, I decided to use Lou's brother Danny. He had been the drummer in our first band in high school. He could play anything and I felt that he was the right candidate for the job. My brother was the obvious choice for bass and Shady (Shoheen), who had a brief stint in the band and played private parties and weddings with us now, was my only choice for keys. We had great chemistry together. They all signed on for the project and I dug into the Shady Groove musical archives for the best-recorded and cleanest versions of the ten songs I intended to record and sent them to everyone. They had a couple of months to listen to them at their leisure and I booked a few mid-week rehearsals during the summer to run through the songs.

Sunday, September 18th was the initial session. I chose Les, the engineer for our first album, as he was fun to work with and knew his shit. He also lowered his hourly rate (friend rate) for tracking, which helped out tremendously as I was funding the project entirely out of my own pocket. I had enough free cash saved up and had been budgeting for a while. Les was working out of DiBella Music, a huge music store up in Teaneck in his neck of the woods. He had a control room in the basement and tracking would be done down there. There was an open space for the drums and rooms for music lessons that we used to isolate the amps. I booked a ten-hour block and maybe got three hours of sleep the night before since I was now sleeping in a king size bed by myself. I didn't know what my fiancée was up to and the resulting anxiety kept me awake.

Danny showed up first since miking the drums and getting sounds and levels takes the longest. Within an hour of Shady, John, and I arriving, we started getting after it. We would play through a song first and make sure everyone had all their parts down and changes internalized before Les hit record. The focus was on getting the drums and bass parts down. All other instrumentation and vocals would be overdubbed later. These songs were not the type that could be recorded live and banged out in one shot. Overdubbing allowed for more freedom and to make sure everything that needed to be recorded in a specific way got recorded. On average, we did between four or five takes per song. If someone fucked up, they owned up and we stopped immediately and started the take over. Les was always active in the takes selection process and he made notes on a pad for everyone. That way, he was able to narrow them down to one or two of the strongest and we'd take it from there. The session was a success. We got through all ten songs in the allotted block of time. Extremely exhausted, I made it home and crashed hard.

~~~

I scheduled an appointment with my psychiatrist whom I hadn't seen in years, as I'd been in a very stable frame of mind for quite a while. Within minutes of sitting down in his office I broke down in tears. I had an inkling of what this major life event would do to me and I needed to take every precaution available. I'd been down in a hole with full-blown depression in college and it was a living hell. The doctor prescribed me Klonopin, an anti-anxiety medicine, and upped my dosage of Wellbutrin to three pills a day. I had been prescribed two a day for as long as I could remember but had been down to one of my own volition for years with the eventual hope of weaning myself off altogether. We agreed to meet three times a week for about a month, then twice a week and to take it from there. He knew my history with drugs and alcohol and didn't have to remind me to take it down a notch. Knowing alcohol is a depressant and I was headed for a major episode, I cut down the booze considerably.

Brendan was running a karaoke/open mic night at Manasquan Beach House every Tuesday night and I started popping in there to sing and play three or four songs at a clip. I had been learning covers in my free time over the past six weeks to keep me busy. Songs by artists such as The Grateful Dead, Phish, Trey Anastasio, The Band, Steely Dan, Steve Winwood, Wilco, George Harrison, and The Beatles all found their way onto the music stand when I performed my mini-set. One night after a gig I was home and threw on The Band's *The Last Waltz* DVD and my X (as she will now be called) walked in while "It Makes No Difference" was on. It was a very emotional moment. It fit my state of mind to a T. I eventually worked that into my repertoire as well as an old bluegrass traditional that Phish covers called "The Old Home Place." It was a song that I started describing as semi-autobiographical due to the singer losing his girl, home, spending all his money at the bar and wishing he were dead. Before heading over to Brophyaoke, I'd stop at Quinn and his girl-friend's place to have some face time and talk about what was going on. I'd pull a couple of tubes, have a beer, and then be on my way. The tubes eventually stopped and I quit smoking grass altogether. I knew I needed a clearer mind to get through the darkening days.

The Klonopin didn't help. In fact, it made things worse. I had days where I was working on less than three hours of sleep because of the anxiety and deepening depression. It became difficult for me to do my job as my mind was all over the place. It seemed like I couldn't focus for more than ten seconds at a time at work. My X's brother and girlfriend were very understanding about where I was coming from and what I was expressing to them during this time. They both thought that it was just a phase and that she'd snap out of it. They believed we'd be able to get through this ordeal and move on to greater and happier times.

During this time, I visited a handful of my crew from my time grow-ing up in Cranford and living on Brielle Road. Two of them were in Point Pleasant, and another was living up in Randolph with his wife. I just needed people I'd been close with my entire life to hear me out and talk things through over a few beers. I needed them to tell me things were going to be OK and that I wasn't crazy. They all knew how much I loved and cared for this woman.

The band had a few gigs that were, well, shitty and at shitty estab-lishments. This made things worse. Bad acoustics, a small number of uninterested clientele, and low energy performances since I was not in the best frame of mind and neither was Brendan whose drug and alcohol consumption made him indifferent and uninspiring to be around. It hurt. I actually told my brother one night that I could just quit everything, never play guitar again, and move to Bumblefuck, Anywhere to start over, because that's how I felt when it came to playing music. I blamed the dissolution of my relationship on my time pursuing the one passion that made me feel completely alive, and in my heart, I knew what I was supposed to do with my life.

I wrote my X two letters. I left them in her car after she went to bed for her to read the next morning at work. Unfortunately, since I'd never been in this situation before, my strategy was not effective. At the time, I believed them to be from the heart however my choice of words and the phrases I used came from a place of bargaining, control, fear, and masculine logic and rationale. I was going through the Kubler Ross stages of grief. We used to leave each other cards celebrating how long we had been together. It didn't matter the specific milestone. They would be random months. It was a nice little surprise to get a card out of the blue and to know we were always on each other's minds. The last card was two days before things went south, 110 months.

To keep my mind from getting into too many dark places, I went down to Barnes and Noble and picked up a handful of books that I thought would be helpful in reducing my stress and anxiety and understanding things about relationships from the other gender's point of view. One was a stress and anxiety workbook with different mental and breathing exercises. The other was a *Men are From Mars, Women are From Venus* series about men and women's viewpoints regarding relationships. I wish I had read the book years ago. It was such an eye opener. It really illuminated the analytical and logical focus of the man and the emotional and creative focus of the woman. The book title and gist of the message didn't lie: men and women are from two different planets!

I was able to recover the security deposit from the wedding reception room. Our homestead refund check came within the next couple of days. I used the money to buy the Mac Book Pro that I used to write the book you are currently reading, obviously not knowing I would ever write this. The sole purpose for the computer was to eventually get back into creating and recording music through software.

~~~

I was over at my brother's house visiting one day and his mother-in-law was there helping out with their little ones. She knew what I was going through and she could sense my stress and anxiety just from being in close proximity to me. She recommended I try yoga and added, "It helps calm the monkey mind." If there was anything I needed help with it was exactly that, calming my monkey mind. My thoughts were all over the place and I was becoming a walking wreck and shell of myself. Every waking second was torturous. My mind was a maelstrom of fear, hopelessness, doubt, and low self-worth. Any negative scenario and emotion you could imagine attacked my body, emotions, psyche, and spirit. It felt like a living nightmare that I would never wake from. I knew very little about the practice but would try anything to get in a better headspace since nothing else seemed to be working, not even doing the one thing I loved the most, playing the guitar.

I went to an intermediate to advanced Vinyasa class held at the Atlantic Club. It was at 11AM on a Tuesday and must have been the first or second week of November. The instructor was an older lady and asked at the beginning of the class if this was anyone's first time doing yoga. I raised my hand, being the only 30-something male in a class full of retirees and stay-at-home moms. The instructor warned that the class wasn't for beginners and asked me if I knew anything about yoga. I said, "I know how to breathe." The entire class laughed, but the instructor did not seem amused. I did a lot of "watch-asana" (looking at other people doing their poses as I didn't know any yoga pose) and kept up as best I could.

The time slot was tough to attend so I decided to try a different instructor in the afternoon. I figured it would be beneficial after a day of work and help to rebalance and re-center myself. I needed to find something healthy to stick to and develop a solid schedule that would keep the worsening depression from taking over my life as it had in college. The instructor was a woman in her early 40s who appeared much more youthful and radiant than someone her age. Her name was Carrie Kecmer-Godesky and she'd been teaching yoga for close to a decade. I liked her vibe and free-spirited approach to teaching and decided I would start attending to her class on Tuesdays and Thursdays. In addition to my regular visits to the psychiatrist, I decided I needed more help and found a local psychologist for additional talk therapy that had no focus on medication.

About a week before Thanksgiving, after one of Carrie's classes, I caught up with her on her way out of the building. Besides calling poses in her class, she drops yoga philosophy knowledge and how it relates to the physical practice as well as other soul-soothing stories. She used the phrase being present and working on reducing the mindless internal dialogue or "citta." This is known as the warehouse of the subconscious mind, where all thoughts, memories, information, and so on floats around. Recently, my internal dialogue was completely negative and full of doubt, fear, and hopelessness. I asked her if she had any tips or pointers to help calm and center my mind as it was all over the place. I gave her a brief description of what I was going through which she kind of already knew given her keen intuition. She recommended Eckardt Tolle's book *The Power of Now* and explained that she had read it numerous times and that it had helped her tremendously. I thanked her for her time and after dinner, ran to Barnes and Noble to pick up the book. I began reading it that night and kept it on my nightstand and read a chapter or two every night before bed.

Thanksgiving came and, per family tradition, I went up to my aunt's house in Ridgefield Park to see the extended family, overeat, and fall asleep watching the Cowboys and Lions. I brought my new book and read it on the way up as well as sneaking to a quiet corner of the house for a few pages here and there.

When faced with the sharpest of pains, one draws much needed inspiration for creative endeavors. My free time at night before reading was dedicated to writing music, much like I had when I was younger. You can't really force the songwriting process. It needs to just happen in the moment. And it did. Melodies and song lyrics started coming to me while outside on the front deck smoking a cigarette and gazing at the stars in the cold November night. I kept my focus and was soon putting the melodies, song lyrics, and chord changes in my music staff book. It was both cathartic and bittersweet. The first through-composed song that popped was titled "Drink These Tears Away." It was written with a little tongue-in-cheek flavor al la Merle Haggard or Willie Nelson with the basis of had I never learned to play the guitar; I wouldn't be in the mess I am now. At this point, I blamed playing music so much on her leaving and the psychological effect was amplified by carrying that around in my head and heart.

We began reviewing our options with the house. After countless phone calls to the bank that held our mortgage and a couple of lawyers, the only recommendations we received was to sell the house. Short sale was another option, but her brother and I didn't want a black flag on our credit reports for however many years. We instead began splitting the mortgage payments in half and it started to strain our bank accounts and spirits.

I booked a trip to Las Vegas to get out of Dodge in early December. My fraternity brother Ernie moved out of the San Francisco area and started working for a high-end steak house a couple of blocks off the strip. We caught up like old times and I ended up finishing second in a Texas Hold 'Em tournament at one of the casinos. I still had it. It was the wrong trip for me to take at the time. I was in low spirits and Ernie did his best to cheer me up, but again, I was just not myself.

Christmas season came and along with it, memories of past Christmas' spending time with my X and waking up in her bed at her parents' house. I was completely miserable, alone, and depressed. I went for a walk with my mother for a much needed mother-son talk. It was uplifting but I still found times where I was crying uncontrollably on her shoulder as the pain in my heart grew and grew. By this time, my energy was low and I had a black cloud following me around. I went over to my brother's to see my nephew and he didn't want to be anywhere near me. I couldn't blame him. Kids have a sixth sense when it comes to sensing energy and my nephew was right on the money.

New Year's signaled my obligatory attendance of as many Phish shows at the Garden as I could manage. It was necessary. If anything was going to lift my spirits it was dancing, singing and drinking, with my good friends and the extended Phish phamily community. They opened the first show with "Free" and I caught a tiny flash of seeing the positive in my current situation.

In February, my X moved out of the house. I had no idea where she was headed or who she'd be living with. I didn't ask any questions. The less I thought about it the easier the whole process would be. Her stepdad was there helping her and most likely to ensure that I would not get in her way or give her a hard time. All I ever wanted was for her to be happy and if she couldn't be happy with me I wasn't going to stop her. Before she left I gave her a hug in the driveway. When I went back inside she had left every photo of us ever taken on the floor in my office. She had taken every single one out of a couple of volumes of photo books. That was another nail in my heart and I looked through the photos with tears in my eyes. The dogs were gone too. I named Bowie and practically raised and took care of him while she was busy with school and work. Anyone who's ever met me knows how much I love animals, especially dogs. With that, more things I loved vanished from my life.

The appointments with my psychiatrist were still scheduled; however, I stopped seeing the psychologist as we had gotten to a point where there was nothing else she could help me with. One day I was sitting on the bed in the master bedroom. I wasn't doing anything except listening to my heart beating in my chest and feeling the continued surge of emotional, psychological, and spiritual pain coursing through my body. All I could think about was the classic expression of dying of a broken heart. It would've been poetic justice. So I focused to see if it was possible and sure enough, my heart started beating erratically like I'd never felt before. It was as if my soul felt I had enough pain in this life and if I chose to exit in that fashion I was free to do so. I freaked out, started deep breathing exercises, and realized that the mind and body have a much deeper and profound connection to the soul.

A couple of days later I found myself with the worst case of stomach flu I had ever experienced. It seemed waste was exiting my body from both ends by the gallons at an uncontrollable rate. My X's brother was spending a few nights a week out of the house over at his girlfriend's place, so it was just me and the walls. I was so drained from bout after bout of it coming out of both ends I collapsed in a motionless puddle on the floor in the master bedroom for about half an hour. Aches, pains, and chills were pulsing in and on every square inch of my body. I couldn't feel any worse at that point. I eventually picked myself up and went on a steady diet of Saltine crackers, chicken broth, and ginger ale for a couple of days. That night I drew a bath and just sat in the tub soaking until I got too pruney to lie there anymore.

By this point, Brendan's addiction to contraband and alcohol had gotten to be the worst any of us had ever seen. His Brophyaoke nights turned into a drunken spectacle (although, miraculously, he never sang or played poorly) and he even started speaking a fictitious language that had an Eastern European or Slavic tinge to it. It scared, stunned, and perplexed the people around him. One day, up at Lou's for band rehearsal, he hit his peak and we knew decisive action was necessary. He had no focus or drive to rehearse, had been drinking coffee spiked with whiskey on the ride up, most likely did a "zanny bar" (multiple pills of Xanax) the night before while drinking, and God only knows what else. He wanted to smoke grass before rehearsal and Lou said there was none to smoke. Brendan became angry, irritated, and would not consider rehearsing before getting high. None of us were able to talk any sense into him. As he became more and more irate, I made eye contact with Lou and my brother that glared code red. As my brother distracted him, I grabbed Lou and went into another room. It was decided that he needed an emergency intervention. Lou secretly called Brendan's sister and she got the ball rolling and contacted their family. Lou received a text back with a plan of attack. It was to get him over to his mother and stepfather's house in Westfield where most of his immediate family would be waiting. It was decided that my brother and I would wait at Lou's while he and Brendan drove to Newark to pick up a bag of pot. Lou got him in his car and took him directly to where his family was waiting.

Since that day, Brendan has been attending and running recovery meetings on a regular basis, been a sponsor to those in need, and has not had a drop of booze or any illicit substances in his body. The emergency plan worked and easily saved his life. If he had continued down that path it surely wouldn't have ended well.

The band had a night off on the second weekend in March, and Hal had an extra ticket for one of Levon Helms' Midnight Rambles up at his barn/house/studio in Woodstock, New York. Quinn's old roommate lived up there and had known members of the Band since the late 90s when he was a teenager. We made plans to eventually meet up after the ramble. This wasn't any old ramble. Mumford and Sons were opening with a set before Levon's band came on and members of Mumford and Sons would be sitting in throughout the evening. The barn held about 260 people and a majority of the seats were folding chairs. There wasn't a bad seat in the house since the entire stage area was viewable from any seat. Levon's was a dream venue. It was full of beautiful old wood, a spacious staging area, and great people who all loved amazing music. The entire show was spectacular and easily ranked in the top ten shows I'd ever seen, given the unique and intimate setting of the event. Levon closed the show playing drums and singing "The Weight". Due to health complications, this would be the last song Levon sang for an audience. He passed away about five weeks later.

After the Ramble, Hal and I met up with Quinn's old roommate at the local watering hole in town. They called last call well past 2:30AM in that town so we were there for a while. I noticed a tall beautiful blonde hanging out with her friend at the bar and started rapping with her. She had an Eastern European accent and we spoke about our heritage. She was of Czech and Slovak descent, which I loved given my paternal ancestral line. Turns out she was friends with Quinn's old roommate and had lived down the shore for a brief stint doing landscaping. I'm sure I had met her on the beach in Manasquan a few years prior. We talked for a while and I got her cell number. Over the course of the next week we texted constantly and I eventually made my way out to her place in Queens where she cooked me dinner. I ended up staying the night and got up early enough to run to the local florist and leave her flowers before she came back for her lunch break. She worked in the office of a construction company but was a brilliant artist and interior designer. Over the course of the next couple of weeks we kept texting and flirting. I went out there a handful of times but it was too much for her. At this point, being six months out of a long-term relationship, I didn't understand the concept of space. She communicated that very clearly as well as the fact she wasn't looking for a committed relationship. Neither was I, but my emotions and mind were still all over the place so I failed to properly communicate and discuss any potential future rules of engagement. It was an easy lesson to learn.

Near the end of March we played at an annual benefit for childhood heart disease. People were getting down and having a blast. One guy, who must've easily weighed over 300 pounds, did a back flip on the dance floor! I'd never seen anything like it before. I had my eye on one particular stunner the entire night. After the charity event, everyone went back to the Manasquan Beach House. When we got there, I went right up to this girl and we started talking. By the end of the night, I had gotten her number and a nice kiss before heading home. We started texting on a regular basis, which led to us going on a few dates. I felt ready and emotionally stable enough to begin dating and becoming intimate with another woman so I went with the flow.

My X's brother and I decided that it would be impossible for us to keep up our mortgage payments with just the two of us paying, so we decided that the best option would be to rent out the house. We would cover the difference to make our number every month while we figured out an end game to our financial problem. We enlisted the same real estate agent who sold us the house and settled on two couples moving in on April 1st. It all happened so quickly but we were desperate since we didn't have the cash flow to handle the payments. We decided on the two couples because one was a lawyer, but there were also four sources of income so we didn't have to worry about if the rent check was going to clear.

I had no idea where I was going to live. The safe bet was to move back home with my folks, but my brother easily persuaded me otherwise since I played in the area so often. I couldn't think of living anywhere but the area between Brielle and Spring Lake Heights. Quinn had recently broken up with his girlfriend of five years and moved into a basement apartment of a suburban home in the Wall section of Sea Girt. I had known the owner, Andy, from when he worked at O'Neill's as a bartender while Brendan and I played there for happy hour back in the day. Quinn had mentioned there may be an open room in his house and gave me Andy's number and a recommendation. I met Andy for dinner one night, explained my dire situation, and he said that if his other roommate and good friend (who was a foot doctor and kept an early schedule) was cool after meeting me, I could move in. The doctor and I hit it off (a huge Allman Brothers and Warren Haynes fan) and Andy was cool with me moving in on April 1st.

Meanwhile, my X's brother and I had to move everything out of our house. We left no nook unchecked and I let him have whatever furniture he needed. It was a lot of stuff and a completely daunting endeavor, but we eventually pulled through. Next thing I know I'm a landlord renting a room in a suburban house with three other bachelors. I had to share a bathroom with two other guys and had the smallest bedroom in the house. I was in a new phase and chapter of my life so it was either adapt quickly or don't. There was a good flow in the house. Rarely did I have to wait to jump in the shower and everyone had their own schedule, so we stayed out of each other's way. My rent included all utilities so it was a nice clean check every month to my landlord.

With my truck being paid off and finally being free of credit card debt, I had extra funds so I opened a brokerage account and tried to put my knowledge of the markets and investing to good use.

I still popped in from time to time at our weekly poker game up in Cranford. It had moved to a different location across town. I was up there one night talking to a friend before the game got going. He knew of my recent run of bad luck and asked how I was doing. I had a short pause before replying, "I'm searching for enlightenment." He found it a little humorous but understood exactly where I was coming from. To be honest, I don't think I knew what it meant but having spoken those words undoubtedly started a spark in my soul and planted a seed in my subconscious mind.

～～

On May 7th, my brother and his wife welcomed their second boy into the family. Christian Eli (named after myself and his wife's sister) was born healthy and happy. Jack couldn't have been more excited to have a baby brother to play with. The scene at the hospital was pretty much exactly as it was when Jack was born, with all the close family members in attendance, sans my X.

The house that I rented a room in was situated close to local eateries, the grocery store, and my gym, and was within biking distance to local indoor and outdoor bars as well as beaches. It felt like I was retired. I was getting my work done late at night and early in the morning when I could, and had time during the day for other activities. In addition to yoga two or three times a week, and returning to my regular gym routine, I started to modify my diet.

The rest of the summer was filled with different activities to keep me focused on not falling back into a deep funk over what had transpired nine months ago. I purchased a beautiful ukulele that was shipped from Hawaii, played a round of golf for the first time at Manasquan River Golf Club, caught a God Street Wine reunion show at the Grammercy Theatre where I met up with my old band mate Josh, and played a hippie wedding for fans of our band and friends of Cranford folk out at the Westhampton Country Club on Long Island. The bride and groom wanted to walk out to Kenny Loggins' "Highway to the Danger Zone" al la Top Gun while approaching the priest for the ceremony, which took place on the 18th hole of the golf course. We set up all our gear outside on a gorgeous late summer day and played the cover with gusto and smiles on our faces while holding back laughter at the absurdity of it all.

Things seemed to be going back to some sense of balance and normalcy. I found myself alone on the Sea Girt beach in early October for a surprise spectacular weather day in the upper 80s. It was soul soothing, serene, and reminded me of how fortunate I was to be able to live where I did and doing what I was doing.

The Saturday of Halloween weekend the band played at Manasquan Beach House, and in customary fashion we picked a theme and threw on some costumes for the show. This year, we decided on Daniel Larusso and three Cobra Kai from *The Karate Kid*. I was Daniel and performed the crane technique for most of the night. The weather forecasters had been predicting a direct hit for the tri-state area from a recently named hurricane Sandy. The information and forecast changed every few hours given the wind and the strength of the cell; however, by Sunday morning it looked like a major destructive storm was imminent and was going to touch down and wreak havoc over a large part of New Jersey.

I decided to pack up some stuff, head up to Cranford to be with my parents, and ride it out until any potential chaos had subsided. I figured there'd be more damage at the shoreline with stronger gusts of wind than up in the northern section of the state. I stopped in at my girlfriend's apartment that afternoon and asked if she wanted to come up with me. She declined. I wished her good luck and would be in touch. I then drove down to the closest beach and headed up to the waterline for a quick glance at the beginning of what Mother Nature had in store for us. The wind was howling, the ocean was churning with water foaming up on the sand, and the waves looked like a violent washing machine spin cycle. It was just awesome.

The storm raged on and by the next morning all hell had broken loose. Every conceivable outcome of what a super-storm powered by the right ingredients could do occurred in the tri-state area. Gigantic trees were uprooted, power lines came down, and cars, houses, and roads were destroyed. It was bedlam. My folks' house had no power but we had gas and running water so my mom was still able to cook. I went out to get a few bags of ice (which at the time was still available at some spots) to save anything that could be spoiled in the fridge. I had to work but my work laptop only held a charge for about four hours. I had a power adapter for the cigarette lighter in my truck, so every other hour I would run the engine and charge my laptop for about 20 minutes and did what I needed to get done so I wouldn't fall behind.

I called my tenants to see how they fared and one of them said that they had all stayed with friends and family the night before as that area of Ocean County was under a state mandated evacuation. He said he was going over to the house later to check on everything. He texted me horrifying pictures a few hours later of the outside property and interior of the house. One photo showed the entire street still under water including a truck in the driveway with water up to the middle of the door as well as over the top step of the front deck. Inside, the water line measured approximately 12 to 14 inches on the wall. This meant there was over a foot of water in my first floor. The line in the garage was even higher. All major appliances were destroyed including the heating and air conditioning system and hot water heater.

The tenant who was a lawyer called and told me that they were breaking their lease since the house was unsuitable to live in. She cited the legal rights of landlords and tenants and I was in no position to have them pay rent while they weren't living on the premises. I wasn't a scumbag landlord and figured I'd be able to negotiate some type of hardship forbearance with the bank while the house was being restored.

Working in the insurance industry for so long, I immediately filed claims with the flood and homeowner insurance carriers. A few of my friends rented a house in Garwood and didn't lose any power. I headed over there to re-charge my laptop, work, and contact Bank of America, the bank that held the note on our mortgage. I explained my situation with the storm and my tenants breaking the lease. I told a very pleasant woman on a recorded line that the property would be uninhabitable until it was restored. She looked up my payment history and told me that my mortgage had been paid on time since we bought the house and was positive that I would qualify for some type of forbearance. I then looked up information regarding FEMA assistance and submitted an online questionnaire/application for whatever I could qualify for. In my head, I told myself I was doing everything I could to get this disaster indemnified without going into foreclosure, declaring bankruptcy, or losing the property and damaging my credit with a short sale.

The power was out at my parent's house for nine days, which is how long I stayed up in Cranford before heading back to Andy's house. I continued the barrage of contact with insurance claims departments and the bank, trying to do what needed to be done as expeditiously as possible. I pretty much set up camp on a daily basis over at my friends' house in Garwood to do my work. I reached out to my girlfriend to see how she was making out and she was furious that I didn't call her sooner. She was holed up in the upstairs apartment of the restaurant with the family that owned and ran the Union Landing. She had never seen the water come up so high before and said that that section of Brielle resembled an extension of the Manasquan River. People were taking canoes and rowboats around the neighborhood, as the town was completely underwater.

By every possible description, hurricane Sandy was the finest example of a super storm. There were four factors that made it so incredibly destructive. I called it a quadruple witching. There was the path and strength of the storm with the added ingredients of a Nor'easter system to the north, a tidal surge due to the full moon, and the timing of the storm hitting the area at high tide. It was just a fucking monster. There was relatively little damage save a fallen tree in my parents' backyard. We took it apart the old-fashioned way with saws, grit, sweat, and muscle. My dad could've easily borrowed a neighbor's chainsaw but we didn't have much else to do that day.

Over the course of the next few weeks I managed to procure a full-service general contracting company (at the referral of my brother and his wife since they were using the same company at their property on 3rd Avenue in Manasquan) that was capable of cleaning, renovating, and rebuilding all that was necessary to get to a place of complete indemnity or to at least make it seem like the storm never landed. It took a couple of weeks for the claims adjuster to come out for the inspection and I wasn't quite sure how much reimbursement we were going to receive from the flood carrier. It was determined that given the age of the original construction of the structure (1966) and the current flood map that was used for the area (1972), our house was grandfathered in. We had "old school" coverage. The entire loss was covered! That was such good news as there was no reimbursement per covered losses in terms of our homeowner's policy. I was still in contact with Bank of America trying to get a hardship forbearance approved. Even if they were able to flip a switch and just let us pay interest on a monthly basis, it would've been an acceptable outcome.

By Thanksgiving, things with my current girlfriend fizzled out. A major catalyst was being MIA up in Cranford while she was dealing with a traumatic experience on the shore. The issue of the "L" word (love) came up as well, but that will be discussed in future chapters. She decided it was time to move on, but I didn't see what the big deal was. This break was much easier than the previous one and I was glad it didn't have a negative effect on my emotions, body, and mind.

I found my way back to Eckhart Tolle's book *The Power of Now* for a second reading. Like listening to music, my brain picked up on things that I didn't notice the first time around. Of course, the first time I read it my mind was all over the map and shot to shit.

By December, the contractor had pretty much gutted the first floor, ripped up the floors, and cut out the sheet rock on the walls about two to three feet above the water line. You could see from one side of the interior all the way to the other side of the house. The bare beams gave it a skeletal look but there was progress and I was impressed at how quickly the contractor had coordinated the work schedule. By this time, we were only two months behind on the mortgage payment; however, since the Bank of America rep advised us not to pay the mortgage until we were approved for assistance, I was getting a little weary that something bad was going to happen.

It wouldn't be New Year's without catching a Phish show at the

Garden, so I hit up the December 29th show to blow off some much needed steam and to embark on some soul healing.

Our parents' good friend's son, who my brother and I had known practically our whole life, inquired about having us up to Killington, Vermont to play a house party at his rental down the road from the mountain. We explained that in order for us to make it worthwhile, we'd have to get at least two gigs at a local bar or club to justify the trip. I emailed the owner of the Pickle Barrel, who also owned JAX and The Foundry as a shot in the dark, and he replied to my solicitation. Next thing I know I'm on the phone with him for 20 minutes and he explained how he had booked Phish in his places back in the late 80s and early 90s. He had a long history with the New England music scene under his belt and we hit it off instantly. He was able to move some people around to accommodate our trip up. We now had a long weekend with gigs at the Foundry as well as The Sugarshack, the famed ski house with a storied history and an impressive list of party people who had once stayed there.

The trip to Killington was a success. We packed everything we needed in my truck and Lou's. The people and clientele at the Foundry dug our acoustic and electric sets, and we played until almost 3AM at the house party with people dancing and playing beer bong all night long. We even got some snow tubing in as we didn't have any room to pack our skis but vowed to eventually make it up again for a little vacation and gig action in the future.

Over the holidays, a good friend of our band mentioned that he was traveling down to St. Thomas to see a mutual friend of ours, Mike. I explained that I had a flexible schedule and plenty of vacation days to burn and asked if it would be cool to meet him down there. He agreed so I contacted Mike and he was excited for the added company. I was craving tropical weather and caught a flight during the last week of January. My friend took a different airline and we arrived separately, but Mike was there with local drinks in hand for both of us before we headed to the far side of the island.

Mike moved to St. Thomas for about six months. He was always on the move, never staying in one place for too long. He worked as a bartender at one of the nicest restaurants on the island and was a zip line tour guide/instructor for a park that had recently opened. He lived with a fellow who surfed and worked for a zip line company tasked with opening parks all over the world. They lived high on the hills on the back of the island in a rental home with a cistern and back patio that overlooked Magens Bay. We dropped off our stuff and headed down to the Hull Bay Hideaway beach bar for a bite to eat. An amazing band from South Carolina was playing. They were doing old Bob Marley (pre-Wailers from the 60s) as well as other rock-steady reggae and covers by the likes of Warren Zevon and the Allman Brothers. We took in the show and headed back to the house to chill out on the back deck in hammocks and listen to tunes.

I didn't take any scheduled vacation days from work, apart from the days I travelled there and back, as I was experimenting with getting my assigned work done throughout the day while down in the tropics. I brought my work laptop with me, logged in, and stayed on top of everything, including responding to emails, throughout the course of the trip. No one knew I was gone since all I needed was an Internet connection to connect to the secure server at work. That evening we all chilled, listened to tunes, and shot the shit for a few hours before turning in.

The following morning I was up early working out on the back deck and taking in the beautiful view before we headed out for breakfast and then Magens Bay for some sun and paddle boarding. I'd never paddle boarded before but was standing up, learning how to maneuver, and turn in no time with minimal falls. It was like walking on water. After lunch and some R&R, we cruised around the back of the island before heading to Hull Bay for a surf session. I hadn't been on a board in about ten years but I had no reservations about paddling out with Mike's roommate and my bud. The paddle out to the break was between a half and three quarters of a mile from the shore and it took me a good 20 minutes to get out there. My bud and Mike's roommate were surfing in no time and by the time I got situated in the line-up; the waves were coming overhead with steady frequency. A handful of locals joined us and by that time I was winded and didn't want to get in anyone's way or get hurt (there was a coral reef where the waves were crashing) and decided to head back in without getting in any solid practice on the board.

We decided to tour St. John the following day and took Mike's truck on a ferry across Red Hook Bay to Cruz Bay. That morning, after getting my work done and before heading out to the port, I witnessed one of the most beautiful sights I had ever seen. It was a perfect rainbow terminating in Magens Bay. I didn't have to look too hard to see a second one (double rainbow) around it either. I snapped a handful of pictures from my phone and took it as a sign that I was right where I was supposed to be.

After landing at the port in Cruz Bay, Mike met a local looking to potentially buy his truck and we grabbed lunch before heading over to Maho Bay for some paddle boarding (Mike brought his), snorkeling, sun, and beers on the white sands. As we were driving on the high pass overlooking Cinnamon Bay, Mike's eyes lit up at one of the yachts that were moored about a mile from the shoreline. It was the biggest boat in the bay and he kept that visual in the back of his mind.

When our day at Maho Bay was over, we hopped on Route 10 passing Coral Bay off to our pre-destined location at Concordia Eco-Resort on the east end of the island. The place was a total hippie-like community and reminded me of the tree village of the Ewoks from *Return of the Jedi*. Our little bungalow had four beds, a mini-fridge, range, sink, and a little back deck that overlooked Drunk Bay and the Ram Head Trail. The toilet and running water for the shower were outside our door and reminded me of an outdoor shower at a beach crash pad in Manasquan. The amenities were minimal but we were there just to be there.

Long story short, we ended up on the biggest yacht moored in Cinnamon Bay, partying with the crew we had met at Skinny Legs on our first night in St. John. We slept in Mike's truck at the plantation ruins because we missed the ferry back to St. Thomas. We went zip lining at the park where Mike and his roommate worked before having a final dinner at Mike's restaurant.

The owner of the clubs up in Killington dug what we did and stayed in touch. We booked three nights up at the mountain, one at the famous Pickle Barrel, with a total of four or five gigs including acoustic work. I had vacation days to burn so I decided to take the entire week off before our birthday and get some skiing in since the conditions looked superb. Our mom's cousin owned a condo right across the road from the main gate (Ramshead) and I coordinated with him in procuring the band's stay there and my early arrival. I packed as much musical equipment as my truck could hold with the inclusion of ski gear, beer, and snacks, and hopped on the road that Monday morning. I planned on getting a four out of five day ski pass for the week and enjoy the most of my alone time before the rest of the guys and Lou's wife came up that Thursday.

The next morning I suited up and headed off towards the mountain. I skied all day, working my way up from the green trails to the blues and covered a wide swath of the area. The next two days were pretty much the same. I had dinner at the Foundry every night and made it over to Jax for some live acoustic music and billiards with the locals. We played The Pickle Barrel on Thursday night to a mostly hippie ski and snow-boarding audience. I got some skiing in with my brother over the next two days, followed by an acoustic happy hour set and live electric sets at the Foundry. Saturday was our 36th birthdays and Lou's wife brought a birthday cake up for the occasion.

I bought a new banjo as an early birthday gift and had a Piezo pickup installed so it could be plugged in and amplified. I settled in with a banjo instructional book once we returned from Vermont and started going through the lessons every night with a couple of beers, followed by my nightly ritual of milk and cookies before bed. I slowly developed my picking, rolls, and alternate tunings.

～～

The band decided it was time to record a legitimate first album. Over the course of the eight years since Brendan had joined us, we had worked up about 11 or 12 original songs primarily based off of his chord changes and lyrics. At the end of February, we began scheduling blocks of studio time with Les, whom I was still producing my album with. We had two or three sessions to focus on three or four songs at a time to get the drums and bass tracking down before going back in and overdubbing guitars, a banjo track, vocals, and keyboards.

In early April I decided that it was once again time to get the fuck out of dodge and decided to visit our old drummer Barry who had been living in California for about a decade doing graphic design and perfecting his golf game and surfing style. I was fortunate enough to work for a company that provided me with a lot of vacation days. By this time, most of my close friends had settled down, started families, or didn't have the resources and freedom that I had to join me on my out of town excursions, so I decided I'd be rolling solo and make the best of my current situation.

I got word that one of the first guitar players I jammed with in eighth or ninth grade was having his band's record release party in San Diego, so I reached out to him and incorporated that into my travel plans. I flew into San Diego, rented a new Jeep convertible, and checked into the Lafayette Hotel in the North Park section of the city a few blocks from the San Diego Zoo.

The following morning I packed up the Jeep, and headed north on the I5 to get to Barry's place in Dana Point. My friend wasn't able to get together and jam, so I hit the road earlier than expected. I got to Barry's, dropped off my stuff, and we headed to Laguna Beach for some lunch, had a little downtime, and then played nine holes at a local golf course. That evening we went to his friend's house in San Clemente for dinner and drinks before calling it a night.

The next day we visited the local beach where he and his friends surfed, cruised into San Clemente, hit up the original Stewarts Surf Shop, and saw the Rainbow Sandal factory (a summer footwear institution of mine). We also grabbed dinner and drinks with a couple of Barry's friends at a swanky restaurant down at the Dana Point Harbor. Barry had a bunch of friends that he used to jam with on occasion and it was decided that we'd all get together at their rehearsal spot that evening for a session.

Barry was pretty much out of the music scene so we had to go to a storage unit to pick up his kit. That night I met a bunch of great guys and solid musicians. There were guitars, basses, percussion, keyboards, and many of the guys traded off instruments whenever they felt like it. We had beer and a hunger to just jam and let it all hang out. We did a handful of Dead covers and a lot of improvisational grooves that I wish had been recorded.

The next morning Barry and I grabbed breakfast and I was off to Santa Barbara. I found a friend of friends from high school that I'd known back in the day who lived up there and reached out to her via Facebook. She was up for grabbing a few drinks and shooting the shit. I always wanted to drive a long stretch of the Pacific Coast Highway and I'd never been to Santa Barbara so I was pumped for the excursion.

On my way up the 405 I swung through Torrance where a business vendor and friend of my father's shop was. I paid him and his wife a visit and shot the shit for an hour before they sent me on my way with a little care package of snacks. I connected with highway 101 past Beverly Hills and eventually made it to Santa Barbara, marveling at the views and scenery. After checking into my beautifully overpriced hotel on Cabrillo Boulevard, I headed down to a café near the harbor and met up with my friend for some light seafood fare and drinks. We then went to a sports bar in town for more beers and shot some darts while taking over the digital jukebox.

My plan was to take a nap and head up State Street to the local brewery, grab a late bite to eat, and drink my face off. My nap turned into four hours and the next thing I know I was up and wired around the time they called last call and only had three beers in my fridge. I laughed it off, cracked a beer, and went outside to have a smoke. Halfway through my smoke, a guy in his early 20s came outside with a girl and we started talking. I explained my evening to them and they invited me into their room since they were partying the entire night. Once inside, I met six blokes from England who were all in their early 20s and three women from Iceland about the same age. We ended up drinking and laughing until the wee hours of the morning.

In the morning, I made my way back down to San Diego, checked back into the same hotel I stayed at a few days ago, and grabbed a nap before preparing for dinner at the hotel bar. I then hit a few of the local bars in the North Park section of the city, walking everywhere. I caught a couple of pretty unique live music acts as well as a DJ spinning old 60s groove jazz guitar tracks including one of my favorites, Grant Green. I tied it on pretty good and went to bed with a smile on my face.

The work on my solo album had been coming along. By now, I had all of the drums, bass, rhythm guitar, guitar solos, and keyboard tracks laid down. I had always envisioned most of these songs with a higher level of production. I loved how Becker and Fagen of Steely Dan had spiced up their tracks with horns, so I asked the musical whiz Bryan Beninghove, who Les had recommended to us when we needed a sax player for a wedding, if he was interested in charting parts for sax and trumpet. He was available and we started with three tracks. I loved how well his writing complemented everything, including the feel and identity of each track, so I eventually asked him to write for three more songs.

While the work on our house was still going on, I began receiving foreclosure notifications from the bank, as the mortgage had not been paid since the previous October. The hardship assistance I had sought was never granted and the bank's only other options were foreclosure, declaring bankruptcy, or a short sale. Those were not viable options for me. I wrote the local assemblyman as well as a state senator explaining my situation. I received correspondence from their offices sating that they had contacted the bank requesting any available leniency for my situation and received no favor or mercy. The only other option was to come up with six or seven months of back mortgage payments. I ended up liquidating my brokerage account and borrowed money from my brother and parents. My X's brother was not in a position to find additional capital, so I started a tab with no interest for him to pay me back half of what was laid out to the bank.

By mid-May, I started working on writing guitar solos and working up other parts for the enjoy! album. My folks went on vacation and left me with Belle, our family's eight-year-old Golden Retriever. She was very mild mannered and exuded love from every ounce of her being. She got along great with Quinn's dog and our other roommates' dog whenever he brought him around. Unfortunately, they had to put her to sleep less than two weeks later. She had a gigantic cancerous tumor growing inside her and the best and most humane option was to not operate. This would be the third time that I was unable to be by the side of a family Golden when they passed. I looked at the brighter side of the story and was glad that she had spent some of her final days with me at the shore. I even got to take her to the Manasquan dog beach where she played like a pup and retrieved the ball I repeatedly tossed in the water.

A week before Memorial Day the band played the post-Sandy re-opening party at the Osprey Night Club. The band's gig-packed summer schedule kicked off and in my free time during the week, if it didn't rain and was in the 70s, I'd hop on the bike after smoking a bowl, throw the ear buds in, and listen to the Bob Marley or the Meters Pandora station while heading to a local outdoor bar to catch up with the locals and watch a Yankees game. I loved paddle boarding in St. Thomas so much that I bought my own board and started taking it out in the Glimmer Glass in Manasquan whenever the sun was out and the wind was low. I started keeping a regular schedule with my physical activities of getting to the gym in the morning for the stepper and weights, paddle boarding before lunch, yoga before dinner, and hopping on the bike for a few beers at night. Unlike my brother who had a wife and kids, I didn't have the same attachments and had not met anyone who was worth pursuing for a traditional relationship, so I kept myself occupied with these activities, as well as writing and working on the songs for both my solo album and the enjoy! album.

〜〜

One of Lou and Brendan's best friends was getting married in Ireland and they were invited to the wedding, leaving us without gigs while they were across the pond. The future groom's sister dated Quinn for about five years and we'd known her since high school. I'd never been to Ireland before and being out there with a big group of people I went to high school with seemed like an adventure. One night on a break at a gig, the future groom was hanging out and I asked if I could come to the wedding if there was an open spot. Yes, I invited myself to a wedding. Without much hesitation he said if I could get there I was more than welcome to come. That's all I needed to hear to get the ball rolling with planning my trip.

The plane touched down at Shannon Airport early in the morning. There was a handful of people from Cranford, including a family that lived a few blocks from where I grew up, on the same flight and I managed to hitch a ride in their rental van to our first stop, Kinvarra, a sleepy town on the western coast about an hour or so north. I checked into my room and crashed for a few hours to assist with the jet lag. After showering, I hitched a ride to the hotel in Gort where a majority of the other wedding guests were staying. Everyone met up there for food and drinks. A couple of musicians were playing Irish standards and everyone was having a ball.

The wedding ceremony was the following day. It was held at a beautiful vacuous church in downtown Gort that was built in the 1830s. After the ceremony, all the guests were shuttled to Lough Cutra Castle not too far south of downtown. The cocktail hour was held in the castle and guests were allowed in most parts of the structure. The actual reception was held in a huge circus-like tent about 75 yards from the castle and in closer proximity to the immense lake that was also owned by the family.

There really was no set time for the duration of the reception. Guests arrived at about 5PM and I took the last shuttle back to Kinvarra at around 2:30AM or so. The time between was spent talking with friends, flirting with the bride's Irish friends, dancing, and drinking my face off. Since I didn't have to worry about driving and was always a happy drunk, I decided to use an app on my phone that tracked the amount of drinks I consumed. It was a rough estimation of blood alcohol content. I registered 19 drinks (mostly beer with a shot or two thrown in) and my BAC hit .38. I was still able to drink, walk, and talk by the time I got back to my room. I'm assuming the app was inaccurate.

The next day I woke up still drunk, ate some food, putzed around for a bit, and then went down for a nap to try to sober up for the "picnic" that was going to be held at the same location under the tent on the grounds of the castle. My nap ran really late, I missed the shuttle to the castle, and ended up taking a cab over. Once I arrived, my friends thought I had disappeared, so I explained what had happened and began to get into much of the same behavior as the night before, only this time the entertainment was traditional Irish musicians in a much more laid back atmosphere.

Our time in Gort and Kinvarra ended the next day. I hitched a ride with a good friend of the groom and his wife and we made the more than two-hour drive east to Dublin where a handful of Cranford people were staying for a few days before heading off to their next destinations.

I checked into a metroed-out, modern hotel on Fleet Street, right in the heart of the Temple Bar neighborhood, and took a nap to the sounds of gypsy street buskers a block away. We all met up at Gogarty's, a bar and restaurant across the street from my hotel, for dinner and drinks and continued celebrating there before heading down the road to pop into other drinking establishments.

The next day, I walked around the local area, stopping to pop into various shops to look for souvenirs. Later, a large group of us headed to the Guinness brewery for their famous tour, which was spectacular. We ended up pretty much doing the same thing as a group that night with the addition of me sitting in for "Dirty Old Town" with a small group of traditional Irish musicians at Gogarty's. A bunch of us had a nightcap at my hotel and then I got a head start on packing so as not to run late for my flight back across the pond the following morning.

Summer came to a close and a few days later the rebuild of our house was completed. Without skipping a beat, I contacted our real estate agent and in no time we had a lease drawn up for a two-year rental agreement. The total rental income was about 85% of what our monthly mortgage payment was, so I split the difference every month with my X's brother to cover the required payment.

Things were looking up after what seemed like an extremely long period of personal hell. With the fall came some down time from gigging, so much so that I had more time to focus on the enjoy! album as well as the production of my solo album. My horn guys were scheduled to lay down tracks for the additional three songs I had contracted them for, and I was able to find two female vocalists as well as a friend-recommended male vocalist to sing on the tracks that Brendan wasn't singing on.

In addition to my two or three yoga classes a week, I trained on the stairs/stepper five days a week and did weight training two or three days a week. I decided to add a cross-fit type workout to the mix. I began a 14-week, five-day a week regiment of T25. These were 25 minute exercises that focused on raising the heart rate up to where I was burning more fat, toning, and strengthening the areas of my body that I'd neglected for so long. My diet became regular, predictable, and I cut out a lot of junk and unnecessary food items and focused on nutrient rich whole foods. I cut down on beer considerably during the week, started reading voraciously at night, and there was times when I was even in bed before 11:30PM. My work schedule was flexible enough to work a little at night to free up time during the day to do whatever I wanted and to keep myself occupied. I was typically up and at the gym by 6:30AM to get the blood pumping. I started feeling noticeably better and stronger, not only physically, but also emotionally and mentally.

One mid-week night in mid-November I was out on the deck at Andy's house having a cigarette and staring up at the stars. It was a crisp, clear evening and the longer I gazed into space, the more my eyes began to adjust, allowing me to see more and more of our galactic neighborhood. At one point, I focused on one area of the sky, east-southeast, and noticed what appeared to be a star moving in a straight line. It was the same size and brightness as an average star, but it moved east-northeast at a rate that was inconsistent with any known aircraft. I knew of no satellites or orbital spacecraft that could've moved like that. I kept my eye on it for a couple of minutes, gazing in awe, and then it stopped moving! I was completely dumbfounded. Meteors and asteroids don't stop moving in space. I've never heard of a star deciding to change its location in the heavens. The only other explanation was a UFO because I couldn't identify it and I doubt anyone else who had seen it would've had a better explanation. I smiled, went inside, and got back to the routine I had adhered to so well over the last couple of months.

A few days before Christmas, I met a girl in the city who I had been communicating with on an online dating site. She lived in Brooklyn, was a doctor, surfed, snowboarded, and played guitar. I found out over a few drinks and some seafood that she smoked marijuana and had the same tastes in music and goofy view on life as I did. She was also beautiful which was an added bonus. We headed over to the Grammercy Theatre afterwards and caught some of the God Street Wine show before she had to make her way back home for an early start at the hospital. While in the lobby, before she had a chance to walk out the door, I grabbed her and planted an unexpected kiss. I was really into her and wanted to make sure she knew it; however, a couple of days later she texted and informed me that she would not be seeing me again. Perhaps she thought I was a serial dater, but the fact of the matter is that in this day and age of social media and instant communication, I really had no idea how to start or maintain a traditional relationship. Old school dating with phone calls and meeting in person was much easier. I wrote back to her on the dating website, wished her all the best in her future endeavors, and began preparing for three nights of Phish at the Garden as I had done so many times in the past.

Chapter 7

THE LIGHT

PLEASE RE-READ CHAPTER 2.

There is no easy way to describe being at/in the Light and where my mind/body/soul was or what I was feeling. I will do my best to describe it, but the mind is but one facet of it all. What was instantly apparent was the fact that the experience was not a hallucination but rather something beyond the natural world. It was a bridge to the soul, a connection to our divine self, and the eternal part of every person that has ever lived: our God-given birthright. I knew/felt/understood the higher plan and purpose of life, reality, and the universe, which is to eternally evolve and create. In the Light I easily viewed the Earth as a school and life as a lesson. On a grander scale, the universe is a school and eternity is the lesson. The Light took all the information and knowledge that I took for granted and that had been relegated and lying dormant in my subconscious and dredged it to the surface of my consciousness. I realized that we are all ONE and came from the same Source/Creator/God/Great Spirit, and that no one is any better than anyone else. WE ARE ALL SONS AND DAUGHTERS OF GOD. We are all equal and part of a bigger picture/plan and purpose and have that spark of divinity within us. Every breath, thought, word, action, and deed carry karmic weight and has purpose so we should make them positive instead of using judgment and negativity. We are what we have been exposed to through our senses, minds, hearts, and experiences. Picture your soul at birth as a container holding past life knowledge, and as we grow older and live our lives, everything that we have learned, loved, and have deep interests in is added to the container and makes us who we are and determines where our Path leads after our soul's earthly journey in our physical bodies. We are consciously creating our reality, destiny, and the universe in real time. The Light is a purifying fire of our connection to the Source/Spirit. In the Light there is no pain, suffering, worry, doubt, fear, hopelessness, anger, judgment, hate, or anything negative. It was all burned away in a flash of light and with it, my ego. The ego is that part of us that, on a subconscious level, separates us from others to make us feel better, safer, and superior. It is a primal part of our personality and a personal defense mechanism. When a person identifies more with their ego than with their heart, they are, on a subconscious level, separating themselves from others. The Light made it clear to me that materialism is an illusion created by man and that the inevitable evolution of the true nature of reality is Spirit and our connection to the Source/Creator/God/Universal Consciousness/ALL. Those driven by the illusions of fame, money, and social status weigh more on the material spectrum, while those who are driven by their hearts with a focus on and pursuit of knowledge and wisdom lie on the opposite end of the spectrum, which is the spiritual.

In the Light, everything and anything is possible. The evolution of the universe and universal consciousness is aimed at togetherness, unity, ONENESS, and unconditional love. In the Light, we realize that heaven or paradise is not a physical destination but an actual state of being. Heaven or paradise can be realized anytime, anywhere, and by anyone in the present moment.

In the Light, my mind, body/heart, and spirit were aligned with the highest good and purpose. I knew instantly why it had happened and where my conscious mind was and what I was thinking right before the Light climbed up my spine. The Light illuminated every lesson I had ever learned and reassured me that I was on the right Path and part of something bigger, something infinite. When I felt as if I was floating above my field of vision, standing a foot and half to two feet above my head, I was pure spirit and detached from my physical body. The feeling and energy were unlike anything I'd ever experienced before, although it felt like I had been there before. It felt like home. I didn't want the feeling to ever go away. I felt that if I could feel like this forever it would be what God feels like. It instantly washed away any fear of death or dying. I can only assume that once the physical body fails, this process begins, time becomes irrelevant, and our connection to the Source/God/Creator/Great Spirit/ Universe is realized as we approach the Light. The Light is in our field of vision, and in a flash our energy signature, heart, and mind determine what is going to happen next. I was conscious while being detached from my body in the Light and then I returned to my physical body. There is no other way to describe it. In the Light I understood that all knowledge inherent in the universe is, at a molecular and energetic level, within us. We all have access to all the information that has ever been or will ever be. A Kundalini awakening expands one's level of consciousness to the cosmos. At/in the Light, I was plugged into the universal consciousness. It is the definition of cosmic consciousness. It is being in a state of super conscious or in the presence of the Absolute Truth.

The next chapter will cover my life from January 1st, 2014 to December 31st, 2015, and encompass what living after having a Kundalini awakening entails as well as being conscious of having active Kundalini energy in my body. The crux of this book will be covered in Chapter 9; the information and knowledge that was buried in my subconscious and brought to the forefront of my consciousness are valuable lessons that can assist anyone in overcoming the fears, doubts, stresses, and anxieties that accompany living on a planet where people are still capable of ungodly atrocities against one another.

From what I've gathered and know in my heart, having a Kundalini awakening destroys blocks in our energy bodies (what we know as the physical body is the gross body; the body that is our connection to the Source/God/Spirit/Creator is our energetic, subtle body or soul) and distributes information between our chakras (energy centers of our subtle body, more information in Chapter 9) and our left and right-brain. There was a free sharing and flow of data between my right and left-brain via the corpus callosum. With that being said, information associated with each major chakra of the energy body was shared with other chakras and my mind scrambled this data through a rational and logical filter (left-brain, masculine energy) as well as a creative, abstract filter (right-brain, feminine energy). It created a unique interpretation that made sense to me, and how it relates to my life in manifesting a reality that allows me to pursue my dreams, and fulfill my destiny with no fear or judgment.

Chapter 8

"Born Again" – Post 12.31.13

I woke up on New Year's Day with the feeling that something spiritually significant had happened to me. I needed to do some research, but I felt like I got hit by a Mac truck. For the next three days, I spent most of my time in bed. I'd never experienced something like this, especially not as far as pain and sickness goes. From my head down to my feet, every major system (nervous, endocrine, digestive, etc.) in my body was under attack and attacking my body. I experienced pain with every breath and every movement. Incessant splitting headaches from every section of my head (top, sides, back, front), pressure in my eyes and nasal passages, pain in my throat, fluctuating and irregular heartbeats, stabbing pains in my gut, and odd bowel movements all presented themselves. It felt like there would be no end in sight. I could hardly eat anything. One minute I was freezing and under the covers, 20 minutes later I felt like I was on fire, sweating my balls off and stripped down to my boxer shorts. This pattern continued frequently. The tips of my fingers and toes were ice cold so I'd throw gloves on and then they felt like they'd been cooked in an oven a few moments later. It was a personal hell and made work that Thursday and Friday unbearable. My concentration and focus was thrown off and I moved at a snail's pace. At one point, as I lay in bed, letting whatever was happening to me happen, it felt like there was an invisible force or energy ping-ponging through my body. One moment I felt a warm, gooey feeling in my right leg and the next I felt it travel up to the left side of my chest, then to the right and back down to my left leg. I knew what it was without having any specific information about it. This invisible force was the light of active Kundalini energy working through my body, repairing and bolstering what was deficient and burning off what was not needed. It was as if my physical body did a hard system reboot or reset back to the template or blueprint of how the human body, and its intended functional design, was originally constructed to operate. My sleep pattern was completely blown apart but I had no stress or anxiety over it as I did in college when I was battling depression.

I immediately found myself on Google searching topics on spiritual awakening as well as ancient yoga philosophy. I came across the diagram of the subtle or energy body that detailed the seven major chakras and three major nadis (channels where prana flows within the energy body; more information on the chakras, nadis, and prana in Chapter 9).

By the end of the third day, all my physical ailments, pain, suffering, body temperature irregularities, and so on had subsided and I felt energetically and spiritually recharged. The information I acquired and felt in the Light didn't disappear and I started to carry this data with me, knowing in my heart that everyone on the planet will eventually have the same experience and feeling. I felt connected and plugged into everything and everyone I came across—like I was living in a different dimension. I touched plants in the house as if they were pets and had love in my heart for everyone I came in contact with. This was not a conscious decision. It was automatic and happened by default. It was as if my highest self was operating in my body with an evolved consciousness. My skin had a dewy complexion, I physically felt lighter, and all my senses were heightened. The food I ate that had impurities seemed out of balance and processed food tasted bitter. My body was able to pick out instantly what the cause of the weird taste was. I instantly craved whole, natural foods including fresh fruit and vegetables, and didn't require a lot to re-energize my body.

With that, my diet changed. It didn't change too much as I had been slowly, over the past year and a half, switching out food that was too fatty, acidic, sugary, and processed for leaner, healthier choices. I opted for water or seltzer over a Coke or a sugary fruit juice. I was super-mindful in my interactions with people to the point where I immediately contemplated how my thoughts, words or actions would affect people prior to engagement. Ultimately, I believed in my heart and soul that I balanced all of my karma and did not want to incur anymore…ever. The dialogue and conversations I had with people exuded positivity and had a spiritual tinge to it but not so much that I sounded like a preacher. I believed that everyone was free to believe what he or she felt in his or her heart without judgment. I understood presence and being present where the mind was only focused on the breath and the five senses and not dwelling on matters of the past or thinking about the future. I felt an inner glow as if the atoms in my body were spinning at a faster rate. I was vibrating at a higher frequency.

That weekend, we played a gig at the Manasquan Beach House and I felt as if I could draw energy up from the Earth from the Native cultures that inhabited the land hundreds of years ago, as well as energies from my musical heroes who had passed away while playing their songs (i.e., George Harrison while playing "While My Guitar Gently Weeps"). I caught flashes of light out of the corner of my eyes as well as in the shower after rubbing them. I was bewildered at the sight of them but had no fear.

I reached out to Carrie, my yoga instructor at the Atlantic Club, via Facebook, and told her I needed to speak to her about matters concerning a spiritual emergency. After one of her classes I told her that I had a spontaneous Kundalini awakening and explained that it felt like every cell in my body simultaneously reaching orgasm. It was the most intense climax imaginable. I told her to picture making love to your significant other for the first time, knowing that you were both in love and there was no greater feeling in existence, and then achieving a simultaneous orgasm while looking into each other's eyes. I told her to picture this scenario, but to multiply it by 100,000. I saw tears well up in her eyes and before we parted she told me to not let it get to my ego. I immediately replied

"What ego? It's gone, completely blown apart." The weather was odd that day as well. There was a polar vortex in the Arctic and the weather app on my phone read a low of seven degrees and a high of 56. (These numbers are associated with synchronicity in my life and will be visited in Chapter 9.)

The following weekend, the band was back up in Killington playing a number of shows at the Foundry. The weather looked perfect as far as skiing conditions were concerned and I decided to take some vacation days Tuesday through Friday to head up early and get in some slope time. I knew there would be less traffic on the mountain as it was between New Year's and Martin Luther King Jr. Day so I was more than excited to set up camp at my mom's cousin's condo.

I was right on. The conditions were optimal and the mountain was empty. I took wider turns than usual given the space and remembered to just consciously breathe in and out through my nose, concentrating on my senses and being of "no mind." I was completely in the present and loved every breath.

On Thursday night, Keller Williams played at the Pickle Barrel and put on an amazing performance. I hadn't seen him since probably 2002 when my X wanted to check him out at the Stone Pony. He busted into a St. Stephen → The Eleven where he was counting one through 11 and putting an emphasis on the 11. (I understood the spiritual significance of the number 11 and will delve more into that in Chapter 9.)

The gigs we played at the Foundry were electric. My thinking mind disappeared and I focused all of my energy on playing completely in the present as if this was the last gig I'd ever play and the world was going to end tomorrow. A woman from Boston came up to me on a set break and explained that she didn't quite know what it was, but she was oddly attracted to me. In my mind I knew why, but it was definitely not a topic for discussion with a stranger on a set break. We were under a hanging house speaker near the stage and the house music was interrupted by an odd hum, almost like white noise but not as annoying. I knew immediately that the heightened amount of energy being emitted from my body was interfering with the speaker magnet and electronics inside. I took a few steps away from the stage, the interference subsided, and the house music came back on.

Later that night after our gig, we were winding down and enjoying some nightcap activities at the condo. I told my brother, Brendan, and Lou what had happened to me and tried to explain what it meant without sounding crazy and discussing a topic such as this out of the blue. It would have any listener scratching their heads. They really didn't have many questions and were more dismissive than interested in what I was telling them. I ended the conversation with the advice to stay positive and for us to keep doing what we were doing.

Back home, I had the urge to take more yoga classes, as the two or three I had been attending weekly didn't seem to be enough. I found a hot yoga studio in Sea Girt that had been open for about six or seven months and made my way down there. I grabbed an unlimited package for the month and began to integrate a couple of classes into my weekly routine. At this point, I was taking between five and six classes a week with two of them at the hot studio. Poses I'd never been able to perform prior to my KA came with little effort. I perspired profusely throughout the classes and had sweat dripping from every pore of my body. I knew it wasn't a glandular problem. My sweat was clear, tasted like water when it touched my lips, and was at times fragrant like flowers! I understood that my body was vibrating at a higher level and generated more internal heat. The sweat was eliminating unnecessary elements from my body, thus purifying it back to its natural and intended operative state.

One Saturday morning as I was beginning to stir in bed to get up and start my day, I opened my eyes to two visions right in my field of sight. There were two circles of images about ten inches from my face at eye level. Each circle was about the size of a half dollar and had what appeared to be golden flames and the brightest light radiating out from the circumference. The one on the left, in front of my left eye, was a playful bust of a man in what appeared to be a Renaissance burgundy velvet hat worn by men of European nobility and dressed in a white shirt from that era. He appeared cartoony but was smiling and winked at me. From what I could tell, he had long brown hair under the hat and his face appeared to resemble mine. I immediately understood that this was an image of me in a past life. *(Or perhaps a future life on a different planet? Time was irrelevant and the visions are open to interpretation.)* I realized that my soul had been born into a noble family where I had more opportunities for growth, development, and education than a lower or middle class person of that time due to previous lives' thoughts, words, deeds, and beliefs. The circle on the right contained a castle with white brick and red turrets. A moat surrounded the castle and the image was as if taken from above because I could see a vast expanse of trees and green fields with a beautiful blue sky. My eyes widened as I continued to stare at both flaming circles in utter amazement. I just smiled. Within about a minute to a minute and a half the images began to fade until they disappeared completely. I got up and went about my day with a huge smile on my face and a boost of energy. I didn't tell anyone about what I saw.

I decided to head down to Barnes and Noble to pick up a book on the topic of Kundalini Energy. I came across the work by Genevieve L. Paulson titled *Kundalini & the Chakras: Evolution in This Lifetime.* Anyone who's ever driven on Route 70 between Brielle and Brick Township knows how out of sync the lights are on that road. My trip to the store and back was miraculous. Every light was green! I didn't even think it was possible. I chalked it up to having a little help from the spirit world and being on the right Path and exactly where I was supposed to be at that point in my life. I included reading this book in my nightly routine before I went to sleep. The winter was perfect for hibernation activities and staying indoors during the week. The material made sense to me. I was as if I'd come across it before and I fully understood all the information and pictures that were included. I even started to meditate with no guide or previous experience. I just calmed my body and focused on love, rhythmic breathing, and the colors and locations associated with the chakras and got to a point of no mind where I felt a warm internal buzzing sensation.

I was searching for information on energy and spiritual topics on my phone one evening and before I fell asleep, I asked my higher self to release and purge all the negative energy and entities from my body. In the dark, I felt a release of darkness from my body and as I stared up from my bed, I saw images of disembodied shapes, much like black cardboard cutouts with menacing faces, floating in my field of vision. The faces resembled a generic Jack O' Lantern face with missing and or sharp, jagged teeth and soulless eyes. My room was dark but these shapes were darker. I stared at them, was not afraid, and believed in my heart that my request had been granted. The shapes eventually disappeared and I fell asleep easily and peacefully.

On another night I was lying in bed preparing to drift off to sleep. As I focused my breath to all the parts of my body and began to relax, I closed my eyes. Within a few minutes, my bedroom materialized as if my eyes were still open! I opened my eyes and what I saw was the same as when my eyes were closed and vice versa. I closed them again and I was still able to view my bedroom. Within a couple of minutes with my eyes closed, everything faded to black but I knew this activity was associated with my third eye being open or the sixth chakra energy.

My sleep time was directly affected by the storehouse of energy that was still present in my body. There were some nights I'd get between two and a half and three and a half hours of sleep, be up earlier than usual, (like 5AM), get through much of my work, and head to the gym for two hours to get my cardio and weights routine in. I'd go through lunch and take a siesta for 75 minutes before checking back in on work and heading to my 4:30PM yoga class. The lack of sleep didn't even faze me. I couldn't wait to get up and begin my daily routine! All my interactions with people were positive and anything negative or judgmental were responded to in the vein of seeing the light in any situation, as a learning experience, or, if something seemed too materialistic, I'd put a spiritual spin on it or drop a hint without sounding too preachy or crazy.

One night the following week I was outside on the deck having a smoke and staring at the eastern and southern skies, marveling at the vastness of space and the stars, when out of the corner of my right eye I noticed a bird flying a little higher than the neighbor's house. It was flying from north to south. I then noticed it would turn around, fly south to north covering a span of about ten to 15 yards, and then turn around and repeat its route. I fixed my gaze on the bird and noticed it appeared to be a dove that had a visible white halo or aura surrounding it. It was the whitest and brightest object in the sky and I knew it repeated its flight a number of times to make sure I saw it. I felt a pulse in my heart and tears began to well up in my eyes given the beauty of this innocent bird and its spiritual significance and symbolism of peace. It almost brought me to my knees. It eventually flew off out of sight to the north but I took it as a sure sign that I was continuing on the right Path.

Over the next couple of weeks I continued my daily routine and my one-month unlimited trial membership to the hot yoga studio was up. I decided to purchase an annual membership that allowed me to attend as many classes as I liked. I quickly became friendly with all the teachers.

When I wasn't reading my recently purchased book at night, I found time to research some yogic and Buddhist terms that I knew, on a subconscious level, were associated with having my Kundalini awakening (KA will be used for shorthand purposes). I eventually came across nine words of personal significance that I wanted to carry with me as a reminder and teaching aid for anyone looking for a spiritual boost or nudge in the right direction. I chose nine for the number of years I was in a committed relationship with my X as this was a primary catalyst of my KA. The number is also divisible by three, which has considerable spiritual significance (information on numbers will be discussed in Chapter 9). I went down to a recommended tattoo parlor in Bradley Beach and explained what I wanted, got a quote, left a non-refundable deposit, and scheduled the appointment for the following week. This was my 37th birthday and my appointment was seven days later.

My tattoo appointment arrived and the Sanskrit words I had sent the artist looked different on the tattoo paper than what I'd originally sent. He must have revised the paper three times because each time he came back with the re-work it looked different. Things finally came together and I had the next 50 minutes or so to enjoy the tattoo needle working on my right side below my armpit and down to my last rib.

~~~

Brendan had been writing acoustic solo material in his free time and put together an ensemble with Danny on drums, an upright bassist, and a female vocalist. It was the perfect opportunity to add a banjo to the mix so he sent me rough cuts of his songs. In my free time I learned the changes and came up with banjo parts. We had a couple of rehearsals and he scheduled studio time to record at Lakehouse Studios in Asbury Park. We tracked everything live and he had enough good takes to work up the tracks and add piano parts prior to working on the post-production process.

At the end of March, my folks brought home a German Shorthair Pointer mix and named her Annie. She must've been about ten weeks old and we already saw the spark of energy, playfulness, and curiosity of the Golden Retrievers we have had in the house over the years. I initially wanted them to get another Golden but they were ready for a different breed to bring into the family and to love.

By April, work continued on post-production for my solo album as well as recording and tracking for the enjoy! material. Les built a home re-cording studio behind his house, equipped with isolation rooms, booths, a bathroom, and refrigerator, and really created a comfortable working environment to record and mix in. We were all pumped for him and it just made the process so much smoother.

I had my eye on a trainer at the gym for a while and never saw her outside the gym in a social setting. I also never had any reason to ap-proach her and strike up a conversation as she was always with clients doing private training sessions. One night, I struck up a conversation at a local pub with a woman who worked in sales at the gym. I'd known her for a while and she dated a local musician I was a friend with. The sole intention was coming up with a way to ask this trainer out. She asked if I had ever had the complimentary health assessment and two sessions with a personal trainer and informed me that every new member has that available to them. I thought it was the perfect idea and went down to the sales lady's office a few days later to schedule my sessions, requesting this particular trainer. I received a call a couple of days later from the trainer and scheduled the sessions for the following week. The first item that was tended to when we met was a health history and family background, exercise, smoking, and drinking habits, and so on. We then started the physical regimen of weights, running on a treadmill, and stretching, all while discussing life. At times, it felt like a date. We were both laughing and goofing around. She told me she was near the end of her time in medical school and had been studying to become a doctor. This blew my mind. Not only was she one of the most physically beautiful women I've come across in a long time, she was funny, down to earth, and had a brain in her head. Near the conclusion of the assessment, I hopped on a metabolic scale that obtained internal data such as percentage of body fat, muscle mass, body composition, body age, strength and cardiovascular measurements, blood pressure, and so on. As we wrapped everything up and she was just about to walk away, I motioned for her to come closer so no one else would hear and asked if she was interested in grabbing a bite to eat or drinks sometime. She said yes. I was elated!

I picked up my assessment information at the trainer desk the following week and was surprised to see that my body age was 26. I had just turned 37 a few months earlier. It would have been 25 but the blood pressure reading was a little high due to smoking a cigarette on the way to the gym which threw things off a bit. My weight was a little below 165 lbs., which is about 22 lbs. lighter than where I was two and a half years earlier. My percentage of body fat was 8.9%. My maximum oxygen consumption (VO2max) from my cardiovascular assessment was 54.2 ml/kg/min that put me in the Elite range. I found this information fascinating. I had been moderately smoking cigarettes, marijuana, and drinking beer for about 20 years. I chalked it up to being near and playing music so often since structured sound/wavelengths have the ability to heal. This was of course in conjunction with having the Light of Kundalini rise up my spine and all the internal work it did and continued to do throughout my body. That, and the fact that in my heart I knew that I was doing what I was born to do: writing, recording, and playing music.

Over the next few weeks I exchanged casual pleasantries with the trainer at the gym, then sucked it up and decided to call her. I got her voicemail and left a rambling message. I sent her a text a week or two later and never received a response. In my heart, I knew that I had the best of intentions with no expectations, so I smiled and let it go.

During this time, I experienced a handful of physical and energetic anomalies that were related to having active Kundalini in the body. One day, after stirring from my post-lunch siesta, I opened my eyes to what appeared to be a vast expanse in my field of vision colored gold and copper. It was reminiscent of when I awoke to the two visions of my past (or future?) self and the castle; however, this vision was not bifurcated or as if it was viewed through binoculars. It was probably a foot across and about nine inches from my face. This vast expanse appeared to be three-dimensional. Within the expanse, algebraic formulas, Greek letters, numbers, and unidentified shapes and symbols colored bright white, gold, and silver were moving from left to right and right to left in the foreground and background. I stared in amazement as long as I could before the vision disappeared. I understood this to be Light language from higher realms of consciousness. A few days later, before drifting off to sleep, I was lying completely relaxed in bed, began a calm breathing pattern, and focused on quieting my mind. I felt a ticklish movement at the base of my spine begin to stir. This is where the Kundalini rises from, the root chakra. I continued my breathing, relaxation, and stilled mind practice and the energy began to rise up my spine. By now, I was quite familiar with the anatomy of the energy body and had a better understanding of how to raise this energy to my crown chakra. I let it rise to between my third and fourth chakra (right below my heart) before I broke my concentration and decided that I did not want to raise the energy all the way to the top and experience what probably would have been complete bliss followed by days of agony. My entire body was humming as my vibration had risen with the movement of the Kundalini. The only way I knew to quell the movement was to rub one out. I experienced the most intense orgasm imaginable and could only imagine what it would have been like to have a partner with active Kundalini and reaching orgasm together with the sole intention of having a child.

I still slept very little at night, averaging between three and a half and four and a half hours and getting a 75-minute nap in during the afternoon. I had so much energy I found myself at the gym at 7AM on a Sunday! That had never happened before and I never thought it would ever happen, but at the time, it was necessary. During this time, before falling asleep, there were plenty of nights where the energy had nowhere to go so it tried to leave my body through my right big toe. This sounds weird but I had what felt like a current of electricity pulsing through my right leg and it would terminate in my right big toe. It felt like a sharp piece of metal penetrating from the top of my nail as well as from the tip of my toe. Over the next few weeks the energy began to turn my toenail black and blue. At first, it was minimal and then it grew larger. The next thing I knew my entire nail was completely discolored. I kept a Band-Aid on it for months. The energy continued to surge down there periodically for months, but I wasn't concerned as I had learned that this type of thing happens with active Kundalini and focused my energy elsewhere.

While continuing my yoga practice at the hot yoga studio, one of the instructors mentioned she and a partner were running a yoga and wellness retreat down in Islamorada located in the Florida Keys. I had plenty of vacation days to burn and that sounded like a nice little respite from the early spring Jersey weather, so I opted to join about 25 other strangers on the retreat. I was looking forward to meeting them all. I flew into Miami, rented a car, and drove down Highway 1, soaking up as much Florida sun as possible. I stopped for lunch, picked up a case of beer, and checked into the resort. There were two daily yoga classes on the beach. One was at 8AM and the other in the late afternoon. All meals were included and the food was spectacular. There weren't that many single people who kept the same schedule as me (boundless energy and late-night activities), so at night after the resort bar had closed I'd walk half a mile or so down a back road that paralleled Highway 1 and would pop into a local bar for a few pints. I'd take over the jukebox and talk with the bartender and whoever else was around. One of the yoga instructors smuggled some medicinal marijuana down and we smoked before she taught a class. Amazingly, she kept it together. That was the first time I had smoked prior to taking a class. She gave me a joint or two to keep me Ire on my own for the duration of the retreat. One day, I went paddle boarding for a good two and a half hours by myself and just took in all the beauty of the Florida Bay. I realized I could've paddled to the Florida mainland had I brought enough water and rations. Another day, everyone hopped on boats that took us out for a snorkeling session. I spent the time between classes and meals reading and lounging on the beach to work on my tan.

Over the next couple of months, I continued with my daily and weekly routines and quest for as much knowledge about spiritual topics as possible. When I was bored, I'd find stuff online that interested me either on Wikipedia or via Google searches relating to yoga philosophy and Kundalini awakening or energy. I picked up the autobiography of Gopi Krishna titled *Living With Kundalini* for additional reference and comparison.

In early June I caught the Avett Brothers for the first time down in Atlantic City. Their uplifting and positive energy brings out the same from everyone in the audience. That summer was full of bar gigs, charity events, weddings, and private parties. My enthusiasm for playing music stayed extremely high and my mindset became that of "play like it's the last gig of your life and the world is going to end tomorrow" multiplied by "you get to do this forever!" We even played a wedding with Shady on keyboards and Bryan Beninghove on sax and melodica, both of whom recorded on my solo album. It was the first time they had met, but both got along like two peas in a pod.

Brendan's solo project, titled Brendan Brophy's Local Honey, was mastered and he wanted to shoot a video for one of the more catchy songs. He hired a professional film crew and we headed to a farm in Wall owned by a Cranford guy who let us use the grounds. The video was to have a very rustic feel so the setting was perfect. I threw on seersucker suit pants, dress shoes, a white dress shirt, tie, suspenders, and my banjo for a Southern gentleman look and we played through the song a bunch of times and let the director tell us what to do. The temperature was the hottest it had been all year with the mercury hitting the mid-90s. I was sweating bullets as my typical daily wardrobe consisted of flip-flops, shorts, and a t-shirt.

The rest of the summer I continued with my regimented weekly schedule and adherence to a stricter, more wholesome/less crappy diet. My free time was spent either paddle boarding or hanging out on the beach with my brother, his wife, and my nephews. On my days off with the weather and temperature being optimal for outside activities, I wanted to do nothing more than take my shirt off, hop on my bike with my ear buds in, and head over to either the Parker House or Boathouse for a few tasty pints and casual conversation with whoever I knew or had the pleasure of meeting. My go-to choice of artists was again either the Bob Marley or Meters Pandora station or my entire catalogue of Bob Marley albums. An odd electrical/digital anomaly started to pop up whenever the Marley from my Google Music was being played. A sound that I can only liken to a digital record scratch started to pop up right when I began my bike ride. This continued a few times throughout a song and happened throughout the summer. It even started happening when I listened to Bob in my truck. I always viewed Bob as a great teacher and one of my all-time musical heroes. There was no doubt in my heart that his spirit had a greater presence in my life and that on the other side of "the veil" between this world and the next he was keeping an eye on me. In addition to this electrical anomaly, the street light on the corner of Old Mill Road and W. Chicago flashed on and off a few times as I approached or passed it on my bike.

Animals that normally wouldn't be spotted every day began to appear on a random basis. One night, during one of my bike rides into Belmar, I biked past two deer hanging out on a suburban front lawn on Old Mill Road. One was an eight or ten pointer and he was a magnificent animal, most likely with his mate in tow. Another night, driving on the same road, a red fox was about to cross my path and suddenly stopped to let me pass. While outside on the back deck having a cigarette, a Praying Mantis paid me a visit. He was hanging out on the floor mat. As I knelt down to take a closer look he paused and turned his head to look at me, acknowledging my presence. A green hummingbird also fluttered about the tall flowers that Andy had recently planted out back. Insects I had never seen before, or didn't think could exist, including what appeared to be a type of moth with translucent sky blue wings and a hybrid ladybug with a longer thorax would pop up randomly. All I could think of when coming across these creatures was how stunning and diverse life was on this planet, and perhaps I was catching a future peek of what beauty awaits from an evolutionary perspective.

By the end of the summer, all the edits and level issues for my solo album were getting wrapped up and the next step was mastering. Les recommended a guy who had plenty of mastering work under his belt that he trusted so I went with him. I needed album artwork done and I asked a local artist if he'd be willing to do some watercolors of photos I had taken over the years. I decided to go with photos I took of the rainbow ending in Magens Bay when down in St. Thomas, a beautiful tranquil sunrise rising from the ocean in Belmar, a random colorful fall sky at dusk in Sea Girt, and a quiet trail at the top of Killington mountain. I gave him complete creative license and just told him to make them look cool. I contacted a photographer from the local Cranford crew and scheduled to have photos of me taken down at the Manasquan beach and doggie beach, as well as some indoor shots of me with my guitar and banjo in my brother's house.

The album artwork and mastering finished in mid-September, which was pretty much exactly three years since our first tracking session. I titled the work *Manifest Destination*. The original phrase was coined by a good friend of Shady Groove while playing his outdoor party (enjoy! also played his wedding). It stems from an existential notion of "You are doing exactly what you should be doing at this very moment as you are the master of your fate and destiny. There are no coincidences." Of course, anything is open to interpretation. At the time, this just made the most sense.

My brother had been doing branch audits for AXA Equitable for the past few years and his territory was the Southeast. He frequented Memphis, Nashville, TN, Austin, TX, and Charleston, SC to name a few. He asked if I wanted to join him for a few days in Tennessee at the end of September. I jumped at the chance to visit the historic music cities of Memphis and Nashville and submitted for days off while traveling. I would bring my work laptop and work from the hotels while my brother was out at the offices he was auditing.

We flew into Memphis, got an early check in at the hotel, and my brother went out to the local AXA office while I caught up on work. That night we hit up legendary Beale Street and had some classic Memphis barbecue for dinner while watching local talent, then hopped in and out of a few clubs before grabbing a nightcap at B. B. King's bar.

The next morning we got on the road for the three-hour ride to Nashville. That night, we drove into downtown Nashville and stopped at the legendary Ryman Auditorium, the birthplace of bluegrass, for a quick photo before popping into a handful of live music clubs on Broadway, including Robert's Western World, Tootsies, and The Second Fiddle. We stopped at those spots up again the next night to similar delight before flying back to New Jersey the following day. That trip was another reason why I loved the freedom of my job. It was flexible enough that I could work from anywhere that had a solid Internet connection or where I would be able to switch over to a 4G hotspot from my Samsung Galaxy.

The final touches were being put on the enjoy! album and it was set for the mastering process. We used a friend who was an amazing photographer, artist, and graphic designer for the artwork design. We agreed on the album title *The Eleven*. Initially, as there were 11 tracks on the album; however, that number grew in significance for me over the past nine months (more on that number in Chapter 9). Our friend photographed 11 phases of the moon and worked a local beach at night into his design. The actual art for the disc was a sand dollar with the names of each track going around the outer edge of the design.

One random Sunday my friend Sean contacted me and asked if we'd be interested in playing for Kevin Statesir's 60th birthday party at

Langosta Lounge in Asbury Park. Kevin was the owner of the live music club, Higher Ground, up in South Burlington, Vermont and Trey Anastasio's brother-in-law. Sean had worked at Higher Ground for close to a decade and had become very close with Kevin. Sean had mentioned that Trey would most likely be there for a brief period and I got really excited. At first it was just supposed to be us as a full band and then other local musicians were added. We ended up just playing an acoustic set as a trio. I brought the banjo to add a little flavor to the mix. During our second song in the set, I spotted Trey walk in. I got super pumped but kept my cool and focused on performing well and having fun without any distractions. Between songs, Brendan leaned over and told me while I was soloing during "The Old Home Place" he looked up and Trey had his head in his hand hunched over a table gazing at my playing. That instantly brought a smile to my face. We played for about an hour and Trey left during our last song so I never got a chance to meet him. The other musicians that were performing after us were chatting him up during our set, but in the end, I was glad he got a chance to see us play.

~

Later that evening, my brother and I grabbed a late bite and some pints at the Annex on Cookman Avenue, and then went home to prepare for an early start to the upcoming week. Around 3:17AM, I happened to wake up from my slumber and spotted an apparition about three feet away standing in front of my nightstand facing the lamp and wall. He was on the shorter side and I propped myself up a bit to try to make sense of everything. The room was dark but that side of the bed was illuminated around this figure. He appeared to have long black hair, was of Native, Central, or South American descent and wearing a black t-shirt. I don't remember what else. I don't even remember seeing his feet touch the ground or if he had feet. The spirit ran his hands through his long hair as if straightening it out or getting any hair stuck inside his t-shirt out so that his hair was resting evenly on his shoulders and upper back. He then put his hands on the nightstand, closed his eyes, and raised his head upwards a little bit. His arms were outstretched on the nightstand and there may have been a large open book that he was standing over. I'm not entirely sure. I rubbed my eyes and re-focused them on the spirit and the next thing I know he was a foot closer to me, bent down a bit, and his head was turned so our eyes were on an even level. Our eyes met and the expression on his face was neither threatening nor joyful. He may have had a tiny smirk on his face. I blinked and in an instant the apparition vanished. I had a bottle of water on my nightstand and it was as if sparkles of light dissipated from the outline of the bottle before disappearing. There was a slight glow emanating from the water bottle and that side of the room when I turned back over to the other side of my bed.

I always told myself that I didn't believe in ghosts since I felt that I was affirming that I never wanted to see or come into contact with one. This event blew that affirmation and belief out of the water. If this had happened before my KA, I would've most likely jumped out of bed, hopped in my truck, and checked into the nearest hotel with plans to move out the next day. I would've been scared shitless. After turning back over, I had no fear. I had a smile on my face and understood that it had happened for a reason. Perhaps the fact that Trey actually saw me play guitar after having seen him perform so many times had something to do with it. On a larger scale, it was a significant event. Perhaps this spirit was a family member or friend from a past life or a guide just letting me know there's more to life, the universe, and reality than most would assume. Or perhaps he was attracted to the light or energy still emanating from my KA that he knew I'd be able to see and potentially help him out with something or relay a message to a loved one in our world. I immediately prayed and asked my higher self, spirit guides, and guardian angels to protect me from and keep all negative entities and energies away. I was no medium nor had I any intention of becoming one. This was not my path; that is what professional psychics and mediums are for. Any spirit looking for help in contacting anyone in this world would be wise in seeking out his or her assistance. I fell back asleep quickly and slept soundly the rest of the night. I understood that having a KA unleashes a large volume of energy in the physical body and also raises the vibration of the body.

At 3:17AM, when I woke up, I was conscious but most likely retained a higher level of brain wave activity, meaning that I was awake with Theta, Delta, or a blend of different frequencies, or that my KA had evolved my brain to emit a different or unknown frequency. Anything was possible so I took the experience at face value and saw the positive in it.

My solo album and the enjoy! album went to the CD manufacturers for production within about a month of each other. Brendan's solo project had been done for a few months. I came up with the idea of having a triple album release party in Asbury Park. Three full albums of original material was a pretty big deal for any musician and the timing couldn't have been more perfect. It had to be at the Stone Pony. I didn't want to settle for a smaller room of lesser significance. I contacted Sean who had contacts with local promoters. He got the ball rolling, procuring an open date at the Pony and incorporated Ed Maier of Elmthree Productions. Ed promoted shows at rooms in Asbury including the Saint, Wonder Bar, and the Pony. He was a die-hard music fan, "head," and the perfect conduit between the venue and us as artists. With the gears in motion, I contacted everyone that I had used on my solo project to gauge their availability. All were available except for one female vocalist who was out of the country. I told them I'd be in touch once a date was nailed down.

Over the next few weeks, I noticed some more odd energetic anomalies. The alarm clock on my nightstand stopped functioning properly. It got stuck on all eights even after unplugging and plugging back in. The light didn't even blink and there were no batteries in it. I figured time was the least of my concerns so I tossed it. My cell phone would shut off without touching it. One morning while logging into to my work laptop, my desktop came up and all my icons were organized on the left hand side of the screen, not scattered all over as I had left them. My TV would shut off randomly. I also found a white feather on the floor of my bedroom. There was no explanation of how it found its way in there. I did a little research online and discovered that it's a sign of being in the presence of an angel. I smiled and felt a warm and fuzzy feeling in my heart just thinking and believing that that was the case.

Keeping with the theme of burning vacation days and getting the fuck out of dodge, I bought tickets for Phish's three-night run in San Francisco and booked a room two blocks from the Bill Graham Civic Auditorium. I hadn't seen the band that far west since Halloween of 1998 in Vegas, and was excited by the possibility of maybe witnessing a Phil Lesh or Bob Weir pop-in as this was their stomping grounds. The shows were great. The band sounded phenomenal and right when the San Francisco Giants took the World Series in game seven, the entire crowd went bananas as the band went into Queen's "We Are the Champions." I didn't do much sightseeing when I wasn't at the shows. I took a Lyft to Haight-Ashbury to grab lunch and some beers at Magnolia, the gastro pub that I had visited when my brother and I came out to see our fraternity brother Ernie about 15 years before. On another day, I walked up Montgomery Street and ducked into a funky little place near the financial district for lunch and a few beers, relishing in casual conversations about life with the bartender and other day drinkers. Overall, it was a pleasurable respite save for the riot; a couple of cars were set on fire and two murders were committed around the corner from my hotel, South of Market, following the Giants win.

Once back in New Jersey, we ran into a couple of snafus regarding pinning down a date at the Stone Pony for our triple album release party. We had two holds that were eventually taken away from us since regional and national acts take priority over local acts. After going back and forth with the powers that be, we settled on January 9th, 2015.

The design for the enjoy! album was finalized and everything was sent to the manufacturer for pressing. Taking pleasure in the fact that things were in a good spot and moving forward for our big gig, I was off to Costa Rica for a real getaway. I found a website that focused on yoga retreats at an affordable rate and settled on Costa Rica. I had only heard good things and was up for another adventure in the sun.

My flight was scheduled for around 5:15AM. I was up staying at my folks' house and had a cab service scheduled to pick me up at 3:30AM to take me to Newark Airport. I went out for a few beers and met up with some friends the night before with the belief that I'd be able to get up with 90 minutes of sleep and hop in the cab; however, my cell phone alarm had other ideas. I set three alarms and none of them went off due to user error. I was woke by my brother who was working in Jersey City that morning. He said, "Doesn't your flight leave in ten minutes?" I checked my cell and saw that I had missed three calls from the cab company. Without breaking a sweat, I logged in and purchased another ticket for a flight that left at 9AM.

I had a shitty seat but my one-stop flight eventually made it to San Jose. The owner of the inn I was staying at in Playa Hermosa had a van waiting to pick me up. After stopping at a supermarket for beer, I made it to my destination a little before 11PM, cracked open a beer, pulled out a joint I had smuggled in my checked luggage, went out back to puff, and threw some tunes on my Bose Bluetooth music player.

The following morning I met my guide and inn owner who was an ex-pat originally from Maryland and around my age. She was bubbling with positive energy and an all-around sweetheart. The other guest and I had a hearty and healthy breakfast before heading out to a yoga class. The inn was situated about 30 yards from the Pacific Ocean and had an amazing break for surfers who were out during all hours of the day. The meals were included in the fee I paid and everything I ate was healthy and delicious. We got around locally via the inn owner and her boyfriend's cars, and when not eating at the inn, we dined at restaurants in the neighboring town of Jaco.

One needed a decent grasp of the Spanish language to really get around in that area. I knew a handful of words which wouldn't suffice had I been going it solo. Thankfully, the inn owner and her boyfriend spoke Spanish fluently and knew all of the locals so I was in good hands.

There were a couple of days where there were two yoga classes, one in the morning and one in the afternoon or early evening. The inn owner's boyfriend was from Florida and an avid surfer. He was also into weird and different shit that I had been drawn to over the past year. He showed me two books he had read and I immediately took an interest in the subjects. The first book was titled, *The Ancient Secret of the Flower of Life Vol. 1* by Drunvalo Melchizedek.

The other was *Your Hands Can Heal You* by Master Stephen Co and

Eric B. Robins, M.D. I tucked the titles away in my memory bank and intended to pick up the books on my return to the States.

One morning I took surf lessons from a local surfer at a teaching beach. I listened with steady concentration to his instructions and within maybe four or five runs and about 15 minutes in the water I was up riding waves on a long board. Surfing had always been on my bucket list and even though I had unsuccessfully tried my hand at it before, I was delighted that my teacher's instruction and guidance made things so smooth. There's nothing quite like catching your first wave at the age 37.

The following day the other guest and I who had paid for the yoga vacation decided to take a guided tour of a local rainforest. Our guide was a 15 year-old native with an encyclopedic knowledge of all the plant and animal life of his country. He explained that most of his knowledge was passed down to him from his grandfather and described all the homeopathic and natural uses of things we passed on the trails. We arrived at a waterfall and had the opportunity to strap into a harness and rappel down to the bottom with water rushing past us.

During the day, between yoga classes and meals, I'd catch some sun on the beach or play along to some Bob Marley songs on my ukulele in the back while watching the surfers tear it up. Since I didn't have a car or speak Spanish well enough, I kept it pretty low key at night and didn't venture into the town of Jaco where all the action was. There was a restaurant with a bar about 20 yards up the road from the inn. I went there a couple of nights for drinks and rapped with some locals as well as ex-pats that had just moved down. On my last night there the inn owner's boyfriend came by my room. We hung out for a bit shooting the shit, and threw back a few beers.

I flew home the next day.

Once back in the States, more prep work and promoting our big gig were priorities. The CD's for my solo album arrived a few days after I got back and within ten days the enjoy! CD's arrived. My friend who designed the enjoy! album artwork put together a colorful glossy postcard to promote the show with pictures of the three albums on it and other important information. Things were starting to fall into place.

In early December, my brother had another audit scheduled in Tennessee. I had such a blast the last time that I joined him again. In the mornings, I was up early at about 5:15AM. I'd run out to the Starbucks down the road, grab a dark roast and oat bar, and start my email review. I found a local yoga studio in the area and hit up a class a few hours later to break up the morning. At night, we had dinner and then headed down to Broadway in downtown Nashville for drinks and live music. One night, we were up on the top floor of Tootsies and a local musician who we had seen playing at the airport bar on our last trip was on stage. During one of his set breaks, my brother approached him and asked if he didn't mind having a couple of New Jersey musicians play a few songs with his band as we'd never played in Nashville before. Tootsie's is such a historic and iconic music venue. Pillars of the music community had always popped in and graced its hallowed stages. We were elated when our new friend obliged and we both dropped a $20 in his tip jar. His lead guitarist handed over his 1951 Fender Nocaster (the precursor to the Telecaster) and said; "Careful with that now, my grand-daddy gave that to me." I told him it was in good hands and I jammed about five tunes with my brother on bass for two or three with the rest of the band. We did Charlie Daniels' infamous "Devil Went Down to Georgia" as well as the likes of Merle Haggard's "Mama Tried" and Johnny Lee's "Looking For Love." That truly was the icing on the cake of our latest out of town musical excursion.

Holiday preparations and gift buying took up a good chunk of December. The rest was dedicated to preparing for our big gig. Brendan held a couple of rehearsals to go over his Local Honey album. We had a rehearsal for the enjoy! material and I scheduled two for my solo album. We also worked on getting the CD's on our website available for purchase, but for the most part we were just excited to have great finished products to share with the world and gave them out freely to family, friends, and diehard fans without batting an eye.

We decided to hire a videographer to record the entire show as well as bring the engineer, Les, we used on *The Eleven* and *Manifest Destination* albums to track the show for a professional mix down during post-production. This would ensure that we'd have a solid finished product to document the entire night.

The tenants renting our house had won the offer they had put in to buy a house, so they gave us 90 days notice. We used the realtors that we had used before and didn't have any issue finding other tenants to move in by mid-March.

Excitement and final preparations mounted for our big gig. We continued to drop off the glossy postcards promoting our show locally as well as distributing our CD's to whoever was interested.

At around 12:50PM on January 9th, the day of the show, I received a phone call from Shady's wife. She told me that Shoheen slipped on a patch of ice exiting a subway station and had dislocated his shoulder. He was laid up in the hospital on morphine and would not be able to make the show. I thanked her for the call and told her to tell Shady to get well soon. I hung up and smiled at the fact that I'd be facing this issue on the day of our biggest gig. With complete calm and determination, I called up Bryan, our sax player and horn arranger for my solo album, explained what had happened, and asked if he knew of any keyboard players who would be able to pull through to the gig. He said he knew of a couple and would call me back in a little while. While waiting, I texted my brother, Lou, Danny, and Brendan and explained the situation. The consensus was "holy fuck, really?!" A little while later, Bryan called me back and said he had contacted Jeremy Beck, a "monster player" who was currently in session in Manhattan, who would be able to make it down to the Pony by about 8:30PM. He gave me his info and told me to send him the tracks he needed to play on, as well as charts for the songs. I didn't have professional charts, only typed out Word documents with chords and song sections (intro, verse, chorus, etc.). I figured that would have to do and crossed my fingers as I emailed the WAV files and Word documents to him.

We headed over to the Pony between 6 and 6:30PM for load-in and sound check preparations. The Local Honey crew was there and I would not be expecting the keyboard and horn players as well as the other vocalist I had used on my solo album until about 9PM or so.

The order of performances would be Local Honey's set, a quick enjoy! set, my solo album, and then another enjoy! set to close out the evening. All the gear was in place on stage and the sound check was complete. This left us with some time to decompress. John and I grabbed a pizza from Porta and relaxed with a couple of beers before the doors opened.

With the exception of a few minor hiccups, the sets went very well. I was up on stage with the mindset of this is what we got and we're going to barrel through it as best we can. Of course, my solo album was something completely different. The keyboardist, guest vocalist, and horn players never rehearsed with us. I went up on stage playing songs live that haven't been played in over a decade, with the inclusion of one that had never been played to an audience. The last enjoy! set was filled with jam-friendly covers by bands such as Phish, Talking Heads, The Who, and David Bowie.

At the end of the night, Ed and Sean came over with the final tally from the door. We were surprised to see that 268 people had paid to see us play. Of course, there were more that got in on the guest list and other friends of Sean and Ed's that came through. All in all, we had over 300 people come out to support us on a bitter, windy, icy Friday in January right after New Year's Eve. We had no help from the Pony or the local radio station in helping us get the word out. We viewed the night as a success and knew immediately that we could have had a bigger turnout with just a little help from the proper channels.

In mid-March, it was time to travel and get some more sun, so I decided to embark on another solo adventure to Barbados. My only plans were to get some good sun, take daily yoga classes, grab another surf lesson, and booze and smoke as I usually do on vacation without a care in the world. I stayed on a property with about 15 rooms, a pool, and a bar/

restaurant in the Silver Sands section of the island, which was about ten minutes to the south of the airport. This was the southernmost section of the island and a quiet section of the country. I immediately realized that calling a cab to take me from point A to B every time I needed to leave the property would get expensive, so I had the property manager call a car rental company and they came down with a cheap little rental that would be perfect for zipping along the south and western shores of the island. They drive on the left hand side of the road with the steering wheel on the right hand side of the car. I'd never driven out of the country before so this was a baptism by fire of the highest degree.

The first night, I had the local favorite mahi-mahi for dinner and proceeded to drink Banks beer until they closed the bar/restaurant. There were two local musicians playing, a female vocalist, and a guitarist who also sang. I approached them during their set break and explained that I was a musician travelling from the States and brought my ukulele if they wanted additional accompaniment while playing locally over the next few days. They said "sure" and told me to head over to a local spot a little west of Oistins on Tuesday night.

There were a few local fellows hanging out that first night and I befriended a Rasta who surfed with the local crew, sold joints of Fanta (a local crop, much like tobacco, that they mixed with marijuana for hybrid joints), and whatever contraband tourists needed while visiting. I grabbed a few more Banks from my room and hung out with my new friend down by the water's edge for a couple of hours just discussing life.

The following day, I drove west towards Bridgetown and rented a paddleboard for a good stint in Carlisle Bay. The next night I met up with my new musician friends and sat in for a set on my ukulele. It was St. Patrick's Day and there were many tourists in the audience. They played mostly top 40 songs with some Motown or Bob Marley thrown in. I kept up with them, as all I needed was to see my guitarist friend's hands or ask what the changes were. It went over well and the crowd seemed to enjoy the added accompaniment.

My surf lesson was the next day but there was a ton of Sargassum seaweed infiltrating the beach where we were scheduled to surf. We agreed to postpone the lesson until the next day and pick another spot. The instructor told me that his half-brother was playing at the Surfer's Café that evening. He said the food was great and that all the locals and surf crew would be there for drinks later. I headed down there for dinner and hung around until his brother went on. My Rasta friend was there too. We hung out and he introduced me to a handful of the locals. My instructor showed up and he did the same. At the set break I asked the musician if I could join him on the ukulele and I ended up playing the entire second set with him doing mostly Reggae tunes.

The following day my instructor picked me up and we headed off to Freights Bay, a quiet spot perfect for lessons. There were two other couples in the van and they hailed from Serbia, Germany, and Russia. After a refresher on the earth we got in the water and I grabbed a handful of waves. There were even a couple of gigantic sea turtles in the area hanging out with us while we surfed. My instructor had a Go-Pro and I was able to get a few decent shots of me in full action mode.

My Rasta friend wanted me to pay him as a tour guide so that he could take me to the clubs in the capital on Friday night, but I opted for a nice quiet last night on the island. I stayed on the property and hit up the bar-restaurant, drinking my Banks, and toking off my last smuggled joint while listening to my favorite albums through my Bose portable Bluetooth device. My Rasta friend asked me for a donation as he had two kids at home and I handed him what I was able to and we said our goodbyes with the intent that I'd be back that way again sometime. I drove to the airport the following morning and returned to the States with a nice tan and some good stories to tell.

Within the next month or two, approaching the upcoming summer season, I noticed a dip in my energy levels even though I had kept up my daily and weekly activities to keep my energy up. It was as if my heightened level of consciousness was reverting back to its normal state in conjunction with my body moving away from its purest state, the one I had before my KA. I discerned that it was the lack of being able to speak freely to friends and family about my experiences and the knowledge I had obtained. I knew talking to them would be beneficial in assisting them in their understanding and approach to "getting them to the Light" (this obviously can't be forced on anyone). I also think that my energy levels had dropped because I was around people who were unconscious of the fact that negative thought patterns, words, and actions carry karmic weight and a negative energy charge. This not only affects their wellbeing but also affects those around them. I had been keeping a digital journal of all the odd energetic and synchronistic anomalies that had been occurring for the past 16 months, as well as the information and thoughts that seemed to have just downloaded into my mind, body, and being. I'll never forget what I saw, how I felt, and what I knew to be true about God, the universe, reality, and a heightened/expanded level of consciousness. It got to the point where I knew in my heart that the only way for me to be truly happy was to pursue my passion and dream of ditching the "9 to 5" corporate gig in the financial services field and to directly pursue music in all its forms and glory. My only out seemed to be writing this book with the hopes that, going forward, the "butterfly effect" will eventually benefit humanity. I would have "killed two birds with one stone," meaning that I'd generate enough royalty income to "buy my freedom" out of the corporate world, to be able to focus my energy on writing, recording, and performing music, and to assist anyone who is pursuing a more spiritual approach to their life with the ultimate goal of having a KA and realizing their eternity. Having enough stories to base a memoir on, I began setting aside 40 minutes to an hour every night when I had the free time, with the focus of getting one solid page of this book completed. I knew my free time would be limited during the summer so I kept a disciplined approach during the week with my schedule. My days consisted of getting up between 6 and 6:30AM, heading to the gym for cardio, getting my work done, hitting a 4:30PM yoga class, having dinner, taking a shower, and then combining my scheduled writing period with reading whatever book I had (by now my reading list included volume two of *The Ancient Secret of the Flower of Life*) and meditating before packing it in by midnight. On most mornings, I'd start the pattern all over again. I projected that, with the pace I was working at and the time dedicated to this project, it would take me about two years before completing the book. I was OK with this timeline and felt it fit perfectly into my schedule. All I needed to do was focus and keep doing what I had been doing.

~~

Summer reared its head once more and the band's work ethic hadn't changed. We added another 15 songs to our band's song list. All the summer seasonal spots were back on our schedule with the occasional private party, charity event, original gig, or wedding thrown into the mix. Aside from being electrocuted at an outdoor gig due to a faulty stage covering on Memorial Day weekend (and actually feeling the current ground itself out of my right foot), every gig was phenomenal. My summer schedule once again included paddle boarding and more biking activity at night if the weather cooperated.

Once all the Benny's were gone after Labor Day, I returned to my fall schedule of staying in more, drinking less, and getting to bed earlier than I had in the summer. We had five weddings booked in September and I knew busting my ass all summer and the added cash flow from the weddings would bring me to a comfortable spot financially, so I booked another yoga retreat for early November to Jamaica with the group I had joined in the Keys a year and a half earlier. After catching Mark Knopfler with my brother at the Count Basie Theatre in mid-October (with amazing second row seats), it was business as usual until the retreat.

This time, I didn't oversleep and made my flight without incident. I flew non-stop into Montego Bay and waited, while enjoying a Red Stripe, for another retreater to arrive from another flight. Within 40 minutes we were on a passenger van headed towards Treasure Beach, which is located on the South Shore of the island. The nearly two and a half hour ride took us through the country and various little towns and villages. We passed Peter Tosh's burial site, which was not too far from Jake's, our destination for the retreat. Once checked in, I got my keys for the second floor villa that had a queen size bed equipped with netting to keep any mosquitoes and other flying pests at bay. Once settled in, I went down to the bar located about 20 yards from my door, had a couple of Red

Stripes, and met up with a handful of familiar faces that I had seen down in the Keys. The owner of Jake's was the son of the fellow who directed the classic Jamaican movie *The Harder They Come*, starring Jimmy Cliff. In the lobby were photos of the owner as a child with his parents as well as photos of his parents with Bob Marley, Jimmy Cliff, and other members of the Wailers.

My days consisted of morning yoga classes followed by breakfast and whatever daily activities were on the docket. One day we all hopped on a few boats and took a cruise up the coast to The Pelican Bar. This place was built on pilings about a good mile and a half from the shore. The only way to get to it was via boat or some other floating device. We hopped off the boats and hung out there for a good two hours, drinking concoctions made with rum and of course indulging in a few Red Stripes. The locals hanging out had sundries for sale and also smoked joints the entire time we were there. They shared with anyone who wanted a toke. After our time at the bar, we were ferried to a shore back south headed towards Treasure Beach where cooks were preparing lunch consisting mainly of local fish, rice, beans, and curry.

The other evenings consisted of dinners on the premises or at Jack Sprat's, which was located up the road within the property. One night during dinner, there was a viewing of *The Harder They Come*. After dinner, I'd get Irie on cannabis I smuggled down and either closed down the bar on the property or headed up the road to the other bars that were within walking distance and relatively safe. The free time during the day allowed for me to work on my tan and continue reading the two books I had brought down with me. One was an illustrated history of music on the Jersey Shore and the other was a biography on Jerry Garcia.

The employees and locals working at Jack's were very polite and I didn't have one bad meal while staying there. It was a pleasurable, relaxing trip and I would recommend it to anyone who doesn't want to stay in the touristy sections of the country. On our last morning, we all had a hearty breakfast before hopping on the bus to take us back to the airport and I returned to the imminent blustery weather of the Northeast.

The remainder of the year was filled with the magic that the holiday season brings as well as the return of Phish to Madison Square Gardens for a four-night New Year's run and prepared for our end of year ritual. I hit the first three nights as we decided to play a gig on the last night of the run. This time, I did not ingest any hallucinogens. I stuck to beer and some grass and relished in the fact that in a few weeks, my brother and I would be off to Aruba for our first legitimate vacation together in close to 20 years. It was just two years before at the same hallowed music venue that I experienced a Kundalini awakening that forever changed my perception of God, my soul, the universe, reality, and my eternal connection to it ALL.

Chapter 9

THE CODE

THIS CHAPTER IS the crux of the book. As I wrote earlier, my KA dredged information and knowledge buried in my subconscious and brought it to the forefront of my mind. For weeks and months after my KA, information seemed to come from nowhere as if telepathically downloaded into my brain, OR, the concept that this information is imbedded in everyone's DNA and the KA triggered a certain frequency or resonance in which I was able to access it. Almost as if the KA unlocked this data so I could re-remember. I was also drawn, like a moth to a flame, to different religious, spiritual and yogic subject matter where I was never that interested in before. A major component of having a KA deals with the energy centers of the subtle (energetic/light/spiritual) body being clear enough of blocks for the Light to rise up the central nadi (Sushumna – more information later in the chapter) located in the center of the spine and pierce the higher chakras for the Light to connect with the crown chakra and – even higher. Once this occurs, the energy body has been activated and in my heightened state of consciousness/awareness with my crown chakra being open, information from the cosmos or universal consciousness found its way into my mind. My left and right brains were able to put the pieces of the data together to form a coherent connection incorporating logical and creative ideals.

The Code represents the notion of what paradise or heaven on Earth (or any other planet or reality) could potentially be if everyone had a basis or goal to strive for and understood that in the end – you can't take any "stuff" with you when you die. Knowledge, wisdom and the right way of living and treating other living beings and our planet are tantamount to any money, fame or materialistic items one accumulates in their lifetime. I like to say, "Earth's a school, life's a lesson." What have you learned while being here? This statement can be expanded to include a spiritual outlook: "The universe is a school and eternity is a lesson." Much as if the universe (macrocosm) has evolved over 13.77 billion years and based on creation, we, as individual souls, race, planet (microcosm) are free to evolve and create as we see fit. This is the basis of existence.

As I wrote earlier, EVERYONE born is created free and equal. We are all free to say, think, do and believe what we want to. With that being said, the information in this chapter is a large cross section of my beliefs and interpretations thereof. The reader (You) is encouraged to read the information contained in this chapter with the following statements as a guide to refer back to if anything seems too outrageous:

1. Believe what you want to believe.
2. Don't judge.
3. Live and let live.
4. We are all ONE.
5. Read and interpret from a place of no ego. (IE No one is "special" or "better" than anybody else.)
6. If you come across something that makes you angry—laugh and realize anger doesn't do you any good and refer back to #'s 1-3.
7. The inevitable ultimate evolution of the universe is the realization that we are all God. God is unconditional and eternal love, therefore WE ARE ALL UNCONDITIONAL AND ETERNAL LOVE!

There are 13 sections to this chapter. Please visualize the top of a pyramid (3 dimensions) or triangle (2 dimensions) corresponding to the first digit, 0, then as you keep reading and accumulating more information you descend the pyramid and triangle until you are at the base/bottom. This visualization will be of assistance later on in the chapter. Each important item that corresponds to a specific number will be bolded with the inclusion of a brief description or reference. Some items will be long, some short. If I expanded on every item, the book would be much larger than it is now however I encourage the reader to dive deeper, and do his or her own research on certain items that are unfamiliar or would like a more in-depth description of. There will also be references and alternate interpretations on religious stories, adages and figures from the past. This is not to be construed as blasphemous in anyway. Remember, these stories were handed down from generation to generation. It would be different if the figure were here today and explained exactly what he meant. I challenge the reader to think freely and creatively, outside the box, to draw your own conclusions and remember – we are free to believe what we want to believe. Every story/parable in every religious text teaches a great lesson however most are steeped in symbolism. Having a KA made it easier to interpret the symbolism of certain stories and lessons that will go against the grain of the collective consciousness and what the general consensus has been taught or socially indoctrinated to understand as the true meaning.

As the previous portion of this book is an autobiography, there will be references to life lessons, as parables for certain sections to explain how all of this fits together like a gigantic jigsaw puzzle. The reader may draw any parallels as he or she sees fit. This chapter could be viewed as kind of a spiritual workbook or checklist. The ultimate goal is to assist the reader in having his or her own KA. From what I gather, they may be similar but each one is specific to the amount of information and experiences one is exposed to in life and past lives. (Yes, I'm going there!) Even if the ultimate goal is not achieved, having read and digested this information, it will dwell in your subconscious (as everything we do, say, think is eternally part of us) and be more of a benefit in the long run than not.

Without further ado – let's get started.

0. Om / Circle / Ring / The Great Void

0 represents the first character of the numeric system (0-9) and nothing, formless—empty. If the only tangible item in reality/universe were nothing there would be no cause for action and with that—no reality or existence.

Om is a sacred and spiritual sound and mantra with origins in Indian religions that represent divinity and the Atman (soul, self within) and Brahman (ultimate reality, entirety of the universe, truth, divine, supreme spirit, cosmic principles, knowledge).

Circle and **ring** go hand in hand. There is no break in a circle or ring. They are connected—like all of us. Mathematically and geometrically, every point from the center out to the edge of a circle is equal—like all of us. We are all equal and connected within the universe.

The **Great Void** is the interpretation of the Buddhist term Sunyata, which means emptiness. (Further research advised.) From a sacred geometric view as described in *The Ancient Secret of the Flower of Life* – Spirit moves in the Great Void by circles and ratios from the center stemming from the center of a circle. (Google search sacred geometry circles). This can also be interpreted as formless or the unmanifested, out of which creation and manifestation arise.

1. God / Love & Light / The Golden Rule

One **God**/Source/Creator/Great Spirit/Brahman/Universal Consciousness that we are all equally connected to. There are numerous gods and demi-gods throughout different cultures and religions but we all come from the same place. Those deities evolved their consciousness enough to do and perform supernatural things. One must believe we are all capable of such feats.

Having a KA and standing in/being part of/merging with/knowing the **Light** is to know God's eternal unconditional **Love**. We are what we choose to experience. The highest evolution attainable throughout the universe is everyone loving everything unconditionally and understanding the Light. You can choose to do it now or some other time but why wait? In the end, from a physical and spiritual/energetic viewpoint—Love and Light is all there is. Smile!

The **Golden Rule** states that we do unto others as we would have them do unto us. (Matthew 7:12) Simple enough. I wouldn't want anyone speaking, doing or thinking negative or bad things about me because I don't say, do or think negative or bad things about them. If everyone on the planet kept this in the forefront of his or her minds there would be nothing evil or negative in the world. No theft, deceit, murder, rape, war etc.

2. Karma / Yin-Yang / Duality / Polarity

Karma as it is defined in Hinduism and Buddhism is the sum of a person's actions in this and previous states of existence, viewed as deciding their fate in future existences.

My interpretations are as such but they all come down to the same thing:

- Receive what you put out there. (IE Give love and kindness, receive it in turn)
- Reap what you sow.

- What goes around comes around.
- Every action has an equal and opposite reaction. (IE standard model and laws of gravity in the physical/material world – what goes up must come down)
- As above, so below. (IE Our thoughts words and actions aren't for nothing. What we do on Earth reverberates in the cosmos and spiritual realm)
- Law of causality. (Cause and effect)
- Ripple (Throw a stone in a still lake. Your action created a ripple. The lake would be still had you not thrown a stone in the lake. Cause and effect.)

A simple example of how karma works in daily life could be losing a limb in a car accident at the age of 16 when, in a past life, you caused someone to lose a limb during a sword fight at that age. Or, losing your sight as a child and in a past life blinding someone. It all balances out.

The core catalyst for my KA was the amount of suffering I experienced due to the dissolution of the relationship with my X. On a physical, mental, emotional, psychological and spiritual level – it almost destroyed me. I knew in my heart that I would've done anything for this woman and I loved her more than I loved myself. This belief had been embedded in my soul before we even met. It is the purest definition of what true love can be. She gave me superficial reasons for ending my relationship that I didn't see were major issues that we/or I couldn't work on. In going over everything in my head, I came to the only conclusion that the amount of pain I experienced due to heartbreak must've been matched in a previous life. Our souls made a contract. I did not witness her suffering while we were together unless it was silent and hidden. I would've done anything to make sure this woman never shed a tear. I deduced that I must've done the same exact thing to her in a previous life and the pain I suffered was equal to hers thus balancing our karmic contract. My only option was to understand my lesson, forgive and forget, not turn the wheels of karma on this situation and hope for the best with her new life without me. Love never dies. What we had for the duration of our relationship will forever be in my heart and soul and I had to accept that as being good enough and smile. This contemplation was one of the last things that went through my mind before my KA initiated.

Another great example of balancing karma would be, on the extreme side, if you murdered someone in cold blood in a previous life, it would eventually need to be balanced. So, maybe not in this life, you will need to be murdered in cold blood to balance that action as well as all other subsidiaries of suffering such as emotional distress caused to friends and family.

Yin-Yang ("dark - bright") as defined on Wikipedia: In Chinese philosophy describe how seemingly opposite or contrary forces may actually be complementary, interconnected and interdependent in the natural world, and how they may give rise to each other as they interrelate to one another.

My interpretations include:
- You cannot have love without hate, light without darkness, up without down, positive without negative etc.
- A balance of opposite forces creates harmony.

A great parable along the lines of this concept that fits perfectly in this section would be the Tale of Two Wolves:

An old Cherokee is teaching his grandson about life. "A fight is going on inside me," he said to the boy.

"It is a terrible fight and it is between two wolves. One is evil – he is anger, envy, sorrow, regret, greed, arrogance, self-pity, guilt, resentment, inferiority, lies, false pride, superiority, and ego." He continued, "The other is good – he is joy, peace, love, hope, serenity, humility, kindness, benevolence, empathy, generosity, truth, compassion, and faith. The same fight is going on inside you – and inside every other person, too."

The grandson thought about it for a minute and then asked his grandfather, "Which wolf will win?"

The old Cherokee simply replied, "The one you feed."

While at/being/in the Light during my KA, I saw and felt this concept and immediately understood opposing forces by such examples as listed below:

Light	Dark
Love	Hate
God	Satan
Good	Evil
Love	Hate
Masculine	Feminine
Spiritual	Material
Church	State
Subtle	Gross
Yes	No
Conscious	Unconscious
Mindful	Mindless
Infinite	Finite
1	0
Positive	Negative
Shiva	Shakti
Empathy	Apathy
Proton	Electron
White	Black
Black	White
Up	Down
North	South
East	West
Right	Left
Right Handed (tantra)	Left Handed (tantra)
Happy	Sad
Courageous	Cowardly
On	Off
Wise	Ignorant
Etc.	

Duality is synonymous with yin-yang, in that it represents opposing forces. Some examples include viewing a glass as either half full or half empty. You can take a non-dualistic approach to any situation, view it as either positive or negative and choose to see the positive in any situation so it mitigates suffering. An example may include losing your job and choosing not see it in a negative light but to view it in a positive one with the notion that it happened for a reason and to move on to a new opportunity. A more abstract view may include losing a family member to cancer, knowing in your heart that you loved them, they loved you and love is eternal, believe you will see each other again and know that they would not want to see you in such pain over what can't be changed so to focus on all happy and positive memories about this person instead of dwelling on the negative. It is possible to flip a switch and take a positive spin on any situation that typically could be construed as negative. This falls along the lines of the Philosopher's Stone in the analogy of turning a base metal into gold.

Polarity deals with the energetic association with duality. A highly charged particle vibrates at a quicker rate than a lower charged particle. Love is associated with the highest energy while hate and fear are the lowest. Are bodies are energy. Sure, we have flesh, bone etc. but at the microscopic level, it's all protons, neutrons, electrons and the subatomic particles that compose them, which is energy. From an evolutionary standpoint, we need to evolve towards the highest energy (love) and reject/move away from the lowest (hate/fear) to survive and achieve our vision of paradise on Earth. Also, you'll notice people that move more (with the view that we are energetic beings) and have a structured exercise plan are happier, healthy and vibrant than those who are slothful and lethargic.

3. PAST-PRESENT-FUTURE / HARMONY-BALANCE / TRINITY: FATHER-SON-HOLY SPIRIT / FATHER-MOTHER-CHILD / SUN-MOON-EARTH / IDA-PINGALA-SHUSUMNA / THOUGHTS-WORDS-ACTIONS / MIND-BODY-SPIRIT / HORACE-ISIS-OSIRIS / BRAHMA-VISHNU-SHIVA / 3 WISE MEN / TRIANGLE-STRUCTURE

Past-Present-Future

As it relates to time, history is in the past, we are living in the present moment and our thoughts words and actions can dictate the future. The past can't be altered and on a larger scale, time is cyclical. If the mind is fixated too much in the past or future, stress and anxiety arise and it makes it difficult to be fully present or to cultivate present moment awareness. Combining lessons learned from Eckhart Tolle's book *The Power of Now* and the concept that heaven is not a place or destination but a state of mind and being – heaven is being fully present with the focus on creating your own vision of paradise.

Harmony-Balance

For one to be in harmony with the universe, one must first understand that we are all equal and no one is any better than anyone else. The ego dictates this. Once the ego is put in place, balance of the physical, emotional, mental, creative and spiritual bodies can develop. If any one aspect is out of line or too heavily influenced or not developed enough, raising the Kundalini energy will be difficult or detrimental to the body or mind.

A structural analogy could be envisioning a plank of wood, perhaps a 2'x4' horizontally balancing on another 2'x4' that is vertical. If the center of the beam is not precisely and mathematically aligned, the beam won't balance and it will tip to one side or the other. As previously mentioned, if we are too fixated on the past or future – balance is not possible.

Trinity

This word is derived from Latin (which translates to threefold) will be used to describe any combination of three concepts that form a clearer or bigger interpretation/meaning.

Father-Son-Holy Spirit

From the Christian doctrine, this is what the Holy Trinity represents.

As put forth in the Fourth Lateran Council they are stated to be one in all else, co-equal, co-eternal and consubstantial, and each is God, whole and entire. As interpreted from having a KA, Jesus may have believed in generational evolution and natural selection. He could have potentially contemplated the concept of bloodlines as it related to biblical and royal persons from studying the ruling classes of ancient Egypt, the Old Testament and other Hebrew texts. (IE Adam and Eve, Ramses II, Moses, David, Solomon etc.) The father teaches the son or daughter about the process of raising Kundalini Energy up the spine, which is an evolutionary mechanism. The Christian Church refers to this energy as the Holy Spirit however it goes by many other names all constituting the same thing: pure consciousness from the Divine. Other names as taken from different cultures and beliefs include prana, Reiki, mana, orgone, chi, qi, ki, orenda pneuma and od.

Father-Mother-Child

Notwithstanding modern science, through procreation, a man and a woman are necessary to bring a child into the world as well as a human in which a soul will inhabit to gain experience throughout its life. As far as we know, we humans, as a race, are the greatest creations in the universe. It takes an equal effort from the father and mother to raise a healthy and energetically balanced son or daughter. Remember, the male represents masculine energy, the female- feminine. With each generation, our species can either evolve or devolve through natural selection. Please keep in mind the goal of our race (and ultimately the universe) is to create and evolve.

Sun-Moon-Earth

The sun and moon play vital roles in allowing life to exist on our planet. We are dependent on the sun for energy and the moon for tidal cycles and weather stabilization. An interconnectedness and symbiosis exists. Without the sun, Earth would be frozen, dark and lifeless. If we had no moon, the oceans would go haywire and weather patterns would go berserk. The sun and moon are our closest celestial neighbors. Throughout time, deities have been associated with these celestial bodies and worshipped/honored. Through the magic of gravity, the moon revolves around the Earth, Earth around the sun, sun around a larger star, Alcyone, Alcyone an even larger star, Sirius and Sirius around the galactic center of the Milky Way.

Ida-Pingala-Shusumna

These are the three main channels (nadis) of the spiritual/subtle/light/etheric body in which prana flows. In conjunction with the chakras, (energy centers of the subtle body – more on these later in the chapter) these channels are used to raise the Kundalini energy from the base of the spine to the crown of the head to obtain Enlightenment. The Ida is on the left, is feminine energy, cold and associated with the moon. The Pingala is on the right, is masculine energy, hot and associated with the sun. The Shusumna is the central channel located in the spine.

Thoughts-Words-Actions

As humans, this is all we have to make things happen. These three things dictate how we operate in this world. Shouldn't we work to make them all be positive? It isn't that hard. It's a choice. From a karmic perspective, our thoughts, words and actions determine our destiny after our souls leave our physical body. From an energetic perspective, they are all energy. This energy is sent out through the universe and adds to the universal consciousness in a positive or negative way. If you live the rest of your life only thinking, speaking and doing positive things for yourself and others – you got nothing to worry about….ever!

Mind-Body-Spirit

Mind, body and spirit are the instruments used for our thoughts, words and actions. These two trinities go hand in hand. Aside from Spirit (soul/connection to Source, which is already perfect and eternal), wouldn't you want a strong mind and body for your thoughts, words and actions? We evolve these through using and developing them. If the mind gets lazy, depression and dementia can set in. If the body gets lazy, disease and illness can materialize. I hated being sick, tired and depressed. I stopped being lazy and did something about it.

Osiris-Isis-Horus

This trinity is an example of the father-mother-child only taken from ancient Egypt to show this union is timeless and universal. Osiris was murdered by his brother, Set, as he was jealous of his reign and wanted the throne for himself. One version of the myth has Set cutting up Osiris' body into 14 parts and spreading them throughout the land. Osiris' wife, Isis, gathered up all but one of the pieces and bandaged them together for a proper burial. This story can symbolize a representation of devotion to unconditional love. The gods were so impressed with this act that they resurrected Osiris and made him god of the underworld.

Brahma-Vishnu-Shiva

The Trimurti, or Hindu trinity, Brahma represents the creator or creation, Vishnu, the preserver, and Shiva, the destroyer or transformer. These cycles are universal and eternal. Keep in mind, the physics law of conservation of mass-energy, which states matter, can neither be created nor destroyed—it just changes form. This applies to everything, including human beings, Earth and the Sun. After experiencing a KA, other corollaries and symbolism became evident: life, balance, waking state/ conscious (Vishnu); death, darkness, unconscious/subconscious (Shiva); rebirth, Light, superconscious (Brahma).

The Three Wise Men

These were men that came from the East to worship the king of the Jews after Christ's birth. They brought frankincense, myrrh and gold – material items. Another interpretation could be that Jesus was taught, at an early age, the wisdom, knowledge and beliefs of other cultures and religions that were foreign to most Jews of the time, as they would have only studied the Torah due to the fact institutions of higher learning were scarce or not even created at the time. If you were raised to be a "son of God" as a child and that was the only upbringing you knew, learned or was conscious of, things may have turned out completely differently on a spiritual level. Who's to say the three wise men didn't bring knowledge of Buddhism, Hinduism, Taoism, Confucianism, yogic philosophy, or teachings of ancient Egypt, Rome or Greece? Who's to say concepts of soul or spiritual growth, evolution, karma etc. were not imparted on to him at an early age?

Triangle-Structure

At the most basic level, the triangle represents structure. On a two-dimensional plane, there would only be two lines. Their only options are to run parallel or cross at an angle for eternity. A third line gives us the possibility of form. There is now length, width and height. The universe is based on concepts of order out of chaos or formless into form.

As shown, the number 3 is significant in relation to a broad spectrum of examples. Even at the sub-atomic level, the first element on the Periodic Table, Hydrogen, has 3 components: a proton, electron and nucleus. On a spiritual level, humans, God and love can be considered a structural basis.

4. THE FOUR NOBLE TRUTHS / CARDINAL DIRECTIONS / ELEMENTS / SEASONS / KNOWN STATES OF MATTER

The Four Noble Truths

The primary teachings of Buddhism; Siddhartha Gautama puts forth that:

<u>Dukkha</u>, incapable of satisfying, painful. Life in this "mundane world", with its craving and clinging to impermanent states and things, *dukkha*, unsatisfactory and painful.

1. *Samudaya*, the origination or arising of *dukkha*. *Dukkha*, and repeated life in this world, arises with taṇha, "thirst," craving for and clinging to these impermanent states and things. This craving and clinging produces karma, which leads to renewed becoming, keeping us trapped in rebirth and renewed dissatisfaction.
2. *Niroda*, the cessation of *dukkha*. By stopping this craving and clinging nirvana is attained, no more karma is produced, and rebirth and dissatisfaction will no longer arise again.
3. *Magga*, the path to the cessation of, or liberation from *dukkha*. By following the Noble Eightfold Path, restraining oneself, cultivating discipline, and practicing mindfulness and meditation, craving and clinging will be stopped, and rebirth and dissatisfaction are ended.

From my perspective, and view of a mundane world, we are born, go to school either attend more school or are thrown right into supporting ourselves by working. We retire and then die. That sounds bleak. If one is consciously striving to obtain his or her version of paradise here on Earth and realize their dream with the belief that it will carry through to the next life, (when the physical body dies and soul moves on) this seems less bleak. One of the last things that I contemplated before my KA, was "Why the fuck does any of this matter?" and "What the hell is the purpose in all of this?" This pertained to the fact that I plan on playing, writing and recording music for the rest of my life and not for fame or fortune but for the sole fact that I love every aspect of it. I felt complete trust in my heart and soul while/in/at the Light. Trust to keep doing what I've been doing, be happy about it, and there is a bigger picture to it all.

Referring back to the Four Noble Truths, from a spiritual point of view and my personal perspective, suffering is a grasping attachment or desire. If one has no attachments or desires, nirvana is attainable. The ultimate attachment is people believe that they are their bodies or minds. You are a soul inhabiting a flesh vessel (body) to obtain knowledge and experience. One day it will return to dust. Other attachments include people, relationships, situations and objects, or material things. The material world is an illusion. (Maya) You can't take anything with you when your physical body fails. There is no sense being too attached to anything, as it is the root cause of suffering. The greatest pain/suffering I experienced was directly caused by the loss of a loving relationship with my X. It took a while but through the contemplation of past life karma, I realized it happened for a reason and made peace of the situation. Of course, there will always be love in my heart (hold space in my heart) for my X as no one ever said you have to stop loving someone after a relationship changes. I believe it's the right thing to do and a requirement for the Kundalini energy to pass through the heart chakra. Forgiveness.

Suffering of the mind affects our emotional wellbeing and can lead to sickness and disease if we let negative emotions get the best of us. My approach to minimize suffering can be viewed as it happened for a reason, make sense of the lesson, learn from it as quickly as possible and move on with pursuing your dreams!

Cardinal Directions

North, South, East and West. The four sides of the Great Pyramid of Giza precisely face each cardinal direction. This is not a coincidence and pertains to a higher consciousness in correlation with sacred geometry. (More on this later in the chapter)

Elements

The four elements of nature include earth, air, wind and water. I will exclude the 5th element, ether/space for the time being. (Ether/Space is associated with Ayurvedic philosophy and medicine, not with the Zodiac or Astrology) Most people believe that there is no rhyme or reason for how these elements react in nature. From the perspective of a higher level of consciousness – they can be manipulated and controlled with the use of prana. One needs to believe in the concept that a group consciousness (many people believing and focusing their intention and energy on something specific) can sway influence of these elements. (IE traverses the course of a hurricane, alter a weather pattern or if you're Moses – part the Red Sea.) Before organic life evolved, these universal elements were all there were in the universe. There is also a correspondence to the Zodiac wheel as each element has three signs associated with them.

Seasons

These include winter, spring, summer and autumn. (Other cultures have a different interpretation and number of seasons such as Ayurvedic and traditional Chinese medicine however four is being used for this example) If you are lucky enough to live in a geographic region that experiences an equal amount of seasonal weather, there is approximately 90 days of each season. This makes it easier to break up the year by activities so one can never get too bored or go stir crazy. I like to ski in the winter, play golf in the spring and summer, paddleboard and bike in the summer and keep a pretty low profile in the fall with leisurely travel mostly done in the fall and winter. Each season has their own specific feel and attributes making them each unique.

Known States of Matter

I included the word "known" as a form of matter exists under different conditions, mostly affected by pressure and temperature. We are familiar with solids, liquids, gases and plasma however, that is what our technology and science can determine from the observable universe. Who knows what lurks out in the ever-expanding cosmos with the variable combinations of unknown pressures and temperatures.

5. The Five Pillars of Islam / Senses / Platonic Solids

The Five Pillars of Islam

A small cross section of laws of the Islamic faith; what I have included are the names of each but with my personal interpretation (as it is much different from a spiritual viewpoint, especially for someone who has had a KA) because just having a basic understanding of these and ones own perspective is better than having no understanding at all.

1. Shahada: Faith (Declaration of Faith)
   That there is only one God. Remember, we are free to believe whatever we want to believe but from my understanding and belief, there is but one Source/Creator/Absolute/God/Great Spirit/ Universal Consciousness and goes by many names throughout various cultures and religions.

2. Salat: Prayer (Obligatory Prayer)
   I've said nighttime prayers before bed since I was a kid. I pray when I visit church. Prayer is asking God for something and the understanding that through him, all things are possible.

3. Zakat: Charity (Compulsory Giving)
   When we get to a point in our lives where we've done enough work to take care of ourselves, we can choose to be selfish and continue to only think of ourselves or understand charity and compassion for those less fortunate who weren't given the same opportunities as the more fortunate had been given. A major factor of this is karma.

4. Sawm: Fasting (Fasting in the month of Ramadan)
   Fasting is apparent in many religions and cultures as a sacrifice to God. A major factor in raising Kundalini is bringing the physical body to as close of a state of purity so there are no impediments and the energy is able to rise to the crown chakra more fluidly.

5. Hajj: Pilgrimage to Mecca

    Men and women of the Islamic faith are required to make at least one pilgrimage in their lifetime to the holy city as an expression and out of devotion to God. Whatever location we feel is dear to our hearts and brings us closer to God should be visited as one sees fit. There are no rules – you can make up your own, as you are master of your own destiny. Whether it is a mosque, church, synagogue, monastery, temple or…Madison Square Garden. This is where I had my KA and I've been there countless times for countless concerts as music brings me closer to my truest self and bliss. There, I can dance, sing, jump up and down without a care in the world and be free to enjoy every aspect of life.

The prophet Muhammad, PBUH, a central figure in the Muslim faith is depicted through various art either wearing a veil over his face, having a halo or engulfed in flames but not burning. These are symbolic of the fire of Kundalini as well as the dissolution of the ego insomuch as once the 'little I' or personality is removed – we are all God and part of the universal consciousness.

Senses

Sight, touch, hearing, taste and smell are how are physical bodies interact with the material world and make "sense" of it as our brains interpret different stimuli.

Platonic Solids

Are the:

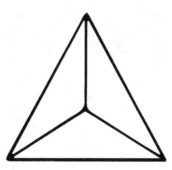

Cube

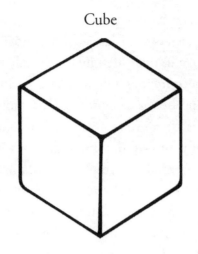

Octahedron

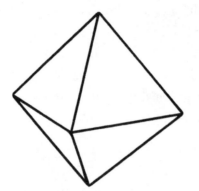

Dodecahedron

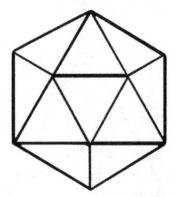

Icosahedron

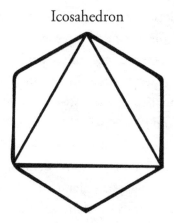

The Greek philosopher Plato theorized that the classic elements of earth, air, water, fire and ether were made of these solid shapes. They are also primal models of crystal patterns that occur throughout the world of minerals in numerous variations. Each shape, through mathematic and geometric symmetry is contained within a sphere. These shapes are included in the study of sacred geometry.

~~~

6. 6ᵀᴴ Sense / Solfeggio Frequencies / 33 / 330° / Star of David / Freemasons-Knights Templar

6ᵗʰ Sense

As we have the five senses of the body that are able to perceive the physical world and have our brains make sense of reality, The 6th sense deals with our ability to sense things other than using our bodily senses and is associated with extrasensory perception and intuition. It is synonymous with the third eye and the 6ᵗʰ chakra. (Part of the subtle body) It is located in the lower center of the brain near the brain stem. It resembles a pinecone. There are historic connections and symbolism found in ancient cultures throughout the world. Osiris as well as the Greek god Dionysus had staffs tipped with a pinecone. In the ancient Sumerian creation myths, the Annunaki are depicted (carved in stone) holding a pinecone at head level as if delivering it to a human being (putting it in their head). This symbolism could be representative of being self-aware. From an evolutionary perspective—this separates us from animals. The pineal gland used to be much larger in ancient times and was more easily accessible for meditating on to have spiritual visions. Through the ages and especially in modern times with the inclusion of fluoride in our drinking water, it has shrunk in size, become calcified and affects certain aspects of the endocrine system. It can be decalcified by drinking filtered water, taking blue green algae supplements, or including cacao in the diet. There are other means to decalcify the pineal gland to bolster and balance the energetic body.

Solfeggio Frequencies

As described by the website Attuned Vibrations, Solfeggio frequencies make up the ancient 6-tone scale thought to have been used in sacred music, including the beautiful and well-known Gregorian Chants. In medieval times, when churchgoers sung in church or listened to these chants, they were, on a subconscious level, healing their bodies. The chants and their special tones were believed to impart spiritual blessings when sung in harmony. Each Solfeggio tone is comprised of a frequency required to balance your energy and keep your body, mind and spirit in perfect harmony.

The primary frequencies are and associated with:

> **Ut 396 Hz** – Liberating Guilt and Fear
> **Re 417 Hz**– Undoing Situations and Facilitating Change
> **Me 528 Hz** – Transformation and Miracles (DNA Repair)
> **Fa 639 Hz** – Connecting/Relationships
> **Sol 741 Hz** – Expression/Solutions
> **La 852 Hz** – Returning to Spiritual Order

You will notice, if you take the digit '0' out of the numeric scale, (1 follows 9) each higher frequency is separated by 111 Hz. That number holds significance and the frequencies can repeat higher IE 963, 1074, 1185, 1296…they all have energetic benefits. Crystal bowls used in meditation and healing practices are tuned to the Solfeggio frequencies as each one resonates a particular chakra. Structured sound/tones have healing properties and evolutionary effects on our DNA at the molecular level. The human body is composed of between 60 to 70% water. Water has consciousness and responds to sound. (Google water has consciousness in respects to Dr. Masaru Emoto's research) As listed above, certain frequencies are associated with the subtle/energy body. Remember, we are spoiled. Recorded music was created less than a century ago. We are making leaps and bounds on the evolutionary scale as opposed to our ancestors who did not have the benefit of listening to recorded music!

'33'

Listed under section 6 for (3+3).

This number has much spiritual significance in that:

1. There are 33 vertebrae that make up the human spinal column. Remember, the main nadis of the subtle body and only way to raise Kundalini is up the spine.
2. The age at which Jesus "died"/crucified.
3. The divine name *Elohim* appears 33 times in the story of creation in the opening chapters of Genesis.
4. Is a numerical representation of the Hebrew Star of David as well as the equivalent of AMEN: 1+13+5+14=33 if a number value is assigned to the alphabet. (A=1, Z=26).
5. A significant number in modern numerology; one of the master numbers along with 11 and 22.
6. Divided by itself yields 11. (More on this later in the chapter)
7. Review section 3 and contemplate randomly grouping two of each reference together to form complex structures of creativity. (IE thoughts, words, actions + mind, body, spirit. Triangle-structure + trinity etc.)

330°

Associated with the Pisces constellation of the Zodiac, which is the last sign (12th house), This is the beginning of the celestial longitude. The Mayan's used a long count in conjunction with the precession of the equinoxes which posits that Earth goes through one such complete processional cycle in a period of approximately 25,920 years or 1° every 72 years, during which the positions of stars will slowly change in both equatorial coordinates and ecliptic longitude. Meaning, a celestial "month" is approximately 2,160 years. (72 years x 30 degrees. 12 Zodiac signs in a year.) Thus representing the change from one astrological age to the next IE The Age of Pisces transitioning to the Age of Aquarius. The constellations of the Zodiac as viewed from Earth are like that of a wheel or circle. A circle precisely divided into 12 sections yields equal sections of 30°. (12 Zodiac signs x 30° = 360° or a complete circle.)

Star of David

This shape is a hexagram, consisting of two equilateral triangles. It is associated with the Jewish faith and was also known as the Seal of Solomon. According to the Hebrew Bible, King David was the second king of the united kingdom of Israel and Judah. His son, Solomon was his successor. The significance of the symbol is that it is a two- dimensional representation of the Star Tetrahedron. (More on this later in the chapter.)

Freemasons-Knights

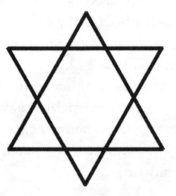

There is no association with the number 6 regarding these two organizations. They are listed here as an association to 1: the Star of David and 2: connection to geometry and creating with numbers and shapes. Hiram Abiff was the chief architect during the construction of the Temple of Solomon. He was considered a master mason and his story and history are included in modern day freemason rituals. The symbol of the freemasons is a compass, square and the letter 'G' in the focal point denoting God and/or Geometry – meaning, there is a grand architect in the universe. Jesus was a carpenter who used these tools to build and as all builders know; tools, measurements, numbers, shapes, angles, precision etc. are all utilized in their craft. It is believed that the Knights Templar (also known as Order of Solomon's Temple) who were officially endorsed by the Roman Catholic Church in 1129, evolved out of medieval guilds of masons and acted as guardians to Christians traveling from the West to the holy land of Jerusalem at the time of the Crusades. They also created an early system of banking and credit. The date associated with their decline is Friday the 13th 1307 by order of King Phillip IV due to claims going against the Catholic Church.

∿∿

7. Days in a Week / Virtues vs. Sins / Colors of the Rainbow / Chakras / Tones of a Music Scale / Liberal Arts of Antiquity

Days in a Week

We have seven days in a week. I pretty much know where I will be at any given time of any day during the week from the moment I wake up Monday morning to the moment I close my eyes Sunday night. The universe responds to structure and order. Having a solid schedule/routine keeps me sharp and focused. I've minimized any types of activities (video games, reading tabloid magazines, total lethargy) that aren't for my greatest good/benefit and what I'm working towards. Once a solid schedule is in place, the weeks begin to fly by without any type of resistance.

Visualize a sound wave that has peaks and troughs. Your days, weeks, months, seasons and years will begin to realign and everything will become an even flow. You will develop a cadence or rhythm/pulse to your life and begin to dance through it! (Order out of chaos)

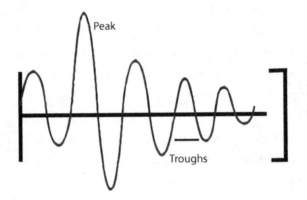

Virtues vs. Sins

These can be traced back to ancient Greek with Plato and Aristotle discerning desirable character traits but ultimately, these are karma based. On an energetic and spiritual spectrum, the virtues are positive, bring us closer to God/Source/Creator/Supreme Soul/Brahman/Great Spirit and the best version of ourselves, the sins are negative, separate us, drag us down to the worst version of ourselves.

Virtue	Sin
1. Chastity	Lust
2. Temperance	Gluttony
3. Charity	Greed
4. Diligence	Sloth
5. Patience	Wrath
6. Kindness	Envy
7. Humility	Pride

These are choices and can be cultivated with mindfulness. Why be lustful when there is love? Why be gluttonous when there's enough to share and moderation is a healthy alternative. Why be greedy when it is right to be charitable to those less fortunate. Do you have a good work ethic and understanding of time management or are you slothful and lazy? Are you jealous of others for what they have or how they look or a certain skill set that is measurably better than your own skill set or can you let it not affect you and be happy for that person? Does your ego and bank account paint the illusion that you are better than other people or are you humble and think of others more and yourself less? Further contemplation, self-reflection and research of these terms are encouraged. I've learned my lessons in this department. It comes from living and experience.

Colors of the Rainbow

Color is derived from the spectrum of light and each has it's own unique wavelength and energetic signature associated with it. They are:

Red
Orange
Yellow
Green
Blue
Indigo
Violet

Red has the lowest wavelength and energy signature. The higher you climb the color rainbow, the higher the frequency and energy signature. These are part of the visible spectrum of light. Our eyes can only perceive certain wavelengths of color as extremely low (infrared) or high (ultra violet) are invisible to the naked eye.

Chakras

Sanskrit for "wheel", these are energy centers of the subtle/energy body. There are many throughout the body but when it comes to raising

Kundalini, there are seven primary ones that are the focus. They are located along the spinal column from the coccyx up through the neck and in the head. Each chakra has a correlation to our physical body. There is extensive information on the anatomy of the subtle body as well as traditional views of the chakra system. While at/in/part of the Light during my KA, I immediately understood the correlation and connection between the physical (gross) and subtle body, what chakra was associated with what aspect of my life, experiences and lessons learned and knew why I had a KA. As I've stated previously, it wasn't a hallucination or fluke. Having a KA combines all aspects of the human experience. I will give a brief description and the primary focus given my first-hand account of what each chakra is associated with. Further personal research is encouraged but my "Cliff Notes" are a great start for a better grasp of this subject.

1. Muladhara – root chakra. This is located at the base of the spine in the coccygeal region. The associated color is red. Here is where dormant Kundalini rests until awoken. This deals with our physical form, flight or fight response when under attack and in connection to evolution, our most basic chakra. Think food, shelter and Cro-Magnon man or Neanderthal before the development of emotions and intelligence. Our connection to Source/soul inhabits a physical form.

2. Svadhishthana – sacral chakra. This is located in the sacrum. The associated color is orange. The primary connection is our emotions. These are developed through life experiences and interactions with others. Throughout my life, I've experience the full spectrum of every emotion possible. On one end love, the other— hate and all points in between. We should be grateful to Source/ Creator that humans are even capable of feeling such a broad spectrum of emotions. There is a correspondence to the seven virtues in relation to good, healthy, positive and loving emotions as well as the seven sins in relation to bad, unhealthy, negative and hateful emotions. (Duality/polarity of section 2) It feels better

and gives us a clean conscience when acting on the positive end of the spectrum. There are examples every day. All you need to do is turn on the 5 O'clock news. People who cannot control their emotional response effectively lash out and perform unconscious acts against others. Murder, rape, racism/bigotry, bullying etc. are all products of negative, unregulated emotions. From an energetic perspective, romantic love and that woozy feeling during the honeymoon period are not only oxytocin levels being effected in the brain but also a boost to our energy/auric field. Near the end of our relationship, I was drinking a little more than I should have been. Alcohol is a depressant. It also lowers our energy field. That strong bond we had had weakened to the point where, as my X was very sensitive to emotions and energy (empath), it assisted on a subconscious level in deteriorating our relationship.

3. Manipura – solar plexus chakra. This is located near the navel. The associated color is yellow. The primary connection is our intelligence. In today's day and age, the more you know the better chances you have at survival. It is getting more and more difficult to find a career and job path without proper training and education. In the West, the first public school system started in Boston in 1821. Throughout history, the primary focus of living life was to survive and procreate. Now, we see an extended range of education programs for all aspects in society. Not everyone has access to all education systems available. If I was serious in my scholarly endeavors and had the financial means available, sure a PhD sounds great but that opportunity wasn't present at the time. We all have brains in our heads and everyone is pretty much capable of learning anything their heart desires given the proper determination, time management, opportunity and will. The kicker here is the development of the brain's hemispheres or left-brain and right-brain. The left-brain is considered masculine and its focus is logic, rationality and concrete thinking. Concrete or permanent attributes can be associated with hard data such as numbers and formulas. The right-brain is considered feminine and its focus is

creativity and abstract thinking. The pinnacle achievements of my left-brain were studying and passing my life insurance license, five FINRA and CFP exams. I crammed a lot of hard data and left grooves in my gray matter. I knew I fucked up in college and didn't learn anything of substance to pursue a career with my degree but I had the intelligence to realize the future value of learning everything I could about the financial services and insurance industry. On the other side, writing and creating music out of thin air. There is also a spectrum associated with intelligence. On one end there is brilliance/genius. On the other there is ignorance/stupidity. Referencing a previous statement from this chapter, "Earth's a school, life's a lesson." Wouldn't it be wise to learn as much about everything as possible? You will keep your brain engaged, firing, functioning on all cylinders and keep dementia and Alzheimer's at bay.

4. Anahata – heart chakra. This is located in the center of the chest. The associated color is green. The primary connection is compassion. Other connections associated with this chakra are empathy, forgiveness and putting others first. One of the last things that went through my mind before the Kundalini rose of my spine was that I made peace with what happened in my relationship with my X. I knew in my heart and soul that I would've loved her forever and put her wellbeing ahead of my own. I felt that she knew this as well however the timing and circumstances just weren't there for the fairytale ending. I had honestly forgiven her for not wanting to work through any bumps in our relationship and I forgave myself in the process. Also, the fact that no one can tell you what to believe and my soul and connection to Source knew how much I loved this woman and at one time, vice versa. I believe love never dies and if there is a heaven it'll all work out in some other time and place. There was no way I was going to be bitter and hold a grudge for the rest of my life but at one time it felt like it. The seat of the soul is located in the heart chakra and forgiving someone who caused you the most pain in your

life balances karma, which is a primary catalyst for my KA. In the long run, it's better to show empathy and compassion than apathy and indifference. The phrase "Have a heart" correlates to this. Another example associated with this chakra is feeling sympathetic for a homeless person, not having the notion in our head and heart that "they got what they deserved." The symbol of the cross, from what Christian dogma states, is the crucifixion of Jesus and ultimately dying for our sins. From a spiritual perspective, it is a primitive representation of a human with arms out-stretched. Where the two lines cross is where the chest and heart chakra are located. Kundalini cannot rise higher than the heart chakra without compassion and ultimately forgiving the source of ones greatest suffering. The Egyptian symbol that is similar to the cross is the ankh, which means breath of life. (Where universal breath of life can be prana circulating through the energy body.) It resembles a human figure with a halo or glow around the head. This symbol-izes raising the Kundalini to the 6th or 7th chakra and is seen in religious art throughout many cultures including Christian saints and Indian sages and gods.

5. Vishuddha – throat chakra located in the throat. The associat-ed color is light or pale blue. The primary connection is com-munication and growth through expression. From a universal a spiritual perspective, the purest form of expression is the use and combination of items that God left for us. If we strip everything man created and found ourselves back before the time of com-puters, plastics, preservatives in food etc., we are left with such

things as wood, stone, metals, water, fire, earth, air, color, sound, dance, plants etc. The human soul knows it is capable of anything and can be a great builder, sculptor, artist, musician, poet, chef etc. Our ultimate purpose besides to evolve is to create. Creating works of beauty is the greatest praise we can give to God/Source/ Creator/Universal Consciousness. We all have souls/connection to Source and are capable of creating anything we put our hearts, minds and bodies into. Music found me at an early age and is my greatest vehicle for expression and creating. This gives greater meaning to the phrase, follow your heart. As we can see, the chakra associated with living your dream of creating does in fact follow the heart chakra. Right before my KA when I was in serious contemplation of God, the universe and reality I found myself saying "this is bullshit" and "I don't get it." I want to create, play and record music forever but after I die that might not be a possibility? Being at/in/part of the Light made those statements completely obsolete. I only understood to trust the process, be patient and everything's all good.

6. Ajna – third-eye chakra located in the center of the head. The associated colors are violet, indigo and dark blue. The primary connection is our intuition, inner guidance as well as extrasensory perception and visual consciousness. The pineal gland is linked to this chakra. While at/in/part of the Light during my KA, I saw two charged particles engaged in a dance, a spaceship as well as a combined vision of the Giza Plateau, Stonehenge and a Mayan temple/pyramid. This phenomenon would be considered extrasensory in that there was remote viewing and retro cognition (perception of past events) taking place. These are siddhis, which are supernatural or paranormal attainments that are products of spiritual advancement. (Trikalajnatvam – knowing the past, present and future; duradarsanam – seeing things far away) I understood these to be linked to time in relation to the past, present and future. I also understood that the ancient Egyptians, Celts and Mayans were on the right track. Everything in the universe,

at the smallest possible level, is composed of the same material and we are not alone in the universe OR there may have been extraterrestrial assistance in the creation and manipulation of our race/species. I also had a clear picture and concept of the story and journey of the soul. Meaning, there was a reason I was born when I was born with the circumstances of my opportunity to education, socio-economic class, body, race, family relations etc. as opposed to being born in squalor or an African village without much potable water, access to education and more exposure to the elements and predators such as hungry lions. The primary reason being karma.

7. Sahasrara – crown chakra located at the top of the head or above the crown of the head. The associated color is white. The primary connection is pure consciousness, enlightenment, issues associated with death of the physical body and liberation of the soul. The pituitary gland is associated with this chakra. In yogic philosophy, meditating on God (Isvara), Samadhi is attainable. A KA is the physical process of raising the Light and energy of pure consciousness up through the chakras where its final point is the Sahasrara or crown chakra, which results in Samadhi. Samadhi can be defined as when the meditator becomes the object of meditation. In my experience, my physical body and mind were in such a relaxed state, while contemplating God, the universe, the Big Bang, energy, matter, karma, eternity, reality, heaven, paradise, immortality—my consciousness merged with ALL and my KA is the result. I was also content in all areas of my life. I had found balance, inner peace and developed a great schedule to adhere to. I just couldn't believe I was supposed to work in a job that wasn't my primary passion and mode for creating for the rest of my life, retire and then "die." I wanted more. I knew there had to be more to this. My KA was direct proof, from a personal perspective, that there IS more. In that instant, eternal faith and hope developed and I knew I would never be depressed again.

The chakra system can be analogous to the Stairway to Heaven or Jacob's Ladder. In order to get to heaven or realize our connection to God/Source/Creator/Universe and our own true divine self, the upper movement of the Light through the chakras can be viewed as a test. The physical body (1) must be strong and as pure as possible from impurities, all emotions (2) must be experienced to understand the human condition, it takes intelligence (3) to assist in survival and to realize negative emotions can bring us down and affect our physical bodies, in order to reach the higher chakras, we must use our hearts (4) and forgive our greatest transgressors and causes of pain, in order to eventually express and create (5) the condition of our circumstances and share this with the world/universe. We use our intuition to realize there has to be a bigger plan and there is no reason to fear if we continue to learn and do good (6) thanks to our eternal connection to God/Source/Great Spirit (7). One of the greatest obstacles to overcome is the misidentification with the ego – or false self. This is the part of the personality (The little 'I') that feels the need to think you are better than someone else. Remember, we are all equal in the eyes of Source/Creator/Great Spirit. The first three chakras are associated with ego. Ego of body/vanity, lack of emotional regulation, and intelligence are all primary blocks, as well as a focus on materialism (IE, I have more money and property than you therefore I am more important and better in my social standing etc.) before approaching the heart chakra and higher.

Tones of the Music Scale

In Western music, (as Eastern music uses quarter tones) there are seven notes of a major or minor scale before the notes repeat at a higher or lower octave. For the basic key of 'C', The notes run C, D, E, F, G, A, B and then repeat at the next 'C' where the frequency is double of the octave below it. A major scale consists of a series of steps to climb to the next octave. W, W, H, W, W, W, H. (W = whole step, H = half step) The 'A' below middle 'C' on a piano is an easier example given the frequency (Hz) is the only pure tone with a whole number. This frequency is 220Hz. Using the major scale formula, the next 'A' above middle 'C's frequency is 440Hz. Above that is 880Hz and above that one is 1760Hz. Tones in music are structured sound in relation to vibrations. As demonstrated, there is math and ratios involved in music.

Liberal Arts of Antiquity

Liberal arts are the term given to an education based on classical antiquity. It is meant to be a practical education, which develops mental capacity. It was designed in the late medieval period (12th/13th centuries) using ideas from Ancient Greek and Roman culture. They were taught in two groups, the Trivium (3 ways) and
Quadrivium (4 ways).
The Trivium consists of:
1. Grammar
2. Dialectic (logic)
3. Rhetoric

The Quadrivium consists of:
1. Arithmetic
2. Geometry
3. Astronomy
4. Music

For the development of the brain (left and right) and a well-rounded and balanced system of worldly and universal knowledge, these subjects are of great importance.

8. Limbs of Yoga / Octave – of Light and Sound / Infinity-Spinal Column / Star Tetrahedron

The Eight Limbs of Yoga

First described in *The Yoga Sutra's of Patanjali*, Astanga (a Sanskrit compound for having eight limbs or branches) is the eightfold yoga path. In combining the philosophy and practice of yoga, the ultimate goal is freedom, spiritual illumination/Enlightenment and the development of a joyful and creative life. This path has its focus on evolution. It can slow or reverse the aging process and is said to add years to one's life and life to one's years. Yoga is derived from the Sanskrit word yuj, meaning to yoke or bind. The practice of yoga is to bind or bring together the body and mind for union with the true self or soul. On a larger scale and from a top-down perspective of the universe – it can be interpreted as bringing together all in manifest reality. We are all One and eternally connected with our Creator.

Before discussing the eight limbs, the following should be contemplated/reflected upon:

Key elements of life include:
1. Aspiring to grow
2. Observing the self (awareness)
3. Discernment – letting go of ignorance leads to wisdom
4. Integrity – synthesis of thought, word and action/deed.

Two aspects of spiritual practice include:
1. Abhyasa – practice
2. Vairagya – renunciation

The four aims of life include:
1. Dharma – observation of spiritual discipline, virtue in one's life purpose

2. Artha – creation of a balanced life
3. Kama – enjoyment of the fruits of one's labors – love and joy
4. Moksa – liberation/freedom

The five afflictions include:
1. Avidya – spiritual ignorance
2. Asmita – pride/egoism
3. Raga (dukkha) – desire, grasping attachment
4. Dvesa – aversion/hate
5. Abhinivesa – fear of death

From a personal perspective/account and system of belief, to show how these elements relate to daily living, examples are as follows:

- Never stop learning.
- Always be mindful of thoughts, words, actions and how they affect others.
- Your word is your bond. I'll believe anything anyone tells me because I'd like to believe they have no reason to deceive or lie. If they do, trust is very difficult to reestablish. In my relationship with my X, I pledged my love forever and she did the same. This was from the heart and soul. My greatest suffering came from that relationship/bond being broken thus throwing integrity out the window.
- Practice makes practice. Keep a steady schedule and incorporate the practice into daily life.
- My greatest obstacle was renunciation. It is the formal rejection of something, most typically a belief. A week before my KA I told my mother I was not a practicing Catholic as I had been raised and she had as well as her parents etc. The biggest belief was that Jesus was the only Son of God. I could no longer get on board with this statement, as, in my heart, I knew we were all equal. I was willing to accept whatever fate would come my way when I died and believed if I were living my life, doing good and what

I loved with the focus on love and togetherness, I would not be thrown into the torments of hell!

- Dharma. What's your purpose for living? We all have one. For some, it takes longer to figure out than others. I boiled it down to this: Pick one dream or vision without the limitations of time (meaning, you know your soul is eternal so if you don't achieve what your goal(s) is/are in this life it will be a closer reality in the next), learn as much as you can about everything, know we are all connected, understand the Golden Rule and the laws of karma while developing your body and mind with the ultimate goal of connecting with your own divinity/connection to Source/God/Absolute/Universal Consciousness. Everyone's Path is different. Discovering and creating one is up to the individual. There is no boilerplate formula.

- Artha/Balance. This took a while for me to develop. It applies to all aspects of being human including: diet, (IE whole foods not tampered with by man, carbs, proteins, good fats, easy on the sugar, bad fats and processed foods) work and play.

- Kama/enjoying the fruit of one's labors makes life all the more worthwhile. While all work is noble, my band plays so often because one of the greatest perks of playing music live is the reaction and joy that is created on the listener/dancer's face. Money is a byproduct of work and enables us to experience more and live a more comfortable life.

- Moksa: We are all born free to think, say and do what we like. Having a good understanding of the laws of society, you will stay out of jail and live freely until it's time for your soul to move on. Liberation of the soul is the ultimate freedom. This is synonymous with a KA.

- Avidya: We are all free to believe what we want but understanding that God exists and the belief there is a bigger picture/plan in the working can wash away any ignorance. It's an individual journey to find your own connection and make sense of it all. Don't tread on that which is sacred to spirit and conscience. Through the years, I've known and had friends of different religious beliefs. I don't judge anyone for what his or her beliefs are.

- Asmita is the affliction of the ego or the false self. Pride is a deadly sin. These are second chakra characteristics. Having a KA dissolves the ego and I immediately understood I am no better than anyone else. We are all equal and the evolution of humanity will eventually come to this realization, as it is necessary for our survival as a race.

- Raga is synonymous with dukkha is grasping attachment and/or desire. Dukkha, the focus of the Four Noble Truths states that life is suffering. To live and know that one ultimately will die is the greatest description of suffering. I believe every breath is a blessing and the experience of living is the greatest gift God/Source/Creator/Universal Consciousness has ever given us. Reverse the polarity on that statement. Life is a gift. Our negative reactions to situations etc. increase our suffering. As far as desire goes, my heart and soul knows what it wants and I know in my heart I will eventually obtain whatever I desire but I'm not going to let it bring me down to the point where I suffer if a desire is not obtained. The hardest attachment to let go is that we are not our physical bodies. We are spiritual/energetic beings that have evolved our levels of consciousness to where we can physically perceive matter. At the substratum: once broken down to the smallest quantum particle—it's all energy of the same vibration/light. Envision all matter swirling into a black hole. The light/energy of a rock, tree, animal or human is at parity before falling in and getting spit out to another universe or Big Bang. Now add this vision to a meditation with the focus on love, unity and the 1st, 4th, 6th and 7th chakras.

- Dvesa: We are all connected. To hate someone is to hate yourself and is to hate God as God is absolute eternal love of the highest order. Hate is the most negative emotion and one cannot evolve with having this sewn into their fabric of being.

- Abhinivesa is the fear of death. We are all born and we will all die. Some of us will go sooner rather than later, and some of us in more horrific or more peaceful ways. Either way, it boils down to karma, as it must be balanced. Having a KA abolishes this fear as my karma had been balanced or burnt up. I started anew with love in my heart for all creation and focusing on positive thoughts, words and deeds. People that focus on acts that separate us (murder, rape, torture etc.) and cause pain on a physical, emotional, psychological, spiritual level are the ones that should be concerned with what happens to their soul after it moves on from this earthly sojourn.

The eight limbs of yoga are:

1. Yamas
2. Niyamas
3. Asana
4. Pranayama
5. Pratyahara
6. Dharana
7. Dhyana
8. Samadhi

Yamas – the five moral restraints
   a. Ahimsa – non-violence, kindness
   b. Satya – truthfulness
   c. Asteya – non-stealing
   d. Brahmacarya – moderation
   e. Aparigraha – non-hoarding, self-reliance, generosity

   » Ahimsa – Besides hitting a cat with my car in my 20's (he survived as he was under the car and the tires didn't squash him.), swatting lightening bugs with a tennis racket as a teen and the occasional mosquito fogger – I don't believe in violence. I've never even really been in a fight – just some horsing around with friends. Society will eventually evolve to non-violence. War will be a thing of the past but it starts on the individual level. Violence is a negative act and will ultimately need to be balanced on a karmic level.

» Satya – If you tell the truth your entire life you will have a clear conscience. There is no reason to deceive anyone if you are always working on doing what's right and good.

» Asteya – The last thing I remember stealing was a book and a couple of CD's in college. If it's not yours, don't take it.

» Brahmacarya – Everything is good in moderation. The body and mind will adapt. Excess may lead to the palace of wisdom however it also creates imbalances in the mind and body. I am a moderate user of tobacco, cigarettes and marijuana. The last time I really got drunk was probably in 2011. I don't like waking up with a hangover, dealing with it the entire day and feeling like shit. I'd rather feel good and keep my wits about me. The same goes with diet. If you are too heavy on red meat, processed foods and sugar—your body will feel the effects as opposed to eating leaner: incorporating more plant based protein, fruits, vegetables etc.

» Aparigraha – Live simply. The tally of personal property I own consists of my truck, clothes, musical equipment, a couple of computers, flat screen, bike, paddleboard, bed, night stand, golf clubs, skis, books and a few personal effects/knick-knacks.

Niyamas – the five observances
   a. Sauca – purity/cleanliness
   b. Santosa – contentment/gratitude
   c. Tapas – zeal, austerity, self-discipline
   d. Svadhyaya – self-study, study of texts/scripture
   e. Isvara-pranidhana – devotion to a higher power, surrender

» Sauca – Don't be a slob. Clean up after yourself! Purity deals with thoughts, words and deeds as well as what we put in our bodies. If you are constantly striving for good and positive purposes in life you have nothing to worry about in this observance. Cleanliness has never been an issue. I shower daily, am mindful of personal hygiene and regularly clean my residence, dishes and clothes.

» Santosa – Through contemplation, I realized I was content in all aspects of my life regarding work, musical ability, recreational activity, income etc. and forever grateful for it all and the opportunities afforded me. However, I was not content in the belief that being happy in life was predicated on working a job while my passion lie elsewhere and not pursuing my dreams. I knew there had to be more than what life currently offered.

» Tapas – Self-discipline deals with time management of priorities as well as a personal moral code. Family/friends, health, work, music are at the top of the list. A moral code comes from experience and living and learning. Life doesn't come with an instruction manual. It's up to each of us to find our own way and Path on this journey. Zeal means enthusiasm and passion. I appreciate the process and have developed a passion for life that will never die and pursuing my dreams.

» Svadhyaya – I've read over half a dozen books on yoga (http://www.hermetics.org/library/Library_Yoga.html) including hatha, bhakti, kriya, karma and Kundalini practices. This observance does not only relate to yoga but all aspects of life. Learning doesn't stop after public school. It's a lifelong process.

» Isvara-pranidhana – This was one of the last pieces of the puzzle regarding the eight limbs of yoga that, after having my KA, I understood that all the components of the Path are there as personal checklist. I just wasn't aware of it prior to my KA. In my life, I've never lost faith in God. Through all the hardships and pain, I never blamed Source/Creator/Great Spirit/Universal Consciousness for any of it. Right before my KA happened, I was at a place of complete surrender. I said in my mind "I don't get it." "This is bullshit." "Some people are completely unaware of the negative things they do and how it affects others." "Haven't I suffered enough hardships in my life?" I didn't ask to be diagnosed with depression or my X to end our relationship or for Sandy to destroy half of my house. I pretty much handed my soul over to God and accepted whatever fate would befall me for striving to do the best I could with what I had to work with. I wasn't expecting Enlightenment/Samadhi/KA. I was completely unaware of the process and not actively trying to arouse the Kundalini energy. This occurred by the grace of God.

Asana – Sanskrit for sitting down; is also defined as seat. In the ancient yoga texts, the primary focus of the asana is a comfortable position to still the mind, focus on the breath and to meditate to obtain Samadhi/enlightenment/liberation. The limb of asana was not as significant in the practice of yoga as the other limbs. In today's world, in the West, most students of yoga focus on the myriad of poses to stretch, tone and strengthen the body. Many are unaware that mindful and conscious breathing into the part of the body while in a pose carries prana to that body part to bolster the energy/subtle body (this improves ones overall health) and assists in the release of energetic blocks – a primary requirement to purify the physical body so the Kundalini energy can move easier up the Shusumna through the chakras. The more one consciously directs the breath to a specific body part during a pose, the more prana can be harnessed and used to heal. Sweating in a hot yoga class eliminates impurities and toxins from the body through the skin. I try to take three hot classes a week. Each day, I sweat out what my body doesn't need and start with a clean slate for the next day. We are given this one body—a vehicle for the soul. It's up to each and every one of us to maintain and honor it to the best of our ability. How you treat it in this life will be a major determinant in what you receive in the next one. Many poses are named for animals and celestial bodies such as the sun and moon. We honor our Creator for even having these things to experience and love in reality. At a structural level, poses are based on alignment, specific angles and symmetry, which are all aspects of beauty in the physical world; from the angles of a constellation, alignment of the sun, moon and Earth during an eclipse and symmetry of geometry that can also be found in the human body.

Pranayama is the expansion of vital energy or life force (prana) through control of the breath. As mentioned earlier, prana bolsters our energy/subtle body and also heals the physical/gross body. There is a direct connection and correlation. The Universe/God/Creator/Great Spirit/Universal Consciousness responds to structure, rhythm and patterns. While breathing during meditation it is of benefit to use a pattern of in-breath and out-breath such as breathe in for 12 counts and out for 12 or in for 16 and out for 12 etc. Holding the breath between inhalation and exhalation is also of benefit. There are no rules when it comes to designing breathing patterns that work best for you. I use 7, 9, or 11 frequently as these numbers have significance for me. The key is where the breath, and with that prana, is directed and why it is directed.

Pratyahara is the withdrawal of the senses to the mind. The yogic limbs are moving from the outside with external awareness towards the inside and internal awareness. With this limb, the yogi should focus on the five senses and stilling the mind of external stimuli/citta.

The next three limbs are all internal. In Patanjali's Yoga Sutras they are described as Samyana, that means holding together, binding, integration. I will list the definitions of the next two limbs then focus on the last one, which is the ultimate goal – Samadhi.

Dharana – concentration, focusing, attention

Meditation – reflection, observation

Samadhi is the union of self with the object of meditation. Tranquility, moksha, spiritual illumination, enlightenment are synonymous with the ultimate goal. As mentioned earlier, the seeker becomes the seer. You will become what you meditate on. The primary focus and concentration is on God/Creator/Great Spirit/Universal Consciousness, the soul, it's connection to Source, the universe, unconditional eternal love, bliss and reality. One can reflect and meditate on an infinite number of things, from physical objects to the yamas and niyamas of the first two limbs. Below is a list that combines dharana and meditation with the ultimate goal of experiencing a KA and obtaining spiritual illumination/enlightenment.

1. Focus on relaxing every muscle in the body. Bliss has no stress, tightness or tension! The vital energy will move more freely if the body isn't locked up.
2. Focus on the five external senses of touch, taste, smell, hearing and sight.
3. Breathing. Pranayama. Deep (breathe into the belly, ribs and chest) rhythmic breathing (ujjayi) as well as alternate nostril breathing. There are many types of pranayama. Example includes hold the right nostril closed with the thumb, breathe for an eight count through the left nostril. Hold for eight counts. Hold the left nostril closed, exhale through the right nostril for eight counts. Switch nostrils and repeat. This will regulate the life force (prana and apana – positive and negative energies) throughout the gross (via the lungs) and subtle/energy bodies (via the nadis).
4. Be "mindlessly present." Only focus on the breath and the five senses. Any thoughts that come up other than these should be observed and discarded as interfering with samyama.

The focus of the next section is on the internal aspect and involves visualization techniques. With practice, these will strengthen over time.

1. Focus on directing prana to each chakra starting with the root or 1st chakra. Prana should be visualized as invisible white light. It

can't be seen and neither can the chakras. Trust they exist. The associated color for each chakra can be visualized. As chakra means wheel, visualize the prana nourishing and spinning each chakra so it can assist in bringing the Kundalini in an upward motion. A silent mantra of OM can also be repeated without speaking it. Chanting is also helpful.

2. As the soul is encased in a flesh vessel or suit (the gross body), visualize the body as having many layers, like an onion. Begin to strip the physical, emotional and mental/intellectual layers away. With each layer being stripped focus on becoming lighter until you are weightless, adrift in a vast ocean of eternal light, love and consciousness.

3. Visualize the eternal journey of the soul. Imagine every human that ever existed started out as the smallest particle of light/energy from the Big Bang. This light was the size of their consciousness and every soul was equal. Over 13.77 billion years, we had to evolve and work together to form bigger pieces of matter in working our way up from IE charm, quark, electron, atom, molecule, cells, rock, plant, animal, human in order to grow and gain experience. This cycle is eternal.

4. Meditate on unconditional love being the final realization throughout the universe with no pain, hate, and fear – anything negative. Now smile!

5. With each breath being drawn in, visualize raising the vibration of cells in the body and filling them with white light. At its tiniest form (substratum), all matter is energy. Prana is pure consciousness from Source/Creator/God/Great Spirit and can be consciously commanded to spin the energy in the body to a higher frequency or vibration. As the subatomic particles of the cells spin faster, internal heat is generated and burns off impurities and cleans up dirty prana that is blocked. Also, visualize acts that incorporate raising one's energy signature. These include singing, dancing, chanting, exercising, yoga, meditating, connecting with nature, hugging, laughing, making love—all positive aspects of

being human with the eventual potential that there will be a reality based more on higher energetic acts and vibrations.

Octave (of light and sound)

After the seventh tone of a musical scale comes the octave. This is double the frequency/vibration of the lower octave. At birth the human range of hearing is between 20Hz and 20,000Hz that decays over time. Animals are more sensitive to certain frequencies as they've evolved this sense over the ages for survival and can hear higher or even lower frequencies. We will eventually evolve this sense as well. It's an evolutionary inevitability. As light and sound are ultimately energy, it is said that we can perceive a certain level of light. There are colors that are outside the visual spectrum of light. Our sight will eventually evolve for our brains to perceive more light. My pineal gland (3rd eye/6th chakra) perceived a higher spectrum of light during my heightened state of consciousness. When I viewed that spirit in my bedroom: that form was from a different octave of light. When the physical body dies, the energy/vibration of the soul evolves higher meaning – we may be able to see them but we can't touch them and vice versa. The frequency of their energy vibrates/spins higher.

Infinity

∞ The symbol is a number 8 on its side. The collective/universal consciousness and with that, reality, is endless and eternal.

Spinal Column

This is the conduit in which Kundalini rises up through the chakras to experience enlightenment/spiritual illumination/KA. Stacking the infinity sign 33 times will yield a representation of the spinal column. There is math and symbols found in the human body.

Star Tetrahedron

Also known as a stellated octahedron, is linked to the Merkaba (Mer Ka Ba) meditation. The Merkaba is the divine light vehicle used to connect with and reach those in tune with the higher realms. In ancient Egypt, Mer means light, Ka means spirit and Ba means body. This is the three-dimensional representation of the two dimensional Star of David and parallels ancient Hebrew mysticism and the visions of the prophet Ezekiel.

9. EXPANSIVE AND EXPONENTIAL NATURE OF THE UNIVERSE / SYSTEMS OF MATH AND SCIENCE / 9 AS IT RELATES TO THE NUMBER 3 / FEMININE FIBONACCI SEQUENCE / YEARS WITH MY X / MY TATTOOS / 36-360° / 72-PRECESSION OF THE EQUINOXES / NUMEROLOGY

I liken this section to a free for all or potpourri. There were some items as it related to my KA that really didn't fit into a specific section that I felt needed to be listed and discussed. Number 9 was the perfect spot for them.

Expansive and Exponential Nature of the Universe

It is believed that the universe is expanding ad infinitum. When we look up at the sky besides space we see points of light. Just as there are only 10 digits that we use (0-9) and then repeat or add to make larger numbers – items in the universe are countable. Distance is measurable and to count and measure we use numbers. As we are all One and connected to Source/Creator/God/Universe we are creating our futures and destinies in real time. Our thoughts, words and actions are all energy and significant. Every person adds to the universal consciousness, whether they are positive or negative and pushes and expands the boundaries of our universe.

Systems of Math and Science

Referring back to section 7 referencing the Quadrivium, arithmetic, geometry, astronomy and music all use numbers to make sense of their art. Systems of math become more and more complex when multiple variables are added. As we can see, moving up the technical scale from arithmetic, algebra, trigonometry, calculus etc. Science also has its relations with numbers and found in biology, chemistry, astronomy, physics etc. Right down from the smallest atomic number of a hydrogen atom to the mass of the largest star in the galaxy – without numbers we wouldn't be able to make sense of much.

9 as it relates to the number 3

The number 9 has it's own peculiarity in it relation to other numbers. It also has a peculiar relationship as it relates with the number 3. Allow me to demonstrate.

1x9=9
2x9=18, 1+8=9
3x9=27, 2+7=9
4x9=36, 3+6=9

5x9=45, 4+5=9
6x9=54, 5+4=9
7x9=63, 6+3=9
8x9=72, 7+2=9
9x9=81, 8+1=9

3x3=9
3^2=9
3^3=27, 2+7=9
3^4=81, 8+1=9
3^5=243, 2+4+3=9
3^6=729, 7+2+9=18, 1+8=9
3^7=2187, 2+1+8+7=18, 1+8=9
3^8=6561, 6+5+6+1=18, 1+8=9
3^9=19683, 1+9+6+8+3=27, 2+7=9
ETC.

There's also:
$\sqrt{3}$=1.73205080757, 1+7+3+2+5+8+7+5+7=45, 4+5=9
$\sqrt{9}$=3
$3\sqrt{3}$=5.19615242271, 5+1+9+6+1+5+2+4+2+2+7+1=45, 4+5=9
$3\sqrt{9}$=9

Feminine Fibonacci Sequence

The Fibonacci sequence appears everywhere in nature including but not limited to the pattern of florets in a flower, the bracts of a pinecone, scales of a pineapple and leaf arrangements in plants. This is not coincidental or random happenstance. A higher evolved consciousness or intelligent designer is at work here. When numerically plotted out on a graph, the design resembles that of a conch shell or a variation of the number 9 spinning inward and outward for infinity.

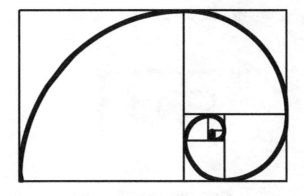

9 Years with my X

This amount of time was significant in my life as without the experience of love as I know in my heart should feel like and be, and amount of suffering due to loss – this book would never have been written.

My 9 Tattoos

Inked 7 days after my 37th birthday on my right side from the top to bottom of my ribs (symbolic of the significance of the breath and prana in yoga), these Sanskrit words are a constant reminder, partial framework and steps towards living a life of peace, love, freedom and eternal devotion to God/Source/Absolute/Creator/Great Spirit/Universal Consciousness. They can be stepping stones for anyone interested in alleviating suffering and bringing themselves closer to their true divine nature. When people ask me what it means I say "It's Sanskrit for don't worry be happy!"

1. **Dukkha**- (review section 4 of this chapter)

दुःख

2. **Karma** – (review section 2 of this chapter)

3. **Prana** –

प्राण

Sanskrit word for 'life force' or 'vital principle'. This is the fifth element and all pervasive cosmic energy that permeates the universe. For *Star Wars* fans, this is the Force used by Jedis in their 'ancient religion'. It is best described as pure consciousness. Direct sources of prana include the sun, with that stars and indirect solar light (IE reflection from the moon), pure water, clean food (not tampered with my man), air and earth. (If one is walking barefoot). When harnessed and directed, it can be used to heal the body. Ancient evolved civilizations understood this and were capable, in conjunction with sacred geometry, different understanding of physics and meditative techniques, among other things, of performing amazing feats such as nullifying the mass of extremely heavy objects in building projects. 50 to 100 ton limestone blocks were not dragged by rope and situated with astronomical precision in the building of the Great Pyramid of Giza or the Temple of Solomon. Modern technology can't even replicate these structures. They were either built by giants or through the application of a more advanced understanding of the laws of physics and prana. For further study, please research the Emerald Tablets of Thoth. The pyramid was not built as a burial chamber but used as an instrument to harness prana from the earth and cosmos.

4. Kundalini –

Sanskrit for "coiled one" this is the latent, dormant, ancient, cosmic, mysterious, universal energy available to everyone. Ramana Maharshi describes this as nothing but the natural energy of the Self, where Self is the universal consciousness present in every being, and that the individual mind of thoughts cloaks this natural energy from unadulterated expression. It resides in the triangular shaped sacrum bone at the base of the spine (1st chakra) in three and a half coils and represents a sleeping coiled snake. It can awaken spontaneously, for no obvious reason or triggered by intense personal experiences such as accidents, near death experiences, childbirth, emotional trauma, extreme mental stress, and so on. Some sources attribute spontaneous awakenings to the "grace of God", or possibly to spiritual practice in past lives. Madness and psychosis can ensue if the physical body and nervous system is not prepared for the huge volume of energy that rises up through the spine. If the body and mind are healthy (free) enough, the energy rises from the root chakra up to the crown chakra where it rests at which time the individual self merges with universal consciousness and bliss, enlightenment and feelings of infinite love and universal connectivity are possible. It is my understanding that the soul has been liberated and through proper meditative techniques can be raised with practice. Like a circuit, the energy body connects the feminine energy (Shakti) to the masculine energy (Lord Shiva) for a complete balance of opposite forces/energies. The chakras must be clear and the energy body healthy. A structured yoga practice, proper diet, exercise and a refrain from negative elements, environments and stimuli are recommended to assist in clearing the chakras and bolstering the energy body. The actual mechanics of the energy rising up the spine through the chakras feels like a snake and is represented in many cultures and religions. The Garden of Eden is symbolic of the divine male energy (Adam) and divine feminine energy (Eve). The snake, as most often misrepresented as temptation and Satan can be analogized as the serpent of Kundalini. The Gnostics referred to it as the Serpent Fire. Kukulkan, the Mayan snake deity means plumed or feathered serpent, which is symbolic of the snake analogy ascending the spine. In ancient Greece, the traditional symbol of Hermes is the caduceus and is represented by two snakes winding around a winged staff. The uraeus, the Egyptian cobra found on the pharaohs' crown represents the Kundalini energy and the 6th chakra. There are ancient serpent mounds found in North America as well as a geoglyph of a snake in Nazca. These physical and tangible examples all have spiritual significance to the representation of Kundalini and awakening or raising it. The Sanskrit word, Namaste, used most frequently throughout yoga studios to practice asana literally means, "bow to you." It can also be interpreted as "I bow to your form", "I honor you" and on a deeper spiritual and energetic platform "The Light in me honors the Light in you." As we are all equal and connected to Source/God/Creator/Universal Consciousness – we all have that Light within us. As put forth in Genevieve L. Paulson's work *Kundalini & the Chakras: Evolution in This Lifetime* – a KA is a marked sign of and mechanism for evolution. Picture a triangle separated into seven layers with the colors of the chakras coloring each layer. The root chakra is most abundant at the bottom in red and as you climb the pyramid, there are less and less of the higher chakras taking up space. Through the physical/survival, emotional, intellectual, heart-centered, expressive/creative, intuitive/6th sense until reaching the summit—there are not many at the top. Remember, there is no ego up there!

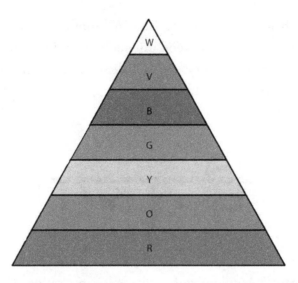

This is a merely a geometric corollary describing human evolution in a single lifetime. Christian dogma teaches the Immaculate Conception when describing Jesus' birth. From an evolutionary perspective envision this: the arrangement of a handsome man (perhaps from the East) of great character, morality, ethics, purity (as the fire of Kundalini renews and burns off impurities, "sins" etc.) strength, intelligence, skill sets and spiritual practice to a beautiful young woman of purity, strength, intelligence, morality and ethics. (Virgin Mary). Jesus' stepfather, Joseph, raised him to be a good man and taught him carpentry. The man insisted that the parents teach the child not only the Hebrew faith but also other faiths, say, Buddhism, Hinduism, knowledge of the ancient Egyptians and Greeks or the 8 limbs of yoga, esoteric, metaphysics of yoga (and with that, siddhis) and explain the concepts of karma/cause and effect and the soul at an early age. This child would evolve much faster than anyone else of his day in his neighborhood. On a molecular and genetic level, there are more than just physical traits that get passed on. An energetic signature from both the father and mother are transmitted as well. While on the topic of Jesus, he claimed to be (or his followers did) the king of the Jews (descended from the bloodline of King David), which in the eyes of the Roman Empire would be considered sedition. Jesus understood this and the punishment at stake. The lessons from the story are 1. He died for his belief and 2. The ego can get you into trouble.

5. **Kaivalya**

is the ultimate goal of yoga, which is synonymous with enlightenment/KA/union with universal consciousness/Samadhi and means solitude, detachment and isolation. This is the realization that the soul has been liberated and freedom from the physical cycle of birth and death. Other terms used to describe this are moksha and the feeling of indescribable bliss of not wanting anything other than that feeling to ever leave – nirvana.

6. **Bodhi**

is the understanding regarding the true nature of things and its closest literal translation means "awakening." I interpret this as being mindful, conscious, awake and aware. Mindful that positive thoughts, words and deeds evolve our reality in real time and aware that we are conscious creators of our own destinies and to pursue ones own dreams with love, freedom and joyful passion. Mindful that negative thoughts, words and deeds are deemed unconscious behavior and does nothing for the benefit of the soul or the universe. Bodhisattva, an enlightenment being that forgoes entering paradise for the benefit of all sentient beings, has its root in Bodhi. When I was at/in/part of the Light and felt as if I was a foot and a half to two feet above the ground and could've just flown or drifted into the Light for eternity (nirvana) but landed back down on the ground was my connection to Source as spirit detached from my physical body and being conscious of this fact with an internal understanding or knowing. Jivanmukta is also associated with this description as it is someone whose soul has been liberated yet still embodied.

7. **Dharma** (review section 8 of this chapter)

8. **Samadhi** (review section 8 of this chapter)

9. **Seva**

refers to selfless service. Who or what do you serve? What do you honor? One can choose to serve and honor their highest potential, embracing God, love, togetherness, unity, light, freedom, hope, the infinite, Spirit and all things positive or Satan (Hebrew for enemy or adversary), evil, hate, fear, separateness, despair, hopelessness, materialism, darkness, oppression, control, finite or all things negative. I choose to serve all things positive in the pursuit of my dreams for the fact that I am grateful for even haven been given the opportunity to do so! One can serve only their self (selfish) or serve others (selfless). This correlates with the 4th chakra – in being heart centered. In order to serve or put others first, one must take care of their own self first and develop enough self-love where they are then capable to love and assist others.

36-360°

The brilliant and enigmatic inventor Nikola Tesla was quoted as saying, "If you only knew the magnificence of the 3, 6 and 9, then you would have a key to the universe." This is along the lines of how the number 3 relates to the number 9 and other technical areas of advanced mathematics and connection to sacred geometry. I was impelled to include this statement as it fits so well in this section of the chapter. 36 (3+6=9) is included as it holds special significance for me: the age I had my KA. When adding a '0' to 36 on the back end we get 360°, which represents the last degree of celestial longitude of the Zodiac in which the constellation Pisces is associated with and coordinating the Mayan long count calendar—the coming end of the Piscean Age. (Age of Pisces)

72-Precession of the Equinoxes

The number 72's association with '9' (7+2=9) represents both equal balance of male and female genders/energies in connection with the seven chakras further adding to the fact that one gender is no more important or dominant than another. We are all equal, connected and capable of evolving our consciousness through understanding the chakras and what they are associated with. For a refresher on precession of the equinoxes and the association with the number 72, please refer back to section 6 of this chapter.

Numerology

As this is the last section of numeric digits (0-9) before the use of compound numbers or double digits, this was the ideal place to include the subject of numerology. As described in Wikipedia, this is the belief in the divine, mystical relationship between a number and one or more coinciding events. It is also the study of the numerical value of the letters in words, names and ideas. It is often associated with the paranormal alongside astrology and similar divinatory arts. Numerology is found throughout the ages with many different cultural and religious associations. The Greek mathematician Pythagoras believed in this as well as St. Augustine of Hippo (A.D. 354–430) who wrote "Numbers are the Universal language offered by the deity to humans as confirmation of the truth." I used Paul Sadowski's website and plugged my name into a numerology engine, removed any negative associations (as those flaws can be worked on, reversed and shown in a positive light – polarity, section 2 of this chapter) and this was the outcome:

You entered: ***Christopher Brian Soltis***
There are 22 letters in your name.
Those 22 letters total to 115
There are 7 vowels and 15 consonants in your name.

What your first name means:

Latin	Male	With Christ inside.
Greek	Male	From the Greek word meaning carrier of Christ, Famous bearer: St Christopher, patron Saint of travelers and bachelors, is believed to have carried the Christ Child across a river.
English	Male	He who holds Christ in his heart.

Your number is: 7

The characteristics of #7 are: Analysis, understanding, knowledge, awareness, studious, meditating.

The expression or destiny for #7:

Thought, analysis, introspection, and seclusiveness are all characteristics of the expression number 7. The hallmark of the number 7 is a good mind, and especially good at searching out and finding the truth. You are so very capable of analyzing, judging and discriminating that very little ever escapes your observation and deep understanding. You are the type of person that can really get involved in a search for wisdom or hidden truths, often becoming an authority on whatever it is your are focusing on. This can easily be of a technical or scientific nature, or it may be religious or occult, it matters very little, you pursue knowledge with the same sort of vigor. You can make a very fine teacher, or because of a natural inclination toward the spiritual, you may become deeply emerged in religious affairs or even psychic explorations. You tend to operate on a rather different wavelength, and many of your friends may not really know you very well. The positive aspects of the 7 expression are that you can be a true perfectionist in a very positive sense of the word. You are very logical, and usually employ a quite rational approach to most things you do. You can be so rational at times that you almost seem to lack emotion, and when you are faced with an emotional situation, you may have a bit of a problem coping with it. You have excellent capabilities to study and learn really deep and difficult subjects, and to search for hidden fundamentals. At full maturity you are likely to be a very peaceful and poised individual.

Your Soul Urge number is: 9

A Soul Urge number of 9 means:

With a 9 Soul Urge, you want to give to others, usually in a humanitarian or philanthropic manner. You are highly motivated to give friendship, affection and love. And you are generous in giving of your knowledge and experience. You have very sharing urges, and you are likely to have a great deal to share. Your concern for others makes you a very sympathetic and generous person with a sensitive and compassionate nature.

You are able to view life in very broad and intuitive terms. You often express high ideals and an inspirational approach to life. If you are able to fully realize the potential of your motivation, you will be a very self-sacrificing person who is able to give freely without being concerned about any return or reward.

Your Inner Dream number is: 7

An Inner Dream number of 7 means:

You dream of having the opportunity to read, study, and shut yourself off from worldly distractions. You can see yourself as a teacher, mystic, or ecclesiastic, spending your life in the pursuit of knowledge and learning.

As shown, the number 7 is highly associated with my name from a numerological position. There is even more significance when we break down my date of birth, February 23rd, 1977, born at 10:06AM.

2+2+3 = 7, year 77, 10+0+6= 7

10. Moses-Commandments / Sephirot (Kabbalah Tree of Life)

The story of Moses as told in the Hebrew bible, is that he was an Israelite prophet, adopted by the Pharaoh's daughter and raised as an Egyptian prince in the royal family. After killing an Egyptian slave master (who was smiting a Hebrew to death) he fled Egypt across the Red Sea where he encountered The Angel of the Lord who instructed him to return to Egypt and free the Israelites from slavery. After the Ten Plagues, Moses led the Exodus of the Israelites out of Egypt and across the Red Sea, after which they based themselves at Mount Sinai, where Moses received the Ten Commandments. The moral of this story is that no person born should ever bear the burden of slavery. We are all born free. Slavery is wrong on every possible level. The 10 Commandments are basically a set of laws based on proper moral and ethical behavior for people to live a life of peace and harmony in civilized society. The U.S. Constitution has its roots in these laws given a majority of our Founding Fathers were very much into Enlightenment ideals. The basis of the Commandments is listed below and there are multiple interpretations of each however we are all free to interpret as we see fit and what makes sense in our hearts regarding civility.

1. I am the Lord, thy God.
2. Thou shall bring no false idols before me.
3. Do not take the name of the Lord in vain.
4. Remember the Sabbath and keep it holy.
5. Honor thy father and thy mother.
6. Thou shall not kill.
7. Thou shall not commit adultery.
8. Thou shall not steal.
9. Thou shall not bear false witness against your neighbor.
10. Thou shall not covet.

These can be viewed as a moral checklist. Four of the five yamas of the eight limbs of yoga are similar in right way of living. Ahimsa—non-violence, kindness (don't kill) Satya—truthfulness (don't lie) Asteya—non-stealing (don't steal) Aparigraha—non-hoarding, self-reliance, generosity (don't covet). I've never given up faith in God/Source/Creator/Great Spirit, no matter how down I was. The worship of false idols is synonymous with materialism. Money and property has its place in life however it can separate an individual from his or her truest and most divine self if there is too heavy a focus on it. There is no fault in pursuing your passion and manifesting your dreams if it falls on a Sunday. My band has played Sunday gigs at the Jersey Shore in the summer for 15 straight seasons. It has become a ritual and I honor my Creator for giving me the opportunity to share that with whoever is present. That's the beauty of rituals as we are free to create our own. Remember, the universe responds to structure! Continuing down the list, I've eased up on my use of obscenities in connection with God/Source/Creator and refrained from being blasphemous. I honor my parents for having brought me into this world and raised my brother and I properly. I don't believe in violence and have never killed anyone. I've never committed adultery. I learned my lessons at a young age regarding stealing, lying and am very mindful about hoarding stuff. Please keep in mind the karmic associations with these from a societal viewpoint as violence, stealing, lying and adultery only create negative energy (pain, suffering, emotional distress etc.) that will ultimately need to be balanced.

Sephirot (Kabbalah Tree of Life)

In the Kabbalah and Hasidic philosophy, the Sephirot are the ten attributes or channels of divine creative consciousness in which the Infinite/God/Source/Universal Consciousness/Absolute reveals itself and continuously creates both the physical world and chain of higher metaphysical worlds. The Sephirot describes the spiritual life of man and the relationship between the human soul and the Divine and has masculine and feminine principles. Listed below are the categories in italics and attribute in their Hebrew words and translations.

Super-conscious
1. Keter - crown

Conscious Intellect
2. Chochmah – wisdom
3. Binah - understanding

Conscious Emotions
(primary)
4. Chesed - kindness
5. Gevurah - severity
6. Tiferet - beauty

(secondary)
7. Netzach - eternity
8. Hod – splendor
9. Yesod – foundation

(vessel to bring action)
10. Malchut - kingship

11. SYNCHRONICITY

A synchronicity is defined as the simultaneous occurrence of events that appear significantly related but have no discernible causal connection. The psychiatrist Carl Jung variously defined synchronicity as an "acausal connecting (togetherness) principle," "meaningful coincidence", and "acausal parallelism." From a spiritual and energetic perspective, these are signs from the spiritual realm reinforcing the fact that whatever is happening in the present moment during a synchronicity has significance in your spiritual life. The most common example is the 11:11 phenomenon where something happening such as hearing a song that has deep meaning or receiving a random call or text to even having a short power outage popping up at that specific time. The simplest and most non-threatening way our spiritual guides, angels and higher selves can send us a sign is through light, sound and numbers. 11 is the most synchronous number as the 1's parallel each other symbolizing that the next life is much like this one and our loved ones that have passed on are there. In numerology, 11 is considered a master number and symbolizes pushing the limitations of the human experience into the stratosphere of the highest spiritual perception; the link between the mortal and the immortal; between man and spirit; between darkness and light; ignorance and enlightenment. (Numerology.com)

11:11 is not the only time they can occur and 11 is not the only number they can occur with. Dates, times of the day, or even random examples that add up to 11 or a specific number sacred to your self may hold some significance. After my KA, I was super aware as synchronicities popped up everywhere with much frequency. Before I even understood this concept, the first example was the date and time of my KA. December 31st, 2013. Remove the millennial year and use the numbers 12/31/13. 1+2+3+1+1+3=11. Also, the row number of my seat was 11 and my KA occurred around 11PM or 11:11PM. The Mayan Long Count calendar supposedly ended on December 21st, 2012, which was 1 year and 10 days (1+10=11) prior to the date of my KA. The first time I saw Phish was at MSG and it was 19 years and 1 day (1+9+1=11) after my first show (12/30/94) that my KA happened. More synchronicities popped into my mind seemingly out of nowhere. Three days after my KA, the low temperature hit seven degrees. My date of birth adds up to seven (2+23=7) and the high of the day hit 56 (5+6=11). My truck was 11 years old, I had met my X 11 years earlier, me and my X's anniversary was July 13th (7+1+3=11), had been using 11 gauge strings on my Gibson ES-335 (3+3+5=11) guitar for 11 years, the year my X left was 2011, my main amp I was using was a '65 (6+5=11) Fender Deluxe Reverb...it fucking blew my mind!

Synchronicities also pop up throughout time signifying important historical events in the planets history such as the date of the infamous 9/11 attacks (9+1+1=11).

After my KA happened, I became super aware of synchronicities on a deeper personal level. The fact that my KA happened at a Phish concert, that these musicians had been a part of my life for so long and that I was a Pisces made complete sense to me from a spiritual perspective.

1977, the year of my birth holds special significance as many bands that had had a profound influence on me released albums that, to this day, I hold dear to my heart including:

Pink Floyd	Animals
Little Feat	Times Loves a Hero
Bob Marley & The Wailers	Exodus
Grateful Dead	Terrapin Station

| Talking Heads | Talking Heads: 77 |
| Steely Dan | Aja |

Other major events in 1977 that I identify with from a synchronistic perspective given their profound effect and influence are the New York Yankees winning the World Series and the release of *Star Wars Episode IV: A New Hope*. (A synchronicity connecting Star Wars to yoga could be Master Yoda (substitute the 'g' for the 'd') being Luke's guru or spiritual teacher). Also, the fact that the number 1 song in the United States on me and my brother's birthday was The Eagles "New Kid in Town" and I have a tattoo of an eagle on my shoulder. In keeping with the theme of synchronicity and tattoos, the sun king tattoo I got inked while in high school is synchronous to the 'Sol' in the first half of my last name. Sol is the Latin name for the Sun (a direct source of prana) and Sol Invictus (meaning Unconquered Sun) is the ancient Roman god of the Sun. Sol is also the Solfeggio frequency that is associated with expression/solutions, cleaning and solving. The frequency is 741 Hz (7+4=11, 1). Take the letters 'c' and 'e' out of the word solstice and move a couple of letters around and it reveals my last name. As one can see from personal examples, synchronicities are apparent and significant in many aspects of our lives. They are there for all to discover. You just need to be aware that they exist in nature, in your heart and connection to Source/God/Creator/Great Spirit/Universal Consciousness.

12. Months in a Year / Signs of the Zodiac / Apostles / Steps / Labors of Hercules / Tones in a Chromatic Scale

Months in a Year

As noted, the universe/God/Source/Creator/Great Spirit responds to structure and patterns. (Order out of chaos) Just as I have filled in my days, weeks, months and seasons with activities to keep me engaged in pursuit of my dreams and living a balanced, creative and joyful life (dharma) – a year encompasses all of these smaller subdivisions of time.

Signs of the Zodiac

The positions of the stars and other celestial bodies/events at the time of birth have a cosmic effect and influence on: us individually, human affairs and the natural world. Just like numerology, the science and study of astrology dates back millennia and is found in many cultures throughout the ages. If you've ever read a generic Zodiac profile of your birthday you will find many similarities on what type of person you are in regards to personality and character traits. Below is the generic profile of my birthday February 23rd taken from gotohoroscope.com. Of course, a more detailed, in-depth reading would be specific to year, time and location of birth given the position of celestial bodies and any other cosmic phenomenon (comet, meteor shower, full moon, eclipse etc.) that may have been occurring.

Birthday Personal Profile

People born specifically on the 23rd of February are envisaged to be compassionate, caring, intuitive and versatile Piscean fish. The ruling astrological planet for this particular day is Mercury and this makes you rational in your thinking and an excellent communicator. If you have this birthday an interest in the metaphysical world and anything unusual seems to fascinate. You are a sensible, quick-witted intellectual who mixes well socially and is quite ambitious. Generous and kind-natured: you also have expansive language fluency and generally have a lot to say. Individual's with a February the 23rd birthday enjoy conversing and exchanging views and ideas with others and are great listeners too. Despite your fascination with mysterious things you are essentially a realist with lots of curiosity and foresighted perception. You like to learn something new every day and have a fairly optimistic outlook but may become restless with dull routines.

Work and Finances

Preferred choices of work to a person born on the 23rd of February are usually within some kind of humanitarian area. Your understanding communicative nature makes you naturally drawn to care or social work occupations. You are capable of multitasking and tend to prefer jobs with plenty of variety in an interesting environment. Individuals with this particular birth date are good managers of money and not often tempted by frivolous spending. Your generosity can sometimes cause you to overspend but your budgeting skills allow you to ordinarily live comfortably financially without any real issues.

Personal Relationships

For a Pisces, the person born on the 23rd of February is unusually rather independent responsively when involved in platonic or romantic partnerships. You are a wonderful friend who will be emotionally supportive, immensely loyal and lots of fun. Your friendly outgoing considerate temperament thrives on interpersonal interactions and hardly ever wants to spend time alone. You have paradoxical behaviors when it comes to intimate friendships and can be described as blowing hot and cold emotions. One minute you are enthusiastic and loving, the next you can be distant and cautious. A long-term soul mate partner must understand this conflicting and sometimes unpredictable part of your personality. They should also ideally be in tune with your open-mindedness in the bedroom and keep the physical side to the relationship stimulating.

Health

Health concerns experienced by those born on February 23rd are sometimes linked to your highly-strung disposition. Although you may not appear outwardly nervous you have a proneness to bottling things up inside. If you are unable to find a release for this pent up frustration in the form of creative expression or gentle exercise it can induce stress related conditions. Massage is something that you are especially receptive to that could help. People born on this day usually possess a good appetite and opt for healthy eating practices. You are likely to find cooking for yourself and others most enjoyable.

Strengths and Weaknesses

The main strengths of your unique character lie in your practical and analytical thoughts and actions. Another major forte of yours is to be found in your agreeableness to reason. These impressive attributes let you make fast easy progress in life and acquire many companions along the way. Negative traits for those born on February 23rd are the tendencies to slip into hypercritical moods and act haughtily occasionally. These personality weaknesses for those born on February 23rd seem to occur at regular intervals if you do not discover an effective method to combat anxiety build ups.

Dreams and Goals

Being born on the 23rd of February bestows you with high levels of intuition and a colorful imagination. These characteristics filter through into your life hopes and aims making you probably have a large number of aspirations. You are highly motivated by goals but tend to make more than you really have time for and rarely accomplish them all. Your dreams are just as plentiful and you have the same enthusiasm to endeavor to make them come true if you possibly can. Your greatest wish is often to be with someone who makes you feel loved, appreciated and complete while truly being yourself.

Birthday Luck and Significance

As you were born on the 23rd day of February, the digits in your birth date equate to a Root number of Five. Inquiry is the special keyword to this numerical reference to your birthday and it accentuates your love of learning and inquisitiveness. The Tarot card associated with your birthday is the 5th in the Major Arcana, the Hierophant. This card highlights comprehension and is a probable symbol of your keenness in investigating the unexplained. The lucky gemstone for February the 23rd birthdays is a sparkly Diamond and wearing it close is thought to attract wealth and happiness.

<u>Summation</u>

All Piscean personalities are believed to be astrologically influenced by the authority of the planet Neptune. The actual day you were born, the 23rd of February, is thought to be governed by Mercury's influence. So the personality differences you notice from others under your Zodiac sign are a result of the combination of these two planets on your day of birth. Your witty sense of humor, ability to interact easily and forward-looking stance helps keep you and those around you cheerful and encouraged. Your realism and perceptive mien assists in maintaining an even balance in your emotions giving you well-balanced priorities and a clear perspective to base decisions and directions on.

Apostles

In Christian theology, the 12 apostles are the primary historical disciples of Jesus. There is a connection between them and the 12 signs of the Zodiac relating to the 12 great ages as well as archetypes of human personality and character traits. They are also symbolic of the dualistic nature (yin/yang, positive/negative) of the six lower chakras with Jesus representing the crown chakra and union with God/Source/Creator/Absolute/Brahman/Supreme Soul/ Universal Consciousness/Great Spirit.

Steps

Below is a list of the original 12 steps of the Alcoholics Anonymous program. These were all reflected upon in the period leading up to my KA after my life began to fall apart and I started to lose my sanity. Take notice of steps 11 and 12.

1. We admitted we were powerless over alcohol—that our lives had become unmanageable.
2. Came to believe that a Power greater than ourselves could restore us to sanity.
3. Made a decision to turn our will and our lives over to the care of

God *as we understood Him.*

4. Made a searching and fearless moral inventory of ourselves.
5. Admitted to God, to ourselves, and to another human being the exact nature of our wrongs.
6. Were entirely ready to have God remove all these defects of character.
7. Humbly asked Him to remove our shortcomings.
8. Made a list of all persons we had harmed, and became willing to make amends to them all.
9. Made direct amends to such people wherever possible, except when to do so would injure them or others.
10. Continued to take personal inventory, and when we were wrong, promptly admitted it.
11. Sought through prayer and meditation to improve our conscious contact with God *as we understood Him*, praying only for knowledge of His will for us and the power to carry that out.
12. Having had a spiritual awakening as the result of these steps, we tried to carry this message to alcoholics, and to practice these principles in all our affairs.

The list made of all people I had harmed in my life was not a physical one. I didn't write any letters or call people on the phone. It was purely contemplative in coming to the conclusion that the sum total of pain and suffering in my life was a direct result of my wrong/negative thoughts, words, actions and pain I caused others. In my heart, I learned my lessons, balanced my karma and knew I would be more mindful and think of others first in future situations and scenarios.

Tones of the Chromatic Scale

In Western music, (as Eastern music uses quarter tones) there are 12 notes of the chromatic scale before the notes repeat at a higher or lower octave. Starting at 'C' and going up in pitch we have 'C#', 'D', 'D#', 'E', 'F', 'F#', 'G', 'G#', 'A', 'A#' and 'B' before hitting the next 'C'. Each step between notes is a half step as opposed to the formula for a major scale. As there are different interpretations and systems of the subtle body (remember, there are more than seven chakras in the body), the ancient Egyptians and Greeks taught a 12-chakra system.

Labors of Hercules

Hercules is the Roman name for the Greek divine hero Heracles, who was the son of Zeus (Roman equivalent Jupiter) and the mortal Alcmene. The goddess Hera made trouble for him in making him lose his mind and in a fit of rage and confusion killed his wife and child. As part of his sentence, he had to serve Eurystheus, the king of Tiryns and Mycenae, for twelve years, in punishment for the murders. The king made him perform 12 labors that seemed impossible. With the help of Hermes and Athena, he beat the odds thus claiming his immortality through virtuous struggle and suffering. The labors can be symbolic of the 12 signs of the Zodiac as well as the 12-chakra system used in ancient Egypt and Greece. Either way, lessons and struggles learned from the chakra system (physical, emotional, intellectual etc.) are instrumental in raising the Kundalini to the crown chakra.

Concluding this chapter is a list of seven recommendations (three were listed earlier) for anyone stuck in life and having a rough go at it. This is a personal mantra I say to myself frequently throughout the day and reminds me to stay present and follow my dreams.

1. Believe what you want to believe.
2. Don't judge.
3. Live and let live.
4. Never stop moving.
5. Never stop learning.
6. Never settle for less than your heart deserves.
7. Always follow your heart and pursue your dreams.

Chapter 10

JOURNAL ENTRIES: ABSTRACT THINKING AND THE EXPANSION OF CONSCIOUSNESS

As MENTIONED IN the beginning of the Chapter 9, a couple of days after my KA, information seemed to telepathically find its way into my mind. I didn't hear any voices and I came to understand that it was the result of my crown chakra being open and allowing for more light, energy, frequency, vibrations etc. to come in and be processed/interpreted. I began saving the writings of what came in on a note pad app on my phone. It didn't take much thought. I was just a conduit. Most were free-form conscious flow from mind, to finger to app. I am leaving a handful out because some are so abstract that I didn't want to expound on the interpretations or meaning, as it would probably add another 200 pages to the book.

These entries are in chronological order beginning on 1.4.14. Some of them have dates included some do not. Some will just be listed for the readers' own interpretation and some will be broken down with added explanation, insight or interpretation. My added explanation, insight and interpretations will be italicized.

Please keep in mind that a KA expands one's consciousness to the size of the universe/cosmos. This is the definition of cosmic consciousness. So there are entries that may sound exotic, very science fictiony or with having no concept of 'time' as we know it. Some may sound like the soul is speaking, as it knows it's eternal, timeless and connected to Source/ God/ Creator/Absolute/Great Spirit/Universal Consciousness. Just a reminder: our thoughts, words, actions and ultimate intentions are ALL significant and add to the universal consciousness. They are not to be taken for granted. With that, another reminder—don't judge them. We are all free to say, think and do as we please. Just be mindful, don't hurt anyone and realize the eventual evolution of the universe is towards Love! We are all creating our destinies in real time. Some of these entries may add some fuel for your mind, heart and soul to burn, will take root in your subconscious and eventually assist in expanding your consciousness and stoke some bigger dreams!

1.4.14
Different frequencies, higher vibration locations on the globe. Electromagnetic law of attraction. MSG. Channeling higher energy at different locations throughout the world. Machu Pichu, Stonehenge, etc.

Prana, the universal subtle energy is more apparent, abundant and capable of being harnessed at locations of higher consciousness. It is easier to feel the subtle energy with focus and intent at ancient places of worship such as Angkor Wat and the pyramids.

1.7.14
Heaven—What dream are you living?

Relates to dharma and if you could think it, why not believe that it will eventually come true in the grand scheme of things? No one says you can't believe and manifest your heart's desire.

1.16.14

Greatest suffering is experienced behind the heart where the seat of the soul/Light is located. Pain from loss is there to learn from it. Heaven is experienced in the present moment. Thinking about the past or future creates more suffering ("hell").

Gravity effects ego.

Through the laws of attraction, light and positivity attract light and positivity and darkness and negativity attract darkness and negativity. Would you rather dance and sing or riot and rampage? This law works at the cosmic level. As above, so below given the sum total of light (stars) in the observable universe and sum total of darkness, void (empty space, dark matter/energy).

People identify and associate with their egos, social status, occupation, income level etc. It's all Maya, an illusion.

Fame, fortune and materialism can only take you so far. Knowledge, wisdom and Spirit are the true keys to evolution.

Divine bliss with everyone. Falling in love with everyone you meet on some level.

This is what it feels like to be in/at/part of the Light.

Routine/schedule—discipline, devotion. Daily rituals to honor your way (dharma)

Your life is your own ritual. The universe responds to structure and how you approach manifesting your reality is ultimately up to you.

There has been either peculiar or extreme weather on major events of life lessons on my Path. Proposing on the beach (double rainbow), two hurricanes (associated with my X leaving and Hurricane Sandy destroying the first floor of my house), arctic vortex (informing my yoga instructor of my KA).

How fast does this planet want to evolve? Societies can no longer advance on a material level with focus on government, corporate greed etc. pursuit of happiness. Mother Earth can no longer support population growth and demands on food supply. People need to understand unconscious living leads to disease, ignorance, and buildup of toxic and negative energy, which directly affects earth's energy field.

Unconscious living. How do you define a great life? Based on the material, keeping up with the Jones's? Measure of virtue to one's self and the Golden Rule.

Evolution of music. The great communicator. Used in ancient spiritual rituals to align brain waves amongst participants. Drums and rhythm – lower primitive man. Melody/structure assisting in higher evolution/new neural pathways being established. Jazz.

Base rhythms and drumming (ritualistic drumming) are associated with lower energy/chakras; music has evolved in complexity incorporating melody and harmony, which assists in the development of our brains (higher energy/chakras).

3.2.14

Working with divine/spiritual energy. Believing in the same result by focusing 3rd eye on all those in a circle or geometric shape having the same pineal ring of Kundalini energy flowing through us. Chanting, music, drumming, certain frequency and vibrations running through us during solstices at sunrise or sunset. Heavenly bodies aligning to which astrological deities are worshipped at these periods for their work with etc. If these beings written about in ancient times did these things, why isn't it happening in modern times? Evolution comes in waves. Need to tap universal consciousness (focus on prana) to see major change happening on this planet.

Higher evolved civilizations based their rituals on togetherness with focus on sacred geometry, structure, pattern, alignments and celestial activity. Items that Source/Creator/God/Great Spirit left us to use and celebrate in our own design/creation. Envision Stonehenge 4,500 years ago as a model of the solar system and celebrators dancing and partying their faces off during solstice and equinox parties in reverence to Creator. Dancing, alone with no focus on mind and just the senses, one creates energy by connecting with Mother Earth.

3.4.14

Black holes are negative energy eaters and advanced civilizations have figured out a way to connect their universal energies and eradicate negative regions of the universe to get sucked in, regurgitated into new big bang and restart or add on to expanding or contracting universe.

All matter is light and energy. Picture black holes as the opposite of another Big Bang with a new universe being created.

Consciousness Creation

You can create your own destiny/universe! Every thought, word, action whether positive or negative carries a certain amount of karmic weight and eventually finds it's way to space. They are brain waves and measurable energy. We could be forming our infinite futures, as there is enough space out there. Dark energy, nightmares, negative thoughts which our karma could catch up to us and enough dark energy forms the eventual catalyst of a black hole sucking a galaxy in to it and starting the big bang or purifying that energy again. This is how our collective consciousness influences the movement of the universe.

3.10.14

When you get enough people that focus on the same task and believe deep down that we are all connected, good vibes etc. through ritual you can influence your destiny/reality. Current psychology of money (material world illusion - non-permanent) can and has been hindering this.

3.16.14

If you need to label anything – love and music are my religions. I'm hearing beautiful soul-drenched stories and lessons every time I am consciously listening to someone offer that much up for the listener. Man created religion and it is just a label for the mind to identify with.

3.19.14

Hell is the realization of the thought that you were doing everything right, positive with loving compassion then finding out you were causing someone you love more than yourself great pain. Then you let it go and see the whole situation in a new light. Learn, change, grow, evolve, create, love.

For what felt like an eternity after the dissolution of my relationship with my X, in my mind I was living and experiencing pure hell. It was a torturous maelstrom of low energy, negativity, doubt, fear etc. then, like the hypothecation and example of what's on the other side of a black hole – everything got spit out, the poles were reversed from negative to positive in/at/part of the Light (KA).

3.19.14

Kundalini energy meditation before bed last night and this morning my work laptop was what appears to have been reimaged.

Mindful breathing with focus on chakras, their associated colors, love and prana. Subtle energy affects electronic devices.

5.17.14
11:45AM
Whispering Pines by The Band came on the radio
Wearing my Richard Manuel t-shirt

Example of synchronicity. The time of day adds up to 11. I'll always hold space for Richard in my heart. Just a little "wink of the eye" from the universal consciousness.

Working with energy on a greater scale is synonymous with how particles interact on a subatomic level. Enough people vibrating at a certain frequency with meditative focus and additional vibrational influence (psychoacoustics/Stonehenge, chanting a certain frequency, pyramids, visuals/fire) during specific celestial events could yield extraordinary results.

If every pyramid on world power/ley line had solstice/equinox parties where KA person was inside or on top and X amount of people (depending on structure—Stonehenge/replace stones with people etc.) meditated on certain consciousness ideals (chakra focus, duality etc.)

Incorporate Fibonacci sequence/structure with Solfeggio frequencies in sacred geometrical patterns. Meditations on themes related to chakras (survival, emotional, mental etc. or ancient deities associated with seasons/elements etc. Neptune, Aphrodite etc.

Everything in manifest reality (this universe) is connected. The more items of divine creation that are brought together and honored, the more energy (prana) is apparent/generated/available.

Conscious Evolution of Humans Without Diseases or Genetic Abnormalities

In a perfect reality, we, as a race, are not supposed to suffer from disease or birth defects. The degeneration accumulates over time on an evolutionary path. People who have genetic abnormalities or defects that procreate will pass those traits on from generation to generation thus weakening the available gene pool. As bringing a child into this world is the greatest gift Source/Creator/God has given us, conscious steps can be taken to minimize future degradation of the gene pool. The universe/universal consciousness responds to structure and pattern. Instead of going out for a seafood dinner, drinking too much, having sex and 9 months later increasing the global population by one or more, contemplate structured schedule incorporating God-made elements into the love making ritual.

The more elements incorporated, the likelihood of a stronger, more evolved offspring. Steps could include:

- Purifying both partners' bodies over the course of one moon cycle. This means eating only food that the Earth provides and not interfered by man. Meals should be eaten at regular schedules. Use of alcohol should be avoided or minimized.
- A sound exercise schedule incorporating cardio, weights, yoga, meditation, and sound therapy with the use of Solfeggio frequencies.
- Planning a birth and preparing to raise a child based on a particular Zodiac sign. Example could include two water signs parents wanting to raise a Piscean child and focus on archetypical traits of a Pisces. They would need to plan to conceive in mid-May.
- Listening to positive music, singing, dancing to raise each parents' vibration/energy.
- Added exposure to natural environments IE hiking in the woods, skiing, swimming, week in the tropics. Sun, Earth, Air, Water.
- Aligning conception with a particular celestial event such as an eclipse or planetary alignment.
- Synchronizing planned date of birth with a particular saint, sage or god's feast or birthday.

7.17.14
Love and Social Conditioning

Look outside the box and unlearn all you've learned and experienced in committed relationships.

If the standard model of marriage was the be-all-end-all of society's loving relationships it would have a 100% success rate or every person lived up to their vows.

7.18.14
Guns, War and Violence

Melt the guns and bombs!
Put mandatory fingerprint signatures on all registered firearms and serial
numbers on bullets. Digital database.
Law enforcement and registered hunters. If someone gets killed—easy to
track.

*It sounds so simple and perhaps one day the world will eventually evolve to
this. Guns, or any weapon for the matter, war and violence (ahimsa) breeds
fear, hate (negative energy) and separates us (Satan/adversary) as a race/
planet (we are ONE), brings pain and suffering (dukkha) and feeds control-
minded egoists. (Ego-illusion/lower evolution).*

8.15.14
Expanding Consciousness
Consciously creating future karmic impressions by dreaming and visual-
izing realities we'd like to ultimately experience.

*Our thoughts, words and actions/deeds are energy. We manifest our own des-
tinies with free will and intent. If it comes from the heart (4th chakra) you're
on the right track!*

8.19.14
Dharma – schedule
This is just an example of honoring the mind, body and connection to
Source/Spirit on a random summer workday by not being lazy.

Abs → weights → stepper → breakfast → work → SUP → lunch →
work → hot vinyasa flow → dinner → work/write/music → bike → bed

Group Consciousness Exercise

As our thoughts are energy, and the four universal elements (earth, air, fire, water) can be manipulated/controlled by prana (5th element), weather patterns can be manipulated/altered or created. Native American cultures performed ritualistic rain dances when they needed rain for their crops during a dry season. If enough people focused a single meditation (and with that similar breathing patterns) with prana on manifesting or controlling a weather event, over time it would eventually be successful. Remember, the universe and universal consciousness responds to structure and patterns.

Human evolution – chakra correlation
Raising an asshole—development of character and personality via alpha male/first chakra upbringing.

Rise above the "me first", ego-based, materialistic, alpha pack leader stereotype. These are rooted in the lower chakras. In order for the human race to evolve, balance and focus of higher ideals/energy is required.

Karma Meditation

What do you do? I'm happy and positive: all the time. In my thoughts, words, actions and reactions to circumstances that affect me on all chakra levels.

Having a KA burns all past wrongdoings from the physical and subtle body allowing one to start new. This is the definition of being "born again." All choices after having a KA can best be approached with a clear conscience from the heart.

9.7.14
Moderation and Lifestyle
At a chemical, biological, physiological level, with proper moderation,

once the light body has been activated and through moderation, we can do anything with proper balance. Hence smoking and alcohol – don't overdo it. The physical body adjusts. I got there by doing the things that bring me the greatest pleasure. Endorphin releases will keep you young and healthy. With proper meditation techniques, we can raise our vibration level at will. Anytime.

9.11.14

Ley lines. Lines and concentrations of conscious energy throughout a plotted area based on sacred geometry. Ancient times were ritual sites such as Stonehenge, Giza pyramids etc. Today, wherever people are doing good, acting civilized pursuing their dreams and assisting in evolving our race. Burlington, Boston, NYC, Brooklyn, Cranford, Asbury Park, Asheville, Charleston, etc.

9.11.14

Grace & Royalty

Grace as it relates to royalty. Compare to fall from with emphasis on virtuous living.

In certain religious beliefs, grace is defined as the free and unmerited favor of God, as manifested in the salvation of sinners and the bestowal of blessings. Jesus believed he was king of his people (and descended from the Davidic bloodline) and the Egyptian pharaohs passed down knowledge of Kundalini energy throughout generations. From an evolutionary perspective, the further down the line generationally, the more diluted and less pure the blood. Before government and separation of church and state, royal families ruled by divine virtue and grace. Throughout the ages, the initial catalyst and knowledge of Kundalini has been lost and with it, the comparison of falling from grace or out of God's favor. A great example is Henry VIII of England. In his prime, he was described as attractive, educated and accomplished. Near the end of his life those traits turned to lustful, obese, egotistical and insecure which are all negative attributes. We are all capable of being the best we can be all the time!

9.14.14

Rainbow Story

Rainbows and I have a special relationship.

I spotted one at high noon and there was no precipitation.

I looked up again and there were two connected at their centers with tails split off in tangent.

I wish I had a legitimate camera to document this, as I had never seen anything like it before in nature. This is just a simple observation but one worth noting!

9.27.14

Universal Consciousness

Unlocking coral castle and the divine connection Edward Leedskalnin made with numbers, geometry, magnetism, math, angles—religions that taught the connection (Egyptians/masons).

Races that connected with nature and influence weather elementals. Praising the fact that math, music, sound, frequency, sun, water, light are universal. Here or some other galaxy or other time. What we are conscious of is the only existence we will know.

The level of awareness one experiences is directly correlated to one's interpretation of reality. An example could include only believing life exists on Earth or believing life is pervasive throughout the universe.

9.27.14

Sloth Rant

Hey, put down that video game controller, wake up an hour earlier, eat better and feel good about advancing our race and you are securing our future on this planet. Rotting your brain will make more analytical robot type personalities. We need more people that would eventually evolve to a consciousness where war never existed on this planet/is just a memory. Time and existence is eternal. Would rather never suffer a war, injury or have children that ever knew to play with guns. Melt the guns.

Of course this sounds judgy but time management, commitment, drive and will are needed to achieve one's dreams, not a focus on slothful activities.

9.30.14
Group Consciousness
If a group of people, or entire world, devoted a fixed amount of time a day towards meditating on 1 thing for the greater good of the race, humanity, planet, evolution, and universe—we can will the outcome to happen. That's how the universe works! You just need to not identify with the ego, personality or be someone who doesn't believe in the concept of group consciousness. If these words make your chakras tingle or feel a little lighter you know at the very core of your being this is true.

9.30.14
Energy and Aging
Rapid effects of physically aging directly coincide with being exposed to negative energy. Thought patterns, energy fields, people, deeds etc.

Search online a before and after picture of a crystal meth addict. Shocking. The same holds true living a life of constant bombardment and exposure to negative elements.

10.1.14
Present Moment Mindfulness Analogy
"What day is it?", asked Winnie the Pooh
"It's today," squeaked Piglet
"My favorite day," said Pooh" A.A. Milne

In correlating this quote with the overall subject matter of Eckhardt Tolle's book "The Power of Now" – live in the present and don't get stuck too much in the past or the future. You could get hit by a bus tomorrow, so live for the day!

10.18.14

Heaven

Our duty to make every persons vision of their own a reality.

10.19.14

Tips for Being Present

Stop thinking. Focus on your chakras and stimuli/given environment affecting them. Breathe and focus on your five senses.

Picture the solar system 1 billion years ago and conscious life thriving on Venus and Mars with healthy atmospheres. Today, Venus' greenhouse gas effect traps heat and toxic fumes under the atmosphere. Mars' atmosphere has been pretty much blown away by solar radiation. What if they are lessons describing what happens to a healthy atmosphere with a buildup up CO_2 (carbon dioxide) (Venus) or a massive nuclear fall out or global war? (Mars)

11.3.14

Bipolar/Manic Depression Diagnosis

We were born to play and spark whatever touches our souls. Eternal children. Dark night of the soul. My higher self was giving me a sign. I got set off in college reading about the French Revolution when I should've been pursuing my passion.

As Source/God/Creator created the soul and man created psychology, psychology is fallible. The symptoms of depression I experienced in college were my higher self giving me a sign that I was on the wrong path. Along with other negative habits such as drinking too much, smoking impure marijuana, sleeping later and later and poor diet – I was completely in my own way and in a low vibratory/energetic state. Dirty prana got stuck in my head (6th chakra) thus experiencing adverse mental states.

11.23.14

Getting Connected Ritual

Global cleansing.

Everyone at every sacred spot, chakra on the planet on same schedule for 7 days involving shared thought, actions, meditations etc. leading up to eclipse, equinox—celestial worship so to speak. Planetary alignments, comets—substance of higher energy (gamma, x, cosmic) anything associated with nature, permanent structures and sacred geometry (forest cut in certain patterns Fibonacci, golden ratio etc.) People who want to worship are welcome. People who'd rather follow their vices can roll the dice.

Just as the humans have a subtle/energy body, the planet has higher points of energy and chakras associated with it. This must mean other planets and the solar system also have higher points of energy and when there are cosmic alignments, that energy is more apparent/abundant. The universe and universal consciousness responds to structure and patterns. Any items that man didn't create (numbers, symmetric patterns, planets etc.) can be honored with intent.

Ahimsa Practice

Last night a bug that resembled a cross between a ladybug and a dragonfly was following me throughout the night. It wound up in a bathroom and I was watching it as I brushed my teeth. Conscious of the fact that it felt trapped I shut the bathroom door as the window was open with a screen that had a hole in it. In the morning, as I was taking a leak, I noticed it was resting on the windowsill. I shut the window to cordon off the space it needed to find its exit. Not a second later, a power surge flashed through the house and the clock on my nightstand began flashing. Reinforces thoughts, words, and actions contributing to happiness, freedom and wellbeing of all sentient beings.

This can be viewed as a test. I was conscious of the fact that this insect wanted to be freed and that I had no intention of killing it and took the time to help it out of a constrictive situation. The light flash and clock reset was a sign that it was the right thing to do. Picture yourself in the bug's shoes. You wouldn't want to be trapped or flushed down the toilet, right?

12.26.14
Cosmic Karma
Think karmically, act locally.
Think cosmically, act globally.
Learn the lessons of love and loss.

1.11.15
Idea of heaven on Earth
Heaven is an ideal reality where everyone is consciously evolving, creating and living their dreams in harmony with one another.

6.16.15
Consciously Raising Kundalini Energy
Last night consciously raised KE to 3rd chakra before calling it off and today was a big day for double rainbows.

6.26.15
Experiencing Active Kundalini in the Body
You can breathe pranically, just think love and make eyes with everyone in the room with a smile on your face, focus on the heart chakra and just know we are all connected. The chakras will start to tingle.

7.8.15
6th Chakra Viewing
Light language encoding waking from my nap last night. Shapes, patterns, lights moving in sequence.

8.11.15
We are gods in training!

Quoted from The Book of Psalms, Chapter 82, A Psalm of Asaph, Jesus said: I have said, Ye are gods; and all of you are children of the most High. What one man/woman can do, another man/woman can do. Never stop learning!

10.2.15

Spun around clockwise with arms outstretched nine times with intention of driving hurricane Joaquin out to sea. It took an eastern turn the next day and a weather forecaster didn't have any logical explanation.

I meditated for three days prior to predicted landfall with focus on Marutas and water (Poseidon) and air deities to alter path of storm. Sole intention was to minimize loss of life and property. Group consciousness study.

10.12.15

Gravity Affects Ego

While contemplating how the sum total of all conscious thought affects the universe, I saw a shooting star or flash in the sky.
The universe will shoot you a sign if you are on the right path.

11.10.15

The Merging or Transition from the Conscious to Subconscious

Your dreams will feel more real, last longer and within time you won't know if you're in dreamland or real life. Dreamland becomes your reality.

12.14.15

Universal prayer at same time, day and specific higher energy/consciousness locations. Stonehenge, Mayan pyramids, Mt. Shasta etc. Focus on timed rhythmic breathing patterns, chakras and direct consciousness towards cosmic love.

1.4.16

Body pulses with prana, Kundalini active when I breathe regularly and rhythmically and think about bigger things. Consciousness can control the way shapes are created in galaxies. Fibonacci sequence. Meditated on love and mental images of shapes, colors and the four elements. Rhythmic breathing with eyes half shut focusing on energy in body. Lights, like stars became apparent in my field of vision and I drew in energy from them as if I was the size of a section of the sky.

3.7.16

Healing Meditation

Twelve Reiki or energy healers meditating on same thing/itinerary at same time. They are all born of different Zodiac signs drawing energy from specific region of the heavens.

3.8.16

Theory on Concept of Multiverse

All learned knowledge, experiences, lessons, relationships etc. get compressed like a black hole and shot out into another higher energy existence/consciousness.

3.23.16

Pyramid as a Pranic Healing Machine/Factory

Mantra repetition. KA person put hands on wounded or sick. Other people put hands on KA person in geometric shapes outwards like a spiral or snowflake.

4.5.16

If you don't value human life, you don't deserve to be human.

7.15.16

Be conscious of the stuff that's in your subconscious as well as cellular memory. Anything accumulated on an energetic, emotional, mental, physical and spiritual level. What have you learned on a structural level? The light illuminates your path on a spiritual level. Ego dies. How would you live forever in every moment? Breathe, light, love, happiness, calm – peace.

12.3.17

Pranayama Practice

Now if you breathe rhythmically to a set count of say, 7 in, hold for 4, 7 out. Focus on your immediate five senses and your breath. No mind. Close your eyes. Bring awareness to the 3rd eye center 6th chakra and top of the head and base of the spine. 7th chakra, first chakra. Fingers

and toes. Envision your chakras spinning quicker and quicker. Breathe…
You'll feel the energy and the grand design. Union with ALL!

3.21.18
11:47PM
Personal Big Bang
Soul's Journey = sum total of available knowledge one has been exposed to over a lifetime converted to energy through our chakras and added to all sources of energy in the cosmos; thus making universe lighter not darker. Once "at the Light" or KA, this energy is disseminated at the speed of light so at time of physical "death", whatever one has in his or hers heart that which one wants to eventually experience over an eternity—your thoughts, words, actions that have been added to the universal consciousness and manifest in the physical world (higher frequency matches that of particular star system by energy signature/size of the star) at the speed of light. Meaning this: dream big, with eternal love in your heart for ALL! Stay present and be patient. You are manifesting your dreams and creating a physical platform for your mind, heart, soul and body to experience in real time. You are manifesting your destiny.

5.29.18
Singularity – Multiverse Theory
As above, so below. Since we are equally energetically connected to the cosmos, there is a correlation between raising one's Kundalini energy to the 7th chakra and where all matter and energy are sent after being pulled into a black hole. You are your own universe!

Cognize the infinite. Realize we will all experience our hearts desires with a clear conscience if it adds light to the universe.

The universe is a puzzle. It's up to each one of us to gather all available knowledge and information and put the pieces in place to cognize and make sense of what reality means to us.

Follow your heart and realize your dreams or bust!

6.5.18

Look up to the sky, remove your interpretation of time, and appreciate the space and the Light.

Think big or don't think at all. We are all building kingdoms, dynasties and our visions of paradise. Now close your eyes, smile, breathe deeply and rhythmically into every cell of your body, with focus on love, eternity and our connection to it ALL!

The universe is your oyster. Shuck the fuck out of it!

Einstein's E=mc2 special relativity equation and correlation with the Great Pyramid, Kundalini and Mer-Ka-Ba

Consider:
Light travels at a speed of 299,792,458 meters per second.

The coordinates 29.9792458° will technically give a hit on the Great Pyramid's latitude.

The Mer-Ka-Ba meditation is based on sacred geometry and the Star Tetrahedron in which the shape of a pyramid is found.

Once Kundalini energy reaches the 7th chakra, one perceives that all matter (including every cell in a human body) converts to divine energy at the speed of light.

I/me = you/us/we = God = Love = universe = eternity

The magic is in the moment.

At the Light, you see a reflection of the highest version of yourself and realize that one day so will everyone else. From a space of equanimity – that's our destiny.

Chapter 11

Song Parables

As life doesn't come with an instruction manual, we are forced to learn many of life lessons through first-hand experiences. How else do we learn? Our parents, immediate family, friends, teachers and books are invaluable resources. We receive what is perceived by our five senses and our brains process accordingly. Another great source of learning is listening to music with lyrics. Instrumental music can evoke certain moods and emotions creating a story with major and minor movements as well as crescendos and decrescendos. Or, playing softly for a section, then louder and more aggressive the next. Songs with lyrics are a little different. The songwriter is offering a part of his or herself out for the listener to connect with on a deeper level. The great thing about song lyrics is the listener can interpret them anyway they choose. The songwriter's message may mean something completely different however; any listener is free to paint their own picture in their mind from what they hear and take or leave whatever they want for better or worse. They are open-ended. Just shut the mind down, let the music flow through and feel the vibrations. All music has a physiological effect on the human body.

The great thing about recorded music is that it is in fact, recorded and will be available forever. The artist leaves their immortal mark on the world and with that; the universe as those vibrations travel out into space forever. As parables, I've listed a bunch of songs by artists that I hold extremely dear to my heart as lifelong teachers. These songs ultimately have a deeper meaning for me and can parallel much of the stuff that was written about in previous chapters. Song lyrics are protected by copyright and the process of obtaining permission from music publishers that handle collection of royalties can be time consuming, tedious and expensive. Therefore, much like a cipher to break, I have listed the first, last and third word (in this order F,L,3) of a particular section of the song to be used as reference points. The reader is encouraged to listen to the song or look up the exact phrase online. Each phrase is associated with one or more items/concepts written about in Chapter 9. Some reference a particular chakra. By keeping the focus on a specific chakra and using ujjayi (yogic) breathing, this exercise is designed to develop neuroplasticity, strengthen a different region of the brain and feel the connection between the corporeal and subtle bodies. It will also assist in breaking up any energetic blocks in the subtle body so the flow of prana can become more fluid. In a sense, you are meditating! They are not listed in any particular order of importance however the first one really says it all. I may expound upon a few and some are left as self-explanatory. Being born, we start out building our world and fill these amazing containers (body, mind, spirit) up with stuff, which makes us who we are on an individual level. Life truly is amazing!

The format for all listed will include the artists name, album and year; song title and some may include interpretations or parallels to what was written in previous chapters.

1. The Grateful Dead
Blues for Allah (1975)
"Help on the Way"

'Without, true, in.'
The basis for this book and ultimately existence.

2. The Grateful Dead
Terrapin Station (1977)
"Estimated Prophet"

'Like, shine, angel.'
How it feels to be in/at/part of the Light.

3. The Grateful Dead
Terrapin Station (1977)
"Terrapin Station"

'The, master, makes.'
There are lessons to be learned every day from everyone from the past and present to assist us in our future. We are all each other's teachers and students.

4. The Grateful Dead
American Beauty (1970)
"Box of Rain"

'Maybe, unclear, tired.'
Confusion, depression, despair, defeated – the only way to go from being at the bottom is to the top.

5. The Grateful Dead
American Beauty (1970)
"Ripple"

'There, alone, a.'
Dharma: follow your own path. Make your own way. There will be light and dark along the way.

'To, follow, must.'
We carry the torch of knowledge and wisdom to honor our great teachers that have come before us.

6. The Grateful Dead
Wake of the Flood (1973)
"Eyes of the World"

'Wake, own, to.'
The beauty and majesty of life is all around us. We all have our vision of paradise in our hearts.

7. The Grateful Dead
From the Mars Hotel (1974)
"Unbroken Chain"

'They're, door, me.'
Kundalini can't rise beyond the 4th chakra (heart) without learning the lessons of compassion and forgiveness.

8. The Grateful Dead
From the Mars Hotel (1974)
"Scarlet Begonias"

'Once, right, a.'
The Light is real and available to all of us.

'Strangers, hand, strangers.'
Humanity will eventually evolve to this reality as we are all connected.

9. The Grateful Dead
American Beauty (1970)
"Brokedown Palace"

'Mama, home, many.'
Wisdom comes from experience.

10. The Grateful Dead
In the Dark (1987)
"Throwing Stones"

'A, waste, place.'
If we can't take care of ourselves, how can we take care of each other and with that our home/Mother Earth?

11. The Grateful Dead
Grateful Dead (1971)
"Wharf Rat"

'But, should, get.'
You are in charge of your own destiny/fate and can start anew at a moment's breath. Sloth and self-destructive behavior are hard patterns to break out of. It takes strength, will, patience and determination.

12. Jerry Garcia
Garcia (1972)
"Bird Song"

'All, on, know.'
People come into our lives for a reason, season, lifetime or eternity. See the positive and learn any lesson you can.

13. Jerry Garcia
Garcia (1972)
"The Wheel"

'Small, ground, turn.'
Symbolic of greater cycles of the universe. From microcosm (sub-atomic particles revolving around a nucleus) to macrocosm (Mayan Long Count Calendar/Precession of the Equinoxes/Zodiac Wheel/Great Cosmic Ages). The wheel is connected and traveling around 360 degrees will eventually find you back at the starting point.

14. Jerry Garcia
Reflections (1976)
"Comes a Time"

'Comes, fill, time.'
With love in your heart, don't ever give up on your dreams or the belief that they will come true.

15. Jerry Garcia Band
Reflections (1976)
"They Love Each Other"

'Don't, do, in.'
From the outside looking in, don't interfere in established relationships built on love. Leave well enough alone.

16. Jerry Garcia Band
Cats Under the Stars (1978)
"Rubin and Cherise"

'If, cold, could.'
In matters of romantic relationships, if you never lie you'll always have a clear conscience! The synthesis of thought, word and action is integrity.

17. Phish
Rift (1993)
"Rift"

'The, ignite, that.'
Having a KA is comparable to the soul catching ablaze.

18. Phish
Rift (1993)
"Maze"

'Inside, maze, a.'
Negative self-talk will make you sick. Insanity is repeatedly doing the same thing expecting different results.

19. Phish
Billy Breathes (1996)
"Free"

'I, free, the.'
The path to total liberation is patience, perseverance and a structured plan (dharma).

20. Phish
Billy Breathes (1996)

"Character Zero"
'Now, yet, convinced.'
Global consciousness has been socially indoctrinated to the point where falsities are believed to be true. It's OK to think outside the box and do a little digging on your own: "against the grain."

21. Phish
Farmhouse (2000)
"Farmhouse"

'Every, dust, rise.'
Like a phoenix rising from the ashes, life can begin anew.

22. Phish
Undermind (2004)
"The Connection"

'Then, new, change.'
Stay present. Don't dwell on regrets or the past. All roads ultimately lead home to Source/God/Creator/Great Spirit.

23. Phish
Joy (2009)
"Backwards Down the Number Line"

'You, friend, what.'

24. Phish
Joy (2009)
"Light"

'I, mind, see.'

We all have the little 'I' of ego/mind and personality. Once that illusion dissolves, it's all Light.

'Obstacles, goals, stepping stones.'

The Path is wrought with highs and lows, ups and downs. Stay focused on the dream and obstacles will be easier to navigate. Understand and appreciate the process.

25. Phish
Joy (2009)
"Twenty Years Later"

'It's, small, small.'

All it takes is a thought and the work to see a dream come true.

26. Phish
Fuego (2014)
"Devotion to a Dream"

'All, dream, was.'

If you have a dream to live, pursue it. Never give up.

27. Phish
Big Boat (2016)
"Breath and Burning"

'Breath, command, Burning.'

The four elements (air, fire, earth, water) are found within all of us. Pranayama (breath) assists in raising Kundalini (purifying fire).

28. Phish
Big Boat (2016)
"Blaze On"

'I, messiah, a,'
Ultimately, you and you alone can only 'save' yourself. Major religious figures throughout the ages are all great spiritual teachers. Knowledge, love and the right way of living (dharma) are primary focal points.

29. Phish
Big Boat (2016)
"Thing People Do"
There is right and wrong, good and bad all around. The ability to be able to discern the difference comes easier with a heart-based approach, knowledge and experience.

30. Trey Anastasio
Trey Anastasio (2002)
"Drifting"

'And, above, fog.'
After the fog of darkness and confusion lifts, the realization that the universe is ours to share and its majesty and simplest pleasures are free for all.

31. Trey Anastasio
Shine (2005)
"Sleep Again"

'Time, again, in.'

Time heals all wounds.
32. The Beatles
Rubber Soul (1965)
"The Word"

'Say, love, word?'

33. The Beatles
Sgt. Pepper's Lonely Hearts Club Band (1967)
"A Day in the Life"

'The, away, army.'
War is wrong and the antithesis of unity. The less energy humanity puts towards fighting, power struggle, materialism and egotistic control peace will eventually manifest.

34. The Beatles
Magical Mystery Tour (1967)
"All You Need Is Love"

35. The Beatles
The White Album (1968)
"While My Guitar Gently Weeps"

'I, sleeping at,'

35. The Beatles
Abbey Road (1969)
"Come Together"

36. The Beatles
Abbey Road (1969)
"Here Comes the Sun"

'Little, sun, its.'
There is always light at the end of the tunnel.

37. The Beatles
Abbey Road (1969)
"Medley"

'And, make, the.'

38. The Beatles
Let It Be (1970)
"I Me Mine"

'All, mine, the.'
This is the little 'I' of ego, personality and 'me first' attitude. The big 'I' stems from the Law of One and that we are all equally connected and should take care of each other.

39. The Beatles
Let It Be (1970)
"Across the Universe"

'Limitless, universe, love.'

40. The Beatles
Let It Be (1970)

"Let It Be"
'And, me, the.'
The eternal Light of the soul that connects us all to Source/God/ Creator/Great Spirit/ Universal Consciousness.

41. George Harrison
All Things Must Pass (1970)
"What Is Life"
It's whatever it means to you. Learn, laugh, love, create, grow, evolve…

42. George Harrison
All Things Must Pass (1970)
"Beware of Darkness"

'Beware of sadness,
It, for, hit.'
Negative stimuli, energy and thought patterns will keep you in a low vibratory state and make you sick. We are not born to be sick our entire lives.

43. George Harrison
All Things Must Pass (1970)
"Awaiting on You All"

'By, see, the.'
Notice George wrote 'names' of the Lord. No matter how you look or interpret it, Source is all the same through cultures and religions.

44. George Harrison
All Things Must Pass (1970)

"All Things Must Pass"
'All, away, must.'
Time heals all wounds. Learn the lessons of love and loss. Change is the only thing that is permanent.

45. George Harrison
Living in the Material World (1973)
"The Light That Has Lighted the World"

'So, world, of.'
Don't judge. Live and let live. Great Spirit/Source/Creator/God is the Light.

46. George Harrison
Living in the Material World (1973)
"Living in the Material World"
Materialism is on the opposite end of the spectrum from Spirit. You can't take physical objects with you when you die. The material world is an illusion (Maya) and money can't 'buy' your way into heaven.

47. John Lennon
Imagine (1971)
"Imagine"

'Imagine, You..., possessions.'

48. Bob Marley and the Wailers
The Wailing Wailers (1965)
"Simmer Down"

'*Simmer, hotter, oh.*'

Think before you act. Rarely do good things come from heated emotions. A clear, calm and intellectual mind can deal with any situation better. Climb the chakra ladder. (4th chakra – heart/compassion; seeing things from another's perspective before your own, 3rd chakra – intelligence is higher than 2nd chakra – emotions where ego/personality has a false sense of "I'm better than you.")

49. Bob Marley and the Wailers
Uprising (1980)
"Redemption Song"

'*Emancipate, minds, from.*'

We are all born free to think about whatever we want. No one can tell you what you can or can't think about or believe.

50. Bob Marley and the Wailers
Burnin' (1973)
"Small Axe"

'*If, axe, are.*'

The meek shall inherit the Earth.

51. Bob Marley and the Wailers
Burnin' (1973)
"Get Up, Stand Up"

'*But, light, you.*'

Find your own version of paradise here on Earth.

52. Bob Marley and the Wailers
Natty Dread (1974)
"Lively Up Yourself"
'Lively, drag, yourself.'
Happiness is a choice. Raise your vibration by doing positive things.

53. Bob Marley and the Wailers
Rastaman Vibration (1976)
"War"

'That, war, there.'
This entire song says it all. We are all equal. Materialism, oppression/ control blind the ego into thinking any one person is better than another.

54. Bob Marley and the Wailers
Rastaman Vibration (1976)
"Rat Race"

'Oh, race, a."
As a race, we created the monetary system however all we ever really need is love and each other.

55. Bob Marley and the Wailers
Exodus (1977)
"Three Little Birds"

'Don't worry about a thing,
'Cause, alright, little.'
God doesn't put obstacles in our Path that are unconquerable. Karma determines how gracefully we navigate our Path. In the present moment, with a focus on the five senses, breath and 'no mind' – there is no worry because you are not thinking!

56. Bob Marley and the Wailers
Exodus (1977)
"Exodus"

Are, from, satisfied.'
We are all free to live the life we want to live. We are all connected to Source/God/Creator/Great Spirit/Absolute/ Universal Consciousness.

57. Bob Marley and the Wailers
Kaya (1978)
"Sun is Shining"

'Sun, now, shining.'

58. Bob Marley and the Wailers
Catch a Fire (1973)
"Slave Driver"

'Ev'rytime, souls, hear.'
Every action has an equal and opposite reaction to balance karma. The brutalizer will eventually need to be brutalized to experience the same pain.

59. Bob Marley and the Wailers
The Wailing Wailers (1965)
"One Love"

'One, right, One.'
The Law of One. We are all connected and in 'this' together.

60. The Police
Ghost in the Machine (1981)
"Spirits in the Material World"

'There, evolution, no.'
We are all responsible for our own growth, development and ultimate evolution.

61. The Police
Ghost in the Machine (1981)
"Invisible Sun"

'There, done, to.'
This is the ultimate Truth; that we are all eternally connected to Source/God/Creator/Great Spirit.

62. The Police
Synchronicity (1983)
"King of Pain"

'But, pain..., my.'
You are responsible for how suffering is processed and dealt with. A life of suffering is living in hell. We are not here to suffer our entire lives. We learn and grow from our experiences. Time heals all wounds.

63. Talking Heads
Naked (1988)
"(Nothing But) Flowers"

'There, it, a.'
Time is cyclical. What has happened in the past can happen in the

future and vice versa. We are all stewards of Mother Earth and must be conscious to take care of her.

64. Talking Heads
Talking Heads: 77 (1977)
"No Compassion"

'So, nonsense, people.'
We need to take care of ourselves before we can begin to take care of others.

65. Talking Heads
Fear of Music (1979)
"Heaven"

'Heaven, happens, heaven.'
The feeling of being in/part of/at the Light where there is nothing more to do but be there forever.

66. Talking Heads
Speaking in Tongues (1983)
"This Must Be the Place (Naïve Melody)"

'The, along, we.'
Life doesn't come with an instruction manual. Enjoy the process and create your own vision of paradise while learning along the way.

'Never, love, money.'
Reject materialism and focus on the other end of the spectrum, which is Spirit. (Liken this to Matthew 21:12 when Jesus overturned the tables of the money changers.)

67. JJ Cale
Troubadour (1976)
"Travelin' Light"

'Travelin', fly, is.'
Live simply. Remove that what doesn't serve you. The less "stuff" and "baggage" we have, the easier life gets. There is no prize for having the most toys before you die. It just serves the ego.

68. Led Zeppelin
Led Zeppelin IV (1971)
"Stairway to Heaven"

'How, all, still.'

69. Led Zeppelin
Physical Graffiti (1975)
"In the Light"

'And, road, you.'

70. The Rolling Stones
Exile on Main St. (1972)
"Shine a Light"

'May, sun, good.'

71. The Rolling Stones
It's Only Rock 'n Roll (1974)
"Time Waits For No One"

'Time, waste, tear.'
Don't sit around and be slothful – it's time to wake up and pursue your dreams!

72. Crosby, Stills, Nash & Young
Déjà vu (1970)
"Teach Your Children"

'You, by, are.'

73. Steely Dan
Countdown to Ecstasy (1973)
"King of the World"

'I'm, die, last.'
One day, in an evolved humanity – this darkness will be a thing of the past.

74. Steely Dan
Pretzel Logic (1974)
"Any Major Dude Will Tell You"

'Any, more, dude.'
Any personal 'hell' doesn't last forever. All things must pass.

75. Steely Dan
Katy Lied (1975)
"Any World (That I'm Welcome To)"

'Perhaps, saying, find.'
Speak more from the heart.

76. Tom Petty
Full Moon Fever (1989)
"I Won't Back Down"

'No, ground, stand.'
Stand strong in the face of adversity.

77. Tom Petty
Wildflowers (1994)
"Time to Move On"

'It's, knowing, to.'
Don't get stuck in the past. Stay present with focus and determination. Whatever happens is going to happen so don't get attached to any outcome that hasn't manifested yet and stay positive.

78. Tom Petty and the Heartbreakers
Into the Great Wide Open (1991)
"Two Gunslingers"

'Two, for, walked.'
Violence is never the answer. There are more productive and creative things to do in life.

79. Pink Floyd
Dark Side of the Moon (1973)
"Breathe"

'Breathe, care, in.'
The easiest way to settle a restless mind is through rhythmic breathing and a focus on the five senses.

80. Pink Floyd
Dark Side of the Moon (1973)
"Money"

'Money, so they say,
Is, today, root.'
Honor love and Spirit, not materialism.

81. Pearl Jam
Ten (1991)
"Release"

'I'll, it, the.'
Go with the flow, believe everything's going to work out and be fine.
Any type of pain is a buildup of energetic blocks that need to be cleared
so prana can flow smoothly through the subtle body.

82. Pearl Jam
Vs. (1993)
"Rearviewmirror"

'Saw, mirror, saw.'
Life is a lesson. Hindsight is 20/20.

83. Warren Haynes
Man in Motion (2011)
"Man in Motion"

'Life, shame, be.'

84. Warren Haynes
Ashes and Dust (2015)
"Company Man" (featuring Railroad Earth)

'Sometimes, man, this.'
Follow your heart and your dreams with no regrets and the utmost determination.

85. The Derek Trucks Band
Already Free (2009)
"Get What You Deserve"

'You, deserve, do.'
Be mindful of thoughts, words, actions and how they will affect others as ultimately, anything negative will need to be balanced. Karma.

86. The Doors
The Doors (1967)
"Break On Through (To The Other Side)"

'Break, side, through.'
There's more to life than working, retiring and dying. Spark your soul and evolve in this lifetime.

87. The Doors
Strange Days (1967)
"People Are Strange"

'People, down, strange.'
Knowing we are all equally connected there are no strangers. Only friends we haven't met yet.

88. The Doors
L.A. Woman (1971)
"Riders On The Storm"

'Into, thrown, house.'
Past life karma dictates our current life's situation(s). Our thoughts, words, actions, deeds and intentions will determine the soul's destination in the next.

89. Jim Morrison
An American Prayer (1978)
"The Ghost Song"

'Thank, light, oh.'
The Light in the field of view when Kundalini energy rises above the 5th chakra.

90. The Allman Brothers Band
Eat a Peach (1972)
"Ain't Wastin' Time No More"

'Last, fly, morning.'
No matter how dark it gets, there is ALWAYS a light at the end of the tunnel.

91. The Allman Brothers Band
Enlightened Rogues (1979)
"Can't Take It With You"

'Can't, go, it.'
In the end, material items are not important. Love, lessons learned and knowledge are.

92. The Allman Brothers Band
Where It All Begins (1994)
"Soulshine"

'Sometimes, control, man.'
Loss of love is supposed to feel this way. Time and surrender to the flow, higher power or Source/God/Creator/Great Spirit can produce the Light.
'He, day, to.'

93. The Highwaymen
Highwayman (1985)
"Highwayman"

'I, again, a.'
Matter and energy may change but consciousness and connection to Source/God/Creator/Great Spirit is eternal.

94. Red Hot Chili Peppers
Blood Sugar Sex Magik (1991)
"The Righteous and the Wicked"

'Killing, peace, future.'
Duality.

95. Red Hot Chili Peppers
Blood Sugar Sex Magik (1991)
"The Power of Equality"

'The, be, of.'

96. The Avett Brothers
The Carpenter (2012)
"Live and Die"

'You, same, I.'

97. The Avett Brothers
The Carpenter (2012)
"The Once and Future Carpenter"

'Well, die, all.'

98. The Avett Brothers
True Sadness (2016)
"Ain't No Man'

'There, there, no.'

99. Mumford and Sons
Sigh No More (2009)
"The Cave"

'And, ways, find.'
Pain can be the biggest catalyst for change and true growth.

100. Mumford and Sons
Babel (2012)
"Below My Feet"

'When, well, was.'

Great spiritual masters are there to guide and teach us. With love in your heart for all there is always hope.

101. Mumford and Sons
Wilder Mind (2015)
"Only Love"

'Didn't, end, say?'

102. Stevie Wonder
Songs in the Key of Life (1976)
"Have a Talk With God"

'Many, God, us.'

103. Bruce Springsteen and the E Street Band
Greetings From Asbury Park, N.J (1973)
"Spirit in the Night"

'And, you, dance.'

For millennia cultures have come together for ritualistic tribal dance to connect to Mother Earth, Great Spirit and raise their vibration. Dancing like no one is watching with a focus on the breath and 'no-mind' will charge up one's energy. It's healthy!

104. John Mayer
Continuum (2006)
"Waiting on the World to Change"

'So, change, keep.'

Everyone has the opportunity to be the best version of themselves.
105. The Jimi Hendrix Experience
Are You Experienced (1967)
"Are You Experienced?"

'Have, have, ever.'
We grow through our life experiences. Try anything once!

106. Eagles
Eagles (1972)
"Take It Easy"

'Don't, crazy, the.'
Be mindful and stay present. Too much negativity via stimuli or thoughts can make you sick.

107. The Band
Music from Big Pink (1968)
"To Kingdom Come"

'Forefather, you, to.'
Reap what you sow. Karma ultimately needs to be balanced.

108. The Band
Cahoots (1971)
"When I Paint My Masterpiece" (Dylan)

'Someday, masterpiece, is.'
We are all capable of creating such beauty!

109. Alabama Shakes
Boys & Girls (2012)
"Hold On"

'So, on, my.'
Patience is a virtue. Never lose faith in God/Source/Creator/Great Spirit. It's a part of us all.

110. Blind Faith
Blind Faith (1969)
"Presence of the Lord"

'I, Lord, finally.'
Love and forgiveness is the key to any door. With the understanding that we are all connected to God/Source/Creator/Great Spirit and striving to do our best in every facet of life – there is no reason to ever have any fear or doubt in our hearts. You are never alone.

111. John Newton
Olney Hymns (1779)
"Amazing Grace"

'Amazing grace! (how sweet the sound),
That sav'd a wretch like me!
I once was lost, but now am found,
Was blind, but now I see.

'Twas grace that taught my heart to fear,
And grace my fears reliev'd;
How precious did that grace appear,
The hour I first believ'd!

Thro' many dangers, toils, and snares,
I have already come;
'Tis grace hath brought me safe thus far,
And grace will lead me home.

The Lord has promis'd good to me,
His word my hope secures;
He will my shield and portion be,
As long as life endures.

Yes, when this flesh and heart shall fail,
And mortal life shall cease;
I shall possess, within the veil,
A life of joy and peace.

The earth shall soon dissolve like snow,
The sun forbear to shine;
But God, who call'd me here below,
Will be forever mine.'

EULOGY FOR BARBARA ANN SOLTIS

My mother passed away before the publishing process of this book began. I've included the eulogy I gave at her funeral mass as I received much thanks and heartfelt responses from family and friends that were there to pay their respects and wanted to share it with you. She truly was an amazing woman.

John really took care of everything. We were blessed to be raised the way we were raised with two caring and compassionate parents. We were spoiled in every way. Mom set the bar pretty high. She exuded love in every cell of her body.

Over the past couple of days, my emotions have vacillated between grief, loss, sorrow and pain to love, hope and positivity. She wouldn't want any of us to suffer one second over her. We actually joked not too long ago if she ended up in the hospital the way she did, what we would have to do. She had such a carefree and light-hearted take on everything.

I've experienced heartbreak, loss and suffering where it felt like a living hell. No one is ever prepared to lose someone that loves you unconditionally so soon out of the blue. I thought I would've been thrown right back down into a dark place. This was completely different. I immediately knew in my heart that it was OK. She's with family and friends. That was good enough for me to keep a smile on my face and cry tears of joy instead of grief. Oh, I can still lose it at the snap of a finger but I know she'll always be with me.

In times of doubt, despair, grief and darkness, we can always find solace, hope, healing, light and pearls of wisdom in our faith in God. I've chosen three passages that have been a great help to me and would love to share with you all.

Psalm 82:6
I have said, Ye are gods and all of you are children of the most High.

Luke 17:21
Neither shall they say, Lo, it is here! Or Lo, it is there! For behold, the kingdom of God is within you.

Matthew 19:26
But Jesus beheld them, and said unto them, with men this is impossible; but with God all things are possible.

Now we are all free to interpret these passages in any way we want so that it makes sense to us. If it is from the heart, there is no fear to think or believe this.

We are all equally connected to God; all his sons and daughters; all given a physical body, thinking mind, compassionate heart and soul. The soul is stainless, perfect and eternal. So, through my thinking mind, heart and soul, I'm free to believe my vision of heaven is a place where all my friends and family, and all their friends and family are. Filled with love, light, laughter, joy, compassion, beauty, no pain or disease. Just perfect in every way.

This gives me hope. My faith in God and the belief that I will be able to give my Mom a big hug and tell her I missed her. That I couldn't wait till the day I'd be able to look her in the eyes again and tell her how much

I love her.

Without hope, love and faith – life wouldn't really make much sense.

Now I'm gonna count to three and with gusto I want everyone to say 'we love you Barbara!' Ready? 1, 2, 3 "WE LOVE YOU BARBARA!"

Love you Mom.

Yogi Musician Mantra

I am God's loving Light. We are all God's loving Light. Spiritually and energetically connected in the universe by divine love. I believe in the Golden Rule, sacred geometry and universal laws of karma and harmony. May my thoughts, words, actions come from the heart, reactions to situations and change be positive and contribute to the happiness, freedom and wellbeing of every being in the universe. Om Namah Shivaya. Shanti, shanti, shanti. Peace, peace, peace. We are love and Light. Namaste.

References / Reading List

What makes you...you? What has shaped your perception of the world, reality and the universe? The beauty of it is that everything we've ever been exposed to has a profound effect on us whether we like it or not. People we meet, television shows we watch, music we listen to, experiences and situations we are exposed to, books and online articles we read etc. One should always be actively engaged in evolving and increasing their knowledge base because well – it's not all for nothing, right? Don't you want to know as much about everything as possible? This is the ultimate path to freedom.

Listed below is a sampling of books (in no particular order of importance) that have assisted me with increasing my knowledge base and shaping my perception of the world, reality and the universe. Asides from biographies and autobiographies on my musical heroes, I find nonfiction books on topics that interest me to be a valuable resource in the evolutionary process.

Tolle, Eckhart. *The Power of Now: A Guide to Spiritual Enlightenment.* Namaste Publishing: Vancouver, 1997

Millman, Dan. *Way of the Peaceful Warrior.* HJ Kramer: California, 1980

Krishna, Gopi. *Living With Kundalini.* Shambala Publications, Inc.: Massachusetts, 1993

Three Initiates. *The Kybalion: A Study of The Hermetic Philosophy of Ancient Egypt and Greece.* Martino Publishing: Connecticut, 2016

Doreal, Michael. *The Emerald Tablets of Thoth The Atlantean.* Source Books, Inc.: Illinois, 2006

Lad, Vasant. *The Complete Book of Ayurvedic Home Remedies.* Harmony Publishing: New York, 1998

Svoboda, Robert. *Prakriti: Your Ayurvedic Constitution.* Lotus Press: Wisconsin, 1998

Bryant, Edwin, F. *The Yoga Sutras of Patanjali.* North Point Press: New York, 2009.

Iyengar, B.K.S. *Light on Yoga.* Schocken Books: New York, 1966.

Co, Stephen & Robins, Eric, B. *Your Hands Can Heal You.* Atria: New York, 2002

Melchizedek, Drunvalo. *The Ancient Secret of the Flower of Life, Volume I.* Light Technology Publishing: Arizona, 1990

Melchizedek, Drunvalo. *The Ancient Secret of the Flower of Life, Volume II.* Light Technology Publishing: Arizona, 2000

Melchizedek, Drunvalo. *Serpent of Light Beyond 2012.* Weiser Books: California, 2008

Skinner, Stephen. *Sacred Geometry.* Sterling: New York, 2006

DeGrasse Tyson, Neil. *Astrophysics for People in a Hurry.* W.W. Norton & Company, Inc.: New York, 2017

Ashley-Farrand, Thomas. *Chakra Mantras*. Weiser Books: California, 2006

Bauvel, Robert. *The Egypt Code*. Disinformation Books: California, 2008

Hancock, Graham. *Fingerprints of the Gods*. Three Rivers Press: New York, 1995

Hancock, Graham. *Magicians of the Gods*. St. Martins Press: New York, 2015

Griffith, Ralph T.H., Berriedale Keith, Arthur. *The Vedas: Rig, Yajur, Sama & Atharva*. Kshetra Books: 2017

Buddhaghosa, Bhadantacariya. *The Path of Purification (Visuddhimagga) Volume One*. Shambhala Publications, Inc.: California, 1976

Wallis, Christopher D., *Tantra Illuminated: The Philosophy, History and Practice of a Timeless Tradition*. Mattamayura Press: Colorado, 2013

Edington, Louise. *Modern Astrology*. Althea Press: California, 2018

Powers, Lisa. *Reiki: Level I, II and Master Manual*. CreateSpace Publishing: California, 2016

Carr, Allen. *The Easy Way to Stop Smoking*. Sterling: NY/London, 1985

Levine, Mark. *The Jazz Theory Book*. Sher Music: California, 1995

Paulson, Genevieve Lewis. *Kundalini & the Chakras: Evolution in this Lifetime*. Llewellyn Publications: Minnesota, 2002

www.atlantis-and-atlanteans.org

ABOUT THE AUTHOR

Born and raised in the suburbs of New Jersey, Chris has always followed his heart in performing, writing and recording music on his own and with his band enjoy! He has an unmatched zest for life and infinitely curious about the universe. He is a Certified Financial Planner registrant, multi-instrumentalist, recording artist and certified to teach Vinyasa yoga. Chris' passions include traveling, paddleboarding, golf, skiing, biking, seeing live music, the beach, New York Yankees baseball and spending time with family and friends as well as making new ones. He is eternally devoted to the discipline and philosophy of yoga. Chris believes in every person's unlimited potential and views humanity as an evolutionary and creative process in which we are all active participants and equally connected to something much bigger.

9 781977 210197